Bomber

The Formation and Early Years of
Strategic Air Command

Phillip S. Meilinger

Air University Press
Air Force Research Institute
Maxwell Air Force Base, Alabama

November 2012

D1473912

Library of Congress Cataloging-in-Publication Data

Meilinger, Phillip S., 1948-
    Bomber : the formation and early years of Strategic Air Command / Phillip S.
Meilinger.
        p. cm.
    Includes bibliographical references and index.
    ISBN 978-1-58566-219-7
    1. United States. Air Force. Strategic Air Command—History. 2. Strategic bombers—
United States—History—20th century. 3. Strategic forces—United States—History—
20th century. I. Title. II. Title: Formation and early years of Strategic Air Command.
    UG633.M329 2012
    358.4'230973—dc23

                                                                2012031465

First Printing November 2012
Second Printing September 2013
Third Printing November 2015

Disclaimer

AIR FORCE RESEARCH INSTITUTE

Air University Press
Air Force Research Institute
155 North Twining Street
Maxwell AFB, AL 36112-6026
http://aupress.au.af.mil

To Barbara

Contents

About the Author

Col Phillip S. Meilinger, USAF, retired, was born in Michigan but raised in Chicago, Illinois. He graduated from the Air Force Academy in 1970 and served 30 years as a pilot, staff officer, and educator. He initially flew as an instructor pilot in Air Training Command, then flew C-130s in the Philippines while also serving in the Pacific Airlift Control Center. Later he transitioned into the rescue version of the HC-130 as an instructor pilot at RAF Woodbridge in the United Kingdom. These overseas assignments allowed him to fly all over the world and further his understanding of geopolitics, history, and culture. During Operation Desert Storm in 1990–91, he was a planner on the Air Staff in the Pentagon while also serving as chief of the Air Force Doctrine section.

In 1975 Meilinger received a master's degree in military history from the University of Colorado and in 1985 was granted a doctorate (also in military history) from the University of Michigan. He has taught at the Air Force Academy and the Naval War College and was dean of the School of Advanced Airpower Studies (now School of Advanced Air and Space Studies, or SAASS)—the Air Force's only accredited graduate school for the education of future strategists. He retired from the Air Force in June 2000 and worked as a defense analyst in the Washington, DC, area for six years. He is now a freelance writer and lives outside Chicago with his wife, Barbara.

Dr. Meilinger has authored 10 books and more than 100 articles dealing with military and airpower operations and theory and has been invited to lecture at military and civilian venues all over the world. Among his books are

Hoyt S. Vandenberg: The Life of a General;
The Paths of Heaven: The Evolution of Airpower Theory;

Ten Propositions Regarding Airpower;
Airmen and Air Theory;
Airpower: Myths and Facts;
Airwar: Theory and Operations;
Hubert R. Harmon: Aviator, Officer, Father of the Air Force Academy; and
Into the Sun: Novels of the US Air Force.

Two of his books to date have been chosen for the USAF Chief of Staff's Reading List, and several of his articles have received awards. This latest book, dealing with the early years of Strategic Air Command, was commissioned by the Air Force Research Institute.

Foreword

It is impossible to think about the Strategic Air Command (SAC) without consideration of Gen Curtis LeMay and his remarkable influence. When he assumed command of SAC in September 1948, LeMay immediately brought dramatic change to Air Force culture and continued to make his mark in the nearly 10 years he served as SAC commander. LeMay extended his influence when appointed vice-chief and then in 1961 as chief of staff of the Air Force and on into retirement—but that is another story. Throughout his tenure at Offutt AFB, SAC was the preeminent Air Force organization. *Bomber*, Phil Meilinger's thorough and well-documented analysis of the formation and early years of SAC, not only informs us on that heroic period in Air Force history, it also provides an understanding of the fundamental and often uncomfortable changes still facing the service in this post–Cold War era.

The drastic reduction of forces at the end of World War II and the onset of the Cold War placed heavy pressure on the Air Force to project power abroad and establish credible deterrence in a dawning nuclear age, to include launching retaliatory strikes should that deterrence fail. It was a heavy responsibility on a newly independent force manned by airmen who had just returned from a long and costly war against the Axis powers.

Bomber attempts to describe SAC in the context of what was then a new global dynamic, later dubbed the Cold War, showing how it faced the continually evolving challenges of its time. Meilinger has illuminated the problems and successes faced during these formative years.

Lt Gen Curtis E. LeMay, just 41 when he came to SAC—the age at which most current officers are pinning on lieutenant colonel—found a few B-29 bombardment groups with half their bombers nonoperational and crews only partially trained. It is debatable as to who was more surprised during an inspection of a hangar full of nuclear-armed bombers, LeMay or the single sentry armed with only a ham sandwich. On a mock bombing exercise against Dayton, Ohio, LeMay was shocked to learn that most bombers missed the target by a mile or more. His command could not express professional expertise.

Forceful and adroit leadership was vital, but the mastering of technology also played a crucial role in SAC's achieving effectiveness.

This included the development of bigger and faster jet bombers, new escort fighters, and a compatible air refueling capability. LeMay also needed better communication capabilities to facilitate command and control. Improved radar and electronic countermeasures contributed to safer penetration of enemy territory. SAC's mission accomplishment was greatly influenced by the advent of nuclear weapons, and, ultimately, ballistic missiles.

All of this was expensive, and by the end of the 1950s SAC controlled one-third of the entire Air Force budget. The Air Force received 50 percent of the DOD budget. SAC was king, placing its personnel in all key command and staff positions. It even developed its own promotion system—spot promotions for its top performers. Other commands envied SAC and LeMay.

In spite of his reputation as demanding, uncompromising, and requiring excellence in performance, LeMay also developed a reputation for exercising concern for the physical well-being of his personnel. He not only encouraged off-duty recreational activities, but also authorized special uniforms, training equipment, and allowances for flight crews. He found many ways to maintain reenlistment rates and retain his highly trained personnel.

LeMay receives abundant credit for developing a highly trained instrument of war. In addition, the circumstance of superpowers challenging each other established SAC as the dominant force of American military policy. Clearly Harry Truman, Dwight Eisenhower, and other national leaders, recognizing the logic of strategic airpower, dictated a strategy and policy that underwrote the nuclear-armed bombers and guided missiles of this new entity called Strategic Air Command. At the time of LeMay's departure to become vice–chief of staff, SAC was composed of nearly 224,000 airmen, 2,000 heavy bombers, and 800 tankers, all dedicated to the preeminent Air Force mission—strategic attack of the enemy's vital centers of gravity in the event of war.

Pres. John F. Kennedy's "flexible response" and a broadened view of national defense, along with the Vietnam War, provided a turning point in the singular mission of SAC. Yet, it must also be said that SAC's decline was a product of its tremendous success. The nuclear-armed warriors of Armageddon were so professional, so accomplished, and so respected by adversaries in Moscow and Beijing that for a while, war was made unthinkable. We can only hope that the Air Force maintains its reputation for effective defense of our nation in this twenty-first century. Toward this end, it is helpful to understand the profound challenges the Air Force faced at the birth of the Cold War and its ability to adapt.

Gen John A. Shaud, PhD, USAF, Retired
Director, Air Force Research Institute

Introduction

This is a story of a major combat organization being formed in the midst of a momentous change in world events. It is not a narrative history. Rather, it is an attempt to place Strategic Air Command (SAC) in the context of its time: what factors led to its establishment; what challenges did it face in its formation and first decade of existence; and what lessons can we derive from that experience? SAC was established in March 1946, soon after the death of one war and at the birth of a new one, the Cold War. The origins of SAC began long before 1946, however.

In 1917 a young Army Air Service officer, Col Edgar S. Gorrell, wrote a memo positing the notion of strategic bombing against the heartland of Germany. His ideas were barely formed and lacking in detail, but they nonetheless offered a vision of war that would be accepted and adopted by most American airmen for the next several decades. It was the belief of Gorrell and those who followed him and thought similarly that the air weapon had fundamentally changed war. It was a strategic weapon in contrast to the tactical nature of armies; moreover, it was far more direct in its application than were navies, which could also be strategic weapons.

For the next two decades, American airmen elaborated on these themes. The inherent characteristics of airplanes—their ubiquity, speed, range, and flexibility—were trumpeted, while inherent limitations such as cost, complexity, impermanence, and the elements were passed over.

In the US Army, a group of eager and driven young officers, led by the charismatic Brig Gen William "Billy" Mitchell, preached of airpower's ability to transform war. Instructors at the Air Corps Tactical School in Alabama, Mitchell's intellectual descendents in many respects, articulated a mission of strategic bombing against an enemy's industrial centers. This was a unique mission that only airpower could accomplish, and because of that, they argued that airpower demanded an independent service run by airmen. An entire generation of aviators—the men who would lead the service during World War II—was educated in the doctrine embodying that mission. Aviators were never bashful about spreading that revolutionary message, a message paradoxically optimistic yet frightening. The bomber defined American airmen.

Besides institutional resistance to their ideas from Army infantry zealots, Airmen continually ran into technological barriers. The visions they proposed were simply not achievable given the airplanes, bombs, bombsights, and navigation gear then available. As a result, theory dominated the debate on airpower, and technology not yet invented was continually put forward as the solution to all problems.

When the United States entered World War II, the military services were surprisingly unprepared, given that fighting had been ongoing for over two years. Airmen, like soldiers and sailors, struggled to catch up. Technology, which lay at the root of air expectations, evolved to the point where armadas of airplanes, thousands in number on any given day, were launched against the enemy. Planners realized, however, that different technologies were necessary—beyond simply the bomb carriers, ordnance, and navigation and targeting equipment—to achieve the strategic goals of the military commanders. These new technologies consisted of intelligence gathering and analysis tools needed to study enemy economies and determine how they worked and what would make them fail. The US Strategic Bombing Survey, the culmination of these analysis efforts, was formed to address and answer the specific and fundamental questions of what the bombers had hit, how badly the targets had been damaged, and, most importantly, what effect it all had on the enemy war effort.

The war ended with the atomic bombs. That fact was to dominate postwar diplomatic and military thinking and in turn had a profound impact on force structure for all the services. Constant struggles over organization, functions, and budgets were continuous and spirited. Airmen's desires for independence were finally realized on 18 September 1947, but their problems were just beginning. The mission of strategic bombing, assumed to include atomic weapons, remained the core tenet of their beliefs, and the bomber continued to define airmen. They kept on preaching this message, much to the irritation of the other services, especially the Navy who saw its two-century claim to being America's first line of defense being pushed aside.

Strategic Air Command was formed specifically to project American power abroad, to assure deterrence, and to launch a powerful retaliatory strike, with atomic weapons, if war came. The main adversary was the Soviet Union, the erstwhile ally. Over the first decade-plus of its existence, SAC's ability to perform this mission, and to do it with a frightening and ever-increasing power, was stunning. Yet it was a rocky road to achieve that level of capability. Postwar demobilization, budget constraints, the secretive atomic community, and questionable leadership all contributed to a Strategic Air Command that was a weak rod when the Berlin blockade occurred in mid 1948. Change was necessary, and it began at the top. Curtis E. LeMay took over SAC in September 1948 and began to transform his command.

Technology remained central to SAC's existence. To reach targets in the Soviet Union, faster and larger jet-propelled bombers were necessary. Hundreds of air-refueling aircraft were built to extend the range of the bombers so that vulnerable bases in Europe were not necessary. Other technologies in the electronic and communications fields were developed to provide long-range reconnaissance, allow the bombers to penetrate enemy defenses—without escort fighters—and maintain command and control with headquarters anywhere above the globe.

And, of course, technology was central to the development of atomic weapons themselves. The bombs dropped on Japan in August 1945 were, for all their extraordinary power, crude devices of great weight and size. As nuclear scientists continued to learn, the bombs they built grew smaller and more powerful, culminating in the thermonuclear revolution that measured power in megatons, not kilotons. At the beginning, however, the secrets of the bomb and its manufacture—indeed, even the number of bombs that existed—were so closely guarded as to cause paranoia among airmen. The basic function of strategic bombing, integral to the Air Force, was dependent upon a weapon over which it had no control and little insight into its design and availability. That would change with the Korean War, but it was not an easy path to that point. Moreover, Korea demonstrated that nuclear war was not inevitable. Major conventional operations could occur under the umbrella of nuclear deterrence. War had stepped back two centuries to the age of limited war, although that was not yet realized at the time.

By the end of the 1950s, the Air Force was officially recognized in US security policy as the dominant player, receiving nearly 50 percent of the Department of Defense budget. Within the Air Force, SAC was king, garnering one-third of the budget and placing its personnel in virtually all the key command and staff positions throughout the service. It even had a "spot promotion" system for its top performers—a perk envied and resented by the rest of the Air Force. Above all of this stood the dominating and larger-than-life figure of Gen Curtis E. LeMay. The second-youngest four-star general in US history at age 44, he always seemed older. He was the acknowledged world expert on strategic bombardment, stretching back to his experiences as a bomber commander in Europe and the Pacific during

World War II. He was controversial because of his outspokenness and the sheer power of his personality, but no one questioned his leadership ability to turn SAC into a potent and professional military force.

This study traces six interrelated themes: mission, message, education, technology, intelligence gathering/analysis, and leadership. All were constantly present in the story of strategic bombing that began in World War I, and all were essential to shaping the deterrence and war-fighting force that would become SAC. It began with the concept of mission—that of strategic bombing against a nation's vital centers. This unique capability was the mission to which airmen clung for decades. It became an almost messianic message that was taught to generations of airmen at the schools in Montgomery, Alabama, both before and after World War II. There were major shortcomings in this message—it too often relied on technologies not yet invented. Yet it remained true that technology, which was continuously evolving at a rapid rate, drove reality closer and closer to theory. By the end of World War II, all recognized the potency, importance, and dominance of airpower. Few argued with that fact; instead, the arguments revolved around who would control airpower and for what missions would it be used.

The successes of strategic bombing in war led directly to SAC. Almost immediately, however, fundamental issues regarding intelligence of the new Soviet adversary, an intelligence bound up with technology to gather and analyze it, were apparent. The wartime intelligence and analysis agencies were recreated after the war and refined, resulting in offices like the Strategic Vulnerability Branch and the Air Targeting Division. Their task was the same as it had been for similar organizations in World War II—to study the enemy's economy, government, and military forces and to determine the best way to make them fail. Eventually, this function would grow to great size and importance: the Joint Strategic Target Planning Staff, which was responsible for developing a single integrated operational plan—a nuclear targeting plan combining the activities of the Air Force, Navy, and allies to carry out a war against the Soviet Union.

As already emphasized, technology was overarching. What outsiders, especially soldiers, viewed as an almost childish fascination with machines and "toys," airmen viewed as a fundamental, healthy interest in the tools of their trade. War had been fought on land and sea since prehistory, but it only moved into the air in the twentieth century, because that is how long it took for the technology to evolve permitting flight. This technology rushed forward at an astonishing pace in the five decades between the Wright Brothers' first flight and the era when SAC was becoming the dominant force in American military policy. Aircraft changed from rickety biplanes built of wood and fabric to sleek jets that could travel at three times the speed of sound and could do so above 70,000 feet. Propulsion went from simple internal combustion engines, not much different than those used in the family automobile, to jet and rocket engines. The space age began with the advent of intercontinental ballistic missiles, weapons that could carry a nuclear-tipped warhead measured in megatons—each missile having more power than all the bombs dropped in World War II combined. Yes, technology was fundamental to airpower, and airmen had no reason to apologize for that fact.

And, of course, throughout this story runs the vital importance of leadership. Sometimes it was inadequate and led to failure and short-comings, while at other times it was wondrously inspired and effective. It is customary to focus on those at the top—especially combat commanders during wartime—but it is essential to note that lower-level commanders were also important. Similarly, the leadership—albeit of a differing kind—of the many staff officers, bureaucrats, and educators who were instrumental in planning, developing, operating, and teaching all the ideas and organizations that went into what would become SAC must not be forgotten. Still, above all was the influence of senior command. Henry "Hap" Arnold, Carl Spaatz, Hoyt Vandenberg, Nathan Twining, Lauris Norstad, and Curtis LeMay play prominent roles throughout this study. Their vision and strength were indispensible. That of LeMay is most compelling and immediate to our story.

Today, it is easy to caricature Curtis LeMay as a cigar-chomping troglodyte with little polish or sophistication who pushed the boundary between civilian and military control. Such depictions were never accurate, but they were especially false for the years covered in this study. LeMay was indeed a tough customer who did not suffer fools lightly. He was an extraordinarily focused individual with both physical and mental courage. He did not shrink from a challenge or from difficulties. It was his unswerving drive that made SAC a professional and highly trained instrument of war. Yet it must be remembered that the choice of making SAC the dominant instrument of American military policy was not made by LeMay or other airmen. Rather, the circumstances of the geopolitical environment—the breakdown of the wartime alliance into a cold war between the superpowers—dictated a strategy and policy that relied on airpower, specifically the nuclear-armed aircraft and guided missiles embodied by SAC. The decision to adopt this strategic posture was made by Presidents Harry Truman and Dwight Eisenhower, former soldiers. The highest military officers in the land during this era were Gen Omar Bradley and ADM Arthur Radford. Civilians, soldiers, and sailors recognized the logic of strategic airpower as fully as did the airmen themselves. When LeMay left SAC in July 1957 to become the Air Force vice–chief of staff, the dominance of strategic bombing was well established in the US military.

The result of all these factors led to an amazingly powerful and professional force whose mission was to keep the peace. What eventually became the motto of SAC—"Peace is our Profession"—was a staggering paradox that was also completely accurate.

The impetus for this study came from the Air Force Research Institute (AFRI) at Maxwell AFB, Alabama. Specifically, AFRI's director, retired general John A. Shaud, saw the need for a book on the formation of SAC and the challenges it faced during its early years. I also give much thanks to Dan Mortensen, the dean of AFRI, and his excellent staff of administrative (Robyn Read) and security (Andrew Thayer) personnel, who ensured the bureaucracy and paperwork flowed with minimum friction. Jerry Gantt and his editorial staff were able to turn my sometimes infelicitous prose into readable copy. Joe Caver and his colleagues at the Air Force Historical Research Agency, especially Sylvester Jackson, Tammy Horton, and Archie Difante, were similarly ever helpful, as was everyone in the magnificent Muir S. Fairchild Research Information Center at the Air University, especially Joan Phillips, Kim Hunter, and Sandy Milladi. At my local library in West Chicago, the research librarians—Sarah, Don, Helen, and Jennifer—were tireless in finding and securing dozens of arcane books through interlibrary loan. As always, the patience and support of my Barbara made everything so much easier. Finally, I wish to thank my son, Phillip S. Meilinger Jr., for designing the beautiful and dramatic dust jacket/cover for this book—the original art work is by Philip Alexander. I told my son I wanted something special, and as usual he exceeded my high expectations.

Phillip S. Meilinger
West Chicago, Illinois

Abbreviations

AAA	antiaircraft artillery
AAF	Army Air Forces
AB	air base
AF	Air Force
AFA	Air Force Academy
AFB	air force base
AFSWP	Armed Forces Special Weapons Project
ACC	Air Combat Command
ACTS	Air Corps Tactical School
ADC	Air Defense Command
AEC	Atomic Energy Commission
AFHRA	Air Force Historical Research Agency
AMC	Air Materiel Command
ASTS	Air Service Tactical School
AWPD	Air War Plans Division
BMEWS	ballistic missile early warning system
BW	bomb wing
CAF	Continental Air Forces
CCS	Combined Chiefs of Staff
CEP	circular error probable
CIA	Central Intelligence Agency
CINCSAC	Commander in Chief, Strategic Air Command
CNO	Chief of Naval Operations
COA	Committee of Operations Analysts
CONUS	continental United States
DDQI	*Declassified Documents Quarterly Index*
DEW (Line)	distant early warning
DOD	Department of Defense
ECM	electronic countermeasures
EOU	enemy objectives unit
EW	electronic warfare
EWO	electronic warfare officer
EWP	emergency war plan
FBI	Federal Bureau of Investigation
FEAF	Far East Air Forces

FM	field manual
FY	fiscal year
GCA	ground-controlled approach
GCI	ground-controlled intercept
GHQ	general headquarters
GPO	Government Printing Office
HMSO	Her/His Majesty's Stationary Office
ICBM	intercontinental ballistic missile
IFR	instrument flight rules
JATO	jet-assisted takeoff
JCS	Joint Chiefs of Staff
JIC	Joint Intelligence Committee
JSPG	Joint Strategic Planning Group
JSTPS	Joint Strategic Target Planning Staff
JWPC	Joint War Planning Committee
LOC	Library of Congress
MED	Manhattan Engineering District
MEW	Ministry of Economic Warfare (UK)
MFR	memo for record
MIT	Massachusetts Institute of Technology
M&S	maintenance and supply
MLC	Military Liaison Committee (to the AEC)
NA	National Archives
NATO	North Atlantic Treaty Organization
NSC	National Security Council
OCAC	Office of the Chief of the Air Corps
OR	operations research
ORI	operational readiness inspection
OSD	Office of the Secretary of Defense
OSS	Office of Strategic Services
POW	prisoner of war
RAF	Royal Air Force (UK)
RBS	radar bomb scoring
RCM	radar countermeasures
R&D	research and development

RG	record group
ROK	Republic of Korea
SAB	Scientific Advisory Board
SAC	Strategic Air Command
SACEUR	Supreme Allied Commander, Europe
SAG	Scientific Advisory Group
SAM	surface-to-air missile
SECAF	Secretary of the Air Force
SECDEF	Secretary of Defense
SECNAV	Secretary of the Navy
SHAPE	Supreme Headquarters, Allied Powers Europe
SHORAN	short-range navigation
SIOP	single integrated operational plan
TAC	Tactical Air Command
TR	training regulation
UPA	University Publications of America
USAFE	US Air Forces Europe
USSBS	US Strategic Bombing Survey
USSTAF	US Strategic Air Forces
VDT	variable discharge turbine (engine)
VFR	visual flight rules
VHB	very heavy bomber
VJ-Day	Victory over Japan Day
WSEG	Weapons Systems Evaluation Group

Chapter 1

The Intellectual and Organizational Imperatives for Bombing

Maj Edgar S. Gorrell arrived in France in August 1917 as chief of the technical section of the US Army Air Service. He was responsible for evaluating Allied aircraft, engines, and other aviation equipment and recommending which of them the Air Service should procure. Almost immediately, Gorrell became interested in the potential of strategic bombing. He met with Italian aircraft builder Gianni Caproni, who, in turn, introduced him to air theorists Col Giulio Douhet and Nino Salvaneschi. The latter was as much a publicist as he was a theorist, and this poem clearly demonstrates his zeal. Such ideas would echo over the next two decades.

> The supreme gallantry of the heroes of so many battles, from
> so many countries, and the sacrifice of those who
> gave their lives, are soon to
> be rewarded with
> victory.
> Where
> could we strike decisively?
> In the air and by the air.
> How can we all concur
> with certainty
> for victory?
> With the bombardment fleets.
> With a single command.
> And a new air
> strategy.[1]

Gorrell met with a number of British airmen as well. One of the most influential of these contacts was Lord Tiverton, who had written a farsighted essay on the subject of aerial bombardment in September 1917. This essay had a major impact on Gorrell's thinking, and in November he wrote a memo to his superiors reflecting the views of Tiverton, Douhet, and Salvaneschi.[2] Gorrell began by noting that three years of warfare on the western front had resulted in a

---

[1] Poem contained in Nino Salvaneschi, "In Defense of True Air War," translation of pamphlet, 1918, nonpaginated, Air Force Historical Research Agency (AFHRA), file 168.661-131.
[2] Biddle, *Rhetoric and Reality in Air Warfare*, 38–40, 54–55.

prolonged and deadly stalemate. New methods of waging war must be found, and the most promising new weapon was the aircraft. The main killer on the western front was artillery—millions of shells were being fired by both sides in a deadly war of attrition that lurched on endlessly. What if, instead of attempting to knock out every enemy artillery piece, aircraft destroyed the relatively few factories that built those guns and shells? Gorrell suggested "strategical bombing" against German commercial centers and lines of communication with the intent of causing "the cessation of supplies to the German Front."[3]

Regrettably, Gorrell's knowledge of the German economy was limited—as was the case with all belligerents. Never before in war had military leaders needed detailed information on an enemy's economy for the simple reason that they could do little about attacking such targets located deep in hostile territory. Aircraft, however, could overfly the front, offering a new way of waging war. Even so, there was little to be done in 1917. The aircraft necessary to drop a significant load of bombs on a specific target were not yet available in sufficient numbers. Nor were there accurate bombsights to put the bombs on those targets. Aircrews trained to conduct precision bombing strikes were similarly unavailable.[4] Besides these very real impediments, Gorrell's memo touched upon the matter of intelligence and its role in targeting. To illustrate just how immature intelligence gathering was at the time, Gorrell could do no better than to suggest four major target areas, each centered on an industrial region in Germany. The "northerly group," for example, contained the cities of Dusseldorf, Krefeld, Elberfeld, and Essen—and each of those cities housed dozens of relevant factories. Which of these hundreds of potential targets were most promising and why? Gorrell had no answer. This was hardly practical as a blueprint for a strategic bombing campaign, but it was a beginning.

In addition, Gorrell advocated bombing both day and night so as not to give the Germans rest. He admitted, however, that a night bombing campaign would require intensive training that American pilots had barely considered. As for the bombs themselves, Gorrell stated blandly that 50-pounders would be adequate for most targets. Echoing a belief held by many airmen at the time, he opined that "after such a bombardment, the manufacturing works would be

---

[3] Maurer, ed., *U.S. Air Service in World War I*, vol. 2, 143.
[4] For the lamentable inaccuracy of British bombing efforts during World War I, see Williams, *Biplanes and Bombers*, passim, but especially chap. 6.

wrecked and the morale of the workmen would be shattered." This effect would be the real payoff: "Statistics will show very easily that, given a fixed amount of explosives to destroy a target, aerial bomb-dropping will reach and destroy this target with less explosive, fewer shells, and less expenditure of money than is required for the artillery and infantry to destroy a target of similar importance."[5] In other words, Gorrell was pronouncing as a verifiable fact that airpower could be more effective and less costly—in both blood and treasure—than were traditional forms of war. It was an argument that airmen would be making for the next century.

Gorrell's memo showed foresight, while at the same time glossing over some real problems. Targeting would indeed be central to a successful strategic bombing campaign, and we shall be revisiting this subject throughout this study. Selecting targets whose destruction would be most important in defeating an enemy was the crux of air strategy, but Gorrell's proposal to bomb four geographic areas in Germany was not nearly good enough. Similarly, the physical effects of bombing needed a great deal of study and practical experimentation—50-lb. bombs would prove useless in war. The psychological effect produced by bombing was another subject causing endless debate—a debate not yet ended. Finally, the notion that bombers could penetrate deep inside hostile territory with impunity also would be revealed as overly optimistic. Nonetheless, Edgar Gorrell was the first American to take a serious stab at the issue of strategic bombing, and his ideas would resurface throughout the next two decades.

The Influence of Billy Mitchell

Brig Gen William "Billy" Mitchell was the top American air combat commander to emerge from the war. Eventually—though not at first—his ideas would evolve toward a position similar to what Gorrell had expressed in 1917. Surprisingly, the two men were never close. It may simply have been professional jealousy—Mitchell did not like anyone around him originating good ideas before he came up with them himself. In any event, Gorrell largely disappeared as a military figure following the war, and Mitchell would become the leader

---

[5] Gorrell's memo is reproduced in Maurer, *U.S. Air Service in World War I*, vol. 2, 145–53.

among Army airmen.[6] This was unfortunate in one sense, because air advocates needed to present a united front—given the number of powerful enemies confronting them. It was distressing to see smart and dedicated airmen fighting among themselves.

Of far-reaching significance, Mitchell was one of the few officers to retain his rank after the armistice. During the war most officers were promoted to temporary rank as the US military establishment exploded in size, but just as quickly, the military contracted after the armistice. Officers who had been rapidly promoted were in for a rude awakening when the conflict ended. Mason Patrick, who had been a major general and chief of the Air Service during the war, reverted to his permanent rank of colonel upon returning to the States. Similarly, Brig Gen Benjamin Foulois and Col Henry "Hap" Arnold dropped back to major after the armistice. Mitchell was luckier; as assistant chief of the Air Service, he was able to retain his rank of brigadier general—and the pay that came with it—due to the position he held. This rank and position gave him tremendous prestige and influence within the Air Service.

It is important to note that Mitchell did not start out as a strategic bombing advocate. Rather, he saw the mission of the Air Service as one of support for the Army. During the war he had written a memo to his superior, Maj Gen Hunter Liggett, stating that the purpose of bombing operations would be "essentially tactical in their nature and directed against active enemy units in the field which will have a direct bearing on operations."[7] In 1919 he published two articles depicting his role in the air campaigns at St. Mihiel and the Meuse-Argonne, and in both essays emphasized that airpower's primary goal was to win control of the air; afterwards, its mission was to attack enemy ground troops and ensure proper cooperation and observation for friendly infantry and artillery.[8] He reiterated these sentiments in his first book, *Our Air Force: The Keystone of National Defense*, published in 1921. In it he stressed the importance of pursuit aviation (what today we would term "fighter aircraft") and especially its role in achieving air superiority: "No navies can operate on the seas, nor armies on the land, until the air forces have first attained a decision

---

[6] Gorrell wrote an invaluable history of the Air Service during the war, which forms the basis of Maurer's work noted above. In 1920 he left uniform and entered the automobile business, later becoming a noted member of the commercial aviation industry. He served as a member of the Baker Board in 1935.

[7] Clodfelter, "Molding Airpower Convictions," 86.

[8] Mitchell, "Air Service at St. Mihiel," 365. These ideas are reiterated in his article "Air Service at the Argonne-Meuse," 552–60.

against the opposing air forces. . . . Therefore, as a prelude to any engagement of military or naval forces, a contest must take place for control of the air."[9] Mitchell went on to state that winning the battle for air superiority would often lead to victory "because the victorious air service will be able to operate and increase without hindrance." The nation with the superior air force would then be able to shower death and destruction on its adversary. Great cities like New York would be particularly at peril; those attempting to escape an aerial onslaught "would be burned like rats in a trap."[10]

Despite this dramatic introduction, Mitchell went on to give a fairly straightforward and dispassionate overview of aviation in the United States. He stressed the need for a strong aeronautical industry, a commercial aviation structure, and a network of modern airfields and weather stations across the country. He noted the benefits airpower could provide to the country during peacetime: aerial mapping, forest patrol, air mail delivery, border patrol, and air transport of cargo and passengers.[11] When discussing the branches of military aviation, he emphasized the importance of pursuit, referring to it as "the major arm of the offense." Pursuit protected observation, attack, and bombardment aircraft while at the same time sweeping the skies of enemy planes. As a consequence, pursuit should comprise 60 percent of a combat air force, with the remainder divided equally between attack and bombardment. In words he would later refute, Mitchell in 1921 argued sternly that "nothing can resist the attack of Pursuit Aviation properly handled, because it utilizes its power of bringing flank, reverse and frontal fire in three dimensions to bear against the air force that it is attacking."[12] To Mitchell, "All other branches of military aeronautics are helpless without an adequate, strong, well-trained and well-equipped Pursuit Aviation. Nothing can contest with it for supremacy in the air. All kinds of Bombardment Aviation are completely at the mercy of Pursuit Aviation."[13]

Mitchell was conservative in his early writings regarding bombardment. The targets he proposed consisted of battlefield facilities, supply convoys, bridges, key road intersections, and enemy troop concentrations. To attack these targets effectively, escort (pursuit

---

[9] Mitchell, *Our Air Force*, xix.
[10] Ibid., xxiv.
[11] Ibid., chap. 13.
[12] Ibid., 46.
[13] Ibid., 53.

aircraft) was essential. Night attacks were potentially more effective—aircraft could be larger and carry a heavier bomb load because they had less to fear from enemy pursuit—but of course, accuracy and navigation difficulties also increased.[14] The following year, Mitchell wrote and distributed a training booklet titled *Notes on the Multi-Motored Bombardment Group Day and Night*. Although nearly three-quarters dealt with administrative and organizational matters—to include supply, maintenance, setting up of an aerodrome, procedures for the inspection of aircraft, and so forth—three chapters were devoted to bombardment, saying it could make certain areas untenable, disperse enemy forces, or intimidate civilian population centers. Of importance, Mitchell argued that "the most effective use of bombardment aviation is the attack of sea craft."[15]

This last sentence indicates that even at this early stage, Mitchell was antagonistic toward the Navy. He argued continually that no warship could survive a determined air attack, yet thousands of aircraft could be purchased for the cost of one battleship. Partly due to Mitchell's negative influence, antipathy between airmen and sailors would often break out in public. The reasons why this distrust and anger occurred are many, but it is possible it hinged on the fact that both services saw themselves as the first line of American defense, and both sides considered themselves as true strategic weapons—as opposed to the Army, which was viewed as a tactical force. In short, airmen and sailors disliked one another because they were so much alike.[16]

When Mitchell demanded the Navy produce obsolete or confiscated German ships to test his theories, the sailors were backed into a corner. They had long argued that no battleship could be sunk from the air, but they were loath to take any chances by allowing the Air Service to conduct such tests. After constant pressure, Mitchell and the Air Service prevailed, and in July and September 1921 and again in September 1923, Mitchell's aircraft did indeed sink several capital ships, including the sturdy German battleship *Ostfriesland*, which

---

[14] Ibid., 64–65.

[15] Mitchell, *Notes on the Multi-Motored Bombardment Group*, 61. See chaps. 5–7 for his observations on bombardment operations.

[16] Mitchell was highly derogatory regarding aircraft carriers. In his view they were the most vulnerable of all surface ships, and even small bombs exploding on the deck would make it impossible for aircraft to land or take off, thus rendering the ships useless in combat. Ibid., 63. Clearly, he was opposed to the Navy having its own air arm and believed all air assets should be centralized in a single, independent air force, as was the situation in Great Britain.

had survived the Battle of Jutland, and the US battleships *Alabama*, *New Jersey*, and *Virginia*.[17]

Mitchell's second book, *Winged Defense*, was more aggressive, but his anger was directed mostly at the Navy. The ability of aircraft to sink any ship afloat—which he had repeatedly demonstrated—meant surface fleets were now obsolete: "the Navy's mission so far as coast defense is concerned, has ceased to exist and its mission must be beyond the zone of aircraft activity."[18] This book was published just prior to his court-martial, so Mitchell was still reticent about attacking his own service—hence, his focus on the Navy. That restraint, such as it was, would soon evaporate. In April 1925, his tour as assistant chief of the Air Service concluded, and he reverted to his permanent rank of colonel and was assigned to Fort Sam Houston in San Antonio. Although, as noted, this reversion to permanent rank was common at the time, Mitchell and his protégés saw it as punitive. He would not go quietly.[19]

The Air Corps Tactical School—The Early Years

Mitchell was idolized by most Army airmen. He was handsome, dashing, aggressive, fearless, brimming with self-confidence, and a devoted believer in the future of airpower.[20] As a result, dozens of young officers gravitated toward him as their mentor and became his advocates. One of these followers, Maj Thomas DeWitt Milling, was given a key post in 1920—he was to establish a new school for airmen. This institution, located at Langley Field, Virginia, was termed the Air Service Field Officers' School.

This was a major step for the fledgling airmen. The Army had always favored education of its officer corps and had founded branch schools for the infantry, artillery, cavalry, and signal corps. In 1901, it established the General Service and Staff School at Fort Leavenworth, Kansas (later named the Command and General Staff School). Soon after, the Army War College was opened in Washington, DC.

---

[17] For descriptions of these tests, see Maurer, *Aviation in the U.S. Army*, 113–27.

[18] Mitchell, *Winged Defense*, 215.

[19] Two days after the Navy's airship *Shenandoah* went down in a storm on 3 September 1925, Mitchell called a press conference from his office at Fort Sam Houston and declared that Army and Navy leaders were guilty of "incompetency, criminal negligence and almost treasonable administration of our national defense." He was court-martialed soon after and found guilty of, among other charges, insubordination. For a good treatment see Waller, *A Question of Loyalty*.

[20] The best source on Mitchell's ideas on airpower remains Hurley, *Billy Mitchell*.

Mitchell was adamant that another school, an *air* school, be established to educate airmen to become senior leaders. The argument for founding such a school was logical: if one believed that the services and even branches within a service were so technically or theoretically unique as to require a separate school for the further education of officers in that specialty, then an Air Service school was clearly necessary. The Field Officers' School opened at Langley Field in November 1920. Two years later, it was renamed the Air Service Tactical School, and four years after that, when the Air Service became the Air Corps, the name changed again. In the summer of 1931, the Air Corps Tactical School (ACTS) moved to Maxwell Field, Alabama.

It is difficult to exaggerate the influence of the Tactical School. The Army took its schooling seriously, and any officer destined for high command or even just a career in uniform was virtually required to attend the professional schools. The list of attendees at ACTS is a veritable who's who of important airmen. All three World War II generals—Joe McNarney, George Kenney, and Carl Spaatz—had attended ACTS, and 11 of the 13 lieutenant generals during the war were ACTS graduates. Indeed, of the 320 air general officers alive at the end of the war, 261 were ACTS graduates.[21] Perhaps of greater importance, the Air Corps recognized that quality education required a quality faculty. Those chosen to teach at Langley and later Maxwell included future four-star generals Hoyt Vandenberg, George Kenney, Muir "Santy" Fairchild, Laurence "Larry" Kuter, and Earle "Pat" Partridge. A host of lesser lights—Harold "Hal" George, Millard "Miff" Harmon, Claire Chennault, Robert Olds, Lewis Brereton, and two dozen others who would eventually wear stars—also taught at the Tactical School.[22]

Milling, as one of Billy Mitchell's trusted staffers, was sent to Langley to see to the school's curriculum. Just as Mitchell himself was largely quiescent at this point in his career, so too was the initial curriculum at Langley fairly benign. Over a nine-month period, students took 20 courses that provided 1,345 hours of instruction. More than half of those hours were spent on nonaeronautical subjects: supply, organization, staff duties, combat orders, and the like. The courses on pursuit, bombardment, and observation were of equal weight and were

---

[21] Finney, "History of the Air Corps Tactical School," 42. The two lieutenant generals who did not attend ACTS were Jimmy Doolittle and Millard Harmon, although Harmon served as assistant commandant in 1941–42. General of the Army Hap Arnold also did not attend ACTS.

[22] See ibid., append. 2, for a list of all ASTS/ACTS instructors and staff members. One non-airman instructor, Courtney Hodges, also became a full general.

followed by a course in "combined air tactics"—the integration of all aviation to achieve a specific military objective.[23]

Over the next two decades, courses would come and go as well as grow or shrink, depending on the beliefs or whims of the commandant, faculty, and air staff in Washington. Even so, over half the classes perennially dealt with the other branches of the Army, the Navy, or various command, staff, and logistical subjects. In fact, airpower was scarcely discussed during the first half of the year; it was not until after Christmas that instruction on air matters began in earnest. Classes on pursuit, observation, and bombardment were vital, but the capstone course at the end of the year, the Combined Air Tactics course, later renamed simply The Air Force, was soon regarded as the most insightful, forward looking, and stimulating of the entire year.

Ideas initially expounded at Langley were conservative and followed Army thinking as expressed in its official doctrine. Moreover, it must be emphasized that official air doctrine was *not* to be formulated by the Tactical School; rather, Army field manuals and training regulations (TR) were designed for that purpose.[24] For example, the War Department's publication TR 440-15, *Fundamental Principles for the Employment of the Air Service* of 1926 categorically stated in its opening paragraphs that the Army's primary mission was to overcome the will of the enemy through the destruction of its armed forces. Consequently, the Air Service's mission was "to assist the ground forces to gain strategical and tactical successes by destroying enemy aviation, attacking enemy ground forces and other enemy objects on land or sea, and in conjunction with other agencies to protect ground forces from hostile aerial observation and attack."[25] The following paragraph reiterated this basic thrust: "The organization and training of all air units is based on the fundamental doctrine that their mission is to aid the ground forces to gain decisive success."[26] Finally, like any good Army briefing, it applied a hammer to nail down its main point for the third time a few pages later: "During an attack by the Army, the Army air force is concentrated on the immediate front to assist the ground forces." If defeat of the enemy were achieved, airpower would then be used to track down and destroy the fleeing enemy.[27]

---

[23] Ibid., 8–12.
[24] Ibid., 69–70.
[25] US Army, *Fundamental Principles for the Employment of the Air Service*, para. 1–3.
[26] Ibid., para. 4.
[27] Ibid., para. 13.

TR 440-15 seemed to leave the door slightly ajar for airmen by noting that once the enemy's armed forces were defeated, bombardment could be used against military industrial centers, mobility and training centers, military shipping and transportation centers, bridges, dams, locks, power plants, and military supply depots.[28] But of course if the enemy's forces were defeated, then in Army thinking the war was over, so such bombing would be superfluous. Airmen resisted such a narrow view of airpower and its role in war. As early as 1921 the Information Group on the Air Service staff published a fiery article stating that the mission of bombardment aviation was to destroy "important centers of concentration behind the lines, or important manufacturing centers in the interior."[29] Maj William C. Sherman, another Mitchell follower, taught at Langley during its first three years. In 1926 he authored a book titled *Air Warfare*, based on his teaching notes. The first several chapters were a primer covering the nature of war, the characteristics of airplanes and what makes them work, basic aerobatic maneuvers, and the missions of observation, attack, and pursuit aviation. It was not until chapter 7 that he began a serious discussion of bombardment.

Sherman began this chapter with a bold statement: "The bomber now stands forth as the supreme air arm of destruction, with vastly enhanced power. When nations of today look with apprehension on the air policy of a neighbor, it is the bomber they dread."[30] He admitted that the practice of bombing as it had been carried out in the world war was rudimentary, inaccurate, and little more than a nuisance to those on the ground. Although technology had advanced little since 1918, he wrote as if the minor steps forward had been revolutionary in scope. Using this alleged progress in the size and speed of aircraft and the development of bigger and more powerful bombs, including chemical bombs, Sherman speculated on the great effects a bombing attack would have on an enemy nation.[31]

The result of these presumed technological advances meant the bomber had become a unique strategic weapon that could strike virtually any target within an enemy country at the outbreak of hostilities.

---

[28] Ibid., para. 16.

[29] "Air Service, Air Force, and Air Power," 522–23. The essay was not attributed to any individual, but the Information Group, which worked for Mitchell, was then led by Maj Horace Hickam.

[30] Sherman, *Air Warfare*, 197. One source claims Sherman was the author of TR 440–15 but had to tone down his comments to pass the Army censors. *Air Warfare* was the unexpunged version. Wray R. Johnson in the preface to the republished edition of *Air Warfare* (Maxwell AFB, AL: Air University Press, 2002), xiv.

[31] Sherman, *Air Warfare*, 202.

One such target was the civilian population, although Sherman noted such a drastic step could only be approved by political leaders. He admitted that if so ordered, "There is nothing inherently impracticable in such an operation as the destruction of a city." In a further step toward this type of air strategy, Sherman noted the modern nation in arms meant "there is no sound reason for granting immunity from attack to any class of enemy subjects."[32] Workers were simply warriors in civilian clothes. He concluded on a somewhat more hopeful note that fear of reprisal would likely serve as a brake on such city-busting tactics—what nation would launch such air strikes against enemy cities if it knew that its own cities would consequently suffer a similarly devastating blow? The answer to that rhetorical question was of course, "everyone." The bombing of cities, even if under the guise of precision bombing against specific military targets, was to be a reality practiced by both sides during World War II. Even so, Sherman's logic was sound. The entire concept of today's nuclear deterrence strategy is founded on the notion that a sizeable nuclear arsenal and delivery capability are the only plausible methods of ensuring such an attack does not occur. Such a deterrence concept—"mutual assured destruction"—has been a major reason why nuclear weapons have not been used since 1945, and it was one of the founding concepts of Strategic Air Command.

By the end of the 1920s, the ideas emanating out of ACTS were becoming markedly more progressive—or radical, depending on one's perspective—than had been the case previously. This was true for several reasons. First, the Air Corps chief, Maj Gen James E. Fechet, had sent a stinging note to the ACTS commandant in September 1928 stating that the mission of the Air Corps was not, as the school's texts implied, merely to serve as an "auxiliary of the ground forces." Fechet argued that "victory was achieved when the enemy's will to resist was overcome; armies and navies were only means to that end, and airpower might achieve it without reference to surface forces."[33] This was a revolutionary call to arms, demonstrating the importance of leadership in the doctrinal process. The chief, in this case General Fechet, provided a clear vision to the faculty at Langley and directed them to revise their thoughts and teachings based on that new vision. The results were to be extraordinary.

---

[32] Ibid., 213.
[33] Greer, "Development of Air Doctrine in the Army Air Arm," 48.

Second, the court-martial of Billy Mitchell in 1925–26 was seen by most airmen as a deliberate attempt to silence dissent within the Air Corps. If that were the intent, the effect on most officers was precisely the opposite. Airmen were angry, not cowed.

Third, the results of the Morrow Board that led to the Air Corps Act of 1926 had been disappointing. Certainly, the renaming of the Air Service to put it on a more even par with the other combat branches was a step forward. So too was the new rule that all flying units were to be commanded by pilots. But in other respects, the results were less positive. Funds were still highly constrained, despite Congress insisting on a larger air arm composed of more modern aircraft. Similarly, the staffing levels within the Air Corps lagged behind the other branches, as did promotions. These were sources of irritation to airmen.

Regarding funding, the Air Corps received less than 12 percent of the Army budget between 1919 and 1941.[34] The low point was 4.5 percent in 1924, and the high was 16.8 percent in 1939. Airmen did not view this as an equitable distribution of funds and blamed the Army hierarchy for deliberately slighting aviation.

An example of the negative light in which Army leaders viewed airpower occurred in 1932. At the Geneva Disarmament Conference that year, a number of proposals were advanced regarding arms limitations. An American delegate, Jay Pierrepont Moffat, was nonetheless stunned when on 4 April the Army chief of staff, Gen Douglas MacArthur, told him he would support the abolition of *all* military aviation. MacArthur said the Air Corps "was already receiving 25–35 percent [*sic*] of the Army budget and was constantly asking for more." The Air Corps was simply too expensive: "money spent on aviation was money thrown away."[35]

One of MacArthur's top subordinates felt similarly. In 1933 MacArthur directed the Drum Board (chaired by Maj Gen Hugh Drum) to study Army aviation needs. It concluded that the Air Corps required 2,320 aircraft to carry out the Army's "Air Plan for the Defense of the United States." Of these, 1,660 should be combat types, and 400 of those—or 24 percent—should be bombers. The Air Corps

---

[34] *Army Almanac* (1950), 692, foldout. Maurer, *Aviation in the U.S. Army*, 475–76, gives different figures and lists the Air Corps' average share between 1923 and 1941 as only 8.8 percent of the Army budget. Remember also this was merely the Army budget, not the entire defense budget.

[35] Hooker, ed., *Moffat Papers*, 60, 63–64, 69, 92; and the diary of Henry L. Stimson (then secretary of state) for 3 June 1932, *Stimson Papers*, Yale University Library. See also US Department of State, *FRUS, 1932*, 65. In 1932 the Air Corps received 9.6 percent of the Army budget, not 25–35 percent as MacArthur stated.

disagreed, stating it needed 4,422 total aircraft, of which 3,719 should be combat types and 716 (19.2 percent) should be bombers. (Note the Air Corps was asking for fewer bombers by percentage than was the Drum Board.) The board ignored the Air Corps' desires while also emphasizing that all combat aircraft would be especially important for land operations. Their purpose would be long-range reconnaissance, interdiction, and support of the ground forces. At that time the Air Corps possessed only 1,685 aircraft—fewer even than the 1,800 authorized by Congress; yet the board was "most emphatically of the opinion" that any increase in airpower should not be at the expense of other Army arms and branches.[36] In 1934 the Army rank-ordered its priorities for modernization: tanks, artillery, field forces, and then aircraft. Three years later, it moved another weapon to the head of the list—antiaircraft artillery.[37]

It is inherent in the Army's culture to place greater emphasis on men than on technology, but this philosophy was disastrous for an air arm dependent on new equipment; aeronautical development was advancing so rapidly that a "procurement holiday" would soon leave the Air Corps with obsolete planes. MacArthur acknowledged this, testifying before Congress that he "endeavored determinedly" to maintain an adequate *personnel* structure, even though that meant "continuing in service obsolete and inefficient equipment" and "slackening technical development."[38] This type of resistance toward airpower from the Army hierarchy is one reason why Congress intervened periodically to insist that more funds be diverted to the air arm.

Manning was also a concern within the Air Corps. Between 1923 and 1941 the Army officer corps was, on average, manned at 95.7 percent of its authorized strength. Within the branches there were two key statistics: the actual manning level of the branch, and the number of officers possessing that specialty throughout the Army as a whole. Thus, although there might be the appropriate number of infantry or cavalry officers in the Army, because many of them served in a headquarters, on attaché duty, in faculty positions, or otherwise, the number actually serving in their home branch would be lower than the authorized strength of that branch. This margin allowed an expertise to reside in the Army as a whole to be called upon in the event of war—a "surge capability." Thus, the infantry had on average

---

[36] Special Committee of the General Council, "Report on Employment of Army Air Corps," 1.

[37] Millett and Maslowski, *For the Common Defense*, 380.

[38] Huzar, *Purse and the Sword*, 140.

106.8 percent of its authorized officers in the Army during the interwar period, but the infantry branch was manned on average at only
68.5 percent in those two decades. The air arm was in an anomalous
position because relatively few aviators were considered worthy of
serving in the staff billets noted above. As a result, the interwar Air
Service/Air Corps averaged only 80.7 percent of its authorized officer
strength, while the branch itself was manned at 78.9 percent—there
were few additional airmen in the Army who could return to their
branch in the event of a crisis.[39] If a surge became necessary, there was
nothing with which to surge. Indeed, until 1929 the cavalry branch
was manned with more officers and at a higher percentage than was
the Air Corps! It should also be noted that on average between 1919
and 1941, the air arm comprised only 9.17 percent of the Army's total
personnel strength.[40]

More important than the number of officers in a given branch,
however, was the makeup of the senior officer ranks. As late as 1939,
of 793 regular colonels in the US Army, only 25 (3.1 percent) were in
the Air Corps. Worse, not one of the 68 general officers of the line
that year belonged to the Air Corps.[41] There were generals in the Air
Corps, usually three or four at any given time, but their ranks were
temporary and went with the position they occupied, not the individual. When officers left a general officer billet, they reverted to their
permanent rank—not unlike what had occurred after World War I,
and to Billy Mitchell in 1925. One incident illustrates that such a system invited mischief. In September 1938, Maj Gen Frank Andrews
was commander of the General Headquarters Air Force, but when his
tour ended he reverted to the rank of colonel. One historian argues
Andrews could have been moved to a general officer billet, but his
well-known advocacy of strategic bombing and the new B-17 bomber
caused him to be reassigned instead as the air officer for the VIII
Corps area in San Antonio, Texas. This was the same position, indeed
the precise office and the same desk, to which Billy Mitchell had been

---

[39] *Report of the Secretary of War to the President* for 1923–41, various pages in each volume.
[40] Davis, *Carl A. Spaatz and the Air War in Europe*, append. 1.
[41] *Official Army Register, 1939*, 2; and ibid., 11. The US Navy did things differently. To ensure there were high-ranking naval aviators available, certain willing senior officers, like Captains Ernest King and William Halsey, transferred to the air arm and became flyers so that naval aviation had its own men in high positions. This negated the seniority problem experienced in the Army, where airmen were told they were simply too junior to be promoted.

exiled in 1925 just prior to his court-martial.[42] The Army's message was not subtle.

In sum, all of these issues and perceived slights led airmen to agitate ever more forcefully for more autonomy within the Army—if not outright independence. At the very least they wanted a greater share of funds allotted to the Air Corps, which would allow them to buy more and better aircraft, and they pushed for a promotion system that gave them a greater say in which airmen were to be promoted. Even so, it would be erroneous to attribute the dramatic change in air doctrine occurring around 1930 simply to negative events. There were two positive developments—one dealing with personnel and the other with technology—which also contributed to an increased awareness of strategic bombing's potential.

The Air Corps Tactical School—The Golden Age

Around 1930 there began arriving on the ACTS faculty a number of original and creative minds who deliberately and effectively altered the debate on airpower. These included George Kenney, Robert Olds, Ken Walker, Don Wilson, Claire Chennault, Hal George, Bert Dargue, Gordon Saville, Robert Webster, Possum Hansell, Larry Kuter, Hoyt Vandenberg, Santy Fairchild, Miff Harmon, and Pat Partridge. All were outstanding officers—all later made general rank—and all thought creatively and deeply about their profession. Most of these men taught in the air force or bombardment sections, but others—career fighter pilots Vandenberg, Kenney, Chennault, and Partridge—were equally important in the formulation of bombing doctrine, simply because their profound knowledge of pursuit and attack aviation was essential in forcing the ideas of the bomber advocates to be more realistic.

At the same time these outstanding officers were arriving at the Tactical School, aviation technology was beginning to make significant gains. The first breakthrough occurred in engine development. Throughout the decades of the 1920s and '30s, engineers were able to produce motors of increasingly greater horsepower that were also lighter, smaller, and more reliable. The Wasp engine of 1925, for

---

[42] Copp, "Frank M. Andrews," 43–71. Chief of staff at the GHQ Air Force was Col Hugh Knerr, also an advocate of strategic airpower. The year following Andrews' demotion and exile, Knerr also reverted to permanent rank of lieutenant colonel and was sent to take Andrews's place in Texas. He, too, occupied the same office with the same desk. Worse, Knerr noted that in the corner of his office was an open-top latrine. He was mortified to find the outer-office clerks walking in and out of his office to use that latrine! Coffey, *Hap*, 235.

example, produced around 500 horsepower, but the Double Wasp of 1939 was able to generate over 2,000 horsepower. This fourfold increase in engine power was of enormous significance. It was a result of developing higher octane gasoline as well as more arcane factors such as hollow valve stems that dissipated heat more quickly, metallurgical breakthroughs that required less metal and therefore less weight, scientifically designed cooling fins and engine cowls, better carburetors and superchargers for high-altitude performance, and the invention of Prestone—a glycol mixture that allowed liquid-cooled engines to run at significantly higher power without overheating.[43]

Streamlining and metal construction were also of crucial importance. Most early aircraft engineers simply did not understand the principles of aerodynamics, which is why most aircraft designed before 1930 or so were marked by multiple wings, struts, guy wires, fixed landing gear, uncowled engines, and open cockpits. All of this changed around 1930. Metal became the material of choice in aircraft because of its strength, reliability, and predictability, replacing wood and fabric on the wings and fuselage of most new aircraft. Biplanes were out, and new designs were built with a single cantilevered wing—it needed no external bracing or struts. Landing gear was retracted into the fuselage during flight, and cockpits and gun ports were enclosed by Plexiglas canopies. All of these seemingly elementary alterations had a profound impact on drag—thus allowing much greater speed and range while also enabling engines to operate more efficiently.[44]

The result of these innovations benefitted large aircraft as well as small; indeed, for a brief time—coincidentally in the mid 1930s—it appeared bombers had a decided advantage over pursuit aircraft. I would argue this was largely due to economic conditions of the Great Depression. The technology for fighter aircraft demanded ultimate performance—high speed, high rate of climb, short turning radius, maximum agility. In the 1930s such demands were simply too risky for most aircraft builders, perpetually on the brink of bankruptcy, to attempt. Instead, the industry favored aircraft that were safe, reliable, and cost-effective and that did not push the envelope on technical development. In other words, the qualities needed in a heavy bomber

---

[43] For overall histories of aircraft engine and fuel development, see Chapel, *Aircraft Power Plants*; Schlaiffer and Heron, *Development of Aircraft Engines and Fuels*; and Setright, *Power to Fly*.

[44] For overviews, see Kelsey, *Dragon's Teeth?*; Schatzberg, *Wings of Wood*; and Launius, *Innovation and the Development of Flight*.

were the same ones required in a viable commercial airliner. The economic conditions of the Great Depression conspired to boost the development of bombers.[45]

In practical terms this meant that new bombers like the Martin B-10 had a performance nearly equal to that of contemporary pursuit planes. The B-10 first flew in 1932 and had a maximum speed of 213 mph. In contrast, the top pursuit plane of the era, the Boeing P-26, had a top speed of 234 mph. In the era before radar, this small speed differential meant pursuit would have an extremely difficult time intercepting and shooting down an attacking bomber force. When the Boeing B-17 flew in 1935 at a speed of over 250 mph, its impact, both physically and psychologically, was profound. As Hap Arnold phrased it, this was "airpower you could put your hand on."[46] The seemingly idealistic and futuristic theories being spun out by the instructors at ACTS now appeared credible.

During the 1930s, classes began at ACTS each morning with a lecture followed by a question-and-answer period; afterward, students broke up into seminars where they discussed the subject of the lecture or worked tactical problems. These problems typically involved half of the class determining the number and type of aircraft and ordnance needed and the tactical formations used by a strike force to hit a specific target. The other half of the class would determine the size and composition of the defensive force needed to thwart such an attack.[47] These detailed and complex tactical problems took several hours to complete and resulted in spirited debate between the two factions. When the students began their instruction on airpower after the Christmas break, they were exposed to strategic bombing theories then being formulated by the faculty.

The thrust of this airpower thinking can be illustrated with a lecture given by 1st Lt Ken Walker, an instructor from 1930 to 1933. Walker began by stating that bombardment was "the backbone of any air force." As such, it must be the dominant arm of the Air Corps, with pursuit and observation units acting in support. Walker argued that, given the defensive posture of the United States, the first and most obvious target for the bombers would be an enemy

---

[45] For this argument, see Meilinger, "Technology and Procurement." For another view, see Vander Meulen, *Politics of Aircraft*.

[46] Arnold, *Global Mission*, 154. The B-17 was significantly larger than the B-10 and weighed nearly four times as much, yet the Fortress was faster and had a greater range and payload than the Martin bomber.

[47] For a typical map problem, see "Solution to Problems," ACTS exercise, 24 February 1933, AFHRA, file 248.101-18.

fleet approaching the coast. Such a fleet would never be able to land an invading army as long as the Air Corps could control the air over the ocean approaches to US shores—naval vessels were helpless in the face of air attack.

Walker then made a statement that would be echoed by airmen repeatedly thereafter: "A determined air attack, once launched, is most difficult, if not impossible, to stop when directed against land objectives." Walker and his colleagues were writing before the invention of radar; therefore, they postulated that aircraft could attack from any direction and any altitude, at any time, thus achieving tactical surprise. Once again assuming the United States would be on the strategic defensive, Walker suggested that enemy air bases near the United States—in Central or South America—would present the greatest threat. The mission of bombers would be to destroy those air bases.

Walker noted that although antiaircraft fire was a threat to bomber formations, it could not stop a determined attack. Pursuit aircraft would be a greater danger, but given that new bombers had a performance nearly equal to enemy fighters and would be equipped with their own defensive guns, even this threat could be discounted.

In summary, Walker argued, airpower had now become the first line of defense for the United States. It would therefore logically follow that an independent Air Force should be created coequal to the Army and Navy, and this Air Force should be built around bombardment aviation.[48] This argument was of course the same one used by Billy Mitchell a decade earlier.

This was typical of the arguments used by bomber advocates at the Tactical School. They were long on passion and theory but short on proof. In 1935, for example, Capt Harold L. "Hal" George, an instructor in the air force section, argued before the Federal Aviation Commission that airpower was not a new weapon; it was a new *force*, "as separate and distinct from land power or sea power as each of these two forces is separate from each other."[49] Three years later 1st Lt Haywood S. Hansell would pontificate that "the air force is capable of conducting the air offensive in spite of any known artificial

---

[48] Walker, "Bombardment Aviation," 15–19. This article is a copy of one of Walker's ACTS lectures. He had been an aide to Billy Mitchell in Washington and would later be killed in action while leading a bombing mission over Rabaul, New Guinea, on 5 January 1943. He was posthumously awarded the Medal of Honor. For bombardment lectures during 1933, see AFHRA, file 248.2202A.

[49] Capt Harold L. George, "Testimony before the Federal Aviation Commission," 7 May 1935, AFHRA, file 248.121-3, 2–3. In a surprising burst of candor, George admitted that to concede that airpower was simply a new weapon would relegate it to being an auxiliary of the land forces.

defenses that can be interposed at that time with the possible exception of barrage balloons." He went on to state sardonically, "Perhaps someone will invent a death ray or some such device that will obliterate airplanes in flight. When that time comes there will be a defense against this new instrument—the air force."[50] Yet not everyone at ACTS subscribed to this belief in the primacy of bombardment. Capt Claire Chennault, a pursuit instructor from 1931 to 1936, argued just as vehemently that the bomber would *not* always get through, and a well-organized and capable defense—armed with first-rate interceptor planes and backed by a ground-observer corps (of the kind used by the British in World War I)—*would* be able to meet and defeat an enemy air attack. In one lecture he dismissed the overly optimistic thinking of those like Walker by sniffing, "This lack of regard for hostile opposition is a theory which has no foundation in experience."[51] Chennault, who would later organize and command the Flying Tigers in China during World War II, was ignored, with devastating results.[52]

Despite dissenters like Chennault, ACTS devised a unique doctrine of war, one dependent on airpower. Rejecting city-busting tactics, the faculty focused on the enemy's industrial infrastructure. In this view, the modern state was dependent on mass production of military goods such as ships, aircraft, trucks, artillery, ammunition, and uniforms. Moreover, most took a broader view and argued that essentials such as electrical power, steel, chemicals, and oil were also military targets and of greatest importance because they were the essential building blocks for other types of manufactured military goods needed to sustain a war effort. Over a period of three or four years, this concept was further refined. Hal George, Ken Walker, Don Wilson, Larry Kuter, Santy Fairchild, Possum Hansell, and others devised a theory that sought industrial bottlenecks—those factories or networks integral to the effective operation of the entire system and whose destruction would have disproportionally negative effects throughout the economic structure.

---

[50] 1st Lt Haywood S. Hansell, "Tactical Offensive and Tactical Defense," ACTS lecture, 28 March 1938, Hansell papers, Air Force Academy (AFA) Archives, box 6, 16.

[51] Capt Claire Chennault, "Pursuit Aviation," ACTS lecture, September 1933, AFHRA, file 248.101-8; and Chennault, "Special Support for Bombardment," *US Air Services*, January 1934, 18–21.

[52] Chennault's memoir discusses in some detail these arguments at the Tactical School in the early 1930s; see *Way of a Fighter*, chap. 2. There have been a number of biographies of Chennault, but the best is Martha Byrd, *Chennault: Giving Wings to the Tiger* (Tuscaloosa: University of Alabama Press, 1988).

A story is told of how one day the school's aircraft were grounded due to a shortage of a particular part used in the propeller pitch-control mechanisms. The instructors discovered that only one company, located in Pittsburgh, produced these parts, and it had been flooded by recent rains. The planes were out of commission until the company was back in operation. The lesson seemed clear: if the objective was to neutralize US airpower, it was not necessary to bomb every airfield or shoot down every aircraft. Rather, destroying a single factory in Pittsburgh could produce the same effect.[53] Using this admittedly simplistic example, the ACTS instructors began to study American industry in an attempt to locate other such bottlenecks. Their doctrinal theory, termed the *industrial web*, envisioned an enemy country as an integrated and mutually supporting system—like a spider's web, a disturbance in any section would reverberate throughout the entire network. The advocates dictated that the bombers would go in at high altitude—at least 20,000 feet. This height would keep them out of the range of most ground fire. To protect against enemy interceptors, they would attack in large formations so their guns could provide mutual support for other aircraft.

Precision was essential. Aside from humanitarian concerns, the principle of economy of force demanded that air planners choose specific targets and then hit those targets accurately so return missions would not be necessary. This would not only save aircrew lives and reduce losses but also provide a more rapid decision. Precision bombing led to the maxim that this offensive campaign be carried out in daylight—attempting to hit specific factories or marshaling yards at night was deemed impossible. And finally, the targets, as noted, would be key industrial facilities, the destruction of which would cause a cascading effect throughout the enemy's economy. In the words of one ACTS lecturer (albeit somewhat inelegant):

> It is maintained that modern industrial nations are susceptible to defeat by interruption of this web, which is built to permit the dependence of one section upon many or all other sections, and further that this interruption is the

---

[53] Greer, "Development of Air Doctrine in the Army Air Arm," 81. In testimony before the Federal Aviation Commission in 1935, Capt Robert Webster used a similar example. Also, several lectures cited a company that made automobile door handles which went bankrupt, shutting down production at several automobile assembly plants due to the absence of those minor but critical parts. Maj Muir Fairchild, "National Economic Structure," ACTS lecture, 3 April 1938, AFHRA, file 248.2019A-10, 33. In addition, one historian notes that this period was dominated by the Great Depression, and airmen witnessed each day the collapse of factories across the country, which in turn had a cascading effect on other factories, financial institutions, the labor force, etc. The American economy did indeed look extremely fragile. McFarland, *America's Pursuit of Precision Bombing*, 92.

primary objective for an air force. It is possible that the moral collapse brought about by the breaking of this closely knit web will be sufficient but closely connected, therewith is the industrial fabric which is absolutely essential for modern war.[54]

By the end of the decade this doctrine was fully and cogently refined—even if still unproven. It was this doctrine that American airmen carried into World War II.[55]

An organization created in 1922 also played a significant role in doctrine formulation. The Air Service Board (later Air Corps Board) was set up as a think tank to study problems given it by the Air Staff (technically, the Office of the Chief of the Air Corps, or OCAC). The issues given to the board included tactics, armament, equipment, aircraft characteristics, and doctrine. The board was collocated with the Tactical School, and its members were virtually all ACTS faculty members.[56] Small wonder the studies produced by the board read much like the doctrine lectures prepared in the school. As a consequence, Langley—and later Maxwell Field—derived a double-weighted influence in doctrine formulation. The staff officers in Washington would perhaps have wanted to write air doctrine, but they were too close to the War Department General Staff's scrutiny to do so. Moreover, they were too busy running the service. Between 1936 and 1938, for example, the OCAC Plans Section, consisting of four officers, was usually working on six or seven different projects simultaneously, most of which dealt with the administrative minutiae of the Air Corps, such as its "Study on the Method of Handling Mail, Routing of Correspondence, and Method of Keeping Records of Civilian Employees in the OCAC."[57] Similarly, operators in the field were practicing and evolving new tactics on a continuing basis, but they were too busy operating (flying) to write most of these new innovations down in the form of doctrine.[58] By default, Maxwell, as

---

[54] "Principles of War Applied to Air Force Action," ACTS lecture, 28 May 1934, AFHRA, file 248.101-2, 3. See also "Air Force Objectives," ACTS lecture, 27 February 1935, AFHRA, file 248.101-1. The lecturer for these lessons was probably Maj Don Wilson. For his story on how these theories evolved at ACTS, see Wilson, "Origins of a Theory of Air Strategy," 19–25.

[55] Maj Santy Fairchild was the leading instructor in the air force section in 1938, and his lectures on the industrial web theory are articulate and well presented, even if overly theoretical. See his "National Economic Structure," 5 April 1938, AFHRA, file 248.2019A-10, and "Primary Objectives of Air Forces," 11 April 1939, AFHRA, file 248-2019A-14.

[56] Finney, "History of the Air Corps Tactical School," 28–32.

[57] Howard and Mooney, "Development of Administrative Planning and Control in the AAF," 10–12.

[58] In his memoirs, Arnold wrote of his experiences with the 1st Wing at March Field, experimenting with all types of new ideas during the mid 1930s, but almost all were tactically focused. Arnold, Global Mission, 150–52.

home to ACTS and the Air Corps Board, reigned supreme in the air doctrine arena.

Although the corpus of thought created by these entities did not constitute official doctrine for the Air Corps, ACTS texts were nonetheless accepted by most airmen as authoritative. This constituted a fundamental error. Sound doctrine must be built upon three pillars to maintain stability. The first of these doctrinal pillars is history. We are all products of our past; we remember the lessons learned earlier in life and often base our future actions upon those lessons. It was not surprising for soldiers to look back at World War I for guidance on how future wars would be fought. That was logical. For airmen, it was a problem, because airpower had been in its infancy during the war and there was little experience and thus few lessons to be drawn from its operations—especially in regard to strategic bombing. Although the Air Corps did conduct periodic maneuvers and exercises—often the students at ACTS participated in these events as part of the curriculum—they were not nearly as realistic as was actual combat.[59] As a consequence, airmen relied almost exclusively on the second doctrinal pillar, that of theory.

Military planners must look forward as well as backward when preparing to fight. Doctrine that relies too heavily on history will condemn a military to "fight the last war"—a common complaint regarding the alleged conservative military mind-set. Airmen between the wars were certainly not guilty of conservatism. In fact, their problem was the opposite—they had so little history to guide them that they relied almost solely on theory. Overdoing this can lead to building a house on quicksand.[60] To their credit, they did lean heavily on the third pillar of the doctrinal edifice, that of technology. Airmen have often been accused of being enamored with technology to an almost childish degree, but airpower was and indeed still is absolutely dependent on advanced technology—there is a reason why it took millennia for man to conquer the air, whereas he adapted to warfare on land and sea in prehistory. The technologies necessary for flight simply did not exist prior to the twentieth century. Aviation technology advanced at a remarkably rapid pace between the world wars. For the

---

[59] In May 1933, for example, the entire ACTS student body flew out to March Field, CA, to participate in a large exercise. "GHQ Air Force (Provisional), Command and Staff Exercises, Critique," 8–26 May 1933, AFHRA, file 248.2122-3.

[60] A related problem was that ACTS wanted to acquire a squadron of modern aircraft of all types so the faculty and students could test out their theories, but funding for these aircraft was never forthcoming, and this forced the faculty into ever more theoretical realms. Finney, "History of the Air Corps Tactical School," 33.

most part, futuristic thinkers like Billy Mitchell, Alexander P. de Seversky, and many of their followers at ACTS understood the rapidity of aeronautical development—they simply misjudged the pace of that evolution. Their prophecies regarding intercontinental range, precision weaponry, supersonic speed, worldwide communications, missile and rocket technology, and even space operations earned them much ridicule.[61] Yet all of these technologies and more were part of the revolution in air and space power that occurred in the 1940s and 1950s. Airmen can be chastised for peering too far into the future and basing their doctrine on unproven theories and on technologies not yet built, but they were closer to reality than most of their adversaries at the time would admit.

There were, however, two related technologies of particular importance to implementing strategic bombing doctrine formulated at Maxwell Field in the 1930s. These technologies related to problems identified but not fully understood at the time, and little was done to address them in the years of peace. It would be the crucible of war that would bring these problems to the forefront. The first dealt with bombing accuracy, and the second concerned targeting.

Bombing Accuracy and Targeting

The key to the airpower theories of ACTS revolved around the issue of accuracy. The industrial infrastructure of a modern nation was large, complex, and interdependent. If a lengthy and costly war of attrition to destroy an economy was to be avoided—the grail of the air advocates—then it was essential that air strikes be massive, rapid, and, most important of all, precise. After all, the aircraft was merely a bomb carrier, and it was what those bombs struck—or did not strike—that determined success or failure. Airmen understood this, but the difficulties involved in bombing accuracy were formidable. Dropping a blunt projectile from high altitude, from a moving and unstable platform, in strong and unpredictable winds, against ground targets four to five miles below that could be obscured by clouds or

---

[61] De Seversky, a Russian fighter pilot and ace during World War I who immigrated to the United States just prior to the Russian Revolution, became a noted aircraft designer and airpower theorist. His most famous aircraft was the P-35, forerunner of the P-47 Thunderbolt, and his most famous books detailing future air and space technologies and their roles in war were *Victory through Air Power* (1942) and *Air Power: Key to Survival* (1950).

smoke, while being shot at, was an extremely complex problem to say the least. How did airmen cope? The short answer is "not very well."

As early as 1919 an Army board determined that the most important problem confronting bombing operations was the design of an accurate bombsight.[62] Airmen agreed, but that did not solve the problem. In December 1927 the Air Corps was informed that a bridge over the Pee Dee River in North Carolina was scheduled for destruction, so they could use it for target practice. Over a six-day period aircraft dropped bombs on the bridge from high and low altitude. The results were not gratifying. There were some hits among the hundreds of bombs dropped, but overall accuracy was poor—and this was in clear skies, in daylight, with no one shooting at them. Airmen did learn, however, that the bigger the bomb the more the destruction—a seemingly logical conclusion not self-evident at the time.[63] In August 1931 they were given another chance to prove their prowess. The Navy had an obsolete cargo ship, the USS *Mount Shasta*, which needed to be sunk—the Air Corps could do the honors. Not only could the airmen barely locate the ship 60 miles out to sea, but their bombing accuracy was abysmal. One bomb hit the ship but did little damage. Much to the airmen's humiliation, the *Mount Shasta* was then sunk by surface ship gunfire. Once again airmen blamed poor weather, inadequate bombsights, and bombs too small for the job at hand.[64] The papers had a field day, and various headlines exclaimed, "The Bomb Flop," "Naval Supremacy Found Upheld by Air Bomb's Failure," and "There She Goes! Dag-Nab, She Missed."[65] Obviously, the Air Corps needed a decent bombsight, better ordnance, and more training if they were to effectively carry out what they were increasingly claiming was their unique and primary mission.

The technological answer to this problem would be the Norden bombsight. Although never as accurate as the propaganda would like to pretend—no, it could not "hit a pickle barrel from 20,000 feet"—it was nonetheless the best bombsight available at the time. Indeed, the theories of strategic bombing were predicated on such a device. This was a clear case of the concept coming before the weapon. Airmen knew what they wanted and expected industry to provide it. The same could be said for the B-17—airmen conjured a doctrine of air

---

[62] McFarland, *America's Pursuit of Precision Bombing*, 27.

[63] Ibid., 40–41; and "Bombing of the Pee Dee River Bridge," 19–28 December 1927, AFHRA, file 248.222-39.

[64] Maurer, *Aviation in the U.S. Army*, 224–29.

[65] Assorted press clippings in "Mount Shasta Bombing," 11 August 1931, AFHRA, file 248.222-29.

warfare dependent upon weapons not yet invented. Eventually, those devices were indeed built, but in the meantime the faculty at ACTS continued to study the problem.

A review of the lectures and student map exercises at ACTS reflects the concern over issues such as accuracy and what types of bombs and fuses would be most effective against a variety of different structures. Unfortunately, although these discussions were a useful start, very little of a practical nature was done. The examples of the Pee Dee River Bridge and the embarrassment with the *Mount Shasta* were two of the few exercises carried out between the wars.[66] Because of this lack of practical experimentation, assertions were made that later proved absurd. In 1938, for example, one ACTS bombardment text stated that 100-lb. demolition bombs were "particularly efficacious against the average factory or warehouse."[67] Such small bombs proved useless in combat. It should also be noted that the Air Corps was not given authority over ordnance development—that was the responsibility of the Ordnance Corps, which was not necessarily responsive to the demands of airmen. This would not be the last time airmen were given responsibility for a particular mission but denied authority over the weapons to be developed and procured for that mission.[68]

Attempts were also made at ACTS to estimate the likelihood of effectively bombing a specific target. 1st Lt Ken Walker, for example, attempted to estimate bombing accuracy using a theory of probabilities employed in artillery manuals. This was hardly satisfactory given the extreme differences between the two weapons.[69] In another attempt at addressing the accuracy issue, bombardment units around the country were required to gather all such data and forward it to Maxwell, where it was collated and the resulting data presumably used to improve results throughout the Air Corps. 1st Lt Larry Kuter, an instructor in the bombardment section, was responsible for this task and forwarded to Washington a chart depicting the results of over 200,000 practice bombs dropped by aircrew members between

---

[66] Not all bombing tests were failures. The Air Corps successfully sank the *Morgan Lewis* in September 1937. A flight of 12 B-10s in four elements of three aircraft each was to use the ship for target practice, but the first element sank it on the first pass in 12 seconds. "Bombing of the Harbor Boat 'Morgan Lewis,' " 18 September 1937, AFHRA, file 248.222-35.

[67] "Bombardment Aviation," ACTS text, 4 January 1938, AFHRA, file 248.101-9, 14–28. This was a remarkably naïve statement at such a late date given the tests against ships and the Pee Dee River Bridge. During the bridge tests, for example, it was determined that anything less than a 600-lb. bomb, even if scoring a direct hit, would do little or no damage. For ships, even larger bombs were necessary.

[68] Only general-purpose ordnance was developed by the Ordnance Corps; chemical or incendiary bombs were the province of the Chemical Corps, and armor-piercing bombs were developed by the Navy.

[69] Hansell, *Air Plan that Defeated Hitler*, 16–18.

1930 and 1938. Kuter's analysis showed that most of the bombs were dropped from between 4,000 and 11,000 feet—almost none were dropped from above 16,000 feet. His calculations revealed that the average radial error from all bombs dropped was around 180 feet; from 15,000 feet the average error increased to 270 feet. Those were not bad results—except of course the higher the altitude the worse the accuracy, and during combat most bombing missions would take place at 20,000 feet.[70] Also, these practice statistics were simply that, practice. No one was shooting at the bombers, and training was carried out in near-perfect weather conditions. Such circumstances were not what crews would experience in combat, and as we shall see, the accuracy achieved during World War II was not as good as that seen in peacetime.

There is also some question as to whether or not the number crunching performed by Kuter and others at ACTS was actually used by anyone in the Air Corps to improve performance. Lt Col Hubert R. Harmon was commander of the 19th Bombardment Group stationed at March Field in California during 1936–37. This was one of the most prestigious units in the Air Corps, part of the elite 1st Wing commanded by Brig Gen Hap Arnold. Harmon had graduated from both ACTS and Leavenworth and in the summer of 1937 was sent to the Army War College. One of his requirements there was to write a thesis on a topic of operational significance. He chose to write on bombing accuracy, a subject of interest when he had been an operational commander. He began by discussing the various forms used to record bombing scores at the unit level, but then noted damningly that there was no agency charged with an analysis of the results! Operational units were required to collect data on practice bomb runs made by their crews and send them to ACTS, believing someone there would collate the statistics from all over the Air Corps, analyze them, and produce suggested corrective actions that were then disseminated back to operational units. Not true, said Harmon; nobody at Maxwell ever provided him feedback on the information he dutifully sent forward! In other words, there is some question as to whether or not the time-consuming efforts of Kuter and his colleagues were ever put to use. If the commander of one of the top bomb groups in the Air Corps never received feedback from all the

---

[70] McFarland, *America's Pursuit of Precision Bombing*, 94–98.

data he was required to compile and send to Maxwell, it is worth questioning if anyone else did either.[71]

The other major problem the ACTS faculty grappled with during the 1930s concerned targeting. The industrial web theory assumed there were bottlenecks, or critical weak points, in an enemy's economy. If planners could determine what those weaknesses were, they could design an air campaign to destroy them. The result would be victory. But such a theory depended on gathering detailed, accurate information on an enemy's economy. This was not something military planners had spent much time worrying about in the past. Certainly, military intelligence organizations had existed for centuries, but the information required was fundamentally different from that needed to plan an air campaign. Spies and intelligence personnel were accustomed to determining the capabilities of enemy weaponry, as well as the location and numbers. Where were the enemy's main combat units stationed, and how long would they take to mobilize? What was their level of training? Where would they deploy once a crisis began? What would be their plan of attack, or what areas would they most vigorously defend? At a higher level, diplomatic intelligence sought to determine a potential adversary's intentions, the mood of its populace, the status of its alliances, and the goals of enemy leadership. All of this information was still necessary as the world stumbled toward war in the late 1930s, but the new air weapon required more. If the doctrine of the Air Corps was to break an enemy's economy and make it unable to continue to fight, then detailed information was needed on that economy. This was virgin territory for intelligence officers.

To address this problem, air leaders had to develop an understanding of what made an economy work. In other words, if you are not sure how an economy functions properly, how can you know what will make it fail—the goal of air strategists? Air planners needed a rudimentary understanding of basic economic theory. The officers at ACTS recognized this problem and attempted to study the workings of a modern industrialized nation during the 1930s. Because of neutrality legislation, the War Department forbade the gathering of intelligence on

---

[71] Lt Col H. R. Harmon, "The Recording and Analysis of Bombing Results," US Army War College paper, 7 May 1938, Harmon papers, AFA archives, annex 4, box 20. The year before Harmon was group commander, he had been the executive officer for the 1st Wing, meaning he saw virtually all incoming and outgoing message traffic for the entire wing. Apparently, none of his bomb groups was receiving feedback from Maxwell. Also of note, when Harmon wrote this report, his older brother, "Miff" (Millard), was assistant commandant of ACTS, so Hubert presumably checked with him to ensure the report's accuracy before submitting it.

foreign economies. So, in 1936 ACTS students and instructors studied the industrial infrastructure of the northeast United States—specifically, the triangle formed between Portland, Maine, Chicago, and the Chesapeake Bay area—including the major industrial centers of New York, Boston, Cleveland, Cincinnati, Detroit, and Pittsburgh, among others. This broad region contained most of America's factories, rail yards, and steelworks. Their investigations led them to conclude that 100 well-placed bombs could shut down 75 percent of the region's electrical generating capacity. Other targets to be struck included rail lines, fuel storage depots, food distribution and preservation facilities, and steel plants. The result of these attacks would be paralysis.[72]

Such talk was not just for the consumption of the students. In a presentation to the secretary of war, the faculty recounted this study, arguing that 20 power plants serving New York City provided electricity for manufacturing, refrigeration, transportation, lighting, and firefighting. It would only take 20 aircraft and 20 bombs "to deprive this area of more than 90 percent of its electric power." The lecture concluded that this attack would be so devastating that "New York City would not exist."[73] Such false scientism, so reminiscent of the exaggerated claims of Giulio Douhet, would prove to be excessively optimistic in actual practice.

This type of analysis was, at best, a humble start. It was also classic mirror imaging—it assumed foreign economies were structured like that of the United States. It also ignored attempts by the enemy to defend, disperse, hide, or otherwise protect its vital industries. All of these problems would confront the American bomber armadas during World War II, and all would cause serious difficulties.

Summary

Even before the US Air Service saw combat action in World War I, one of its leading thinkers was seriously considering the importance of strategic bombing as a major component in the US plan for winning the war. In short, as early as 1917 some airmen had already begun to equate airpower with strategic bombing.

---

[72] "Committee Study on the Northeastern Theater," 31 January 1936, AFHRA, file 248.501-33; "Electric Power Industry in Northeastern United States," Memo for Commandant, 14 February 1935, AFHRA, file 248.211-29; "Thesis on the Attack of New York City from the Air," 16 February 1931, AFHRA, file 248.211-28A; and Kreis, *Piercing the Fog*, 26–27.

[73] "Program for the Secretary of War," ACTS briefing, 2 December 1937, AFHRA, file 248.2018A-50.

Such a conclusion was not foregone. In the Navy, airpower was seen as an extension of the fleet and used to achieve naval objectives. In the Army, the situation was different—or at least it evolved differently over time. This was to a large extent due to the way in which airpower and airmen were treated within the service. The statistics regarding funding, manning, and promotion inequities were too obvious to ignore—little wonder airmen were bitter toward Army leaders. One officer had the candor while testifying before the Federal Aviation Commission to exclaim, "It [the air arm] must be free from the army incubus!"[74] Add to that the courts-martial of Billy Mitchell and Ben Foulois, Air Corps chief from 1931 to 1935, and airmen quickly began to look beyond the limited scope delineated for them by the ground zealots who controlled the Army.[75]

One study of ACTS argues that airmen between the wars had four broad and related goals: to redefine America as an air nation rather than a maritime nation, to demonstrate the benefits of peacetime aviation, to achieve independence from the Army, and finally, to develop a unique theory of air warfare that would demonstrate the dominant role airpower would play in future wars.[76] The last was the most important, because it determined the future of the air arm; airmen needed a doctrine and a justification for their calls for autonomy or perhaps even independence. It therefore became essential for airmen to posit a unique mission, one that transcended merely assisting the ground forces to achieve their goals. Certainly, airpower could do that, but it could do far more. Before the guns of World War I had fallen silent, there were airmen in the United States proclaiming that airpower—specifically, strategic bombing—could offer an alternative to the hecatomb of the trench stalemate on the western front that had slaughtered millions. Aircraft could fly over stagnated armies, rivers, mountains, and oceans; it could strike at the very center of an enemy nation; and it could do so at the opening of hostilities. A corollary of this message was that airpower, not sea power, was to be the new first line of American defense. Airpower's unique offensive and defensive capabilities offered enormous hope to those who had just endured the horror of the trenches. It was even believed by some that,

---

[74] Capt Robert Webster, Testimony before the Federal Aviation Commission, 7 May 1935, AFHRA, file 248.121-3. These were strong words to utter in public for a junior captain.

[75] Shiner, *Foulois and the U.S. Army Air Corps*, chap. 7, argues that although the court-martial was ostensibly conducted due to alleged procurement irregularities, Foulois was simply a scapegoat for other problems within the Air Corps. Although acquitted, Foulois retired shortly after the proceedings in June 1935.

[76] Faber, "Interwar U.S. Army Aviation and the Air Corps Tactical School," 186.

paradoxically, the enormous latent power of strategic bombing would in fact help to prevent war from even breaking out. As French aviation pioneer Clément Ader phrased it,

> The great bombing planes will become veritable terrors! I am convinced that their awesome power and the fear of seeing them appear will provoke salutary reflections among the statesmen and diplomats who are the real dispensers of peace and war, and that in the final analysis these airplanes will serve the cause of humanity.[77]

This was a utopian ideal not to be realized during this period, but it is important to note again that such thinking underpins nuclear deterrence theory even today—a nuclear exchange would be so horrifying as to be unthinkable. Therefore, building such a nuclear deterrent is essential to maintaining the peace. Airpower is so horrible it is humanizing. This truism remains one of the great paradoxes of modern air and space power.

Airmen therefore worked assiduously throughout the 1920s and 1930s to formulate a message emphasizing the importance of strategic bombing and how it could, in the long run, save lives. The Air Corps Tactical School was essential in devising a doctrine articulating this message and disseminating it to the generation of air officers who would soon be called upon to fight a major world war against powerful enemies. Yet ideas alone were not enough to realize this dream. The technologies necessary to build aircraft that could carry the requisite bomb load over long distances and do so without incurring prohibitive losses to enemy defenses were not yet available. Moreover, even if such aircraft could be built, the ability to put bombs on target with great precision presented entirely different types of technical challenges.

All of these doctrinal and technological issues were addressed in the two decades between the world wars. Leadership was crucial in this effort. Men like Billy Mitchell, James Fechet, Ben Foulois, Frank Andrews, Hap Arnold, and the dozens of junior officers at the Air Corps Tactical School labored tirelessly to make these dreams reality. To give one rather unusual example, Maj Gen Benjamin Foulois was chief of the Air Corps when the industrial web theory of strategic bombardment was taking hold at ACTS, yet the American policy at that time was one of defense and isolationism. How, then, could Foulois justify a doctrine that depended upon offensive weaponry? Foulois

---

[77] Ader, *Military Aviation*, 27.

simply changed the semantics. Rather than base a force structure upon known *threats*—which appeared minimal at the time—he focused on building a force structure that emphasized *capabilities*. His memoirs are revealing:

> Up to this time my air staff planners had been stressing the need for bombers in offensive operations and gotten nowhere with the General Staff. Discouraged, they came to me and I could see only one way out: "Stress *defense*, not *offense*, and stress re-enforcement of the Hawaiian Islands," I told them, "and maybe that will work." It did, and the climate became more favorable as we dropped the word "offense" from our justification papers. . . . As I saw it, if we could get bombers that could carry bigger bomb loads and fly greater distances this way, what difference did it make what words we used?[78] (emphasis in original)

Perhaps things did improve as Foulois states, but the effects were barely noticeable at the time. When World War II erupted in Europe during September 1939, the Air Corps was nowhere near ready for combat. As will be explained in the next chapter, procurement of the B-17—the vital cog in the airmen's view of airpower—was deliberately suppressed by the Army hierarchy, with significant ill effects.

The Army airmen of the interwar period have often been described as zealots—and the term is not used favorably. But the Army's ground officers, especially infantrymen, were equally zealous in defending their beliefs and refusing to think ahead to the next war or to see the emerging dominance of new technologies like the airplane and the tank. This zealotry, which looked backwards to an outmoded form of war, would cause unpreparedness and needless cost to American forces at the beginning of World War II.

Two other problems—besides the doctrinal and technological ones noted—had to be met and overcome. Airmen had to be able to drop their bombs with great precision, and they needed to drop them on the appropriate targets. These tasks required an intelligence-gathering network and an analytical capability that could tell air commanders if their bombing efforts were having the desired effect on the enemy. The next chapter examines how all of these challenges were met and overcome by the Army Air Forces—the new organization that evolved from the Air Corps in June 1941.

---

[78] Foulois, *From the Wright Brothers to the Astronauts*, 227.

Chapter 2

The Realities of War and Strategic Bombing

Despite the strategic bombing doctrine devised during the 1930s, a heavy bomber force needed to carry out that doctrine did not exist at the beginning of World War II. When Germany invaded Poland in September 1939, there were only 27 strategic bombers in the Air Corps—26 B-17s and an experimental XB-15.[1] The United States then began to rearm, and airpower enjoyed a large buildup. In the two years prior to Pearl Harbor, the Air Corps, soon to become the Army Air Forces (AAF) in June 1941, purchased nearly 21,000 aircraft. Of those, 374 were strategic bombers—197 B-17s and 176 B-24s—a mere 1.8 percent of the total aircraft bought during that period.[2] The AAF was not able to realize its dream of a heavy bomber force, and the intransigence of the ground officers who dominated the Army was partly to blame. It is instructive to review the history of B-17 development.

The Martin B-10 was the Air Corps's first all-metal monoplane bomber and also had an enclosed cockpit, retractable landing gear, and an internal bomb bay. When it entered the inventory in 1934, it was faster than most pursuit planes and could carry a ton of bombs over 1,200 miles. But the Air Corps was already looking ahead and, in August 1934, circulated a proposal for a new aircraft. Builders were instructed to have designs ready for a flying competition in October 1935; the desired aircraft would be capable of flying 2,000 miles with a 2,000-lb. bomb load at a speed of 200 mph.[3]

Martin and Douglas proposed variants of existing designs: Martin's bid was an improved B-10, and Douglas offered a military version of its DC-2 airliner. Initially, Boeing engineers were thinking along the same lines, suggesting a version of their new twin-engine Model 247 airliner. They quickly realized, however, that their two-engine design would offer only marginally better performance over the B-10. Boeing designers therefore wondered if "multi-engine" could mean four engines.[4]

---

[1] Craven and Cate, *Army Air Forces in World War II*, vol. 1, 69–70.
[2] Holley, *Buying Aircraft*, 550.
[3] For an overview of B-17 development, see Freeman and Osborne, *B-17 Flying Fortress Story*.
[4] Some contemporary aircraft, like the Ford Tri-Motor, had three engines, but the engine in the nose was unsuitable for a bomber because that area was needed for a bombardier position and defensive guns.

They discreetly asked Air Corps officials for an interpretation and were told a four-engine bomber was indeed acceptable if it met all performance criteria.

Boeing's four-engine Model 299 had its maiden flight on 28 July 1935. The all-metal plane had wing flaps for better performance at slow airspeeds, electric trim tabs on its control services for improved handling characteristics, a hydraulically operated constant-speed propeller, and positions termed "blisters" for five defensive machine-gun posts. When Richard L. Williams, a newsman for a local Seattle newspaper saw the plane for the first time, he promptly dubbed it "a flying fortress."[5] The name stuck.

On 20 August, the 299 made a nonstop flight from Seattle to Dayton—2,000 miles—at an average speed of 233 mph. This performance, coupled with its size, weight, armament, looks, and four engines, created a sensation. The Martin and Douglas entrants at Wright Field were good aircraft, based upon proven concepts, but Boeing's Flying Fortress was in a class by itself. Ten days later the B-17 taxied out for takeoff at Wright Field. A crowd gathered to watch. The aircraft roared down the runway and took off. It then climbed very steeply, too steeply, to around 200 feet where it stalled, rolled to the side, and crashed back on the airfield and exploded. Two crewmembers died and three escaped.[6]

The crash was doubly tragic because of its impact on the Air Corps. The Fortress prototype had crashed, so the winner of the competition was the Douglas B-18 Bolo. Air Corps leaders tried to place an order for 65 of the revolutionary B-17s, but the War Department, which controlled the Air Corps purse strings, refused. The plane had crashed; moreover, it would cost $197,000 per copy, whereas the smaller B-18 would cost only $99,000. The Army ordered 133 Bolos. Fortunately, a legal loophole allowed the Air Corps to buy a small number of test aircraft—13 to be precise, enough to equip one squadron. These planes, designated YB-17s, were to prove of enormous importance. As one author phrased it, "By the frayed thread of a loophole purchase, the dream machine stayed alive."[7]

---

[5] Underwood, *Wings of Democracy*, 66. The Plexiglas and metal blisters were later abandoned because of their complexity.

[6] Copp, *A Few Great Captains*, 326–31. The Fortress crashed because the elevator controls were locked—the pilot could not lower the nose, so the aircraft stalled. The locking mechanism was controlled from the cockpit, but no one had remembered to disengage it prior to takeoff.

[7] Perret, *Winged Victory*, 28. The Y prefix stood for "service test status." A 14th YB-17 was used for static tests only.

Over the next four years the Air Corps would log over 9,200 flying hours on their squadron of YB-17s without experiencing a major accident. Airmen continually asked Army leaders to buy more of the big bombers, but ground commanders were not receptive. Instead, they ordered more B-18s.[8] It appears the Army's policy was based on the beliefs that quantity was more important than quality and long-range bombers would embolden airmen to continue to think beyond the battlefield—something not to be encouraged. Airmen countered with fiscal and efficiency arguments. In one report they posited a combat scenario requiring bombers to fly a specified number of miles and deliver a required tonnage of bombs. Comparing B-17s to B-18s in such a scenario, the report concluded that it would take fewer B-17s to do the job; the cost would be about the same in procurement dollars, but the heavy bombers could complete the mission more quickly and with significantly fewer personnel. Gen Malin Craig, the Army chief of staff, was unmoved.[9] In truth, it was not the Army alone that insisted on quantity over quality. Congress also was inclined to procure hundreds of B-18s, simply because they were relatively cheap and it could then be claimed the Air Corps was indeed procuring a sizable number of aircraft each year, despite their inadequacies.[10]

So, when World War II broke out in Europe in September 1939, the Air Corps had barely two dozen of the new B-17s, and by Pearl Harbor, two years later, there were still only 200. It would not be until 1944 that the Fortresses were available in sufficient numbers to make a decisive impact in the bombing campaign against Germany. Besides the B-17, the Consolidated B-24, which first flew in December 1939, would comprise the backbone of the bomber force until 1944. The nagging problem of doctrine—how the new bombers would be employed—was wrapped up in the matter of organization. An independent air force was not in the cards during the two decades between the world wars, but organizational progress was made nonetheless.

Organization for Combat

The War Department General Staff, which had jurisdiction over Army doctrine, dismissed the theories developed at Maxwell. As late

---

[8] Underwood, *Wings of Democracy*, 66–67; and Craven and Cate, *Army Air Forces in World War II*, vol. 6, 203–4.

[9] Maurer, *Aviation in the U.S. Army*, 360–61.

[10] Futrell, *Ideas, Concepts, Doctrine*, vol. 1, 79–83; and Holley, *Buying Aircraft*, 76–77.

as March 1939, it rejected a manual submitted by the Air Corps that referred to "independent air operations." This phrase was anathema to ground officers, and the offending passage had to be removed.[11] Army doctrine was clear throughout the interwar period: the mission of the Air Corps was to support the ground forces in achieving their objectives. Army Field Manual (FM) 1-5, *Employment of Aviation of the Army*, dated 15 April 1940, stated that air forces would receive their targets from the "field commander," a soldier, and their first priority was to "decisively defeat important elements of the enemy armed forces."[12] This wording was little changed from that of the previous two decades, and these priorities and command relationships were demonstrated in the Louisiana Maneuvers of 1941. The Army commander used the air assets at his disposal—600 aircraft—exclusively for ground support. The General Staff devised a scenario that assumed an invasion force had already landed in the United States and it was the Army's task to expel it. Consequently, strategic air operations were specifically precluded.[13]

Despite these limitations, the Air Corps was able to experiment and practice with its baker's dozen of YB-17s and devise concepts of operations. More importantly, in 1935 it was able to form a combat organization tailored to adopt and adapt these bombers—as well as other Air Corps combat aircraft—into a coherent operational concept. This organization, the General Headquarters (GHQ) Air Force, was a crucial step toward independence.

The Air Corps was divided into two types of aviation. The "air service" consisted of observation aircraft for visual and photo reconnaissance, artillery spotting, and combat patrols. "Air force" aviation consisted of combat aircraft—the bombers, fighters, and attack planes that would carry out offensive operations. Fighters would ensure air superiority; bombers would strike targets within the theater; and attack planes would strike enemy troop formations and positions. Around 80 percent of the Air Corps consisted of air force assets, but they were neither centrally located nor controlled. Instead, units were parceled out to the overseas possessions and to various Army corps in the United States. In all cases, they were under control of local ground commanders. There were no provisions for aircraft from one

---

[11] Futrell, *Ideas, Concepts, Doctrine*, vol. 1, 84.

[12] FM 1-5, *Employment of Aviation of the Army*, 15 April 1940, 13. A revised version appeared in 1943 but still emphasized this targeting precedence. FM 1-5, 18 January 1943, 14.

[13] Gabel, *U.S. Army GHQ Maneuvers of 1941*, 55, 179–82.

corps area to join together with those of another to conduct strategic air operations.

Airmen disliked this organizational concept because it violated the principle of unity of command while also denying airpower one of its great strengths—the flexibility of aircraft based in different locations to converge over a single target hundreds of miles distant. Airmen wanted centralized control of airpower. Support for this concept was provided by a 1934 commission headed by former secretary of war Newton Baker. It agreed with the airmen's thinking regarding centralized control but stopped short of advocating a separate service. Army maneuvers in 1931 and 1934 had tested a concept in which air force assets were centralized under an air commander reporting directly to the theater commander.[14] The results were excellent, and this, combined with the recommendations of the Baker Board, prompted General MacArthur to establish a GHQ Air Force. During peace, the unit would report to the Army chief of staff. When deployed during war, it would report to the theater commander.

The new organization was established on 1 March 1935, and MacArthur chose Lt Col Frank Andrews as its commander; he was immediately promoted to temporary brigadier general. Andrews set up his headquarters at Langley Field, Virginia, and organized his forces into three wings—one on the west coast, one on the east, and the third in Louisiana. Altogether, the air force consisted of nine combat groups totaling 38 squadrons.[15] The GHQ Air Force was a major advance organizationally, administratively, and philosophically. Despite Army reservations about the aspirations of its airmen, it allowed the new organization to exist, though giving it scant support. The tiny contingent of YB-17s remained the airmen's main jewel, while ground officers continued to order marginal B-18s by the score. Even so, the GHQ Air Force was crucial because it allowed airmen to begin training and experimenting with large, composite air units. It helped prepare them for war.[16]

By the beginning of 1941 the Air Corps had its doctrine (albeit not officially sanctioned) and organizational structure—which would be

---

[14] Maurer, *Aviation in the U.S. Army*, 246–53, 323–25.

[15] The US-based GHQ Air Force consisted of 38 airplane plus two airship squadrons in March 1935; that number dropped to 31 the following year and 29 by 1939. Counting aircraft overseas, there were only 55 heavier-than-air squadrons in the 1939 Air Corps, along with 10 balloon squadrons and 9 observation squadrons. Maurer, *Aviation in the U.S. Army*, 467–73.

[16] For overviews of the organization and operations of the GHQ Air Force, see Maurer, *Aviation in the U.S. Army*, chap. 18; Shiner, *Foulois and the U.S. Army Air Corps*, chap. 8; Craven and Cate, *Army Air Forces in World War II*, vol. 1, 49–51, 63–64, 69–70; and Futrell, *Ideas, Concepts, Doctrine*, vol. 1, 68–74.

further advanced that June with the formation of the Army Air Forces—and two heavy bomber models that, although not yet procured in sufficient numbers, would be the workhorses of the strategic bombing campaign against Germany. The next step was to develop a specific plan for directing those bomber assets against specific targets.

Planning the Air Campaign—AWPD-1

In July 1941 President Roosevelt believed it prudent to begin planning for conflict. On the 9th of that month he directed the War Department General Staff to begin drawing up overall production requirements for a war that assumed Germany would be the main enemy and Britain the main ally.[17] Col Clayton Bissell, an airman in the War Plans Division, went to Gen Hap Arnold, the commanding general of the AAF, and suggested he ask to have his own staff draw up the air annex to the war plan. Ordinarily, the Army's Plans Division had this responsibility, but Arnold agreed with Bissell's suggestion and approached Gen George C. Marshall, the Army chief of staff, on the matter. The request was granted.

To author it, Arnold turned to Lieutenant Colonels Hal George and Ken Walker and Majors Possum Hansell and Larry Kuter. All had been instructors at ACTS and had played key roles in formulating the doctrine of high-altitude, daylight formation, precision bombing of an enemy's industrial centers. Now they were tasked to put their ideas into practice. Over a dozen other officers from various divisions on the Air Staff, as well as procurement specialists from Wright Field, assisted on various parts of the plan. These officers drew up what was termed an aircraft production plan but was actually far more detailed; it was to be the air war plan for the defeat of Germany—AWPD-1.

The task was enormous. They approached it by relying on their own experiences—which were minimal; their belief in the efficacy of strategic bombing—which had not yet been put to a serious test; and their academic studies at Maxwell. That was a weak base, but they pressed on. Their first task was to articulate the strategic objectives derived from existing plans: to defend the Western Hemisphere, defeat Germany and its allies while maintaining a strategic defensive in

---

[17] The strategic plans were color-coded—Red (Great Britain), Red-Orange (add Japan), Green (Mexico), Black (Germany), etc. These evolved into the Rainbow Plans. For their details, see Ross, *American War Plans, 1919–1941*; and H. G. Cole, *Road to Rainbow*.

the Pacific, and provide close support to the ground forces in preparation for an eventual invasion of Europe. For airpower, the goal was to destroy the industrial war-making capacity of Germany and restrict Axis air operations.[18]

Following their doctrinal beliefs from ACTS, planners studied information on the German economy to determine what made it tick. Once they understood how that economy worked, it would be easier to figure out how to break it. Hansell had recently been assigned to the intelligence section of the Air Staff and had been in Britain observing the Royal Air Force (RAF) bombing campaign against Germany. The British were helpful and shared much sensitive information. The knowledge Hansell gained in these duties would prove extremely useful. In addition, planners turned to American industrialists and bankers for assistance in understanding the US economy, assuming the operations of modern industrialized societies were similar. The airmen knew that many of Germany's factories had been financed or built by American banks and companies. Therefore, they were able to obtain detailed blueprints of many industrial facilities from sources on Wall Street.[19]

Planners sorted and prioritized this data to project an image of Germany as an industrial web. Using this as a prism, their examination led to the 154 most important targets in Germany. These were grouped into six major target sets: electrical power plants (50); transportation networks, including railroads and internal waterways (47); synthetic oil refineries (27); aircraft assembly plants (18); aluminum plants (6); and "sources of magnesium" (6).[20] Using data from bombing tests before the war and from combat operations already conducted by the RAF, planners determined the weight of ordnance needed to destroy a variety of structures. They projected loss rates in planes and crews and then estimated how many aircraft of all types would be needed, as well as the number of personnel required to fly, maintain, and support such an air force. Although later critics have claimed that the planners were overly mechanistic and approached the bombing campaign as a science problem rather than a Clausewitzian

---

[18] A-WPD/1, "Munitions Requirements of the Army Air Forces to Defeat Our Potential Enemies," August 1941, AFHRA, file 145.82-1. The authors were inconsistent with their nomenclature, and the plan was variously referred to as A-WPD/1, AWPD/1 and AWPD-1 throughout the document. The last is the conventional designation and will be used here. Also, the actual plan is a bewilderingly large document of nearly 1,000 pages with countless tabs, annexes, appendices, and indexes, most of which are not paginated. It is therefore impossible to give accurate page citations.

[19] Hansell, *Air Plan that Defeated Hitler*, 50–52; and Gaston, *Planning the American Air War*, 27–31.

[20] AWPD-1.

exercise in friction, they did take unknowns into account. Based on prewar experiments, they determined accuracy estimates and loss rates and then multiplied these peacetime accuracy numbers by 2.25. They also employed an attrition figure of 20 percent per month for all units—a figure derived from a study of RAF combat operations.[21]

Putting this together, planners came up with a needed force of 6,834 operational bombers organized into 98 groups—although 37 of these groups would be dedicated to hemisphere defense and the Pacific. The officers assumed an additional 1,708 aircraft would be located in depot reserve, and they projected a monthly replacement rate of 1,245 aircraft. For defense of the air bases in England, they would need 3,400 fighter aircraft. (Significantly, the planners thought there would be a shortage of bases in Britain and therefore called either for more bases elsewhere or a bomber with twice the range of the B-17 and B-24.) Given the planned force, they estimated it would take six months to destroy those 154 targets once the bombing campaign was fully operational. They predicted that a token force of three bomb groups would be able to begin operations in April 1942, but an all-out offensive could not begin until April 1944; hence, the 154 targets would be eliminated by September 1944.[22]

The numbers they deduced were enormous: over 63,000 aircraft, more than 135,000 pilots, and over 2.1 million total personnel. Considering the AAF had ordered only some 300 heavy bombers for 1941, the vision and audacity of these planners were remarkable.[23] Even so, AWPD-1 underestimated the number of aircraft needed. By the end of the war, the AAF had purchased over 231,000 planes, of which nearly 35,000 were strategic bombers.[24]

As for targets, the planners decided the first priority was to gain air superiority. Without it, a bomber offensive would be long and bloody; therefore, they listed the Luftwaffe and its factories as a crucial objective. While the air superiority campaign was ongoing, the bombers would also be attacking the vitals of the German economy. Planners

---

[21] Ibid. For the critique, see Watts, *Foundations of US Air Doctrine*, passim. As it turned out, the 2.25 factor used by the planners was too small, but that is not the same as claiming they did not understand friction.

[22] AWPD-1. The projected aircraft numbers were significantly off, but the projected dates were fairly accurate—the first bombing mission of the Eighth Air Force was in August 1942, and the crescendo of bombing began in the summer of 1944—by late fall the German economy was devastated.

[23] Ibid.; Craven and Cate, *Army Air Forces in World War II*, vol. 1, 146–50; and Hansell, *Air Plan that Defeated Hitler*, chap. 4.

[24] Holley, *Buying Aircraft*, 550–51. Planners did not factor in the buildup of the Twelfth Air Force for the North African invasion, which siphoned off a large number of assets from the Eighth, or a major war with Japan, which also threw off their calculations.

addressed the issue of escort fighters for the bombers, admitting that while such aircraft would be desirable, they did not yet exist; they recommended such a plane be developed immediately. Meanwhile, they believed the combination of speed, altitude, defensive guns, and tight formations would be adequate to get the bombers to their targets and back. Remaining overly optimistic, while the planners assumed an invasion of the continent would take place, they suggested that "if an air offensive is successful, a land invasion may not be necessary."[25]

AWPD-1 was completed in nine days, briefed up the chain of command, and approved by Secretary of War Henry Stimson on 12 September 1941. The blueprint it laid out was a good starting point, although the priority assigned to specific target systems would vary during the war, and though daring in its materiel and personnel projections, it underestimated the resources needed. In a prescient statement, the warning that long-range escort fighters might be necessary proved all too true. There were, however, other errors in the planners' thinking—German industry and morale were tougher and more resilient than expected, and bombing accuracy was worse than projected. Nonetheless, AWPD-1—a descendent of the ideas formulated at ACTS—remained a reasonably accurate forecast of the US strategic bombing effort against Germany.

Problems and the Development of Operations Research

One by one the problems encountered during the bombing campaign were met and overcome. The question of escort, for example, had dogged airmen for a decade. Although Chennault had questioned pronouncements of the unstoppable nature of a bomber formation, he was ambivalent on which direction to take and rejected the concept of fighter escort. To him, that was a defensive mission not suitable for aggressive pursuit pilots. Instead, he argued the only way to ensure the bombers would "always get through" was to build more bombers to compensate for the attrition that enemy fighters would cost an attacking force![26] Similarly, when Hoyt Vandenberg took over the Pursuit section at ACTS in 1936, he was given a written directive to teach that pursuit was an element of antiaircraft defense; it was not

[25] AWPD-1.
[26] Chennault, "Special Support for Bombardment," 18–21.

for protection of the bomber force. Escort was not a suitable mission for pursuit.[27] Army doctrine entering the war acknowledged the escort mission, but saw it in purely defensive terms. FM 1-15, *Tactics and Techniques of Air Fighting*, stated that the role of escort was "to ensure the success of the forces they support. Their firepower may be considered as replacing or augmenting the defensive firepower of the supported forces. Their mission *precludes* their seeking to impose combat on other forces except as necessary to carry out their defensive role" (emphasis added).[28] Combat would demonstrate that this mind-set was incorrect.

The issue was settled once and for all in early 1944 when Maj Gen James Doolittle took over command of the Eighth Air Force. When walking into the headquarters of his fighter command, he noticed a sign that read, "The First Duty of the Eighth Air Force Fighters Is to Bring the Bombers Back Alive." He ordered it removed and replaced with one stating, "The First Duty of the Eighth Air Force Fighters Is to Destroy German Fighters." The semantic distinction went to the heart of the debate regarding the proper role of fighters in an escort role. To Doolittle, the issue was one of capitalizing on the innate aggressiveness of fighter pilots. By unleashing them to seek out and destroy enemy aircraft, whenever and wherever they were located, he ensured the bombers would indeed be protected. Doolittle later wrote that he thought this decision was his most important and far-reaching of the war.[29]

The problem also involved technology. Before the war it was generally believed impossible to build a fighter plane incorporating both the range and agility to engage enemy interceptors on equal terms. An aircraft with the range to escort the bombers had to be large enough to carry a great deal of fuel and would thus need two engines. To compensate for the lack of maneuverability of such a design, the aircraft would need flexible gun positions and extra crewmembers to man them. Chennault described such a "special support" aircraft as being a "multi-seater with at least four gun stations so placed as to afford the maximum field of fire for each. The crew will consist of four gunners, a radio operator, pilot, and co-pilot." In short, the escort

---

[27] Wilson to Vandenberg, letter, 26 August 1936, AFHRA, file 248.2806. Vandenberg took this advice to heart and while serving on the Air Staff in March 1941 advised against the use of drop tanks for fighters, stating that the escort mission was "incompatible with the mission of pursuit." Holley, "General Carl Spaatz and the Art of Command," 31–32.

[28] US Army, FM 1-15, *Tactics and Techniques of Air Fighting*, September 1940, 2. (Emphasis added)

[29] Doolittle, *I Could Never Be So Lucky Again*, 380–81.

would soon look much like the bombers it was protecting. In fact, Chennault concluded dryly that building such an aircraft would be a technical challenge, but the real difficulty would be in preventing bombardment from adopting the design for itself.[30]

Alexander P. de Seversky disputed such thinking. An aircraft designer as well as a theorist, he concluded that those denying the possibility of building an escort fighter able to contest with the best interceptors available did not know what they were talking about.[31] In 1936 he designed the P-35—the ancestor of the P-47 Thunderbolt. The P-35 was not only extremely fast—it won the Bendix Air Race three years running—but also had unusually long range and could fly from coast to coast with only two refuelings. De Seversky's secret was to build fuel tanks within the wings that dramatically increased range.[32] Even so, it became apparent during the war that even the P-47 did not have the legs to escort bombers all the way to the target. The solution was the drop tank. Cheap, disposable tanks were slung under the wings of fighters, and the pilots would drain the gas from these tanks first. When empty, the tanks were jettisoned and the planes would still have a full internal gas load. The results were dramatic. By the end of the war P-51s were able to escort the bombers all the way to Frankfurt and back.[33]

The strategic bombing offensive encountered other challenges during the war. The first chapter referred to the importance of accuracy, targeting, intelligence, and analysis. These concerns were recognized to some degree before the war, but little was done. When advance units of the Eighth Air Force arrived in England in mid 1942, it became apparent these issues were crucial. Bluntly, the ideas devised at ACTS in the 1930s were a "faith-based theory," unsupported by hard evidence.[34] Because the United States had not conducted strategic bombing before 1942, it was inevitable that things would not work out as planned.

Air commanders realized that basic questions regarding tactics, procedures, and cause and effect still begged answers. How did one, for example, disrupt a rail transportation system, or what size and

---

[30] Chennault, "Special Support for Bombardment," 19.

[31] For de Seversky's beliefs on aircraft range, see his articles, "My Thoughts on the War," 18–19, 86–88, and "Ordeal of American Air Power," 7–14, 127.

[32] For a good description of the P-35 and its successors, see Stoff, *Thunder Factory*.

[33] For charts showing the ranges of US fighter aircraft with and without drop tanks, see Davis, *Carl A. Spaatz and the Air War in Europe*, 362–63.

[34] I will always be grateful to Dan Kuehl for coining this term.

type of bombs are most suitable for putting an oil refinery out of commission? What is the ideal bomber formation to maximize accuracy while also minimizing exposure to enemy defenses? As we saw, these types of questions had been asked at Maxwell—as well as by airmen in operational units—but funding shortages and other priorities meant that little was accomplished. Once the war began, a new discipline was founded called operations research (OR) that addressed these questions. Essentially, OR applied scientific and mathematical methods to the study of military operations to make them more efficient and effective.

The concept of OR was first tested in World War I but was largely forgotten after the war. World War II quickly identified the need for such methods once again, and OR units were formed in the Royal Air Force's (RAF) operational commands. The leading members of these sections were scientists, while the rest of the staff consisted of personnel trained to "think numerically."[35]

The problems studied by the OR sections were largely tactical or technical—the most effective use of aerial photography, camouflage, radio, radar, and so forth. General Arnold liked this idea and in mid 1942 established the Committee of Operations Analysts (COA) in Washington, composed of mathematicians, lawyers, physicists, and engineers. The types of problems examined by the COA and its detachment at Eighth Air Force were similar to those studied by OR sections in the RAF. In September 1942, Maj Gen Ira Eaker, the Eighth's commander, directed his OR section to study bombing accuracy and loss rates. Using automatic cameras that took photos during bomb runs, analysts found, not surprisingly, the better the weather, the greater the accuracy. Electronic bombing aids were therefore essential, because the weather over Germany was usually miserable. Nonetheless, bombing through weather never equaled visual bombing in accuracy, regardless of the radio or radar aids employed. By October 1944, 41.5 percent of the Eighth Air Force's bombs were falling within 1,000 feet of the aim point when bombing visually. Using only radio or radar aids, accuracy plummeted to 5 percent within that range.[36] In addition, after studying poststrike photographs, the COA determined that, contrary to popular belief, bombing accuracy would be enhanced if an entire

---

[35] Air Ministry, *Origins and Development of Operational Research in the Royal Air Force*, xvii–xx. For the OR story at Bomber Command, see Wakelam, *Science of Bombing*.

[36] McArthur, *Operations Analysis in the US Army Eighth Air Force in World War II*, 214, 235.

group dropped on its leader's mark, rather than every bombardier choosing his own drop point.

Analysts also tackled specific problems dealing with range extension, bomb weights and fuses, incendiary bombs, optimal formation size, and the like. A typical problem involved determining the relative danger of enemy fighter planes versus antiaircraft artillery (AAA) fire. After interviews with crew members, especially those who had been shot down and lived to tell of it, the COA discovered that the worst danger was faced by stragglers. When a bomber fell out of formation, enemy fighters quickly pounced on it.[37] Bombers usually fell out of formation, however, because their engines had been hit by AAA, resulting in fires and power loss. The solution: put armor around the engines to reduce AAA damage, which would in turn reduce the number of stragglers downed by enemy fighters.

These technical problems had not been ignored before the war. A review of the lectures and map exercises at ACTS reflects the concern over such issues, but solutions were not forthcoming. It was precisely because of such neglect before the war that OR was so essential to the success of the strategic bombing campaign during the war.

It must be remembered, however, that air commanders faced greater problems. Their theories and doctrine *assumed* that strategic bombing against the industrial infrastructure of an enemy would have decisive results: that it would sap and eventually break both the will and the capability of the enemy to resist. This was an assumption, not a fact. Eventually, OR was able to provide commanders and planners guidance on how best to destroy specific parts of an infrastructure most effectively and efficiently. The broader question remained: What effect did destroying an oil refinery or railroad marshaling yard have on the overall goal of breaking the enemy's will and capability? In short, because you know *how* to destroy a factory does not necessarily mean you *should* destroy it. OR told air commanders how to hit the target right; they now needed to know how to hit the right target.

Air Intelligence and Targeting

The industrial web theory postulated that certain targets were more vulnerable or vital to the enemy's war effort than others.

---

[37] Perera, *Leaves from My Book of Life*, vol. 2, 77–80. Perera was the senior military member of the COA during the war.

Unfortunately, prior to World War II airmen did not have the analytical or intelligence tools necessary to determine the effectiveness of strategic air operations. Using OR techniques, they began solving various tactical and technical problems, hoping that by doing things efficiently they would also do them effectively. The issue revolved around targeting. What were the most appropriate facilities, systems, or networks to bomb to diminish the German war effort? Were there "bottlenecks" within the enemy economy? AAF doctrine offered little more than laundry lists of broad categories: rail communications, bridges, tunnels, rail yards, power plants, oil refineries, and "other similar objectives."[38] Such bromides were insufficient.

After war broke out in Europe in September 1939, the AAF expanded its efforts at planning and measuring the effects of its air operations. OR helped, but two organizations were established to study vulnerabilities within the German economy. The first was formed by the British government prior to the war, the Ministry of Economic Warfare (MEW); a second group, created in late 1942 in the American Embassy in London, was the Enemy Objectives Unit (EOU). The EOU's official history summed up its purpose artfully: "a precision bombing operation would be extraordinarily dependent on detailed intelligence concerning the location and importance of the elements in the enemy's war production structure." It was the EOU's task to search, criticize, organize, and advise air leaders to help them select the most appropriate targets.[39] For the remainder of the war, these intelligence and planning units would serve Allied air leaders, but they all suffered from similar problems. They did not have access to the types of information necessary to make reasoned judgments on the German economy. As the AAF official historians eloquently phrased it,

> But there existed in almost every instance a serious shortage of reliable information, and the resulting lacunae had to be bridged by intelligent guesswork and the clever use of analogies. In dealing with this mass of inexactitudes and approximations, the social scientist finds himself in a position of no special advantage over the military strategist or any intelligent layman; and an elaborate methodology may even, by virtue of a considerable but unavoidably misdirected momentum, lead the investigator far afield.[40]

---

[38] FM 1-5, *Employment of Aviation of the Army*, 11, 36.
[39] "War Diary," 1.
[40] Craven and Cate, *Army Air Forces in World War II*, vol. 2, 369.

One such "misdirected" avenue was the misconception that the German economy was drawn taut and therefore susceptible to attack with devastating results. Early in the war that economy actually contained a great deal of slack. Because the economies of the Allies were on a wartime footing, they assumed Germany's was as well. This was not the case. As an example, Germany's automobile industry, the largest sector of its economy in the 1930s, was utilized at barely 50 percent of capacity during the war.[41] On the other hand, some air planners believed that oil offered a special case.

Germany had extremely limited oil sources within its boundaries; 93 percent of its peacetime needs were imported, but once war broke out the British blockade removed these options. In 1940, therefore, Germany formed an alliance with Rumania to gain access to its vast oilfields, which then supplied 60 percent of German crude oil supplies.[42] At the same time, German scientists perfected a method of producing oil from coal in a process called hydrogenation—a highly inefficient and expensive process.[43] Air planners thus saw Germany as highly vulnerable in the area of oil. It was not known, however, how much oil Germany had in reserve when entering the war, nor how much it had produced and consumed since then. Indeed, based on little more than guess work, in 1942 the COA estimated Germany had somewhere between 2.4 and 6.0 million tons of oil in reserve. That was quite a range. The MEW put the figure at 3 million tons.[44] Because there was no agreed formula for determining which group's methodology was superior, the issue was decided by picking a number in between the two estimates—4 million tons. As a result, when air planners met at Casablanca in January 1943 to determine targets for the Combined Bomber Offensive, they placed oil fourth on the list—Germany had so much oil in reserve it did little good to make it a high priority. This decision, at least as far as the Americans were concerned, would later be seen as an error.

---

[41] Hinsley, *British Intelligence in the Second World War*, vol. 3, 1, 54; "History of the Organization and Operations of the Committee of Operations Analysts (COA)," 29 November 1945, AFHRA, file 118.01, 28, 52; and Overy, *Why the Allies Won*, 203.

[42] Craven and Cate, *Army Air Forces in World War II*, vol. 2, 358.

[43] US Strategic Bombing Survey (USSBS), "Over-All Report (European War)," 39–40. Another process, Fischer-Tropsch, was also used, but hydrogenation remained far more important while also providing all of the Reich's synthetic aviation gasoline.

[44] The planners of AWPD-1 had expressed ignorance on the subject. See Rosen, *Winning the Next War*, 161–63. USSBS, "Over-All Report," 39, states that Germany had only 1.6 million tons of fuel in reserve at the start of the war—less than six months' supply of wartime requirements. However, this figure actually grew over the next several years despite the demands of military operations, because Germany captured more refineries and hence more fuel than it consumed.

As time went on the COA, EOU, and MEW became more capable in determining the effects of air attacks. The economists, engineers, and mathematicians who comprised the bulk of these organizations defined their field as they went, looking at such issues as the indispensability of the product to the war economy, total production of a given commodity, minimum operational requirements, surplus capacity, ability to substitute other materials, time needed to repair damaged facilities, the actual degree of damage sustained, and the ratio between "pool and production."[45] This last was important because it noted the distinction between commodities that could be stored, stockpiled, or simply used for an appreciable length of time versus a commodity where such activities were impractical. Thus, the oil reserves noted above were seen as a large "pool" and destruction of production would have little immediate effect—hence, the initial decision to give it a low priority. Similarly, U-boat production was slow, and most submarines were actually in service or in port, so hitting the factories building the boats would have little immediate effect on operations.[46] On the other hand, German aircraft were used up quickly in combat; there was no real pool from which to draw. In this case, destroying the factories would have a significant and almost immediate effect on the Luftwaffe's combat status.

Once planners had determined which industries, systems, or commodities were more important than others and OR provided guidance on how to attack them effectively, they then had to ascertain if the bombing was actually working. There were two fundamental questions to be answered. First, were air strikes actually destroying or neutralizing their intended targets, and second, if they were tactically successful, was that destruction or neutralization having the intended ripple effect throughout the German economy or war machine that had been predicted?

The first question—Were the bombers actually hitting and destroying their targets?—did not have an obvious answer. In 1943 the COA formed a subcommittee on "probabilities" to determine the accuracy of Eighth Air Force strikes, but the data proved "too pessimistic as a criterion for the future."[47] In addition, the related question of how

---

[45] "War Diary," 36–37; and "History of the COA," 43. See also Rostow, *Pre-Invasion Bombing Strategy*, 99–104; and Olson, "Economics of Target Selection for the Combined Bomber Offensive," 308–14. Rostow was a member of the EOU and authored the "War Diary."

[46] "War Diary," 43–46.

[47] "History of the COA," 20. For the accuracy of the Eighth Air Force, see USSBS, "Bombing Accuracy, USAAF Heavy and Medium Bombers in the ETO."

much damage was achieved when the bombs did hit the target was not obvious either. Poststrike photographs showed, for example, that the bombing raids against Schweinfurt's ball bearing factories in 1943 caused extensive damage. However, after the war it was discovered that many bombs detonated upon hitting the factory roofs. This collapsed the roofs, and such damage appeared impressive in photos, but in reality the machines on the floors below had been largely untouched—less than 5 percent were damaged, and most of those were quickly repaired.[48]

The answer to the second question, regarding bombing's effect on the German economy, was even more problematic and caused a great deal of disagreement. One notable dispute revolved around the oil plan versus rail plan controversy of spring 1944.[49]

The argument over targeting traces back to the Casablanca Conference of January 1943 when the objectives of the Combined Bomber Offensive were formalized. RAF and AAF bomber operations were to be a coordinated effort, "each operating against the sources of Germany's war power according to its own peculiar capabilities and concepts—the RAF bombing strategic city areas at night, the American force striking particular targets by daylight." Yet, air planners were also directed to "prepare the way for the climactic invasion of Europe."[50] These differing objectives meant differing strategies, which in turn demanded a different set of targets. Would these varied strategies work in harmony or at cross-purposes?

By early 1944 planning for the Normandy invasion was in full swing, including the question of how best the bombers could complement the landings. By this point, American analysts had revised their estimates of the German oil situation and decided the reserves available were not as great as originally thought; therefore, oil should become a top priority for Allied bombers. If the oil refineries in Rumania were knocked out, along with the hydrogenation plants in Germany that produced synthetic fuel from coal, the German war machine would be halted. Other planners focused on the German rail network. Troops, supplies, and raw materials all moved around the Reich primarily by train. If rail lines could be cut and trains stopped, so this argument went, the German war machine would stop as well.

---

[48] Perera, *Leaves from My Book of Life*, vol. 2, 139; USSBS, "German Anti-Friction Bearings Industry," 31, 38.
[49] "War Diary," 39.
[50] Craven and Cate, *Army Air Forces in World War II*, vol. 2, 665.

This debate broke along national lines with the Americans pushing for the oil plan and the British—notably Air Marshal Arthur Tedder—advocating the rail plan. The question of oil versus rail was resolved on 25 March 1944 when Gen Dwight Eisenhower agreed to the rail plan.[51] The critical factor was time. He wanted Allied air superiority to isolate the beachhead from German reinforcements before the invasion, not during the months that followed. Tedder's rail plan won the day because it promised a more immediate solution.

Another difficulty often experienced in targeting debates was that of mirror imaging. Allied air planners and analysts, in the absence of hard data or intelligence, often made decisions based on their own experience or common sense. Sometimes this worked, but on other occasions it induced errors. For example, German hydrogenation plants were assumed to operate similarly to Allied oil refineries. They did not. The Germans, in the interests of efficiency, folded rubber and chemical production into their hydrogenation plants. Thus, an air strike on one of these facilities affected not only gasoline production, but that of rubber and chemicals as well. In turn, these chemicals (notably methanol and synthetic nitrogen) were used in other applications, so there was a cascading effect in the explosives industry. Allied planners were not aware of this symbiotic relationship until after the war.[52] This is precisely the type of cascading effect prewar planners had hoped to achieve. Had this information been available in 1944, it would no doubt have moved the oil targets higher up the priority list.

Attempts to organize intelligence to better serve air planners continued for the rest of the war. Tedder, for example, renewed his efforts to prod US Strategic Air Forces (USSTAF) commander Gen Carl Spaatz into a greater emphasis on rail targets. Although he had won the earlier battle over the oil proponents, Tedder had seen his influence slipping since 14 September when the heavy bombers passed from Eisenhower's control back to Air Chief Marshal Arthur Harris and Spaatz. Initially, they were not responsive to Tedder's urgings, but after the first of the year he received unexpected support.

The Allies had broken the German Top Secret codes, transmitted by "Enigma" machines and whose products were referred to as "Ultra"

---

[51] For the best overall discussion see Ehlers, *Targeting the Reich*, chaps. 9–10. Also, Craven and Cate, *Army Air Forces in World War II*, vol. 3, 42–64; Webster and Frankland, *Strategic Air Offensive against Germany*, vol. 3, 42–64; Tedder, *With Prejudice*, 513–24; Zuckerman, *From Apes to Warlords*, chap. 12; and, Rostow, *Pre-Invasion Bombing Strategy*, 88–98.

[52] USSBS, "Oil Division Final Report," 1, 3; Klein, *Germany's Economic Preparations for War*, 226; and Rostow, *Pre-Invasion Bombing Strategy*, 165.

intelligence, early in the war. The importance of this special intelligence is well known. In January 1945 the German railroad system, which had been using its own teletype network for transmitting status reports, began using Enigma. Signals intelligence personnel had been largely ignoring rail traffic messages, believing them of little import, but the change to Enigma caused them to pay attention.[53] Decodes then revealed the crucial role played by coal in the German economy, powering virtually all industrial production. Indeed, 90 percent of Germany's energy derived from coal; without it, there was no economy. Coal was moved around the Reich largely by train ever since Bomber Command had effectively mined the rivers and canals, thus eliminating barge traffic.[54] Since the rail plan had been in effect, coal movement had slowed, causing a serious decline in production. The implication was clear. To deliver a death blow to German industry, the Allies had to stop the flow of coal. The best way to do this was to stop the trains.[55]

In sum, the first question air planners confronted in World War II centered on knowing the structure of an enemy's society and economy. The second big question was whether or not they could hit and damage selected targets. The final question involved determining if hitting the targets achieved the desired results.

Analyzing the Effects— the *US Strategic Bombing Survey*

In early 1944 certain airmen pushed for a major study to ascertain the effects of strategic bombing on Germany. This study, to become the US Strategic Bombing Survey (USSBS), was the intellectual brainchild of Maj Gen Muir S. "Santy" Fairchild. Santy had been an instructor in the Air Force section of the ACTS in the late 1930s and served most of the war in Washington in key positions on the Air Staff and Joint Staff. He remained very interested in the bombing offensive and, more importantly, in what effect it was having on the German economy. He had been instrumental in forming the COA,

---

[53] Mierzejewski, *Collapse of the German War Economy*, 167–69.

[54] Around 60 percent of the oil from Rumania was transported to Germany via barge on the Danube River. When the RAF mined the Danube, it brought this traffic to a halt. When one realizes that a single barge of oil was equivalent to a 100-car train, it becomes obvious how important these mining operations were in throttling Germany's oil supply. Goralski and Freeburg, *Oil and War*, 271; and Cooke and Nesbitt, *Target: Hitler's Oil*, 70.

[55] This argument is spelled out in detail in Mierzejewski, *Collapse of the German War Economy*.

and in early 1944 believed a bombing survey was essential to answer questions regarding the effectiveness of airpower. At the same time, members of Spaatz's staff in England were having similar thoughts. Spaatz sent letters to Arnold in April suggesting a study, emphasizing that it must be done by impartial civilians. He also wanted the survey to be an American effort, arguing that the differences between RAF and AAF efforts were so distinct as to demand separate studies.[56] Arnold approached Robert Lovett, the assistant secretary of war for air, who approached the president. On 9 September, Roosevelt gave his approval to form a bombing survey team.

The following month Arnold offered the job as survey chief to Franklin D'Olier, president of Prudential Insurance Company. D'Olier expressed his unsuitability for the job—he was not an aviator. Arnold countered that was precisely why he was ideal; he wanted "a nationally prominent man of affairs, with no axes to grind, pro or con." Arnold argued the AAF needed an impartial report to be used "as a basis for planning the postwar composition and strategical principles of the Army Air Forces." The survey would also guide the bomber offensive against Japan. The general concluded by stressing, "This is your job, and when you're finished, you report not to me, but directly to Secretary Stimson and the President."[57]

D'Olier organized his team—which would eventually number nearly 1,600 officer, enlisted, and civilian personnel—into three broad groups dealing with military, economic, and civilian studies, with those divided into 13 smaller divisions for categories such as physical damage, oil, munitions, transportation, morale, and so forth. All of the groups and divisions were headed by civilian businessmen, lawyers, or bankers. The quality of the men chosen was exceptional and included Paul Nitze, John Kenneth Galbraith, Henry Alexander, George Ball, and Edward Meade Earle. Each was chosen for his specific expertise; for example, Robert Russell of the Standard Oil Company was to be director of the oil division, and Frank McNamee, deputy head of the US Civil Defense Agency, was named director of the civilian defense division.[58]

Over the next year USSBS teams roamed Europe, visiting hundreds of bombed sites, measuring, photographing, and collecting data,

---

[56] MacIsaac, *Strategic Bombing in World War Two*, 32–36. The British authorized their own bombing survey. For the RAF's effort, see Cox, *Strategic Air War against Germany*.

[57] MacIsaac, *Strategic Bombing in World War Two*, 52.

[58] Ibid., 68–70; and Daniels, *Guide to the Reports of the United States Strategic Bombing Survey*, xxiii.

while also interviewing thousands of individuals, from top generals and diplomats to civilian workers. In June 1945, D'Olier and some of his division chiefs met with Spaatz—who was scheduled to take command of all AAF forces in the Pacific—and advised him on targeting priorities for the bombing campaign over Japan. D'Olier said based on the findings in Germany, the target that should be given the highest priority was the Japanese transportation system, specifically the railroads and coastal shipping assets. At a lower order of priority, he listed oil and chemical plants and the electrical power system, especially transformer stations.[59] For reasons discussed below, the targeting priorities set forth by USSBS directors were scarcely used.

D'Olier and his staff deployed to Japan upon enemy surrender and conducted a similar survey of the Japanese economy and its destruction by the bombing campaign. Overall, they published 324 reports on the air campaigns—216 for the European theater and 108 for the Pacific. These reports were often controversial, especially in the Pacific theater. The US Navy had played a supporting role in the defeat of Germany but felt it had exercised a dominant role in the Pacific. It therefore insisted on writing a lengthy report detailing naval operations in the theater, including the amphibious operations in the South Pacific and Central Pacific areas. In the Navy view, these operations were essential preludes to the bomber offensive that began in November 1944 from bases in the Mariana Islands.[60] Clearly, both services were looking ahead to peacetime when the major issue of a separate air force would be decided.

So what were the bombing survey's findings? Regarding the war in Europe, survey writers concluded that "Allied air power was decisive in the war in Western Europe."[61] Airpower was not, however, the only decisive factor; the massive Soviet army on the eastern front was chewing up German divisions at an astonishing rate. The American, British, and Free French forces in the west were facing far fewer German troops, but the offensive beginning on D-day caught Germany in the jaws of a vice it could not escape. Even so, strategic bombing had a catastrophic effect on the German economy and transportation system, and this in turn had a fatal impact on German armed forces.

---

[59] Daniels, *Guide to the Reports of the United States Strategic Bombing Survey*, 101.

[60] This report, no. 73, "The Campaigns of the Pacific War," was published over the objections of Paul Nitze, the deputy head of USSBS. MacIsaac, *Strategic Bombing in World War Two*, 128–30.

[61] USSBS, "Summary Report (European War)," 15.

The USSBS presented scores of charts, graphs, and tables illustrating the impact of bombing. At its peak, the air campaign employed 1.34 million personnel and over 27,000 aircraft. Bombers flew 1.44 million sorties and dropped 2.7 million tons of bombs—54.2 percent of that by the AAF. The bombing campaign was costly—nearly 160,000 airmen were lost by the British and the Americans (almost exactly the same number by each), and 40,000 aircraft were destroyed (22,000 RAF and 18,000 AAF). Losses for the Eighth Air Force were staggering: 44,472 men.[62] Indeed, the Eighth Air Force suffered greater losses than did the entire US Marine Corps or Navy during the war.[63] Of great significance, 85.9 percent of all bombs dropped by the AAF on Germany fell after D-day.[64] In a true sense, the Combined Bomber Offensive did not really begin until the spring of 1944—just as predicted in AWPD-1.

Bombing survey graphs regarding production in key industries are dramatic—virtually every major commodity necessary to sustain the German war effort began a severe decline by summer 1944, which is when the bombing of Germany finally began in earnest. Production of aviation fuel, for example, plummeted from a peak of 316,000 tons/month to 107,000 tons in June and 17,000 tons by September. Synthetic fuel dropped from a high of 175,000 tons in April 1944 to 30,000 tons by July and 5,000 tons in September—a 90-percent drop in four months. The effects of this fuel drought were felt throughout the Wehrmacht—aircraft stopped flying, and tanks stopped driving. In March 1945 the Soviets overran 1,200 German tanks that had run out of gas.[65]

Bombing attacks on the German transportation industry were even more profound: "The attack on transportation was the decisive blow that completely disorganized the German economy." The survey noted that 40 percent of all rail traffic was coal—21,400 train carloads per day at the beginning of 1944. By the end of the year, that number had fallen to 9,000 cars daily.[66] Steel production was related to this collapse, reflecting an 80-percent drop in three months. Similar drops were experienced in the production of explosives, synthetic rubber, chemicals (nitrogen, chlorine, methane, etc.), powder, and combat munitions.[67]

---

[62] USSBS, "Over-All Report," 1; USSBS, "Statistical Appendix," 1–9.

[63] The US Marine Corps lost 24,511 men to all causes during World War II; the US Navy lost 36,950.

[64] USSBS, "Statistical Appendix," 13.

[65] USSBS, "Summary Report," 8–9.

[66] Ibid., 12.

[67] See the devastating charts depicting this collapse in USSBS, "Over-All Report," passim.

The survey also gave some overall conclusions. Air superiority was essential to the bombing campaign's success. This air dominance was not achieved until the spring of 1944, allowing the bombing campaign to achieve its dramatic success. Analysts concluded that it was better to focus on one target system and destroy it rather than hit numerous systems simultaneously with a relatively small amount of tonnage on each. Each industry had built-in slack so that a small degree of bombing was simply absorbed, resulting in little decline in overall production.[68] As noted, the transportation network, which was the recipient of greater tonnage than any other target system—32.1 percent of all bombs dropped—was the key to the enemy economy because it moved resources to the factories and finished goods to the front. Disruption of railroads brought everything to a crawl—especially important was the movement of coal that powered the entire German economy. Close behind the destruction of the transportation system was the demise of oil refineries, which was especially fatal to the Wehrmacht's mobility on land and in the air.

Area attacks were deemed less effective in reducing industrial production than were "precision" attacks.[69] In fact, the survey concluded that area attacks by the RAF had only a minor impact on German production. Analysts determined that German morale fell precipitously as a result of bombing, causing "defeatism, fear, hopelessness, fatalism, and apathy." Yet the coercive practices of the Nazi regime—relying on slave labor and a 72-hour work week—kept factories operating.[70] The survey also confirmed the notion of an industrial web focusing on key targets within the overall system that had a disproportionate importance to the whole. In the USSBS phrasing, "The most serious attacks were those which destroyed the industry or service which most indispensably served other industries."[71] This finding speaks to the synergism existing between target sets; bombers destroyed the steel mills as well as rail lines leading to and from those factories, along with marshaling yards serving the railroads. Taking down the oil refineries meant there was little fuel to power the airplanes and tanks that were produced, and, of course, tactical aircraft destroying military equipment in combat also contributed to the

---

[68] USSBS, "Summary Report," 16–17.
[69] Ibid. Somewhat surprisingly, the British Bombing Survey arrived at a similar conclusion. Cox, *Strategic Air War against Germany*, 69.
[70] USSBS, "Effects of Strategic Bombing on German Morale," 1; Tooze, *Wages of Destruction*, 632.
[71] USSBS, "Summary Report," 16.

German military collapse. In other words, rather than specific bottle-neck targets existing as predicted by prewar theorists, it took re-peated, heavy attacks against several components of the industrial system to collapse the entire enemy infrastructure.

USSBS analysts claimed some targets were overlooked that should have been struck more heavily during the war. The primary "lost tar-get" was the German electrical system. It had been considered early on as a bottleneck target (it had topped the AWPD-1 list), but its widely dispersed nature and the small size of individual power plants made it a low-priority target. This system, "with minor exceptions, was never made a primary target for strategic bombing," but analysts argued it should have been—a relatively small amount of bomb ton-nage would have had "catastrophic" and cascading effects throughout the economy.[72] Similarly, the USSBS argued that the ball bearing in-dustry, hit hard in the fall of 1943 but at grievous cost to the AAF, was indeed a choke-point target system that should have been revisited.[73] Other potential key nodes susceptible to heavy damage and cascad-ing effects were aircraft engine factories, fuselage assembly-jig plants, propeller facilities, and tetraethyl lead plants.[74] Nonetheless, the over-all effect of strategic bombing on Germany, while concentrated in the last nine months of a six-year war, was devastating.

USSBS findings regarding the strategic bombing campaign against Japan revealed that problems in the Pacific were difficult from the beginning. As noted, the AAF entered the war seriously deficient in stra-tegic intelligence, but that problem was greater in terms of Japan because of the closed nature of its society. In many cases, air planners had to rely on old maps, an occasional tourist report, or prewar insurance data.[75] There were also mechanical teething troubles with the new B-29s re-quired to span the great distances inherent in Pacific theater opera-tions and meteorological phenomena, like the 200-mph, high-altitude jet stream, that played havoc with navigation and bombing accuracy.

Initial operations out of the Marianas were not a success, and the commander there, Brig Gen Haywood Hansell, whom we have met elsewhere in this study, was relieved. He was replaced by Maj Gen

---

[72] USSBS, "German Electric Utilities Industry Report," 5–7.

[73] Webster and Frankland, *Strategic Air Offensive against Germany*, vol. 4, 384.

[74] USSBS, "Strategic Bombing of the German Aircraft Industry," 7; USSBS, "Oil Division Final Report," 2, 43–46. Tetraethyl lead was a chemical that raised gasoline's octane rating, making it essential for high-powered aircraft engines.

[75] For more on the problems with air intelligence before and during the war, see Kreis, *Piercing the Fog*, chaps. 1, 2, 6, and 7.

Curtis E. LeMay. In a stunning reversal of two decades of air doctrine, LeMay jettisoned the teachings of ACTS, and for that matter, most of what he and other combat leaders had learned over Germany. He stripped his B-29s of guns, ammunition, and armor plating and launched them at night and at low altitude in area bombing attacks, using incendiaries against Japanese cities. The Japanese were unprepared for fire bombing, and the results were devastating to the Japanese economy and its military capability.[76]

On 8 August 1945, a B-29 dropped an atomic bomb on Hiroshima. Three days later a second atomic bomb hit Nagasaki. The Japanese announced their surrender on 15 August, their emperor citing the new bomb as his reason for capitulating.[77]

The USSBS team arrived in Japan shortly afterward and began collecting data and interviewing key individuals in the political and military hierarchy. Statistically, the numbers were illuminating. B-29s dropped 91 percent of all bombs on Japan, and 96 percent of all tonnage dropped on the home islands fell in the last five months of the war.[78] The attacks destroyed 600 factories and thousands of "feeder shops." The Japanese attempted to disperse into underground factories and caves to avert the air attacks, but this only further dissipated scarce resources. Overall, production dropped by 53 percent between November 1944 and July 1945. In cities that had *not* been bombed, production in July 1945 was at 94 percent of its wartime peak, but in cities that had been bombed, production had fallen to 27 percent of its acme.[79] By July 1945 aluminum production was at 9 percent, while oil refining and ingot steel production were at 15 percent of their high points.[80] The USSBS concluded, "By July 1945 Japan's economic system had been shattered. Production of civilian goods was below the level of subsistence. Munitions output had been curtailed to less than half the wartime peak, a level that could not support sustained military operations against our opposing forces. The economic basis of Japanese resistance had been destroyed."[81]

---

[76] The exception was Nagoya. Although hit by nearly the same amount of bomb tonnage as Tokyo throughout the war, it suffered only one-tenth the casualties due to a more effective and efficient fire department and civil defense system. USSBS, "Effects of Incendiary Bomb Attacks on Japan," chap. 8.

[77] "Emperor's Rescript," 191–92. For one of the better discussions of the Japanese surrender, see Coox, "*Enola Gay* and Japan's Struggle to Surrender," 161–67.

[78] USSBS, "Summary Report (Pacific Theater)," 16. Only 7,180 tons of the 160,800 tons dropped on Japan fell prior to 9 March 1945.

[79] USSBS, "Effects of Air Attack on the Japanese Urban Economy," 11.

[80] USSBS, "Effects of Strategic Bombing on Japan's War Economy," 43; and USSBS, "Summary," 88.

[81] USSBS, "War Economy," 2.

An estimated 8.5 million people evacuated Japanese cities. This was one-quarter of the entire urban population of Japan, although in big cities like Osaka and Kobe, over half fled. One-third of the 8.5 million evacuees were factory workers, and this was evidenced by an absentee rate in the factories of 49 percent by the end of war.[82] Morale and hope plummeted.

Overall, at least 400,000 Japanese civilians were killed in air attacks—about the same number as Germans, although the losses occurred in much less time with only one-tenth the tonnage. About 2.5 million homes were destroyed, as well as over 600,000 that were pulled down by the government to build firebreaks.[83]

The air campaign was not, however, an unmitigated success. The biggest strategic errors made by airmen, according to the USSBS, were that the B-29s should have struck railroads and inland waterways much sooner.[84] These attacks would have thoroughly disrupted internal transportation and significantly curtailed the influx of reinforcements to Kyushu—site of the proposed invasion in November 1945—that so concerned Army planners. As in Europe, such a transportation plan would have made beachhead defense much more difficult. Even so, results of the bombing campaign, especially atomic strikes, were disastrous for Japan. Surrender occurred without a bloody invasion being necessary.

Summary

American airmen, like soldiers, sailors, and marines, were unprepared for the magnitude, complexity, and viciousness of the war they would face. For airmen, the newness of their weapon and its largely unexplored capabilities compounded problems and introduced others not anticipated. Airmen started with ideas—long before technology existed to realize those ideas. At the Air Corps Tactical School, as well as on isolated airfields scattered across the country, visionaries posited new ways to wage war—not merely new methods to fight wars in the traditional fashion. In truth, this was the easy part. Sitting behind their desks or at bars, these men engaged in spirited debates

---

[82] USSBS, "Effects of Strategic Bombing on Japanese Morale," 13; and USSBS, "Urban Economy," 25.
[83] The USSBS gives a total of 330,000 civilians killed, about 1 percent of the total population, but other estimates run higher. Approximately 45 percent of those killed were part of the Japanese labor force. USSBS, "Summary," 20.
[84] Ibid.; and USSBS, "War Economy," 61–65.

with other equally intelligent operators and hammered out a logical and coherent theory of air warfare. These theories were not based on experience or even a great deal of experimentation; rather, they were Aristotelian logic exercises—the same type of mind patterns that would be used by atomic warfare theorists two decades later. Yet the theories were not far wrong. More importantly, they served as a polestar to guide airmen through and around myriad difficulties.

The first of these difficulties involved technology, and the most important technology was the airplane itself. For the first three decades after the aircraft was invented, engine performance grew steadily. As engineers better understood the principles governing lift and drag, they improved streamlining, which in turn increased performance. By 1935 the builders at Boeing made a significant leap, designing what would become the B-17. The performance of the Flying Fortress was greater than any other bomber in the world at the time and surpassed that of most pursuit planes as well. It was the aircraft that air theorists had been postulating. For that very reason, the ground zealots who dominated the Army hierarchy resented and opposed it. The result: the United States entered a world war with a pitifully small number of heavy bombers—bombers that could have been built six years earlier. In mid 1943 the Allies together could muster barely 1,000 heavy bombers on a given day. One year later that number had tripled. By the fall of 1944, the combined bomber forces numbered 5,250 aircraft.[85] That is why the "Crescendo of Bombing,"[86] which began in mid 1944, was so utterly devastating. Air strategists wondered if those astounding results could have been achieved earlier and with less loss of life.

There were other technologies that needed to be developed to fulfill the airmen's theories. Accuracy was essential to the doctrine formulated at Maxwell Field. Coincidentally, the Norden bombsight was invented around the same time as the B-17. Although the precision desired for the bombing offensive was never as good as hoped or desired, the combination of the heavy bomber with the Norden device enabled destruction of the German and Japanese economies. Other technologies that advanced rapidly during the war included those which enabled long-range escort fighters, radar, advanced fuels, and jet engines. Airmen have often been labeled as technological determinists,

---

[85] Tooze, *Wages of Destruction*, 649.
[86] Meilinger, "USSBS' Eye on Europe," 76.

but the truth was simple: bombing campaigns required advanced technology. The B-17 had barely flown when airmen were already contemplating aircraft with twice its range—the B-29 was to be that aircraft, and right behind it would come the behemoth B-36.

Doctrine combined with technology, and these in turn were mated to an organizational structure that maximized the effectiveness and efficiency of airpower. Before the war, this structure was the GHQ Air Force. During the war itself, it was the numbered air forces—composite air units containing a mix of bombers, fighters, cargo planes, and reconnaissance aircraft. Some of these air forces, like the Eighth, Fifteenth, and Twentieth, were focused on strategic bombing; whereas, the Fifth, Ninth, and Twelfth were more tactically centered and contained greater numbers of fighters and medium bombers. An unusual but important anomaly was the command structure used to command these air forces. On 1 January 1944, the US Strategic Air Forces was established under the command of General Spaatz, consisting of the Eighth Air Force based in England and the Fifteenth Air Force based in Italy. Cutting across theater boundaries, USSTAF ensured unity of command of the strategic air forces, but ingeniously focused that unity on the target—Germany—rather than in the different theaters where the bombers were based. This system was modified prior to the Normandy invasion, when General Eisenhower was given temporary targeting authority over the heavy bombers. He relinquished that control in September 1944.[87]

The Pacific situation was similar. In April 1944, B-29s began deploying to India, and staging bases were established in China. The bombers of XX Bomber Command flew from India to China to refuel, continued on to hit targets in Japan, and then returned to India via China. In October 1944, the Mariana Islands were liberated, and airfields were built on Guam, Saipan, and Tinian to accommodate the XXI Bomber Command. This meant that B-29 bases were established in two different theaters—South-East Asian Theater and Pacific Ocean Areas—while transiting the China Theater.[88] Who was in overall command of the B-29s?

In an unusual move, General Arnold formed the Twentieth Air Force, composed of the XX and XXI Bomber Commands, and then

---

[87] Craven and Cate, *Army Air Forces in World War II*, vol. 3, 79–83.

[88] Technically, China was part of the South-East Asian Theater, but Generalissimo Chiang Kai-shek seldom took advice, much less orders, from outsiders. To help smooth relations, Gen Joseph Stilwell, Chiang's chief of staff, was dual-hatted as the deputy of the South-East Asian Theater.

elected to command the Twentieth himself. Arnold argued that, as in Europe, unity of command over the *target area*—Japan—was more important than unity of command in the *basing areas*. He maintained that it would be impossible to delegate command authority to three different theater commanders and have any hope for an effective, co-ordinated strategic air campaign against Japan. (When selling this idea to his fellow chiefs, Arnold noted that much the same system in the US Navy allowed ADM Ernest King to command the US Anti-submarine Command, Tenth Fleet, while remaining in Washington as commander in chief, US Navy.)[89] As in Europe, however, if the ground situation were such that strategic bombers were needed, Arnold would place them at the disposal of the theater commander. This happened in March and April 1945, when the Twentieth Air Force was diverted from its strategic bombing campaign to support the invasion of Okinawa.[90]

In sum, in both Europe and the Pacific, strategic air forces operated side by side with theater commanders, all of whom took their guidance from the joint or combined chiefs. If the situation required, forces or resources were shifted from one theater to another, or air assets were temporarily placed at the disposal of a theater commander if the tactical situation deemed it necessary. The system worked and would serve as an important precedent for Strategic Air Command a few years later.

One of the great challenges faced by air planners during the war revolved around targeting and intelligence for the bombing offensive. Planners of AWPD-1 ran into this problem as soon as they began their project. It proved a difficult challenge. As described above, the types of targeting, intelligence, and analytical bodies necessary simply did not exist prior to invention of the airplane. They had to be invented, and, as with the technology of the airplane itself, these creations developed with remarkable speed. Operations research and its work in rationalizing and improving the mechanics of air warfare came first. Immediately thereafter, targeting and intelligence agencies were formed to guide planners and commanders in their conduct of the bombing offensive. Targeting was the key to everything, and intelligence was essential to conduct that function; analysis was then needed to ensure the

---

[89] Baer, *One Hundred Years of Sea Power*, 203; and Hansell, *Strategic Air War against Japan*, 26–27. Hansell was on the Air Staff at the time Twentieth Air Force was formed and soon after took over XXI Bomber Command in the Marianas. King's position of commander in chief and the authority it carried was dissolved after the war, and the head of the Navy then became simply the chief of naval operations.

[90] Craven and Cate, *Army Air Forces in World War II*, vol. 5, 630–31.

targets were indeed the correct ones, which in turn required more intelligence. It was an iterative and complex process. In brief, OR was instrumental in studying the *tactics* of air warfare, but for matters of air *strategy*, a higher level of analysis was necessary. Going into the war, air planners had no precedents for determining appropriate objectives, targets, or measures of effectiveness for strategic bombing. At the same time, they had almost no experience with gathering the types of intelligence necessary to conduct such a campaign. These processes, which required massive resources and conceptual skill, had to be created from scratch. As we shall see, they would become integral to the functioning of Strategic Air Command.

The largest of all the analytical agencies formed to study the results of airpower was the US Strategic Bombing Survey. Although USSBS was supposed to be apolitical, this hope was naïve. The entire subject of strategic bombing was freighted with politics: inter-Allied (US vs. UK), interservice (AAF vs. Navy), and intraservice (bombers vs. fighters). No matter what the survey teams wrote, they would offend someone. Moreover, the USSBS did have inherent problems: its focus on strategic bombing tended to slight the achievements of tactical airpower. Civilian specialists chosen were from the management side of things—there were no labor representatives on the teams. And then there were the virulent exchanges between sailors and airmen over which airpower—land-based or sea-based, strategic or tactical— was more important to victory.[91] This fight, which had been ongoing since the early 1920s, would continue unabated. We will soon see another of these confrontations—the "Revolt of the Admirals"—which would become one of the most vocal and nastiest interservice fights in American history. Despite these cavils, the overwhelming authority of the Strategic Bombing Survey is unassailable. Nothing like it had ever been attempted after a war. The mountain of evidence obtained, the thousands of interviews conducted, the painstaking measurements taken, are simply too massive to refute. More importantly for our purposes, the USSBS provided airmen in the immediate postwar years the unimpeachable evidence they needed to carry on the fight for institutional independence. The survey's reports, and especially the easy-to-read, concise, and readily obtainable summary volumes, were widely circulated and quoted in the years to follow.

---

[91] MacIsaac, *Strategic Bombing in World War Two*, 157–60. See also, Gentile, *How Effective Is Strategic Bombing?* chap. 4.

Then there was leadership. In this chapter we saw it first with Frank Andrews. A contemporary of Hap Arnold and one of the most senior and important airmen of his era, Andrews was the driving force behind the GHQ Air Force. He pushed incessantly for autonomy of the air arm, but also for the B-17. It nearly cost him his career. When he left Langley Field in 1939 after four years as commander, he lost the stars of a major general and reverted to his permanent rank of colonel—all because he refused to quell his advocacy for strategic airpower. Leadership then emerged from an unlikely place. Gen George C. Marshall was appointed chief of staff in September 1939 and almost immediately recalled Andrews from exile in Texas to become the War Department's G-3—the first airman to hold that position. As the Army's operations chief, Andrews again pinned on a star (and a second one soon after) and was instrumental in pushing the service into modern war. Not only did the Army now begin to purchase B-17s and B-24s, but Andrews also insisted it begin buying another machine that infantry and cavalry zealots had refused to embrace: the tank.[92]

Leadership was crucial at all levels. The four officers mainly responsible for authoring AWPD-1, but also the many anonymous staff officers assisting them, worked with remarkable poise and self-confidence in devising a blueprint for a strategic air campaign against Germany. During the war itself, the tireless efforts of a host of air commanders—Spaatz, Eaker, Doolittle, Kenney, Twining, and many others—made the difference between victory and defeat. In addition, unsung staff officers, especially Santy Fairchild, proved essential in pushing airpower to become more efficient and effective.[93]

Along these lines, it is useful to reflect on the situation in the Pacific Theater. When the XXI Bomber Command was formed on Guam in mid 1944, Brig Gen Haywood Hansell was chosen for command. It seemed an ideal choice. Hansell had been a main proponent of strategic airpower at ACTS; he had helped author AWPD-1 and its successor AWPD-42; he had commanded a B-17 bomb wing in combat while in England; and he had served on the Air Staff as both a planner and an intelligence officer. What better officer to lead the new B-29s into war against Japan? Yet Hansell failed. He followed the dictates of doctrine and experience from the European war but was unable to

---

[92] Johnson, *Fast Tanks and Heavy Bombers*, 141–44. There has never been a biography of Andrews, a huge gap in the historiography of airpower, but for an enlightening essay, see Copp, "Frank M. Andrews," 43–71. Andrews was a lieutenant general when he died in an airplane crash near Keflavik, Iceland, on 3 May 1943.

[93] There has not yet been a biography of Fairchild, but for a good article, see Schaffel, "Muir S. Fairchild," 165–71.

adjust to the new war against a different enemy. His replacement, Maj Gen Curtis LeMay, was not known as a thinker, but he too had been a bomb commander over Europe. He was a tactical innovator who was both physically and mentally courageous—he frequently led his group in combat. In the Pacific he unceremoniously jettisoned two decades of doctrine and adopted what was essentially the tactics of RAF Bomber Command: area bombing of urban centers. It was a gamble, but it worked. Atomic bomb strikes against Hiroshima and Nagasaki were merely LeMay's tactics writ large.

When the airmen returned home from war in the fall of 1945, they basked in the glow of a job very well done. It had not been easy, but it had been done. Their accomplishments were apparent to all, in and out of uniform. It seemed inevitable that a separate service, formed around the nucleus of a strategic bomber force, was in the offing.

Chapter 3

Formation

When the Air Corps became the Army Air Forces in June 1941, it moved closer to the goal of independence. Hap Arnold became the commanding general of the AAF while wearing a second hat as the deputy chief of staff for air. He also became a member of the Joint Chiefs of Staff (JCS); the RAF's chief of air staff attended meetings of the Combined Chiefs, so Arnold did as well. In December 1944, Arnold pinned on a fifth star—the only American airman ever to hold that rank.

Arnold had great respect for Marshall, and the feeling was mutual, so there was no agitation for a separate Air Force during the war. That did not mean airmen failed to plan for the future. In April 1943, Arnold formed the Special Projects Office for postwar planning under Col F. Trubee Davison, who had been assistant secretary of war for air from 1926 to 1932. Two months later Brig Gen Larry Kuter, Arnold's assistant chief of staff for plans, formed a Post War Division within his office, headed by Col Rueben C. Moffat, to look at the matter as well. Kuter was replaced by Maj Gen Lauris Norstad in spring 1945. These four men—Davison, Kuter, Moffat, and Norstad—would plan the future of the postwar air arm.

Postwar planning included force structure, budgeting, personnel allocations and training, basing, procurement, and research and development (R&D), among other issues. In truth, air planners focused primarily on the matter of independence, and all other questions were viewed through the prism of how they impacted or were impacted by the drive for a separate service.[1]

At this point most postwar planners had no knowledge of the atomic bomb. That subject was so highly classified that only a few high-ranking officers had access to such information. Norstad and Kuter had the necessary clearances but would not have shared that intelligence with their subordinates, so Davison and Moffat were not privy to such knowledge. Nonetheless, planners envisioned an Air Force in which bombardment was the main arm. This rationale had been consistent over the previous two decades. To justify independence,

---

[1] This theme runs throughout the study by Perry Smith, *Air Force Plans for Peace*.

the air arm needed a unique mission; that mission was strategic bombing—the ability to strike the vital centers of an enemy nation at the outset of war. In the whole history of war only airpower offered this capability, and airmen trumpeted this uniqueness. Although the war was still in progress, planners were confident airpower would demonstrate its decisiveness. They operated on the belief that a bomber force would form the core of a postwar Air Force.

When envisioning a postwar world, air planners posited potential threats. Although a resurgent Germany or Japan could be a problem, they quickly shifted their fears toward the Soviet Union. By mid 1944, relations between Washington and Moscow were beginning to chill, and it became obvious that although the Soviets had a huge army and tactical air arm, they had no strategic air force. US bombers would serve as a counterbalance. As early as April 1943, chief of plans Brig Gen Orvil A. Anderson (Kuter's predecessor) predicted that once Hitler and the Nazi regime fell, chaos would result, and "Russia may have sufficient provocation to alone occupy and assume control of not only all [of] Germany, but all of Central and Eastern Europe now under Axis domination."[2] This would be a fairly accurate prophecy. The concept of airpower as the equalizer would therefore be a common theme for airmen in the years ahead.

Maj Gen Thomas T. Handy, chief of the Army's operations division, looked at the postwar question from a broader perspective—there was no assurance the AAF would become independent. Handy therefore posited a postwar Army consisting of nearly 1.6 million personnel, part of whom would be allocated to the AAF, and this would permit 105 groups—42 of which would be strategic bomb groups.[3] Although this was less than half the number of total groups in the wartime AAF—the peak was 232 in early 1945—airmen realized a force this size in peacetime would be impressive.

There was also talk in diplomatic circles of a United Nations to be formed following the war. Such a concept had been hinted at in the Atlantic Charter of August 1941 signed by Winston Churchill and Franklin Roosevelt. Although vaguely worded, the concept of a world organization persisted. Unlike the failed League of Nations following

---

[2] Brig Gen O. A. Anderson, "A Study to Determine the Minimum Air Power the United States Should Have at the Conclusion of the War in Europe," April 1943, AFHRA, file 145.96-125.

[3] Smith, *Air Force Plans for Peace*, 48. In the parlance of the day, "very heavy bombers" (VHB) were B-29s; "heavy bombers" were B-17s and B-24s. "Strategic bombers" almost always referred solely to the B-29 VHBs. In 1948 the B-36 would become the VHB, and the B-29 and B-50 would be downgraded to medium bombers. The term *heavy bomber* was no longer used.

World War I, this notional body was to be equipped with a military force to deter aggressors or punish them if deterrence failed.[4] As early as 1942, joint planners assumed an international police force would be in the offing once the war ended, and airpower would play a major role. One journalist imagined airpower as the primary arm of a new "aeropolitics," with strategic airports scattered around the world to dominate key oceanic choke points from which "air police" would deploy when necessary.[5] AAF planners expected that the bulk of the air forces assigned to this world police force would be provided by the United States. The airmen folded this idea into their plans: it might be possible to secure a peacetime Air Force that included 78 groups for national defense and a further 75 groups for international policing.[6] Planners quickly realized, however, that an international police force would not be forthcoming.

By late 1944 the high hopes of airmen were being severely dashed. General Marshall balked at the figures proposed by Handy. He thought it impossible that Congress would approve such a large and costly peacetime military force and insisted planners drastically scale back their estimates. Over the next several months, air planners steadily trimmed their numbers. When Handy told the AAF it could hope for no more than 400,000 personnel in a postwar force, planners calculated that such manning would support only 70 groups, barely; 25 would be strategic bombers. In total, the air arm would include nearly 18,000 aircraft, although well over half of those would be assigned to the Air National Guard and Air Reserve.[7] From August 1945 on, these numbers were to be touchstone figures for airmen, but as we shall see, even these reduced goals would be unattainable. Another problem facing airmen in the immediate aftermath of Japanese surrender involved the impact of the atomic bomb.

The Bomb and Its Relevance

Theoretically, it had been known for decades that splitting the atom (fission) would release enormous power—far greater than any explosive ever invented. In the 1930s, the theories of nuclear fission

---

[4] Beaumont, *Right Backed by Might*, 77; and Converse, *Circling the Earth*, 6–10.

[5] Smith, *Air Force Plans for Peace*, 83.

[6] Ibid., 51.

[7] Wolk, *Struggle for Air Force Independence*, 54–63, 67–73. See also Schnabel, *Joint Chiefs of Staff and National Policy*, vol. 1: *1945–1947*, 102–3.

began to take definite shape as scientists in Germany, the United States, and elsewhere undertook experiments that revealed the secrets of the atom.

It became apparent in early 1939 that war was coming in Europe. It was also obvious to a group of scientists in America, some of whom had recently fled Germany, that the Nazis were working toward an atomic bomb. Faced with this frightening possibility, these individuals, led by Albert Einstein, wrote President Roosevelt warning him of the peril represented by the German research. The United States *must* beat the Nazis to the atomic bomb, but it would take immediate action and vast funds to do so. In October 1939, one month after war erupted in Europe, FDR directed the Army to study the matter.

For the next five years, the Army managed the "Manhattan Project" to build an atomic bomb.[8] This was the most secretive and costly weapon-development program of the war—although it later proved not secretive enough; spies working for Moscow infiltrated the program and passed on crucial information. The Manhattan Project was enormous, requiring not only secretive laboratories, "heavy water" plants, and vast amounts of silver to produce the required electrical coils, but also mining operations to obtain the required uranium.

On 2 December 1942, a team of scientists, led by Nobel Prize winner Enrico Fermi, huddled in a secret lab beneath the football stadium at the University of Chicago and produced the world's first self-sustaining nuclear reaction. A year later, scientists at Los Alamos, New Mexico, under the leadership of J. Robert Oppenheimer, began producing a weapon from Fermi's achievement. On 16 July 1945, an atomic device was detonated at Trinity Site in the New Mexico desert. The blast was seen as far away as Albuquerque and El Paso and entailed the now familiar ball of fire and mushroom cloud. One observer described the blast as "unprecedented, magnificent, beautiful, stupendous, and terrifying."[9]

Pres. Harry Truman was in Potsdam discussing the postwar settlement of Germany with Joseph Stalin and British prime minister Clement Atlee when he was told of the Trinity blast. According to Truman, there was never any question in his mind that he would use

---

[8] For the development of the atomic bomb and the Manhattan Engineering District, see Vincent Jones, *United States Army in World War II*; and Hewlett and Anderson, *History of the United States Atomic Energy Commission*, vol. 1.

[9] Jones, *United States Army in World War II*, 516.

the atomic bomb against Japan.[10] The issues now dealt with delivery and the appropriate target.

Because of its size and weight, the bomb could be carried only in a B-29; even so, the bombers had to be specially modified and the crews specially trained to handle this new weapon. In the summer of 1944, Arnold chose Lt Col Paul Tibbets, a superb pilot with a distinguished combat record, to head the unit that would deliver the bomb. The 509th Bomb Group was activated on 17 December 1944, and after training in the United States, Tibbets moved his unit to the island of Tinian in the Marianas. Once oriented in-theater, the 509th flew a number of combat missions against Japan, utilizing large conventional bombs that resembled the atomic bombs in size and shape.[11]

The target question involved several factors. President Truman and his advisors decided to hit an actual military target rather than attempt a demonstration, such as exploding a bomb off the coast of Tokyo. There were too few bombs available to waste on empty space. They also feared that since the actual bomb had not yet been tested—Trinity involved a huge, static device detonated under laboratory conditions—the psychological and propaganda harm of announcing a demonstration only to have the bomb fail to explode was too great a risk. This concern was not trivial; even the head of the JCS, ADM William Leahy (who considered himself an ordnance expert), predicted failure.[12] In addition, military planners and scientists wanted an untouched target so it would be easier to determine the effects of the atomic blast. Secretary of War Henry Stimson then crossed Kyoto off the target list because of its historical and cultural significance. The name then coming out on top was Hiroshima—Japan's eighth largest city, a large seaport, headquarters of the Second Army, and a major war industry center.[13]

In late July, Truman warned the Japanese they must surrender or face terrible consequences. He was ignored. On 2 August, Tibbets received orders to drop the bomb. The *Enola Gay* took off from Tinian at 0245 on 6 August 1945. The flight en route was uneventful, and at 0815 the bomb exploded above Hiroshima at an altitude of 1,900 feet—to maximize the blast effect. The bomb, nicknamed "Little Boy," had a uranium core and detonated with the equivalent force of 12,500

---

[10] Truman, *Memoirs*, vol. 1, 419.

[11] Tibbets, *Return of the Enola Gay*, chaps. 24–28 (509th's training), chap. 30 (Hiroshima mission).

[12] Leahy had expressed this opinion to President Truman in April 1945. Truman, *Memoirs*, vol. 1, 11.

[13] Jones, *United States Army in World War II*, 528–34.

tons of TNT—equal to the conventional bomb loads of over 3,000 B-29s. Tibbets described the blast as a "giant mushroom" that quickly rose to a height of 45,000 feet—three miles higher than the aircraft's own altitude—and even from several miles away appeared to be "boiling like something terribly alive." It gave the unsettling appearance of a phenomenon about to engulf the plane.[14] In the city below, virtually everything within a one-mile radius of the blast was destroyed.

A second bomb, a more advanced plutonium design nicknamed "Fat Man," was dropped on Nagasaki on 9 August. Japan surrendered five days later.

Debate still rages over whether atomic bombs were necessary to force Japan to surrender, but it was not a serious question at the time. President Truman had no regrets over his decision—the invasion of Japan scheduled for November would have cost millions of lives, on both sides.[15] He was not willing to pay that price. Japanese leaders interviewed after the war agreed the bombs had been the final straw that had broken their will.[16] The enormous power of the atomic bombs had as much psychological effect as it did physical. Virtually everyone believed atomic weapons had fundamentally altered the conduct of war. There would have to be new strategies, new weapons, new organizations, and new doctrines.

Planning the Atomic Air Force

In October 1945 General Arnold directed three of his top men— Generals Spaatz, Vandenberg, and Norstad—to study the impact of the atomic bomb on the AAF. The result of their efforts, referred to as the Spaatz Report, was a frank appraisal of where the air arm should proceed in the years ahead.

The report stated that atomic weapons had revolutionized warfare with their awesome destructiveness; they could devastate a four-

---

[14] Tibbets, *Return of the Enola Gay*, 233.

[15] For projected Allied casualty figures, see Giangreco, "Casualty Projections for the U.S. Invasions of Japan, 1945–1946," 521–82. For the Japanese decision to surrender, see Asada, "Shock of the Atomic Bomb and Japan's Decision to Surrender," 477–512. The invasion of Kyushu, set for 1 November 1945, envisioned 767,000 Allied troops participating; Honshu, planned for February 1946, would have involved over one million Allied troops. Over three million Japanese defended the home islands. On average, the United States suffered 35 percent casualties attacking Japanese positions throughout the war (about 30 percent of which were deaths); Japanese losses were far higher—95 percent dead (very few Japanese surrendered or were captured). If these averages held true for the projected invasions of the home islands, the Allies could have expected around 180,000 dead, while the Japanese would have lost nearly three million military. Civilian deaths—based on the Okinawa campaign—would have been horrendous.

[16] US Army Air Forces, *Mission Accomplished*, 39–40.

square-mile area, and future designs would be of greater power—able to obliterate an area of 10 square miles. Yet, because of the secrecy surrounding the atomic program, the Air Staff had not devised a plan for development and employment of the new weapon. The bombs were large and weighed 10,000 pounds, which meant only specially modified B-29s could deliver them. The Air Force needed a robust fleet of such planes and a sizable atomic stockpile to serve as a deterrent. This was problematic, because the enormous expense of the atomic weapons meant they would remain "definitely limited in availability."[17] Nonetheless, the planners assumed that at some point in the not too distant future other countries, including adversaries, would also possess the bomb.

An enemy surprise attack—if it began with atomic weapons— could decide the war, because the United States would not have time to mobilize. That meant the United States must be prepared at all times for war, which in turn pointed to the requirement for a large and capable air arm equipped with an atomic delivery capability, perpetually on alert to either smash an enemy offensive or retaliate with an irresistible attack of its own: "no longer can we expect to have the grace of a few months to prepare defenses after war is started."[18]

There were other important aspects to the Spaatz Report. First, it called for a number of overseas bases which would not only provide a defense in depth, but also serve as staging points for atomic-laden B-29s. The range of the Superfortress was over 4,000 miles, not enough to rely solely on bases in the United States. The generals noted that given the scarcity of the bombs, it was still necessary to maintain a large conventional bombing force to hit such targets as fuel production and refining plants, bridges, tunnels, surface vessels, enemy air installations, and similar objectives. To carry out such a conventional bombing campaign, control of the air was essential. Other findings included the need for an effective air defense, a vastly expanded intelligence network, and upgrading of the air arm's research and development effort.

These findings reflect the logic, experience, and foresight of the three generals chosen to conduct the study. Spaatz had been the top American air commander of the war and perhaps the only officer that Hap Arnold totally trusted. He had been the initial commander of the Eighth Air Force, then commander of USSTAF, and finally deployed

---

[17] Spaatz Report, November 1945, AFHRA, file 145.86-104, 1.
[18] Ibid., 5.

to the Pacific to head the strategic air forces there as well. He was respected not only by Arnold, but also by Dwight Eisenhower, who would succeed Marshall as Army chief of staff in November 1945. Spaatz would become commanding general of the AAF the following February, although by fall 1945 he was already beginning to assume Arnold's duties—Arnold, who had sustained four heart attacks during the war, was not a well man. Norstad, a consummate planner, had been on Arnold's staff and, as chief of staff of the Twentieth Air Force at the end of the war, was familiar with the details of the atomic bomb and the B-29 unit that dropped it. Vandenberg, besides commanding the Ninth Air Force, had also been one of Arnold's top staff officers.

The three generals noted the urgency of R&D. Airmen were always cognizant of the role that advanced technology played in their service. The outcome of the war had impressed on them the necessity of having the best aircraft and engines and now the atomic bomb that had transformed war. This technical advantage had to be maintained. Maj Gen St. Clair Streett, deputy commander of the Continental Air Forces, wrote a letter to Arnold in August 1945 detailing the need for an enhanced emphasis on R&D: "The Army Air Forces is, in a scientific sense, on trial for its life. The whole concept of air warfare is undergoing a rapid change and unless we grasp the impact of these changes and adapt ourselves to them quickly, they will be lost to us." He went on to fret that if the AAF did not act quickly on these advances—obviously referring to atomic weapons—"they will be snatched at random by all other branches, and the confusion and loss of effectiveness will be tremendous."[19]

Therein lay a problem. Airmen had been frozen out of atomic development. Maj Gen Leslie Groves, commander of the Manhattan Engineer District (MED), had put a near-total clamp on all matters regarding atomic weapons.[20] This put the airmen in an uncomfortable position: their future was dependent on atomic weapons, but they had no input or insight into that critical field. Spaatz and his colleagues therefore suggested that a new post be created on the Air Staff for a deputy chief of staff for R&D—a position also recommended by Streett. They envisioned this person's duties including not only the "exploitation" of atomic energy, but also the direction of research and development of future "special weapons." They suggested that this officer

---

[19] Streett to Arnold, letter, 31 August 1945, AFHRA, file 415.85-1.
[20] Events would later show that the Soviets had a number of high-level spies in both the US and UK atomic bomb programs. See Albright and Kunstel, *Bombshell*; and Weinstein and Vassiliev, *Haunted Wood*.

be a member of the MED to "represent the Air Force in the highest councils." Most unusually, they recommended a specific senior officer for the position, Maj Gen Curtis LeMay.[21] Perhaps they hoped that if anyone could break through the barriers installed by Groves, it would be the gruff, no-nonsense LeMay. Arnold agreed with the report, noting at its bottom, "I approve this report without qualification, and I strongly emphasize that the national interest demands relentless efforts, operationally and technically, in research and development, especially as they relate to future air weapons."[22] Soon thereafter, the position was announced, and LeMay was given the task. Picking the atomic lock installed by the Army would not be easy.

The inclusion of comments regarding intelligence is significant. All three men had been involved in intelligence activities during the war, had been privy to "ultra" intelligence, and, more importantly, had seen how deficient the Army and AAF had been in this field. Significantly, Vandenberg was also a member of another committee, appointed by Eisenhower, which was studying the issue of Army intelligence at that same time. This three-man committee reported that Army intelligence was dangerously inadequate for the tasks lying ahead of it. During the war there had been an "incredible" lack of cooperation between intelligence users and intelligence producers. G-2, although a major division on the War Department staff, was not seen as an equal by the other divisions. There was not even a career field in the Army for intelligence experts—those chosen for these positions were either reservists, part-timers inducted from other divisions, or civilians. The committee concluded that these defects were so fundamental that the entire G-2 function had to be totally reorganized. Obviously, these complaints were seen to apply to the AAF's intelligence function as well. In the atomic era, such deficiencies could be fatal.[23]

Vandenberg would soon leave the Air Staff to take over the War Department's G-2 division and be charged by Eisenhower to fix the problems he had just identified. Following that tour President Truman appointed him director of the Central Intelligence Group, forerunner of the Central Intelligence Agency (CIA). In June 1947 he would return to the AAF as deputy commanding general. He succeeded Spaatz as Air Force chief of staff on 30 April 1948. His deep involvement in

---

[21] Spaatz Report, 9.

[22] Ibid.

[23] G-2 to Assistant Secretary of War for Air, "Report on Intelligence Matters," 26 October 1945, AFHRA, file 170.2204-5B; and Sidney Shalett, "Army Intelligence Being Reorganized," *New York Times*, 6 May 1946, 14.

intelligence affairs would be a crucial asset in running the Air Force. As we have seen, intelligence gathering and analysis are fundamental to the issue of air strategy.

Before departing the Air Staff, however, Vandenberg had another task to perform. In January 1946, he was tapped by Lt Gen Ira Eaker, Spaatz's deputy, to conduct a study on atomic weapons and the AAF. Vandenberg responded with a memo suggesting guidelines for the "atomic strike force." He suggested an elite unit equipped with the most advanced aircraft and the best crews, equipment, and training. This unit, the 58th Bomb Wing, would consist of three groups, including the 509th that had dropped the bombs on Japan. Each would consist of four squadrons of B-29s. The wing should be based at Roswell Field, New Mexico, so it would be near Los Alamos—where the atomic bombs were built. This would provide "extremely close and continuous coordination and liaison with the Manhattan District Project with particular regard to development, manufacture, handling, and general technical aspects of the bomb itself."[24] The atomic strike force must be ready for immediate deployment worldwide on short notice, once the decision to deploy came from the president. Vandenberg expected that aircraft and personnel would move to bases near the crisis area, and the weapons themselves would follow. Loading atomic bombs on the specially modified B-29s would take place at these forward bases.

Vandenberg emphasized that operations must be capable of implementation within "a few days from any established VHB base in the world." The 509th would form the core of the atomic strike force, but the other two bomb groups should also be trained for that mission, and at least one squadron in each should be modified to carry the atomic bomb. Eventually, all bomb groups should be trained and equipped for the atomic delivery mission. Tactics were discussed—formation attacks versus single aircraft, sometimes at night and sometimes in daylight. Radar bombing would be essential: "reliance on visual bombing should be discarded altogether and accurate radar bombing *can* and *must* be attained and relied upon as a primary method of dropping." Unfortunately, current B-29 radars were "definitely unsatisfactory" and were in the process of being replaced.[25] This was an important memo from an important officer—he coordi-

---

[24] Vandenberg to Eaker, memorandum, 2 January 1946, AFHRA, file 179.061-34A, 3.
[25] Ibid., 4–5. Emphasis in original.

nated it with LeMay, the new deputy chief of staff for R&D. Spaatz would soon act, and over the next decade this atomic strike force would become the elite unit Vandenberg proposed.

Reorganization and Strategic Air Command

Two months after Vandenberg's memo, General Spaatz reorganized the AAF. The roots of this administrative shuffle were planted during the war as airmen recognized that the prewar organizational structure was outdated. Looking to the postwar world they realized restructuring was necessary even before independence was gained, and the Air Staff came up with various schemes. One proposal entailed an Air Combat Command containing all the bombers, fighters, and long-range reconnaissance aircraft, while a second command would include training and airlift functions and other service organizations—a suggestion reminiscent of the "air force" and "air service" distinction of the 1930s. The proposal initially implemented in December 1944 was the formation of Continental Air Forces, which contained Troop Carrier Command, air defense units, all agencies responsible for redeployment for overseas theaters, and a "continental reserve" of various combat units.[26] The matter continued to evolve.

One year later, on 11 December 1945, Eaker formed a committee to look at postwar reorganization. It came up with several ideas, because the ideal solution was not obvious. One of these was a functional corps system, like that of the Army, where combat commands would coexist with service units for ordnance, engineers, quartermaster, and so forth. Others favored a "semicorps or service-type structure in which specialized activities would be represented by special staff agencies through the command up to the top."[27] General Spaatz, not enamored with either proposal, discussed the matter with Eisenhower.

Ground officers were sensitive about tactical airpower and whether it would be available to support their operations in war. Spaatz recognized the concern, and his close working relationship with Eisenhower during the war was a factor in favor of air interests. True, Spaatz had commanded the strategic bombers, but he was always willing to use those bombers to support ground operations, even when unconvinced it was wise. During the breakout from St. Lo, for example, the Eighth

---

[26] Wolk, *Struggle for Air Force Independence*, 123–25.
[27] Ibid., 126–28.

Air Force carpet-bombed German positions just prior to "the break-out from Normandy" made by Gen Omar Bradley's First Army—the bombers blew a huge hole in German defenses, allowing American troops to pour through.[28] More importantly, the massive support of the Ninth Air Force was well recognized. The Ninth, under Vandenberg, consisted of over 4,000 aircraft and 200,000 personnel—it was the largest tactical air unit in history, larger than the entire combat strength of the Luftwaffe. The three tactical air commands comprising the Ninth were each assigned to a field army, and the cooperation between these units became the stuff of legend. During the drive across France by George Patton's Third Army, the XIX Tactical Air Command, led by Maj Gen Otto P. "Opie" Weyland, served as Patton's right flank. The airmen's mission: keep all German units at least 30 miles away.[29]

It is reasonable to conclude that it was this close and continuing relationship between airmen and soldiers—Spaatz, Vandenberg, Weyland, Eisenhower, Bradley, Patton, and others—that reassured Army leaders and persuaded them to support AAF independence. Even so, soldiers were concerned, and some senior Army leaders talked of retaining tactical air forces within ground units—much like the Navy and Marine Corps insisted upon organic air assets to support maritime operations.[30] To airmen, this was an unacceptable option.

From August 1945 onward, senior air leaders therefore talked increasingly of the necessity to establish a major command within the AAF—and subsequent Air Force—with the responsibility of supporting Army ground forces. This was the genesis of Tactical Air Command (TAC). Lt Gen Elwood "Pete" Quesada, who had commanded the IX TAC under Vandenberg during the war, later stated, "Bradley and Eisenhower were assured by Spaatz that the Air Force would always honor and always meets its commitments to the Army and provide strong tactical air forces." Quesada further contended that Spaatz promised such a tactical air force and, in turn, Eisenhower agreed to an independent Air Force.[31]

The other two major combat missions of the AAF were air defense and strategic bombing. The air arm also had major responsibilities in

---

[28] D'Este, *Decision in Normandy*, chap. 23.

[29] Spires, *Air Power for Patton's Army*.

[30] This was the opinion of, among others, Gen Jacob L. Devers, commanding general of Army Ground Forces immediately after the war. Wolk, *Struggle for Air Force Independence*, 128.

[31] Quesada, interview, 32–33. In truth, Eisenhower had gone on record supporting an independent Air Force long before Spaatz moved to reorganize the AAF into combat commands in 1946.

the areas of airlift, R&D, supply, training, and education. In March 1946, Spaatz announced the new setup: there would be three combat organizations—TAC under Quesada; Air Defense Command (ADC) under Lt Gen George E. Stratemeyer; and Strategic Air Command (SAC), led by Gen George C. Kenney. SAC would be based at Bolling Field in Washington, DC—taking over the offices of the now defunct Continental Air Forces. Supporting commands were established at the same time: Air Materiel Command, Air Transport Command, Air Training Command, Air University, and AAF Proving Ground Command.[32] When announcing this reorganization, Spaatz emphasized the need for an "air force in being," because the next war would "certainly" begin in the air and, therefore, "America's best insurance is an adequate, alert force." That force would consist of 70 groups—21 of which would be VHBs—manned by 400,000 personnel and entailing some 14,200 aircraft.[33]

The "atomic strike force" was a reality, and Spaatz defined its mission:

> The Strategic Air Command will be prepared to conduct long-range offensive operations in any part of the world either independently or in cooperation with land and naval forces; to conduct maximum range reconnaissance over land or sea either independently or in cooperation with naval forces; to provide combat units capable of intense and sustained combat operations employing the latest and most advanced weapons; to train units and personnel for the maintenance of the Strategic Forces in all parts of the world; to perform such missions as the Commanding General, Army Air Forces, may direct.[34]

This was an interesting directive. It specified that SAC would have a worldwide mission, it would have the most advanced weapons (atomic bombs), and, most significantly, it should be prepared to carry out this global mission independent of land and sea forces. Clearly, Spaatz was intent on carving out a unique mission for SAC, and by extension, the AAF.

Soon after, the joint chiefs began discussing the matter of unified commands, and Spaatz suggested that Northeast and Alaskan Commands be directed "to support the strategic air commander in his

---

[32] W. H. Lawrence, "Regrouping of Army Airmen in 3 Commands Set by Spaatz," *New York Times*, 3 March 1946, 1, 15.

[33] Sidney Shalett, "Spaatz Shakes Up Army Air Forces," *New York Times*, 13 March 1946, 16. Spaatz stated that 8,000 aircraft would be in the regular AAF, with the other 6,200 going to the National Guard and Air Reserves. Note that Spaatz dropped the number of bomb groups from 25 to 21. There were still 80,000 airmen overseas at the time: 30,000 in Europe and 50,000 in Alaska and the Pacific.

[34] Spaatz to Kenney, letter, 12 March 1946, contained in "Strategic Air Command—1946: Organization, Mission, Training and Personnel," *Official History*, vol. 2, exhibit 3. (Hereinafter the annual official histories will be referred to as, for example, "*SAC History—1946*." All are located in AFHRA, call number 416.01 or K416.01 followed by the year and volume number.)

mission." He emphasized the global mission of SAC that transcended geographic boundaries. He referred to the command arrangements of the strategic bombers in Europe and the Pacific during the war, which he labeled an "overwhelming success." Not unexpectedly, the Navy demurred, arguing testily that the "confused command relationships" in the Pacific during the war had not been ideal from their viewpoint, and problems had arisen with the inception of the Twentieth Air Force—the very example that Spaatz was hailing. By December 1946 the chiefs came to an agreement: geographic unified commands would be established for the Far East, Pacific, Alaska, Northeast, Caribbean, and Europe. The Atlantic Fleet was designated as what was later termed a *specified* command, as was Strategic Air Command, consisting of "strategic air forces not otherwise assigned." SAC, like the unified commands, would be under the direction of the joint chiefs, who "will exercise strategic direction over all elements of the armed forces." This unified command plan would remain in place "as an interim measure for the immediate postwar period."[35]

The man chosen to lead SAC was one of the premier airmen of the war—George C. Kenney. He grew up outside of Boston and, after attending MIT for three years, went to work for the railroad. When the United States entered the world war, he joined the Army and chose the aviation section. Upon winning his wings, he was sent to France, where he flew 75 combat missions, shot down two German aircraft, and was awarded the Distinguished Service Cross. Between the wars he flew attack aircraft, taught at ACTS, and attended the Army Staff School and War College. In 1939 he was assigned to the Engineering School at Wright Field, Ohio, because of his background at MIT. In August 1942, Kenney, now a major general, was sent to the Southwest Pacific Area to take over AAF units there under Gen Douglas MacArthur. After fleeing the Philippines for Australia and beginning the process of building up Allied forces for a counterattack against the Japanese, MacArthur ran afoul of his air commanders. After going through two others, Arnold sent him Kenney.[36] The two men hit it off immediately. Kenney was the type of aggressive, focused leader MacArthur wanted.[37]

---

[35] Ibid., vol. 1, 42; and Schnabel, *Joint Chiefs of Staff and National Policy*, 84–87. The executive agent for the JCS regarding SAC would be the AAF.

[36] Maj Gen Lewis Brereton was the commander of AAF units in the Philippines at the time of Pearl Harbor; he left for the Middle East in March 1942. He was replaced by Lt Gen George Brett, who never won MacArthur's confidence and left in July. MacArthur then asked for Frank Andrews, but he was unavailable, so Marshall offered him either Kenney or Jimmy Doolittle: MacArthur chose Kenney. James, *Years of MacArthur*, vol. 2: *1941–1945*, 197–98.

[37] For Kenney's biography through World War II, see Griffith, *MacArthur's Airman*.

Kenney was the second-ranking four-star general in the AAF at the end of the war (behind Joseph McNarney), but it was apparent Arnold had misgivings about his vision and perhaps even his loyalty— he was seen as working a bit *too* closely with MacArthur. It was not lost on Kenney that when the B-29s were deployed to the Pacific, Arnold ensured they were not put under his control. Moreover, despite Kenney's seniority, Arnold chose Carl Spaatz as his deputy and eventual successor.[38] Kenney nonetheless hoped he would be given Air Combat Command—recall this was the proposed super command of all combat units in the AAF. Instead, Kenney was given SAC—the plumb of the major commands, but still consisting of only a portion of the AAF's combat strength. As a potential consolation prize, Kenney was also named commander presumptive of the new International Air Force to be formed by the United Nations. In this dual-hatted situation, Kenney would divide his time between Washington and New York. That would eventually cause problems.

For his deputy at SAC, Kenney turned to Maj Gen St. Clair Streett, a veteran pilot from World War I who had led a flight of aircraft to Alaska in 1920, earning him the Mackay Trophy, and then served as an aide to Billy Mitchell. During World War II he had tours on the Air Staff and then became commander of the Thirteenth Air Force under Kenney in the Southwest Pacific. Streett had been the deputy commander of the Continental Air Forces, headquartered at Bolling Field, so he simply remained in place when SAC and Kenney arrived. The headquarters moved to nearby Andrews Field in October.

Initial Problems

SAC was the dominant of the three combat commands, with an authorized personnel strength of 84,231; TAC had only 26,000 people and ADC a mere 7,000.[39] On paper SAC consisted of 1,300 aircraft, although only 221 were B-29s. On V-J Day the AAF had nearly 3,000 B-29s in the inventory, and this alarming drop in quantity and capability was evident in the type of personnel retained—or rather *not*

---

[38] After the war it was the "Europeanists" who dominated the AAF—Spaatz, Eaker, Vandenberg, Quesada, Weyland, et al. Those who fought in the Pacific—Kenney, Whitehead, Harmon, Streett, and Chennault— were nudged aside. Exceptions were Twining and LeMay, who fought in both theaters. The same was true in the Army as a whole; the postwar service was led by Eisenhower, Bradley, Collins, Clark, and Ridgway; not MacArthur, Stilwell, Krueger, or Eichelberger.

[39] Sturm, "Organizational Evolution," 59.

retained—in the aftermath of the Japanese surrender. The number of qualified mechanics in the AAF fell from 350,000 to 30,000 during the following year. This dearth of skilled technicians resulted in an aircraft readiness rate of a bare 18 percent. The historian for one bomb group noted that "due to the fact that there are but 17 enlisted men assigned to Aircraft Maintenance Division instead of the 473 authorized, efficient maintenance has been impeded to say the least."[40] Another report stated that "radar bombardment and navigational aids cannot be kept in operating condition with the present number of trained personnel now available."[41] By the end of 1946, in-commission rates for SAC aircraft averaged an anemic 42 percent.[42]

Administrative problems surfaced immediately when orders arrived from the Air Staff directing SAC headquarters to move to Colorado Springs. This was a major change of plans, and dozens of civilian personnel resigned rather than move; others sold their homes or moved out of rented accommodations and planned to accompany the command on its move west. Then orders arrived cancelling the move; headquarters would remain at Andrews Field.[43] This was the type of inexplicable staffing snafu that caused untold hardship on countless people and was easily avoidable. SAC was off to a bad start.

The command was divided into two numbered air forces—the Eighth and Fifteenth, although only the latter was active—but the heart of SAC was to be the atomic-capable 58th Bomb Wing.[44] Its mission was similar to that of SAC itself: be ready for global deployment to conduct conventional or atomic strike operations. The wing was also to be the AAF liaison with the Manhattan Engineering District.[45] Despite this charge, problems regarding access to atomic secrets and the weapons themselves remained. General Groves continued to keep the AAF, the only organization capable of delivering bombs, at arm's length and in the dark. This caused airmen to become increasingly irritated and paranoid. Kenney and his command had little or no insight into the atomic program, and LeMay, deputy chief of staff for R&D, was similarly ill informed.

In January 1947 Groves and the MED gave way to the Atomic Energy Commission (AEC), but secrecy increased. The official historians

[40] Moody, *Building a Strategic Air Force*, 65.
[41] Wagner to Spaatz, letter, 9 September 1946, in *SAC History—1946*, vol. 3, exhibit 55.
[42] *SAC History—1946*, vol. 1, 28.
[43] *SAC History—1946*, vol. 1, 15–16.
[44] The Eighth Air Force was not actually manned until November 1946 and then only partially.
[45] LeMay to Kenney, letter, 13 June 1946, in *SAC History—1946*, vol. 2, exhibit 13.

of AEC noted, "It seemed that the Commission had the exaggerated idea that its control of atomic energy information was a sort of sacred trust which took precedence over even military requirements."[46] Airmen's concerns were not trivial; everything connected with the training, loading, aircraft configuration, and delivery of atomic bombs was so highly classified it was extremely difficult to get anything done. The AEC had a monopoly in the control of atomic matters: all fissionable material and the exclusive right to produce such material; all facilities for the research, manufacture, and storage of atomic weapons; the weapons themselves; and all information regarding atomic issues.

In these early postwar years, there was as yet no talk of peaceful uses for atomic energy; its only purpose was for weapons of war. Yet the military tasked to employ those weapons was frozen out. Congress sympathized with the military's plight and insisted on the formation of a Military Liaison Committee (MLC) to advise the AEC on such matters as the design, development, manufacture, and storage of atomic weapons.[47] The MLC had the right to appeal directly to the secretaries of War and Navy (and later Air Force) if it thought the AEC was insufficiently attentive to military needs. General Groves, who was appointed a member of the MLC, stated bluntly that the committee "should be a watchdog for the armed forces."[48]

The military arm of the AEC was the Armed Forces Special Weapons Project (AFSWP), composed largely of former MED personnel. This group, headed by Groves, ran the facilities that manufactured and stored the bombs—under supervision of the AEC. The AAF pushed to have the AFSWP under its control but was resisted by the Army and the Navy. Not until August 1948 did the other services relent, and the project was placed under the Air Force for implementation of the emergency war plan.[49]

An example of how this bureaucratic web of secrecy impacted the AAF is the B-29 fleet itself. When SAC was founded, the 509th was its only atomic-capable group, although plans were in place to upgrade its two sister groups. In early 1946, only 22 B-29s had been modified—a simple, inexpensive, but highly classified alteration. The most important modification to Silverplate bombers involved fuel-injected

---

[46] Hewlett and Duncan, *History of the Atomic Energy Commission*, vol. 2, 130.

[47] The first head of the MLC was Lt Gen Lewis H. Brereton.

[48] Little and Bowen, *History of Air Force Atomic Energy Program*, vol. 2, 53. Of the five volumes, only two have been declassified, and those were sanitized.

[49] Ibid., 42–43.

engines. Also, gun blisters were removed (the tail gun remained in place); the bomb bay was modified to carry the large and unusually shaped atomic bombs; and the bomb bay door opening mechanism was changed to speed opening and closing. Additional braces were installed inside the bomb bay to keep the weapon stable during rough flight, new propellers were mounted with a reversible pitch mechanism that allowed greater braking power, and another crew position was inserted next to the radio operator—an "electronics test officer"—to monitor the condition of the atomic bomb in flight. Finally, most of the armor plating was removed, resulting in a lighter, faster aircraft that could cruise at higher altitude—over 30,000 feet—which put it out of range of both enemy aircraft and AAA.[50]

Atomic bombs necessitating these Silverplate modifications were initially of two types. The Little Boy model dropped on Hiroshima was a "gun type" device. In this design, "two subcritical masses of nuclear material are placed at opposite sides of a long tube. To produce detonation, an explosive charge at one end of the tube fires, shooting its nuclear material across the tube into the other subcritical mass."[51]This bomb used 135 pounds of uranium 235 to create the nuclear chain reaction; its yield was 13 kilotons. Little Boy was 10 feet long, 28 inches in diameter, and weighed 8,900 pounds.

The Fat Man bomb dropped on Nagasaki was an "implosion" device, in which a sphere of nuclear material—13.5 pounds of plutonium—was surrounded by high-explosive "lenses." When fired simultaneously, the lenses compressed the plutonium core and initiated the nuclear chain reaction. This device was more powerful than the gun-type design and produced a yield of 23 kilotons. Fat Man was nearly 11 feet long and 5 feet in diameter—hence, its nickname—and weighed 10,800 lbs. Because this design required less fissionable material than the gun type, implosion weapons were used almost exclusively after 1945. The problem with Fat Man was its poor aerodynamic shape, which caused accuracy problems—a situation not fixed until later models were developed.[52]

Silverplate modifications were essential to drop the atomic bombs but were not overly complicated. Except for redesign of the bomb

---

[50] Campbell, *Silverplate Bombers*, 1, 15.

[51] Gibson, *Nuclear Weapons of the United States*, 85–88.

[52] Ibid. When preparing for the atomic strikes, the 509th used shapes the same size and weight as Fat Man bombs but filled with high explosives. These "pumpkins" gave the crews a feel for the size, weight, and stability conditions they would encounter when dropping the atomic bombs.

bays themselves, the only significant change was the additional electronics needed to arm and monitor the bomb during flight. Removal of the gun blisters and armor and adoption of new engines and propellers were hardly difficult. The modifications cost $32,500 per aircraft—not an exorbitant sum. The 509th had 15 Silverplate bombers in August 1945, and only seven more were added over the next six months.[53] From the airmen's view, this was an unacceptably slow rate, but because everything connected with the atomic program—including the Silverplate modifications—was so highly classified, it was difficult to secure clearances for mechanics to perform the alterations. The AEC insisted on controlling all atomic security clearance requests but quickly proved unable to handle the flood of applications. It took up to six months for mechanics to obtain clearances allowing them to work on Silverplate aircraft. By March 1947 the AEC had formally approved only 124 clearances—it had over 3,200 on backlog.[54] Therefore, by the end of its first year in existence, SAC had only 23 modified aircraft; 15 months later it would still have only 35.[55] As an example of the absurdity of the classification issue, when the new North American B-45 was first delivered in early 1947, the AAF discovered it could not accommodate the atomic bomb—due to security issues, the manufacturer had not been told the size of the weapon its aircraft were specifically designed to carry![56]

Not just SAC suffered from the dislocation and confusion of the postwar period. The entire AAF was devastated by demobilization. The AAF went from 2,253,000 personnel on V-J Day to 303,000 by the end of May 1947. Readiness was even worse—the number of combat-ready groups plummeted from 218 at the end of the war to only two by December 1946—one of those was the 509th.[57] The AAF's budget was cut by 38 percent for FY 49. The reasons were twofold. First, the country was tired of belt-tightening. After a decade of depression, followed by war, the American people were loath to spend money on defense when it could be spent on domestic programs. The American public was not yet as concerned with the problems presented by an antagonistic and powerful Soviet Union as were its

---

[53] Ibid., 22.

[54] Little and Bowen, *History of Air Force Atomic Energy Program*, vol. 2, 203.

[55] Rosenberg, "U.S. Nuclear Stockpile," 30.

[56] Little and Bowen, *History of Air Force Atomic Energy Program*, vol. 2, 196–99.

[57] Goldberg, *History of the United States Air Force*, 105; and "Notes of AAF Commanders Conference," 19 November 1946, AFHRA, file 168.15-10.

political and military leaders. After all, wartime propaganda had stressed repeatedly that "Uncle Joe" was our faithful ally.

Second, it is a traditional American trait that all wars are "crusades"—the country is slow to provoke, but once it is, the war is pursued with ferocity and drive.[58] The corollary of such a notion is that once the war is over, peace and tranquility are demanded—the country is expected to return quickly to normalcy. A large standing military force was anathema to the American tradition, and although some would argue things had dramatically changed in the aftermath of two world wars, the people had not yet accepted that premise. This meant the millions of husbands and sons who had gone off to war were expected to come home. Now.

Military efficiency dictated demobilization of entire units, composed of both old-timers and newcomers. But the civilians in the military believed they had enlisted "for the duration," and now that the war was over, they expected those who had served longest should be discharged first. Eventually, a system was devised that allotted points for various categories, such as length of service, combat time, overseas time, age, rank, marital status, combat decorations, and job specialty. When a certain number of points were attained, the individual was eligible for discharge. Unfortunately, the criteria and weights assigned to these factors changed frequently, and operational considerations were crucial. What if, for example, following the point system would result in the majority of radar operators being discharged at one time, thus rendering a night-fighter interceptor squadron non–combat ready? In April 1945 AAF policy stated that "military necessity" would take precedence over all other considerations.[59] The AAF established lists of indispensable job specialties that automatically extended individuals with a designated expertise for six months.[60] With the surrender of Japan, this entire process became a severe headache—not least for those sitting in tents on Pacific islands waiting to go home. When all was said and done, America, as it had in the past, simply ignored talk of military necessity and operational requirements—it wanted its troops home. General Marshall's view of the problem was painful but accurate: "For the moment, in a widespread emotional crisis of the American people, demobilization has become, in effect, disintegration, not only of the armed forces, but

---

[58] Recall that the title of Eisenhower's war memoir was *Crusade in Europe.*
[59] Jones and Sanders, "Personnel Problems Related to AAF Commissioned Officers, 1939–1945," 166.
[60] Ibid., 167–68.

apparently of all conception of world responsibility and what it demands of us."[61]

The Deployment Challenge

The mission statement given to SAC called for worldwide deployment. Initially, this meant that the B-29s would be based in Germany and Japan in support of the occupation forces. That was called into question in mid 1947 when President Truman announced two key programs. The Truman Doctrine called for military aid to Greece and Turkey, both in the process of resisting widespread communist uprisings. Such aid would not be cheap, and it would not be limited to those two countries. The Marshall Plan—named for George Marshall, who soon after military retirement became secretary of state—was a massive aid program to help countries devastated by the war get back on their feet. The Marshall Plan would eventually cost $13 billion.[62]

For the military, this meant that budget restrictions would grow even worse. It was not that Truman was indifferent to the military and its needs; rather, he believed a strong economy was the first step toward national security. Moreover, he believed this to be the case not just for the United States, but for other countries as well. The Army emphasized the importance of its occupation forces in these schemes. If soldiers wished to maintain as large a share of the defense budget as possible, they needed a mission, and occupation of defeated enemies would suffice for that mission. For airmen, this meant air units in Germany and Japan.[63] This seemed neither unreasonable nor disadvantageous to AAF leaders. SAC was formed for worldwide deployment; assisting the Army in its occupation duties would allow this forward basing. In fact, whereas Eisenhower had wanted two B-29 groups in Europe, the AAF pushed for five, arguing they were required to "combat any possible threat from the East."[64] The difficulty would be in keeping enough air groups combat ready to support such deployments.

Kenney favored deployments to the Pacific area, perhaps because he had served there during the war and had such a high regard for Lt Gen Ennis Whitehead, commander of Far East Air Forces—B-29

[61] Marshall, "Responsibility of Victory," 77.
[62] For the Truman Doctrine, see Howard Jones, "A New Kind of War"; for the Marshall Plan, see Behrman, Most Noble Adventure.
[63] Schnabel, Joint Chiefs of Staff and National Policy, 102–3.
[64] Moody, Building a Strategic Air Force, 53.

squadrons that rotated to Guam and Okinawa throughout 1946–47 and experienced few problems. Diplomatic concerns did not arise, and Whitehead (who had been Kenney's deputy during the war) kept the SAC crews busy. Deployments to Europe were another matter. Kenney was concerned about the "do nothing policy" of the air leaders in Europe, who did little to foster an energetic or professional attitude toward their mission.[65] Nonetheless, the primacy of Europe in US political and military diplomacy could not be ignored.

As early as mid 1945, AAF planners had anticipated deploying five groups of B-29s to Europe in Project Wonderful. Units were scheduled to begin moving that September. Almost immediately, however, demobilization chaos imposed reality. Deployment was delayed a month, then another, then two more; in January 1946, Wonderful was postponed until the summer. The planned deployment was causing chaos in SAC.[66] At the same time, political factors arose among former allies. France and Britain wanted no "atomic bombers" on their soil. Norway and Denmark were concerned with the message such aircraft would send to the Soviets—distressingly nearby. Politics would remain a concern for the next two years, and in mid 1947 Spaatz wrote Kenney that due to "sovereignty sensibilities," the number and scope of deployments to Europe would have to be curtailed. Thus, deployment to Europe often meant Germany, simply because the defeated could not object.[67] Unfortunately, German bases presented their own problems. The new Allied commander in Germany, Gen Joseph McNarney, told the AAF he saw no role for B-29s in the occupation force. Moreover, he feared bomber airfields would be vulnerable to Soviet attack, and he did not have the ground forces to protect them. The AAF countered with a plan to leave some aging B-17s in place, but to rotate B-29s into Germany on a periodic basis for training and familiarization purposes. This would ease the concern over their safety while also lowering distress among Europeans regarding the bombers that had flattened Hiroshima and Nagasaki being permanently based within their midst.[68] In May 1946, Wonderful was cancelled.

Alaska was also a planned deployment area. Air leaders realized by war's end that the maps used to visualize worldwide operations

---

[65] Borowski, *Hollow Threat*, 74.
[66] *SAC History—1946*, vol. 1, 67–68.
[67] Spaatz to Kenney, letter, 2 July 1947, in *SAC History—1947*, vol. 4, exhibit 122.
[68] Moody, *Building a Strategic Air Force*, 78–79.

were no longer satisfactory. Mercator projections were adequate when planning military operations within a theater, but intercontinental flight if the adversary were to be the Soviet Union was another matter. The shortest distance between the United States and potential targets in Russia was over the North Pole. Polar projection maps became the new standard, and this was largely uncharted territory. During Project Eardrum in 1947, SAC reconnaissance aircraft began mapping Greenland, Iceland, and the polar region to become more familiar with those areas.[69] This geographic imperative also meant bases were needed in Alaska and the northern United States. This in turn required cold-weather operations to become commonplace in SAC. Bases in "the northern tier" would require new techniques and facilities to ensure combat readiness year round in subzero weather conditions.

In mid 1946, SAC ordered the 28th Bomb Group to deploy from Nebraska to Elmendorf Field, Alaska. Problems arose because many in the group had expected to deploy to Europe as part of Wonderful; they had no desire to head for the Arctic instead. Fifteenth Air Force commander Maj Gen Charles Born visited the 28th in Nebraska, listened to their grievances, and stressed the importance of SAC's worldwide mission. He asked for volunteers to complete the move north, and about half the group agreed. The result was delay, as the unit needed to rebuild its strength and begin training for cold-weather operations.[70] The 28th moved in October 1946 and remained in Alaska for six months. It was the first time a SAC group had deployed outside the continental United States (CONUS). Even so, the drive to acclimate SAC to Arctic conditions would be long and difficult. Conditions were grueling, not just due to the extreme cold, ice, fog, winds, and darkness, but because suitable facilities for the airmen and required maintenance activities were lacking. Communications with CONUS were slow, and parts usually took six weeks to arrive.[71] These problems would take months to solve. In the meantime, "The eternal cold, the monotonous terrain, the fear of crash-landings on the polar ice cap, the general lack of recreation, were not calculated to keep crew morale at a high level."[72]

---

[69] Bohn, *Development of Strategic Air Command.*
[70] Ibid., 80.
[71] *SAC History—1946*, vol. 1, 118–19.
[72] *SAC History—1947*, vol. 1, 145.

General Streett wrote Spaatz that his plan was to rotate units through the north periodically, but this would take three years. Streett noted hopefully that he expected a three-to-five-year period of peace and relative calm in the global situation allowing SAC to "man, equip, and operationally train a strategic force without material interference from outside elements."[73] This was wishful thinking, and Streett soon realized it. Two months later he wrote that suddenly the picture looked "pretty dark." He lamented, "I think we have allowed our confusion occasioned by lack of a program and by changes in direction caused by the fluid international situation, and other causes with which you are familiar, to take greater toll of efficiency than was necessary." He blamed much of this on poor leadership. Streett confessed that from his viewpoint, "Our boys in the field have failed to do everything that could be done and have failed to use the imagination and ingenuity which we have expected of them."[74] In truth, Arctic operations were far more difficult than air leaders had anticipated. Although "polar air attacks" looked logical on maps—some maps— the realities of the harsh climate on both men and machines were underestimated. Eventually, Alaskan air bases were indeed established and made effective, but the real solution to Arctic operations was long-range aircraft.

As deployment plans foundered, the AAF continued to spiral downward in capability. The 70-group plan of 400,000 personnel was soon seen as unrealistic. As overall AAF strength fell toward 300,000, the "interim" goal of 55 groups was announced, but even that was passed, and by August 1946 AAF strength was down to 52 groups and would eventually fall to 48.[75] SAC was hard hit. By the end of 1946, the command had fallen to half strength in personnel and had only 279 aircraft assigned—148 of which were B-29s. Of the nine bomb groups in the command, only six actually possessed airplanes.[76] Even worse was the dearth of skilled personnel. Many new recruits had marginal test scores on their entrance exams and were unqualified to be aircraft mechanics. In September, the entire Fifteenth Air Force had only nine men qualified to work on B-29 radar equipment, with the result that nearly half of the bomber force was grounded at any

---

[73] Streett to Spaatz, letter, 25 July 1946, in *SAC History—1946*, vol. 2, exhibit 23.
[74] Streett to Born, letter, 30 September 1946, in *SAC History—1946*, vol. 3, exhibit 62.
[75] Wolk, *Struggle for Air Force Independence*, 81.
[76] Bohn, "Development of Strategic Air Command," 1.

given time.[77] By the end of 1946, only three bomb groups could report an operational effectiveness of between 60 and 69 percent.[78] In September, General Streett wrote an acerbic memo to General Born at Fifteenth Air Force criticizing his command for slovenly personnel policies that added to SAC's dismal operational readiness posture. "I realize that the job of accounting for personnel, filling out forms and knowing what the hell they are all about may be beneath the dignity of our base commanders," Streett fumed, but "personnel accounting, for some devious and dark reason which I have been unable to fathom, is still a mystery to most of our people."[79] SAC was having a difficult time getting untracked; turmoil was endemic, and it was aggravated by SAC's other major commitment of 1946.

The Bikini Atomic Tests

On 25 August 1945, Senator Brien McMahon, chairman of the Special Committee on Atomic Energy, suggested to President Truman that captured Japanese and German ships be taken out to sea and bombed with atomic weapons to prove "just how effective the atomic bomb is." The joint chiefs agreed, and in December Secretary of War Kenneth Royall and Navy Secretary James Forrestal sent a memo to the president emphasizing that such tests were necessary "to determine, among other things, the consequences of this powerful aerial weapon with respect to the size, composition and employment of the armed forces and should particularly facilitate an analysis of future naval design and tactics."[80] In January 1946, President Truman approved tests to be carried out at Bikini Atoll in the Pacific; their codename was Crossroads.

These atomic tests would be conducted jointly by the Army and Navy, because the main targets were to be surplus American ships and captured enemy vessels. The plan called for one air burst over the ships themselves—to be dropped by a B-29 from the 509th—and two

---

[77] Moody, *Building a Strategic Air Force*, 81. On a lighter note, SAC headquarters was informed in April that the command's venereal disease rate was more than twice the overall AAF average. Obviously, SAC was keeping its end up in some areas. Hewitt to Kenney, letter, 9 April 1946, in *SAC History—1946*, vol. 3, exhibit 78. In 1949, SAC set up "Character Guidance Councils" at all of its bases to help alleviate the morals problem.

[78] *SAC History—1949*, vol. 1, 90.

[79] Lloyd, *Cold War Legacy*, 75.

[80] Schnabel, *Joint Chiefs of Staff and National Policy*, 130–31.

underwater detonations arranged by the Navy.[81] VADM William Blandy would be the overall commander for Crossroads, with Maj Gen William Kepner from the AAF as his deputy and Maj Gen Roger Ramey leading the AAF contingent of 2,200 people. Ramey, who commanded the 58th Bomb Wing, was responsible for all air transport to the test site, the bomber aircraft, and the drones that would take photographs and collect air samples. Shortly before the test, Col Paul Tibbets, commander of the 509th and pilot of the *Enola Gay*, was relieved of command due, he claimed, to AAF politics. He had been slated to drop the bomb at Bikini but was removed from that task, again according to Tibbets, because of machinations by Ramey and his cohorts.[82]

The first test, termed Able, was scheduled for 1 July. The 509th had been practicing at Roswell Field for several months, dropping "pumpkin" dummy bombs in the desert. Accuracy remained a concern. The horrible aerodynamic shape of the Fat Man bombs had been troublesome ever since Nagasaki, but little had been done to correct it. Nonetheless, the B-29 crews felt confident as they prepared for the trip out to the Marshall Islands. Prior to the actual drop, crews from the 509th dropped 27 practice bombs on the target to refine their skills. Even so, it appeared trouble was brewing when Kepner received a memo stating that "the scoring system, which worked so well in the States, seems to be giving trouble at Bikini. Of the seven releases, it was possible to measure the accuracy of only four, and those were estimated." According to the practice scores obtained, Tibbets's crew was the best.[83] Nonetheless, he was bypassed. The day of the drop he and his navigator noted the winds and computed when and where to drop the bomb—their calculations were far different than those of the assigned drop crew. He offered his advice to the chosen crew but was ignored. Tibbets's navigator predicted the bomb would fall 1,600 feet short and to the left of the target.[84]

Meanwhile, secrecy remained a problem as Groves continued to maintain a tight clamp on security. He relented in early 1946, under pressure from LeMay and the AAF, and agreed to train 11 officers as

---

[81] Only one underwater detonation was carried out because the first was so successful a second was deemed unnecessary, and it was desirable to conserve the small atomic stockpile. Only nine bombs were extant at the beginning of the tests.

[82] Tibbets, *Return of the Enola Gay*, 259.

[83] Woods to Kepner, memorandum, 15 May 1946, AFHRA, file 179.150061-2.

[84] Tibbets, *Return of the Enola Gay*, 263.

weaponeers for the Crossroad tests. These officers would arm the bombs in flight. Ramey discussed their training with them and reported to LeMay that the procedures were not nearly as complicated as Groves had claimed.[85] One weaponeer later discussed his six-month training and admitted it was excessively detailed for the simple tasks he was required to perform—place the atomic "insert" into the bomb casing while in flight and then monitor a number of electrical consoles; if something was amiss, he would check the wiring.[86] As with the Silverplate modifications, the heavy layers of secrecy gave an illusion of complexity that was not really justified.

On the morning of 1 July 1946, a B-29 arrived over the USS *Nevada*—painted bright red to be visible from 30,000 feet—and dropped its bomb. The device was to explode 550 feet over the top of the battleship and sink it immediately. It did detonate at 550 feet, but it missed its target by nearly half a mile—as Tibbets's navigator had predicted. The *Nevada* was still afloat—although five other ships were sunk and others were heavily damaged.[87] It was as embarrassing as the *Mount Shasta* failure of 1934. Despite months of practice and two dry runs immediately prior to the actual drop, the bomb still missed its target—in perfect weather—by six football fields. The Navy was much amused. As a research boat approached the barely scorched *Nevada*, one sailor mused, "Well, it looks to me like the atom bomb is just about like the Army Air Force [sic]—highly overrated."[88] What had gone wrong? Fingers were pointed at the aircrew, plane, bombsight, and the bomb itself. LeMay ordered tests of the aircraft and bombsight immediately, but they showed no malfunction. Crew error was also ruled out, although as noted, some believed that was the culprit. The SAC official history blamed unpredictable winds.[89] A report of the incident concluded lamely that "some unusual force affected the bomb causing it to veer off in an unpredictable manner, giving a point of impact somewhere left and short of the theoretical

[85] Moody, *Building a Strategic Air Force*, 116. After the test, the SAC operations analysis office wrote a report attempting to explain the "Ballistic Winds" computation that was used—against the advice of Tibbets. Operations Analysis Office, "Radar Bomb Scoring in Operation CROSSROADS," 1 November 1946, AFHRA, file 416.310-2.

[86] Harris, interview, 36–37.

[87] Schnabel, *Joint Chiefs of Staff and National Policy*, 133. Also embarrassing, the miss meant that the bomb detonated over ships loaded with measuring devices to evaluate the detonation—these were destroyed by the blast. Weisgall, *Operation Crossroads*, 189.

[88] Bradley, *No Place to Hide*, 58.

[89] *SAC History—1946*, vol. 8, section 6, n.p.

one."[90] The AAF blamed the poor aerodynamics of Fat Man and used this as an argument for greater transparency in the atomic weapons program. If the AAF were to be responsible for dropping the bombs in war, it should have greater insight into their construction. Divided authority over development and delivery was a recipe for disaster.

In the aftermath, the AAF continued to hammer away at Groves to gain greater access to the atomic program. By November 1946, Groves agreed to train more bomb commanders—air officers who would assemble the bombs—as well as weaponeers.[91] This was a major step forward. At the same time, despite the embarrassment of the errant bomb, the test gave the services and policy makers an opportunity to witness the power of the new weapon. Many found this sobering. One naval officer at Bikini commented privately that the Navy was much chastened by the tests. It had expected to sail the target fleet back to San Francisco to demonstrate the negligible effects of atomic weapons against naval vessels, but the radioactivity on the ships was too severe. That plan was abandoned, and the fleet had to be sunk—the contamination could not be removed despite countless attempts. This was, as the naval observer noted, "a momentous decision, a momentous admission."[92] The official committee tasked to examine the results of Crossroads painted the significance of the atomic bomb in stark terms: "If used in numbers, atomic bombs not only can nullify any nation's military effort, but can demolish its social and economic structures and prevent their reestablishment for long periods of time." The report went on to state that there was no defense against the bomb; therefore, the only choice for the United States was to stockpile enough weapons so it could overwhelm any potential enemy.[93]

Summary

The goal of independence had been on the minds of airmen since the end of World War I. Administrative reshuffling in the two decades

---

[90] Moody, *Building a Strategic Air Force*, 121; and Commander, Joint Task Force–1, *Report on Atomic Bomb Tests*, vol. 1, 152–54. Some speculated that a fin on the bomb was damaged when leaving the bomber, thus causing a veer off course.

[91] Little and Bowen, *History of Air Force Atomic Energy Program*, vol. 2, 88–90; and "Atom Bombing with B-29s," *SAC History—1946*, vol. 8, n.p.

[92] Bradley, *No Place to Hide*, 116.

[93] "The Evaluation of the Atomic Bomb as a Military Weapon: The Final Report of the JCS Evaluation Board for Operation Crossroads," 30 June 1947, in Ross and Rosenberg, *America's Plans for War against the Soviet Union*, 12–13.

following saw steps in that direction, but as most airmen would have privately admitted, the air weapon was largely untested. The innumerable committees and studies conducted between the world wars concluded that the air arm was simply not yet ready for separate status. Part of this reticence was due to inexperience and lack of actual combat proof of airmen's theories, and part was due to technology—planes, bombsights, navigation equipment, and ordnance were simply not yet available. World War II was the turning point. Airmen realized this almost immediately, and, as a consequence, early in the war began planning for a postwar world in which airpower would be recognized by all as an equal if not dominant partner to land and sea forces.

The development of atomic weapons, which took all but the most senior diplomats and military officers by surprise, was recognized as a defining moment in history. The detonation of a single bomb carried by one aircraft that destroyed a large portion of a major city while killing tens of thousands of people had a profound psychological effect on everyone. Cities and people had been destroyed before—Carthage was leveled in antiquity and its soil sown with salt so nothing would grow, and 50,000 Roman soldiers had been slaughtered in one afternoon at the Battle of Cannae—but the impact of such destruction occurring virtually instantaneously by such a relatively small device shook the foundations of military theory. Carl Spaatz noted this belief when he wrote in April 1946, "Strategic bombing is thus the first war instrument of history capable of stopping the heart mechanism of a great industrialized enemy. It paralyzes his military power at the core."[94]

Airmen believed this, and because initial atomic bombs were so large and cumbersome—weighing over 10,000 pounds and measuring 10 feet long by five feet wide—the only way of delivering them was via large aircraft. Specially modified B-29s, then the largest aircraft in the world, were the sole carriers of the bomb, and they belonged to the AAF. This gave airmen a sense of both euphoria and of paranoia. Although they owned the aircraft, they did not own the bombs. The Manhattan Engineering District under the command of an Army general, Leslie Groves, controlled all aspects of atomic bomb development, construction, and assembly. In January 1947 the MED was disbanded and its functions absorbed by the AEC. The cloak of secrecy draped over the program by Groves and then the AEC was so

---

[94] Spaatz, "Strategic Air Power: Fulfillment of a Concept," 388.

total the AAF was kept almost completely in the dark. Indeed, not just airmen were in this state; when President Truman was briefed by the AEC in April 1947, he was told the atomic stockpile was "very small." Worse, no bombs were actually assembled, and few personnel were trained to do so. Truman, who had been president for two years by then and should have known better, was nonetheless visibly shocked.[95] At that time there were no more than 13 unassembled atomic bombs in the American arsenal.[96]

In hindsight, it is apparent there was a great deal of institutional jealously and gamesmanship being played by the atomic gatekeepers. The complexities of the bomb's assembly and arming, as well as the modifications carried out on the B-29s used for delivery, were not as great as pretended. Moreover, secrecy was hardly airtight—the Soviets infiltrated the Manhattan Project early in the war, and spies passed on invaluable secrets to Moscow. As early as 1942, Groves knew the Russians were attempting to infiltrate the Manhattan Project, but little was done. In fact, one historian labeled the MED's attempts at counter-espionage as "amateurish."[97] The heavy mantle of secrecy was most successful in keeping information from the airmen charged with de-livering the bomb, not from Soviet adversaries. Airmen would fight against this bureaucratic barricade for two years.

When the war ended, the men who had led the services through-out began to retire. George Marshall would leave uniform to take over the State Department, and Dwight Eisenhower became Army chief of staff. Admiral King gave way to Chester Nimitz. Hap Arnold, shaken by four heart attacks during the war, would turn over the AAF to Carl Spaatz. As Arnold moved toward retirement, he directed Spaatz to form a small board to study and forecast the future of the AAF. Spaatz selected two of his brightest and most energetic young officers, Hoyt Vandenberg and Larry Norstad. Their deliberations called for an independent Air Force composed of 70 groups, 25 of which would be strategic bombers. They also noted the vital impor-tance of intelligence to the strategic bombing mission, as well as con-tinued research and development. The latter was no doubt a reflec-tion of their belief in the importance of atomic weapons to the future of the air arm. They were already beginning to fret over being ex-cluded from atomic development and therefore suggested that a new

[95] Schnabel, *Joint Chiefs of Staff and National Policy*, 134–35; and Rhodes, *Dark Sun*, 283–84.
[96] Rosenberg, "U.S. Nuclear Stockpile," 26.
[97] Herken, *Winning Weapon*, 123–25.

position on the Air Staff be created specifically for the purpose of exploring this new field. Their suggested occupant of this new position, Curtis LeMay, was another young officer of enormous capability and drive.

Soon after, Vandenberg was tasked to think specifically about an "atomic strike force." His memo on the subject called for an elite, dedicated force that would form the core of the Air Force. He, too, emphasized the need for intelligence. This was not coincidental; he was at the same time studying the problems of intelligence for Eisenhower and would soon be named the War Department G-2. After he reorganized that division, President Truman would appoint him the director of Central Intelligence. These high-level forays into the arcane world of intelligence were crucial because they would give Vandenberg insights into diplomatic and technological areas normally outside the purview of military officers. These insights would in turn prove invaluable when he returned to uniform in mid 1947 to become Spaatz's deputy.

Meanwhile, studies done by the Air Staff during and after the war, including that which he chaired, prompted Spaatz to reorganize the AAF into functional commands in early 1946. There were three combat commands, the largest and most important of which was Strategic Air Command, the atomic strike force suggested by Vandenberg. To command SAC, Spaatz chose Gen George Kenney, one of the Old Guard officers who had seen combat in World War I and who had commanded the Far East Air Forces under MacArthur during World War II. The combination of the largest combat unit with one of the most prestigious and experienced combat airmen augured well for the new bomber command. However, events would show that real problems would need to be solved.

The disintegration of America's armed forces after V-J Day was predictable given past history but was still devastating to military capability. All the services were affected, but airmen, perhaps believing the events of the interwar years were about to be repeated, felt themselves especially hard hit. Plans calling for over 100 groups in the postwar world were relentlessly chopped. The bottom line of 70 groups, seen by airmen as the bare minimum to assure security, was seen only in passing as the AAF plunged from 232 groups during the war to 52 by August 1946, and it would go even lower. Worse, the clamor of the American people meant it was impossible to conduct an orderly demobilization process. Seniority in time served counted most as the nation demanded the return of its husbands, fathers, and sons. The result was a deplorable drop in combat capability. This drop was experienced even by Strategic Air Command, which saw its top mechanics mustered out regardless of the effect such discharges had on unit readiness. This situation, combined with the persistent inability to crack the barrier of secrecy surrounding the atomic program, led to widespread frustration. This depression was not helped by difficulties encountered in deploying overseas and to Alaska or by the embarrassing failure of an atomic bomb test at Bikini Atoll in July 1946. In truth, the notion of SAC as an elite command within the AAF was lip service. As we shall see, SAC was not given the priority and resources commensurate with its alleged elite status.

The notion of "mission" remained a talisman throughout this period. Strategic bombing, even more so than in the past, was the key advantage airmen possessed over the traditional services. The formation of SAC, with its global reach and focus, was specifically designed to accentuate that unique mission and capability. Not unexpectedly, that mission was tied to technology. The near-magical properties of atomic energy put military strategy and theory on a new plane, and the airmen scrambled to gain insight into this new field. Knowledge was power, and the airmen had little, but the connection between airpower and atomic power was too obvious for them to curtail their efforts. They were determined to break the atomic lock.

As always, leadership was in the forefront of everything that was achieved—or not achieved—by the AAF during this period. The strong guidance of Hap Arnold in the months following the war, followed by the wisdom and experience of Carl Spaatz, was basic. Not all was a success story, however. As we shall see, the new leaders that emerged in the postwar world—and that would lead to an independent Air Force and the dominance of Strategic Air Command in that Air Force—were not all up to the task.

Chapter 4

Independence Mixed with Challenges

The AAF emerged from war with newfound respect among political and military leaders and the public. Even so, there were persistent struggles. The air arm was not as large as airmen had hoped, nor was it given the resources they thought necessary. Airmen believed they needed an independent service, equal to the Army and Navy and complete with a separate budget and cabinet department. The drive for a separate service was bound up with what was termed "unification"—the formation of three coequal branches of an army, navy, and air force united in a single department of defense.

Unification was a bitter process. Separate departments of the Army and Navy had existed for nearly two centuries, and although a joint board had been formed in 1903 to smooth coordination between soldiers and sailors, it produced scant success. Between 1921 and 1945, Congress examined nearly 50 bills to reorganize the armed forces and move toward a unified department of defense. All were opposed by the Army and Navy, and only one even reached the floor of the House, where it was defeated in 1932.[1] Land and sea were separate domains, and there seemed little reason why "coordination" would not continue to prove sufficient.[2]

The airplane changed everything, because it could fly over oceans, mountains, and front lines—it united the globe. Even before World War II, the Army and Navy realized the need for airpower to achieve their objectives, but the question of demarcation—so obvious in the era before airpower—was a concern when land-based airplanes could fly hundreds of miles out to sea and aircraft based on carriers could fly far inland. Overlapping command and control sectors, as well as redundancy and inefficiency, were problems demanding solutions. Old command organizations and structures seemed obsolete in modern war. Moreover, World War II presented the United States with the largest, most ferocious, and most capable enemies it had ever faced. Bland talk of cooperation and coordination was no longer adequate

---

[1] Rearden, *History of the Office of the Secretary of Defense*, vol. 1, 17.
[2] Cline and Matloff, "Development of War Department Views on Unification"; and Sander, "Truman and the National Security Council."

in a world war against powerful enemies. Unity, both at the theater level and also in Washington, was essential.

On a more practical note, the United States was fighting as part of a major alliance, and this meant periodic high-level meetings between American military leaders and those of its partners. This matter came to a head when US and British leaders met in July 1941 at the Argentia Conference in Newfoundland. Due to security concerns, little advanced warning was given. Marshall told Hap Arnold to pack a bag and prepare to travel—he was not told where he was going or for how long. The result was predictable: "The Americans arrived without any serious consultation or staff work among themselves or, more importantly, any idea of what the president desired or hoped to accomplish."[3] The Americans were unprepared. The Joint Chiefs of Staff—consisting of ADM William Leahy, chief of staff to the president, ADM Ernest King, Gen George Marshall, and Gen Hap Arnold—was soon formed to complement the efficiency of the British. A significant decision coming out of the periodic meetings of the Combined Chiefs of Staff—as the group of Americans and British was termed—was the formation of theater commands. These geographic entities consisted of a combined force of sailors, soldiers, marines, and airmen, sometimes from several different countries. One commander was appointed to head this theater, and all were expected to work harmoniously together under that commander. Thus, for example, Gen Dwight Eisenhower was the supreme allied commander of Northwest Europe, and Field Marshal Harold Alexander held the same title and position in the Mediterranean. These unified theater commands would be important precedents in the debates on unification.

In early 1943, General Marshall directed his staff to explore postwar reorganization, and it quickly decided the Joint Board arrangement of the prewar era was inadequate. The unified theater commands received direction from the JCS and sometimes from the Combined Chiefs. It seemed to the Army that such a command setup was a logical model to follow after the war. Moreover, Army planners—especially those in the AAF—were aware the JCS organization was a wartime expedient without firm legislative foundation. Indeed, the War Powers Act and Executive Order 9082 stated that the JCS would automatically dissolve six months after the end of hostilities.

---

[3] Huston, *American Airpower Comes of Age*, vol. 1, 207–10. See also Vernon Davis, *History of the Joint Chiefs of Staff in World War II*.

Marshall deemed a unified defense establishment necessary.[4] The Navy rejected such a notion. The sea service was not convinced of the need or desirability for unification; moreover, it understood that such a plan would entail a separate Air Force—a notion anathema to it.

Nonetheless, pressure from Congress prompted the JCS to form a joint committee in early 1945 to study unification. The four-man group, chaired by ADM James O. Richardson, submitted its report on 11 April 1945. It had interviewed 56 high-ranking officers, including theater commanders Generals MacArthur and Eisenhower and Admirals Chester Nimitz and William F. "Bull" Halsey. All supported the majority opinion that there should be a unified defense establishment after the war—Richardson, however, dissented. Admirals Leahy and King sided with Richardson, whereas General Marshall concurred with the majority and in a memo to the JCS stated, "I concur emphatically in the basic recommendation of the majority report of the Special Committee on the Reorganization of National Defense that there be established a single department system of organization for the armed forces with equal and coordinate land, air, and sea components."[5] In October 1945 the joint chiefs submitted the report along with the Navy's dissent to President Truman.[6]

The House and Senate then held hearings on the subject, and debate conformed to service lines. The Army supported unification and a separate Air Force. The Navy was implacably opposed, and its rationale was blunt: it feared losing naval aviation to the Air Force; it feared losing the Marine Corps to the Army; and it feared loss of budget share.[7] Admiral King called for integration, not unification, and he saw no need for an independent Air Force—the Navy Department contained the Marine Corps as an autonomous organization, and the Army and its air arm could use the same model.[8] ADM John Towers was more blunt: "I fear—and I have good reason to fear—that the Army Air Force advocates of a separate air force have well established in mind the plan, upon realization of a separate service, to absorb naval aviation."[9]

---

[4] Edwin Williams, "Legislative History of the AAF and USAF," 42; and Schnabel, *Joint Chiefs of Staff and National Policy*, vol. 1, 6, 95. The chiefs advised President Truman not to use the phrases "end of the war" or "termination of hostilities" after V-J Day for fear they would trigger the six-month clock ending their existence.

[5] Marshall to JCS, memorandum, 10 October 1945, in Bland, *Papers of George Catlett Marshall*, vol. 5, 327–28.

[6] Caraley, *Politics of Military Unification*, 35–38.

[7] Schnabel, *Joint Chiefs of Staff and National Policy*, vol. 1, 110–11.

[8] US Congress, *Hearings before the Senate Naval Affairs Committee on S. 2044*, 127–46.

[9] Ibid., 278.

The congressional hearings revealed the chasm existing between the services. President Truman was losing patience. As vice president he had supported unification, and in December 1945 he wrote a strongly worded letter to Congress on the subject stating that during the war there was insufficient coordination and collaboration between the services. This lack was "costly and dangerous," and victory was achieved only "in spite of these handicaps." The cooperation sometimes exhibited during the war was inadequate for the future, and there was ample evidence "to demonstrate beyond question the need for a unified department." He also insisted on a separate Air Force with responsibilities equal to those of land and sea power.[10] After listening to the back and forth between the Army and Navy for two years, Truman had enough, and in early 1947 *directed* the services to reach agreement or he would reach it for them.[11]

To comply with the president's wishes, the Army appointed Maj Gen Lauris Norstad to work with VADM Forrest Sherman to reach a compromise. After several months the two reported they had reached agreement "on all aspects of the unification problem."[12] The breakthrough occurred when the Army dropped its call for a defense department with three coequal services; instead, there would be three cabinet-level departments for the Army, Navy, and Air Force to be coordinated by a secretary of defense. This was not the organization desired by soldiers and airmen, but it answered the Navy's concerns regarding access to the president and Congress. The Army also dropped its demand for a chairman of the JCS who would be the ranking military officer and advisor to the president. This position was actually formed, but it did not have the authority the Army sought; rather, it was the same "chief of staff to the commander in chief" position that Admiral Leahy had held during the war. This individual would be a primus inter pares and serve as spokesman for the three service chiefs but could not override them or impose decisions on them.[13]

On 26 July 1947, the National Security Act became law. It was a compromise, leaving none of the services satisfied. There were to be three executive departments for the Army, Navy, and Air Force, and these would be administered by a national military establishment. The secretary of defense had an office but no staff; moreover, the

---

[10] Truman, "Our Armed Forces Must Be Unified," 16; and Cole et al., *Department of Defense*, 7–17.

[11] "State of the Unification," 893.

[12] "Chronology, Functions and Composition of the Joint Chiefs of Staff," JCS Historical Study, 1979, 30.

[13] Of interest, the law mentioned the position of chief of staff to the commander in chief, "if there be one."

service secretaries had the right to go over his head to the president. General Eisenhower remarked that the defense secretary was "nothing more than a damned switchboard operator."[14]

Truman picked Navy secretary James Forrestal to be the first secretary of defense. Forrestal achieved unification, but it would be a shaky edifice for the next several years. More ominously, the specific roles and functions assigned to each of the three services were not spelled out in the National Security Act. Truman intended to address that minefield by executive order, arguing that such matters were part of his responsibility and not that of Congress. The issue would prove thornier than expected.

Roles and Missions

A frequent justification for unification was efficiency, which would result in budget savings by reducing duplication. Congress agreed with this rationale, but this placed even greater strain on the services.[15] Fiscal austerity and demobilization left the military reeling, and all in uniform believed their combat capability was at a dangerously low level. Although such beliefs no doubt resulted in a self-serving parochialism in some quarters, most soldiers, sailors, or airmen sincerely believed their special expertise was vital to US security and that expertise was in danger of being eroded away.

Precise roles and missions assigned to the services were therefore of enormous import. None of the services wanted its budget cut, but if tasks were taken away, cuts were inevitable. There were many areas of disagreement that needed to be addressed, but the two biggest concerned naval aviation and the Marine Corps—could the nation afford another air force and "private army"?[16] In truth, these questions were quickly answered in the affirmative. Although some in the Army and Air Force may have harbored designs on the marines and naval air, these forces had strong constituencies in Congress and among the American people. The issue causing the most debate was more fundamental to the ethos and structure of the Air Force.

---

[14] Kintner, *Forging a New Sword*, 24–27; and Childs, "Battle of the Pentagon," 48.

[15] Rearden, *History of the Office of the Secretary of Defense*, vol. 1, 385–93. Truman had trumpeted efficiency in his letter to Congress in December 1945, and the assistant secretary of war for air, Robert Lovett, testified that "substantial economies will be gained by unification." US Congress, House Select Committee on Post-War Military Policy, 50.

[16] Kenneth Condit, *Joint Chiefs of Staff and National Policy*, 163–67.

In March 1948, Secretary Forrestal gathered the chiefs to Key West to hammer out decisions and compromises regarding roles and missions. One result of these meetings was a statement defining "primary" versus "collateral" functions.[17] A primary function was one in which a particular service had a clear-cut responsibility, whereas in a collateral function, a service supported whoever had it as primary. Forrestal admitted such definitions were fluid and a clear distinction was not always possible—the function of close air support, for example, was something the Air Force, Navy, and Marines might all claim as primary, depending on the situation. Yet the secretary's intent was to preclude one service from using a collateral function "as the basis for establishing additional force requirements."[18] When building a budget request, a service would see to its primary functions first; if these were adequately covered and there were funds remaining, those dollars could be spent on collateral functions. If there was disagreement as to whether or not the primary functions were adequately covered, the JCS or the secretary of defense would decide. This was important: the JCS or defense secretary could prevent a service from funding a collateral function if he determined money was better spent covering a primary one. This provision would cause a major interservice fight one year later.

The services were assigned functions, but some were vaguely worded and invited trouble. The Navy, for example, was given the primary function of conducting air operations "as necessary for the accomplishment of objectives in a naval campaign." The Air Force was given the primary function of "strategic air warfare," defined as:

> Air combat and supporting operations designed to effect, through the systematic application of force to a selected series of vital targets, the progressive destruction and disintegration of the enemy's war-making capacity to a point where he no longer retains the ability or the will to wage war. Vital targets may include key manufacturing systems, sources of raw material, critical material, stock piles, power systems, transportation systems, communications facilities, concentrations of uncommitted elements of enemy armed forces, key agricultural areas, and other such target systems.[19]

---

[17] The terms *missions*, *roles*, and *functions* are often used interchangeably but have separate meanings: a *mission* is a task assigned to a unified or specified command; a *role* is a broad and enduring purpose for which a service was established; and a *function* is a specific responsibility assigned to a service that permits it to fulfill one of its roles. Trest, *Air Force Roles and Missions*, ix.

[18] Forrestal to Truman, "Functions of the Armed Forces and the Joint Chiefs of Staff," letter, 21 April 1948, in Wolf, *United States Air Force*, 155.

[19] Wolf, *United States Air Force*, 165–66.

This definition described the AAF's bombing campaigns against Germany and Japan, but what of naval aviation? Carrier aircraft had flown thousands of missions against land objectives in the Pacific. Were the sorties flown against Japanese airfields an example of targets "necessary for the accomplishment of a naval campaign," or were these strikes against "uncommitted elements of enemy armed forces"? Target definitions were in the eyes of the beholder. Nonetheless, Forrestal noted in his diary that the chiefs had reached an oral understanding recognizing "the right of the Navy to proceed with the development of weapons the Navy considers essential to its function, but with the proviso that the Navy will not develop a separate strategic air force, this function being reserved to the Air Force."[20]

This was fundamental: strategic air warfare was a primary function of the Air Force, and Strategic Air Command would carry it out. At Key West the Navy had seemingly acknowledged this supremacy. The Navy could not build a "separate strategic air force," and indeed could not even allocate funds to that function until all its primary functions—for example, the protection of shipping, antisubmarine warfare, or mine-laying—were adequately covered. Even so, the Navy had its foot in the strategic bombing door and would soon seek to wedge it open a bit further.

The Key West decision regarding strategic bombing was immediately challenged. The Navy had its eye on the mission, and VADM Daniel Gallery wrote a memo stating, "The Navy was the branch of the National Defense destined to deliver the Atom Bomb." To Gallery, this function was crucial, because the next war would be dominated by atomic weapons, and if the Navy did not participate in strategic bombing, it would be obsolete. He continued, "The time is right now for the Navy to start an aggressive campaign aimed at proving that the Navy can deliver the atomic bomb more effectively than the Air Force can."[21]

Using Gallery's logic, ADM Louis Denfeld, the chief of naval operations (CNO), attempted to renege on the Key West agreements by submitting a memo to Forrestal on 22 April seeking to "clarify" the decisions just reached. Denfeld argued that targeting for strategic air warfare should be a joint Air Force/Navy responsibility, and the Navy should be allowed to strike any targets, anywhere, without reference

---

[20] Millis and Duffield, *Forrestal Diaries*, 392.
[21] This memo was leaked to the press on 10 April 1948. Hammond, *Super Carriers and B-36 Bombers*, 14.

to the Air Force. Denfeld wanted his interpretation accepted as official policy. Vandenberg, the new Air Force chief of staff, protested that Denfeld's suggestion would undermine the entire basis of Key West—if the Navy were allowed a free hand in strategic air warfare, then what was the point of assigning primary and collateral functions and attempting to eliminate redundancy? General Eisenhower and Admiral Leahy agreed with Air Force reasoning, and Denfeld's ploy was brushed aside.[22] The issue did not, however, go away. Further meetings were held in Newport, Rhode Island, in late August in an attempt to further clarify the roles and functions dispute. Even so, Forrestal noted glumly but presciently in his official report that the most divisive issue remained "What is to be the use, and who is to be user of air power?"[23]

Planning for Atomic War

The basic issue of airpower's role in war came to the fore when the joint chiefs began drawing up war plans after the war. They did this largely in a vacuum because Pres. Harry Truman remained detached from atomic issues and war planning. Indeed, it was not until September 1946 that General Eisenhower briefed him on atomic stockpile issues.[24] The political climate between the United States and the Soviet Union was already hardening, so the chiefs wanted options. The planners' first response noted that air-delivered atomic bombs—196 to be exact—would be used to devastate 20 urban targets in the Soviet Union. These strikes would severely cripple Soviet industry by dramatically decreasing production—aircraft by 90 percent, tanks by 46 percent, trucks by 88 percent, steel production by 36 percent, and so forth. The attacking B-29 force, based in England, Italy, India, and China, would sustain heavy losses (up to 35 percent), but it would get through.[25]

This was a useful start, establishing strategic air attack with atomic weapons as the primary response to Soviet aggression, although the president had not yet approved the use of atomic weapons. The planners,

---

[22] "Chronology of Changes in Key West Agreements, April 1948–January 1958," JCS Historical Study, 7 February 1958, National Archives (NA), RG 218, file CCS 337, box 96.

[23] Rearden, *History of the Office of the Secretary of Defense*, vol. 1, 402.

[24] Rosenberg, "Origins of Overkill," 11.

[25] JWPC 416/1, "Military Position of the United States in the Light of Russian Policy," 8 January 1946, NA, RG 319, file "ABC 384," box 469. At the time, there were no air bases in Italy, India, or China that could be used as forward staging bases.

who did not have information on the atomic stockpile, assumed a large number of bombs would be immediately available, but at the time the entire US stockpile consisted of no more than nine atomic bombs.[26] The reasons for the small atomic stockpile are unclear. General Groves's successor, Maj Gen K. D. Nichols, later recalled that the "turnover period" when the Manhattan District gave way to the AEC was one of confusion and intense turmoil—demobilization chaos affected the atomic program as well. Also, the Fat Man bombs were the only atomic devices in the inventory, and all knew they were inefficient and outdated. As he summed the problem, "The lack of urgency and reluctance to stockpile obsolete weapons delayed production and stockpiling of weapons."[27] Whatever the reasons, the result was an atomic stockpile growing very slowly for the first four years after the war, while few in power were even aware of the problem.

Soon after, the Joint Strategic Plans Group wrote *Pincher*, a war plan which assumed the Soviet Union invaded the Middle East to secure oil resources and then turned on Western Europe. The prognosis was grim: the Soviets would overrun most of the continent, although the Allies hoped a toehold could be maintained in either the Italian or Iberian Peninsula. Britain would remain the major base from which to launch counterattacks. *Pincher* called for the defense of the Western Hemisphere as primary, but then envisioned a gradual buildup of forces, a blockade of the Soviet Union, and an air offensive against the Soviet war-making capacity. The plan noted that likely targets would be located in the Moscow and Caucasus areas, but no detailed target analysis was presented. Although the president had not issued a formal statement on whether or not atomic weapons would be authorized in the event of war, *Pincher*'s wording implied they would be used from the outset: "No war with the USSR can be less than a total war, requiring the full utilization of the entire US and Allied war potential." The Soviet forces would be formidable, consisting of 113 ground divisions with their satellite republics providing an additional 84 divisions. In contrast, the allies would be able to muster but 17 divisions—airpower would have to be the great equalizer. After the air campaign, the United States would carry on "as resources

---

[26] Rearden, *History of the Office of the Secretary of Defense*, vol. 1, 439. There was at least one bomb available after Nagasaki, and there were nine bombs in June 1946; it is unknown how many were available five months earlier at the time of the above study.

[27] Nichols, *Road to Trinity*, 228. Nichols became head of the Armed Forces Special Weapons Project in January 1948 after Groves retired.

permit."[28] *Pincher* also noted that forward air bases, not then available, would be necessary to carry out the atomic air offensive.

This was merely a rough sketch outlining the size of the forces needed—far in excess of what were then being planned—and did not include targeting data for the air offensive; once again, 30 major cities were targeted. Intelligence data on the Soviet Union was not available in sufficient detail to allow other than generalities.[29] The JCS never approved *Pincher* or the subsidiary studies deriving from it that dealt with specific areas such as Italy or China, but they did approve it for "planning purposes." Of note, the Navy was not involved in the air campaign: its mission was to sink the Soviet fleet and blockade the country.[30] Vandenberg expressed frustration at the slow pace of war plan development in November 1947, and Thomas K. Finletter, chairman of the President's Air Policy Commission, also expressed his concern. When the JCS attempted to brief Finletter's group on the status of current war planning, General Eisenhower quickly confessed, "I think we really owe it to them to tell them that there is no war plan."[31] Secretary Forrestal was equally frustrated at the state of US war plans, noting they were "a source of embarrassment" when he was required to brief Congress on the subject.[32]

Vandenberg's main concern was that the services had no "definitive statement of the long-range objectives of the United States," nor did they have a reasonable estimate of the nation's industrial and manpower mobilization capabilities. This lack was fundamental: it made a huge difference to planners whether the objective was to destroy Soviet industry, the armed forces, the Communist Party and hierarchy, the Russian people, "or a combination of these." Moreover, what was the goal? Occupation and reconstruction of the country with a view toward establishing a viable democracy? In the absence of guidance, the Air Force had developed rough outline plans showing how it would be committed "in the event of an emergency." *Harrow*, *Makefast*, and *Earshot* were early Air Force efforts at articulating how SAC's air campaign would evolve. Vandenberg admitted these plans

---

[28] JCS 789/1, "Concept of Operations for PINCHER," 2 March 1946, in *Records of the Joint Chiefs of Staff*, Part 2, microfilm collection, reel 2.

[29] JCS 789/1, "Problems Deriving from PINCHER," 13 April 1946, in *Records of the Joint Chiefs of Staff*, Part 2, microfilm collection, reel 2.

[30] JWPC 432/3, "Joint Basic Outline War Plan Short Title: PINCHER," 27 April 1946, in *Records of the Joint Chiefs of Staff*, Part 2, microfilm collection, reel 2.

[31] Finletter, interview, 36–37; and "Lack of Strategic Plan Hampers Development of U.S. Air Power," 11–12.

[32] Kenneth Condit, *Joint Chiefs of Staff and National Policy*, 275.

lacked logistical specificity and urged work to begin on a joint plan "to develop ways and means of exploiting the great shock and destructive power, as well as the psychological effect, of atomic weapons with a view to defeating the USSR within six months after D-day."[33]

As tensions mounted in Europe in 1948, the joint planners presented *Bushwhacker*, a long-range war plan speculating that if war erupted in 1952, the Soviets would not yet have the atomic bomb but might use either chemical or biological weapons. Allied goals would be to push the Soviets back to "at least" their 1939 boundaries. This plan also relied on a strategic air campaign for the main offensive, but Navy aircraft carriers would take part, although "there is a divergent opinion" on whether they would be confined to conventional operations or could employ atomic weapons. The Air Force's strategic offensive was expected to begin "within a matter of hours." The plan suggested that aerial refueling would be "technically feasible" by 1952. As we shall see, this indeed would be the case.[34]

Two months after *Bushwhacker*, joint planners submitted *Halfmoon*, a short-range plan covering the first year of a projected war with the Soviet Union. Like its predecessors, the plan posited a Soviet invasion of Europe. Vastly outnumbered, the Western allies would retreat to the Rhine and then offer whatever resistance possible. Planners expected the Soviets to overrun most of the continent, and Allied forces would be evacuated from French and Italian seaports. Britain would probably remain secure, and it was from there and bases in the Middle East and on Okinawa that the United States would retaliate on D+15 with an atomic air offensive—*Halfmoon* was specific on the use of atomic weapons. Once again, it would be a long slog. Significantly, although the JCS relied on SAC to do the heavy lifting early in the conflict, the new plan postulated that eventually there would be a role for everyone to play: the Navy would sweep the seas of the Soviet fleet, institute a blockade, and even contribute to the air offensive. At an unspecified point there would be a land invasion to retake the continent.[35]

---

[33] Vandenberg to Symington, memorandum, 5 November 1947, Declassified Documents Quarterly Index (DDQI), 1976, 241B.

[34] JSPG 500/2, "BUSHWHACKER," 8 March 1948, in *Records of the Joint Chiefs of Staff*, Part 2, microfilm collection, reel 2. Keeping track of these early war plans is difficult because of their rapidly changing names and foci. For example, the predecessor of *Bushwhacker* was another long-range plan termed *Charioteer*, which went in and out of consideration in a matter of months. *Broiler* was a short-range plan replaced by *Frolic*, which in turn was superseded by *Halfmoon*, whose name was changed to *Fleetwood*. Et cetera.

[35] JCS 1844/0, "HALFMOON," 18 June 1948, NA, RG 319, file 312TS.

Halfmoon was not well received by the chiefs: it had no projections beyond the first year of operations. Yet, despite its shortcomings, it was the first postwar plan to be approved by the JCS. In early 1949 the plan was updated, expanded, and renamed *Trojan*. This effort was a major step forward because it included a detailed targeting annex for the air offensive, which targeted 70 urban and industrial centers for atomic attack by SAC bombers. These attacks would require 133 atomic weapons—eight of which would be dropped on Moscow and seven more on Leningrad. The first air strike would occur on D+9 and involve 25 atomic bombs. B-29s and B-50s would launch from bases in the UK, Middle East, and Okinawa, while B-36s would come from the United States. The lack of detailed targeting data in earlier war plans had been noticeable; *Trojan* helped remedy this problem. In a side comment, planners noted the crux of what would become nuclear deterrence policy: "not the slightest doubt can be allowed to creep into Soviet minds that we will use the bomb, or they may miscalculate and start the war we are trying so hard to avert."[36]

Deterrence was not a new concept, but *nuclear* deterrence would soon take on enormous significance. For one nation to deter another, several conditions had to be met. First, a would-be deterrer must have the capability to actually inflict grievous harm on an enemy. Second, determination to use that capability had to be unequivocally communicated to the target nation; there could be no doubt in the mind of the adversary that the threat to use force was credible—the concern noted above by JCS planners. Finally, the target nation must agree to be deterred; it must accept that harm to it would be so severe as to make an aggression unwise and costly.

War plans between 1945 and 1950 were alike in assuming war would begin with Soviet aggression, leading to a global war involving atomic weapons and lasting for three or more years. All of the services would play a role, although the first US response would be an atomic air offensive led by SAC. Eventually, naval aviation was included in these strikes. Planners assumed a protracted conventional bombing campaign would begin simultaneously with the atomic phase. This meant that a large bomber force was necessary—regardless of the number or availability of atomic weapons. In essence, the war plans imagined an updated World War II scenario bringing Allied

---

[36] JCS 1935, "U.S. Policy on Atomic Warfare," 3 September 1948, in *Records of the Joint Chiefs of Staff, 1945–1953, Strategic Issues*, Part 1, microfilm collection, reel 1.

victory after prolonged, combined arms employing atomic and conventional weapons from all the services. Significantly, although early plans called for a virtual abandonment of Europe—except for Britain, which would be essential as a forward base—the founding of the North Atlantic Treaty Organization (NATO) in 1949 changed things. Europe would not be abandoned; it would be contested, and the debate now centered on how far forward the Allies would attempt to halt the Soviets and how many atomic/nuclear weapons would be used in "retardation"—the blunting of the enemy offensive.[37]

These war plans were rudimentary, and military leaders knew this, but the planning *process* was essential. Atomic weapons forced military planners to start over with a blank sheet. It was a lengthy process: logistics and mobilization plans could not be written until a war plan had been completed, but when they appeared, the logisticians often declared them infeasible and sent them back for revision. This iterative process resulted in a succession of hastily prepared plans submitted and then retracted.[38] Traditional war-planning assumptions and constraints no longer seemed valid, and military leaders groped to find their way in this new environment. They did not expect that *Halfmoon*, for example, would be a blueprint for future war—these men had seen too many such plans evaporate during the just-concluded world war when the realities of combat intruded into the realm of war on paper. Nonetheless, as one historian of the war plans of this period accurately notes, "If war plans do not establish the precise course of a conflict, they do set the general course of strategic operations."[39] Of perhaps greater significance, *Halfmoon* was on the table when the United States faced its first significant postwar crisis.

The Berlin Crisis and the Rebirth of SAC

Tensions had been rising in Berlin since the end of the war, when it was divided into four occupation zones. The divided city, in the midst of a divided country, was the focus of conflict between the West and its erstwhile Soviet ally. Gen Lucius D. Clay, the military governor of Germany, wrote Washington on 5 March 1948 that tensions were rising and war could come with "dramatic suddenness."[40]

---

[37] Borgiasz, *Strategic Air Command*, 14–16.
[38] Little, "Organizing for Strategic Planning," 43.
[39] Ross, *American War Plans*, xi.
[40] Jean Smith, *Papers of General Lucius D. Clay*, vol. 2, 568.

Although the CIA concluded war was unlikely "within the next sixty days," it admitted that the Soviets might blockade West Berlin in an attempt to apply pressure on Western leaders and isolate the city.[41] There had never been a formal agreement assuring land access to Berlin from West Germany, and on 30 March the Soviets used this loophole to impose restrictions on traffic into the city.

The cause of the trouble centered on the future of Berlin. The Soviets saw the division of the city as temporary; they expected the West to withdraw and Berlin to become incorporated into the eastern zone. The West had no such intention and announced it would introduce a new currency into West Germany to show its long-term commitment. The Soviets vigorously objected, and tensions escalated in mid June when the Soviets cut off all passenger trains and road traffic to Berlin and limited freight trains to one per day. On 24 June they stopped all rail and barge traffic into the city.[42]

President Truman was adamant that the West would not abandon Berlin, but the use of armed force was too risky. The West was vastly outnumbered in Europe, and although Clay favored an aggressive response to Soviet affronts, those in Washington thought otherwise.[43] The response was to be a massive airlift to keep Berlin supplied with food and fuel for as long as necessary. Clay then asked for the deployment of a B-29 group to Europe as a show of commitment to the Berliners' plight. Truman approved, although he refused to transfer custody of atomic weapons to SAC, as the Air Force requested. As the president put it in his typically pithy way, "I don't propose to have some dashing lieutenant colonel decide when would be the proper time to drop one."[44] Vandenberg was receptive to the idea of sending over the bombers; recall that the Wonderful project had called for the deployment of up to five B-29 groups to Europe. Although that large deployment had been scrapped as impractical, the idea of establishing a SAC presence in Europe was still in his mind.

Spaatz had discussed basing B-29s in Britain in July 1946 when he met with Air Marshal Tedder. They agreed that four airfields in East Anglia would be refurbished and made available for SAC B-29s. Both sides assumed these bases would be used as staging points in the event of war and the B-29s would then be carrying atomic bombs on strike

---

[41] "CIA Review of World Situation," 8 April 1948, NA, "Special File 4A: Berlin Crisis."

[42] For a good account of the crisis, see Shlaim, *United States and the Berlin Blockade*.

[43] Jean Smith, *Papers of General Lucius D. Clay*, vol. 2, 599–604.

[44] Miscamble, "Harry S. Truman, the Berlin Blockade and the 1948 Election," 310.

missions against the Soviet Union. The first deployment of B-29s to England was in June 1947—nine aircraft from the 97th Bomb Group, which were not atomic capable, deployed to RAF Marham.[45] B-29s were to be stationed in Europe at all times, but none on a permanent basis. In truth, the use of these bases by SAC aircraft was to be a matter of high diplomacy for several years. The original Spaatz/Tedder agreements were deliberately vague, and British political and military leaders soon found it desirable to nail things down a bit more solidly.

The catalyst for talks was the Berlin crisis. The United States asked to deploy B-29s to the bases previously agreed to, but now the British wanted to discuss details. The talks ran on for several years as the British, who were kept in the dark regarding the US atomic program and war plans, pushed for greater transparency. American leaders were reluctant to share information, partly because they were ill informed on atomic matters, but also because they did not trust their allies to keep secrets. Finally, the Americans said they could not be more forthcoming because the McMahon Act of 1946 prohibited them from sharing atomic secrets. The positions of both sides were understandable. The Americans believed the brunt of fighting in a future war would fall on them; the least the British could do was allow them the use of air bases to launch the atomic strikes that would be the best hope for victory. To the British, it was a question of sovereignty—the bases were on their soil—as well as practicality. Britain would undoubtedly be sucked into a war involving the United States and the Soviets, but the presence of SAC bases would guarantee England would be in Soviet crosshairs. They wanted a voice in basing, at the very least, but also insight into the war plans that could involve them in a future conflict.[46]

As these larger talks continued, the British government agreed to a limited deployment, and on 17 July two squadrons of B-29s from the 301st Bomb Group arrived in England. Within weeks the 28th Bomb Group was established at RAF Scampton and the 307th Bomb Group at Marham and Waddington.[47] All remaining SAC units, including the 509th, were put on 24-hour alert. Retired general Carl Spaatz

---

[45] Young, "No Blank Cheque," 1139–41. B-29s had deployed to Germany in November 1946 in response to the downing of two C-47s by the Soviets. The B-29s, which were not atomic capable, flew along the Soviet border as a show of resolve. The SAC history notes this was the first time B-29s were deployed as a political statement. Bohn, *Development of Strategic Air Command*, 5.

[46] Young gives an excellent overview of this entire basing issue in "No Blank Cheque," 1133–67.

[47] At the beginning of the crisis, one squadron of B-29s from the 301st Bomb Group was already in Germany on a training exercise. It remained there and was joined by its sister squadrons. Bohn, *Development of Strategic Air Command*, 11.

wrote an editorial in *Newsweek* heralding the importance of the deployment, stating that a group of B-29s, armed with atomic bombs, would have the potency "comparable to a fleet of 79,200 fully loaded B-17s carrying TNT . . . and these demonstrations have not been lost on the rest of the world, including Soviet Russia."[48] In truth, the B-29s deployed were not atomic capable—the Saddletree modification program (formerly codenamed Silverplate) had not been completed. The crews believed they were on a training exercise and were not equipped to take offensive action.[49] General LeMay, who was then commander of United States Air Forces Europe (USAFE), later commented that the aircraft sent to his theater "weren't too much good" and, not only were they not atomic capable, "they [also] didn't have the capability of much of anything." He added, "USAFE would be stupid to get mixed up in anything bigger than a cat-fight at a pet show."[50] Even so, the deployment was portentous and had wide implications. Maj Gen Leon Johnson, the air commander in England, later stated: "Never before in history has one first-class power gone into another first-class power's country without an agreement. We were just told to come over and 'we shall be pleased to have you.'"[51] The two countries drew closer.

The first atomic-capable unit from the 509th was not deployed until July 1949—after the crisis was over—so the events of 1948 were saber rattling. The reasons for this tepid response are clear: the United States, and SAC, had only a very weak capability to take offensive action.[52] In a candid letter to Vandenberg, Lt Gen Joe Cannon (LeMay's successor at USAFE), stated that his air units were unprepared for war. He had one fighter group assigned plus some transports—the SAC B-29s were his only offensive weapons. If war broke out, he could evacuate his forces and that was all.[53] The war plans noted above were frighteningly accurate: if the Soviets attacked, continental Europe would almost certainly be lost. The West was not ready for war. In fact, the joint chiefs were doubtful an airlift would work. In a memo written on 19 July, they concluded glumly that "continued air supply for Berlin as a long-term

---

[48] Spaatz, "Era of Air-Power Diplomacy," 26.

[49] London newspapers echoed this story on several occasions. See articles in the *Times* for 17, 19, and 30 July 1948: p. 4 for the first two articles, and p. 3 for the latter.

[50] LeMay, interview, 9 March 1971, 8–12. Assembly facilities and loading pits for atomic bombs had already been built at the bases in England. LeMay and Kantor, *Mission with LeMay*, 411.

[51] Twigge and Scott, *Planning Armageddon*, 31.

[52] *SAC History—1949*, 91–94; and Borowski, *Hollow Threat*, chap. 7.

[53] Cannon to Vandenberg, letter, 16 November 1948, Vandenberg papers, Library of Congress (LOC), box 32.

operation is not feasible. Hence, unless ground routes are established, our position in Berlin will eventually become untenable."[54] As events turned out, the chiefs were wrong. The resulting Berlin airlift was a measured and tremendously successful response.

Maj Gen William H. Tunner, commander of the Hump airlift across the Himalayas in World War II, was summoned to run "Operation Vittles." Soon, a fleet of 300 US and British cargo planes were delivering over 5,600 tons of coal, food, and other supplies daily. Overall, the airlift moved 2.5 million tons of cargo in 275,000 flights; however, the campaign claimed the lives of 60 airmen in crashes. Morale within the beleaguered city soared, and the clumsy aggressiveness of the Soviets backfired.[55] It was apparent to all that the West was moving mountains to save the city and its inhabitants, while the Soviets were trying to destroy them. In May 1949 the Soviets conceded and reopened the land lines into Berlin; the blockade was over. The Berlin airlift was perhaps the greatest Western victory of the entire Cold War, not in the least diminished because it was achieved by airpower without a shot being fired.

The Berlin crisis also had a great impact on SAC. For one thing, the 3rd Air Division was established in England, giving an air of permanency to the continual deployments to the United Kingdom.[56] There was another important side effect on SAC from the Berlin airlift. To explain, it is necessary to discuss the United Nations.

The UN was an effort at world peace. The idea was not new: after World War I, the League of Nations was formed for the same purpose, but it had systemic problems that spelled its doom. When Japan invaded China and Italy went into Ethiopia in the 1930s, the League did not punish the aggressors. When civil war broke out in Spain and foreign powers intervened, the League again stood aside and soon became irrelevant.[57] Some world leaders vowed during World War II that next time things would be different. As a result, representatives from several dozen countries met in San Francisco between April and June 1945 to hammer out a charter for a new United Nations; its charter was signed by 50 countries in October 1945.[58]

---

[54] JCS 1907, "U.S. Military Courses of Action with Respect to the Situation in Berlin," 19 July 1948, in "JCS Strategic Issues," reel 5.

[55] For the best history of the Berlin Airlift, see Miller, *To Save a City*.

[56] Bohn, *Development of Strategic Air Command*, 13.

[57] See Northedge, *League of Nations*; and Scott, *Rise and Fall of the League of Nations*.

[58] For the origins and organization of the UN, see Goodrich, *United Nations*; Patterson, *Oxford 50th Anniversary Book of the United Nations*; and Kennedy, *Parliament of Man*.

The UN has six major organs, the most important being the Security Council. It consists of representatives from 11 countries, five of which are permanent members—the United States, Great Britain, France, China (then led by Chiang Kai-shek), and the Soviet Union. The "big five" have veto power over resolutions submitted to the council. To redress the primary deficiency of the League, the UN charter included Article 43, stipulating that armed forces—land, sea, and air—were to be assigned to the Security Council for maintaining international peace and security. The wording of Article 43 is vague, however, and implementation has proved impossible.

Gen George Kenney, the SAC commander, was the senior military member of the US delegation to the UN and was also slated to lead its air force—should it ever be formed. It was soon apparent there would be no such air force, but Kenney still spent much of his time in New York City rather than at SAC headquarters at Andrews AFB. He was relieved of his UN duties in November 1946 but still remained away from headquarters a large part of the time. In fact, Andrews was a poor choice for a headquarters; the airspace was too congested in the Washington zone, and Vandenberg thought there were already too many military personnel stationed in the capital area. He wrote to Kenney in December 1947 that he should begin planning a move. Kenney replied he did not want to move; Andrews was "close to the center of government." If a move were nevertheless required, he preferred Mitchel AFB on Long Island—a suggestion even less to Vandenberg's liking. The following June, Vandenberg *directed* Kenney to prepare for moving SAC to Offutt AFB near Omaha, Nebraska.[59]

SAC had other concerns besides its venue. As we have seen, the entire Air Force, including SAC, was hard hit by demobilization and budget constraints following the end of the war. These problems lingered into 1948. The command was deficient in modified bombers—there were still only enough to equip one group, the 509th. Although the 43rd Bomb Group was in line to transition to the atomic mission, there were not enough modified B-29s to even begin the process.[60] In July 1948, Vandenberg wrote AEC chairman David Lilienthal urgently

[59] Vandenberg to Kenney, letter, 17 December 1947; Kenney to Spaatz, letter, 15 January 1948; and Vandenberg to Kenney, letter, 3 June 1948, all in Vandenberg papers, LOC, box 52. One of Kenney's wing commanders believed his boss simply did not care anymore once the war was over, and he was happy to let his deputy run SAC. Irvine, interview, 17 December 1970, 17. This was also the view of Col Paul Tibbets, a SAC group commander. Tibbets, interview, 7 February 1985, 43.

[60] Bunker to Spaatz, letter, 28 March 1948, NA, RG 18, file AAJ, box 799; Brereton to Spaatz, letter, 7 July 1947, NA, RG 341, file DCS/O, box 10; and *SAC History—1948*, 147.

requesting that more aircraft be modified; an additional 82 Saddle-tree bombers were necessary to carry out the war plan.[61] By January 1949 the number of bombers modified would increase to over 120, but this was still too few to carry out the SAC mission.[62]

SAC was also deficient in trained atomic aircrews, having only six available in January 1948. The number of atomic weapons was similarly small, with only 13 devices in the US stockpile on 30 June 1947, a number that would increase to 50 a year later. Moreover, joining the bomb canisters with their atomic cores was a time-consuming operation. Exercises in early 1948 demonstrated that one assembly team, consisting of 39 people, required two days to prepare one weapon. Once the new Mk. IV bombs became available in late 1948, assembly time was cut to less than 24 hours.[63] Unfortunately, there were no military assembly teams in 1947, and the only team at the start of the Berlin crisis in March 1948 was then in the Pacific preparing for the Sandstone atomic tests. It took six months to train an assembly team, and the first one did not begin training until February 1948. An estimated five days would be required to get the first bomb assembled and delivered to the 509th at Roswell Field. It was doubtful if 20 bombs could be built in 30 days.[64] Also lacking were the bomb commanders and weaponeers necessary to monitor weapons loading and in-flight status. Putting this data together, we can see the United States possessed a very small atomic punch at the start of the Berlin crisis and was not able to react quickly. An atomic strike would have taken weeks to implement and consisted of only a few dozen bombs. Kenney, however, said he would need at least 200 bombs, delivered simultaneously, to carry out a successful strike.[65]

These difficulties were not all Kenney's fault. As we have seen, the AAF and then the Air Force were largely frozen out of the Manhattan Project and its successor, the AEC. When General LeMay, while still deputy chief of staff for R&D, attempted to gain information on the size of the atomic stockpile in April 1947, General Groves responded:

---

[61] Vandenberg to Lilienthal, letter, 12 July 1948, Vandenberg papers, LOC, box 32.

[62] Rosenberg, "U.S. Nuclear Stockpile," 30.

[63] JCS 1745/5, "The Production of Fissionable Material," 21 January 1948, "Records of the JCS Part 2: Strategic Issues, Part 1" microfilm collection, UPA, reel 1; and Rearden, *History of the Office of the Secretary of Defense*, vol. 1, 439. In June 1948 the Air Force requested that it be allowed to arm the bombs in flight. This would provide a safer alternative to performing that operation on the ground. Tests showed this to be feasible. Kepner to Wilson, memorandum, 1 July 1948, AFHRA, file 143.5191.

[64] Little and Bowen, *History of the Air Force Atomic Energy Program*, vol. 2, 90–91, 102–9, 223, 375; and Rosenberg, "U.S. Nuclear Stockpile," 29.

[65] MFR, by Vandenberg, 7 July 1948, DDQI, 1978, 149B; and Rosenberg, "US Nuclear Stockpile," 26–28.

"That information is quite complicated and is based on many factors. I cannot answer your question because I force myself to forget the numbers involved."[66] James Forrestal, then the Navy secretary, admitted he did not know the size of the atomic stockpile either.[67] It is probable this information was kept from Kenney.

There were, however, SAC deficiencies that could have been corrected. In January 1947, Kenney replaced Streett as his deputy with Maj Gen Clements McMullen, who had been his logistics chief in the Pacific during the war. McMullen was known as an uncompromising and difficult man, earning him the nickname "Concrete." He soon alienated many in SAC. In an effort to streamline operations at headquarters, he eliminated a host of offices and positions and in March 1947 assumed the position of chief of staff while also maintaining his role as deputy.[68] In those roles McMullen essentially ran SAC.

McMullen was concerned with efficiency and often intervened to manage the affairs of subordinate commanders. He claimed his motto was, "Give them half of what they ask for; work them twice as hard; and they will get twice as much done."[69] In one letter to a group commander, McMullen complained the supply situation was poorly handled: "I have received several reports which indicate that the commanding officer of your M&S [maintenance and supply] Group is incompetent. It might be a good idea to change him." McMullen noted there was a lieutenant colonel serving as a deputy commander in the 4th Fighter Group. "I don't like deputies," intoned McMullen. "Why don't you make him your M&S group commander?"[70] To another commander he expanded on the problems of supply: "In general, the supply officers that I see in this command are long-faced, non-flying officers who try to make an aurora over their head out of the mystery of supply. There is no mystery in the business of supply." He then wrote, "I desire that you take steps to see that the most intelligent officer in your command is assigned as supply officer." McMullen went further; he noted that five lieutenant colonels in the group were being utilized as operations officers and executive officers. This was a

---

[66] Rosenberg, "US Nuclear Stockpile," 28. Rosenberg argues the stockpile total was the most closely guarded of all atomic secrets and the number of devices was seldom even written down. Within the military, Groves would brief Eisenhower periodically but not the Navy or AAF; the AEC was not even required to brief the Army.

[67] Ibid., 27–28.

[68] Bohn, *Development of Strategic Air Command*, 6–7.

[69] *SAC History—1947*, vol. 1, 42.

[70] McMullen to Taylor, letter, 10 October1947, in *SAC History—1947*, vol. 4, exhibit 195.

waste: "I see no use for an Operations Officer and Executive Officer." He closed by stating that if the colonel could not find more gainful employment for his men, then he would do it for him.[71]

One member of SAC headquarters later said people learned to work around McMullen. One of the deputy's rules was to have the gate guards at Offutt AFB stop cars each morning beginning at 0752 and issue "late citations" to people on their way to work. McMullen deemed it impossible for people to make it to their desk by 0800, the required work time, if they were not on base at least eight minutes earlier. After three such citations, the individuals would be required to report to McMullen with an explanation for their tardiness. Late-comers soon learned how to beat the system; they would wait until 0900—when the guards stopped issuing citations—with the result that some arrived even *later* to work.[72]

One problem was McMullen's undisguised disdain for nonrated officers. The Air Corps and AAF had few nonflyers because the Army's corps system provided quartermaster, ordnance, or logistics experts to run things, allowing the operators to operate. In the new Air Force, nonrated officers were essential for these types of tasks. McMullen thought pilots could handle these responsibilities in their spare time, and Kenney agreed. Indeed, Spaatz had counseled Kenney on this very issue; yet, when some nonrated officers transferred over from the Army in 1948 and were assigned to SAC, Kenney rejected them. Spaatz was mightily irked, writing Kenney, "I have made an effort to explain to you" the Air Force policy on nonrated officers, but Kenney obviously did not get it. "If it is not clear to you at this time, come to me, so report and I will endeavor again to make it clear." The chief of staff expected his SAC commander to follow orders.[73] Kenney was not paying attention.

McMullen hoped to alleviate personnel shortages with a cross-training program. All pilots would train as navigators, bombardiers, flight engineers, and radar operators and become familiar with the gunners' duties. All bombardiers were to be proficient navigators, flight engineers, and radar operators—all crew members were to be cross-trained in several different specialties. McMullen believed this cross-training scheme would negate the effects of personnel short-ages—if a squadron were low on bombardiers, it could temporarily

[71] McMullen to Hudnell, letter, 8 October 1947, in *SAC History—1947*, vol. 2, exhibit 4.
[72] Zimmerman, *Insider at SAC*, 25.
[73] Vance Mitchell, *Air Force Officers*, 69–70.

solve the problem by having a surplus navigator or pilot fly in that crew position instead. McMullen expected it would take four years for the average pilot to complete scheduled training, with less time required for the other crew positions.[74]

The result of this unusual experiment was predictable. Aircrew members were spending so much time learning how to do someone else's job, they forgot how to do their own. Proficiency in SAC's primary mission plummeted. Worse, commanders took to subterfuge. Accurate bomb scores were deemed important by headquarters, so commanders had their crews drop from 15,000 feet—far below what they would be doing in combat—to ensure better scores. Radar bombing was a delicate skill requiring a great deal of practice to distinguish specific targets from normal ground clutter or other geographic features. Crews therefore practiced in good weather so they had a visual backup for their radar drops. When actual radar bombing was required, special reflectors were installed near the Gulf Coast to serve as "targets." Even cross-trained pilots could find the reflectors on their radar scopes.[75] In short, such ploys and Mullen's cross-training program made SAC's combat capability a scandal. Even the official history confessed that it "furthered the cause of breakdown in stability . . . and added to the confusion. . . . It almost destroyed all proficiency in the combat units of SAC."[76]

Kenney was also a concern. He loved to give speeches, especially when he could give dramatic accounts of a future atomic war. Symington encouraged him in this activity—the Air Force needed publicity[77]—Kenney did, however, get carried away. The public relations director at the time, Steve Leo, later testified regarding his "problem child": "George . . . used to think that the way to promote air power was to make speeches before the largest possible audience in which he could forecast that as soon as the enemy bombers dropped a bomb on New York City, radioactive taxicab fenders would be found out beyond Danbury, Connecticut."[78] Leo told Kenney he gave too many speeches and should spend more time at his command. Whitehead concurred, writing his old boss, "If anything should happen and units of the Strategic Air Command be called upon for combat operations, the only

---

[74] SAC History—1947, vol. 1, 85–98. See also Borowski, Hollow Threat, 57–60.

[75] LeMay, interview, 9 March 1971, 37–39.

[76] SAC History—1947, vol. 1, 85.

[77] Kenney, interview, 125.

[78] Leo, interview, 77.

thing which people would remember would be that George Kenney was the commander."[79] Kenney was still not listening.

As the Berlin crisis began to simmer in the spring of 1948 and there was talk of war, SAC's ability to carry out its mission was questioned. General Norstad, then the deputy chief of staff for operations, recalled Secretary Forrestal asking him about SAC's readiness. Norstad replied that the reports stated they were ready for war. Forrestal retorted that he did not care what the reports said; he wanted to know if SAC was ready. Vandenberg, the new chief of staff, thought it prudent to dig more deeply and sent Maj Gen Frederic Smith, his chief personnel officer, to evaluate the SAC manning situation. Smith reported back that it was very bad: in some units one-quarter of the personnel had turned over in a two-month period.[80]

Vandenberg then called in an old friend, Charles Lindbergh, and asked him to investigate SAC readiness. He chose Lindbergh for this and other fact-finding missions because he was a world-renowned aviator. If SAC pilots could not fly or navigators could not navigate, Lindbergh would know quickly. Second, he had enormous prestige and would command respect wherever he went. Third, although a colonel in the Air Force Reserve, he was considered an outsider—he had no axes to grind and would readily gain the confidence of the SAC crews he met. Finally, he was known as an honest straight shooter.[81]

After 10 weeks and over 100 flying hours with SAC crews, Lindbergh returned to Washington and met with Vandenberg. The report was not positive. Lindbergh began by bluntly stating that the standards of performance for an atomic strike force were "inadequate" and the average SAC pilot was less skilled than the average airline pilot. Pilot proficiency was "unsatisfactory, teamwork is not properly developed, and maintenance of aircraft and equipment is inadequate. In general, personnel are not sufficiently experienced in their primary mission." Lindbergh also noted that SAC accident rates were too high, reflective of poor training, and those training missions flown did not simulate combat conditions. He scored the cross-training scheme and the extracurricular activities that interfered with a crew member's primary mission of atomic weapons delivery. He proposed

[79] Whitehead to Kenney, letters, 5 June and 4 July 1948, Whitehead papers, AFHRA, file 168.6008-3.
[80] Vandenberg to Kenney, letter, 10 May 1948, NA, RG 18, file AAJ, box 799; Vandenberg to Kenney, letter, 9 June 1948, Vandenberg papers, LOC, box 32; and Borowski, *Hollow Threat*, 46–47.
[81] Berg, *Lindbergh*, 475–77.

the "integral crew concept"—as in World War II, crews should be standardized and fly together as a unit so they would become familiar with each other's capabilities and habits. This made it more difficult for the squadron scheduler, but the benefits in teamwork and camaraderie were worth the inconvenience. In sum, Lindbergh stressed the need for SAC to concentrate on its primary atomic mission, to do so under simulated wartime conditions, and to eliminate the extraneous activities and counterproductive cross-training program that were wasting valuable time and detracting from mission accomplishment. He also stressed that SAC personnel policy be stabilized and the command be given a higher priority.[82]

At the same time, Vandenberg called in Col Paul W. Tibbets, pilot of the *Enola Gay* and the 509th's first commander. He directed Tibbets to inspect SAC headquarters. Tibbets, like Lindbergh, was well known among SAC aircrews, and he too had a reputation for speaking his mind.[83] His report to Vandenberg was as damning as Lindbergh's: "There isn't anybody out there that knows what the hell they are doing. The crews don't know how to fly an airplane. The staff officers don't know what they are doing."[84]

During this period, the JCS told Vandenberg they wanted a briefing on atomic readiness. Nerves were on edge because of the Berlin situation, and the chiefs wanted to examine SAC's status in the event matters escalated. Vandenberg notified Kenney of the required briefing on 15 September. Norstad later recalled that Kenney's performance was poor; he seemed ill prepared and uninformed. The combination of this gaffe in front of Vandenberg's peers and the negative reports from two of his trusted agents forced action. On 21 September Vandenberg summoned Kenney to his office and relieved him of command. His replacement at SAC was to be Lt Gen Curtis LeMay. That same day Vandenberg ordered the cross-training scheme scrapped and directed SAC to begin concentrating on its primary duties.[85]

This was an important decision. SAC was in trouble, and although not all of it was Kenney's fault, command—by definition—

[82] "Lindbergh Report," 14 September 1948, LeMay papers, LOC, box 61. Another officer, a bomb group commander at the time, later stated Kenney's problem was that he was not a long-range bomber man; he was a medium-bomber expert. Irvine, interview, 16.

[83] In his memoirs, Tibbets wrote of a vocal run-in with Larry Norstad during World War II; speaking his mind had delayed his promotion to brigadier general for several years. Tibbets, *Return of the Enola Gay*, chap. 18.

[84] Tibbets, interview, 43–45. Tibbets does not mention this inspection assignment in his memoirs. In his oral history, he stated that he reported to Gen Nathan F. Twining, but at the time Twining was a commander in Alaska, so his memory was incorrect on this detail.

[85] Norstad, interview, 22 February 1984; and *SAC History—1948*, vol. 1, 265.

means responsibility. Had SAC passed muster, Kenney would have received the accolades; so, too, he had to accept the arrows when things went wrong. After more than two years in command, Kenney had been unable to put SAC on a sound footing. He was absent from headquarters too often and left too much of the day-to-day operation to McMullen, whose cross-training program had become an obsession and a disaster.

The firing rippled throughout the Air Force. Kenney was a decade older than Vandenberg and thought he had been misused since the end of the war; he had not gotten the Air Combat Command he desired, and the UN air force was going nowhere. He was a senior general—he had even outranked Spaatz—and believed he should have been named chief of staff when Spaatz retired. He had backers throughout the service—there were others who believed the Air Force "youth movement" had gone too far and the old guard was being shunted aside.[86] Ennis Whitehead wrote Kenney speculating that the Navy was behind the relief, and Vandenberg—whom he considered a pawn—was forced into action. Whitehead opined that Fairchild (the vice chief of staff), one of the old guard and thus presumably sympathetic to Kenney, was powerless to stop the action, and an ambitious three-star—Norstad apparently—was involved in setting it all up so he could succeed Vandenberg as chief in four years.[87] Whitehead misread the entire incident. Vandenberg was no one's pawn, and it was Kenney's failures that pushed him into action, not the Navy. Those on the scene were aware of SAC's problems—highlighted by the Berlin crisis—and realized that change was necessary.

Before leaving Germany to take up his new command, LeMay called Maj Gen Leon Johnson, who had recently commanded Fifteenth Air Force, and asked him what was wrong with SAC. Johnson replied simply that the cross-training program and the resentment felt by Kenney and McMullen toward all nonflying officers had created a poisonous atmosphere throughout the command. LeMay said that was pretty basic, and Johnson replied, "Yes, Curt, that's all that is wrong with SAC. They are just emphasizing the wrong things." McMullen's training program, for instance, was a sincere attempt not only to do more with less, but also to build a strong officer corps for the future by making it more well rounded and

---

[86] The Air Force was led by a host of unusually young generals during the decade following World War II: Vandenberg, Norstad, LeMay, Twining, Rawlings, Kuter, Quesada, Weyland, Armstrong, et al.

[87] Whitehead to Kenney, letter, 24 September 1948, Whitehead papers, AFHRA, file 168.6008-3.

knowledgeable. This was a useful and visionary goal, but it worked at cross purposes with the immediate goal of making SAC combat ready. It was a question of emphasis.[88] LeMay was listening. He hit SAC like a whirlwind and began to turn it around. The golden age of Strategic Air Command was about to begin, but it would take time, energy, resources, and leadership.

Summary

The Navy feared unification of the armed services. The Army was supportive of reorganization, and Generals Marshall and Eisenhower threw their considerable prestige behind the idea early on, but Navy leaders were able to fight a delaying action for two years. Their reasons for opposing unification were various, and it would be hasty to malign their motives. The admirals sincerely believed unification would be harmful to the Navy, and anything bad for the Navy was also bad for the country. For the AAF, the decades-old dream of independence was synonymous with unification.

The momentum building for change proved irresistible. Soldiers and airmen pushed for unification; so did Congress, and President Truman expressed his strong support. The result was inevitable, although a series of compromises were essential. The Air Force became a separate service. The defense secretary had little real power, and the secretaries for the Army, Navy, and Air Force were of equal cabinet rank with access to the president. In Congress, the committees for War and Navy were combined into an Armed Services Committee in both houses. The secretary of defense was James Forrestal, former secretary of the Navy, and the chairman of the House Armed Services Committee was Carl Vinson—former head of the Naval Affairs Committee.[89] The National Security Act guaranteed that the Marine Corps would not be disbanded and naval aviation would remain with the fleet.

Time would reveal that the establishment was flawed—the National Security Act was revised in 1949 to give the secretary of defense and the new chairman of the Joint Chiefs of Staff more authority. Unfortunately, these changes came too late for Forrestal; he committed

---

[88] Johnson, interview, August 1975, 145–46. Of note, LeMay would later institute a similar cross-training for the B-47; all officers were to be triple rated as pilots, navigators, and bombardiers. Gunderson, interview, 22–23 October 1987, 42.

[89] Two of Forrestal's top three advisors were also former Navy Department officials: Mark Leva, his legal advisor, and RADM Wilfred J. McNeil, the budget director.

suicide in May 1949, overcome by the burdens of a powerless office he had labored so hard to create.

It was not just lack of power that brought down the secretary; it was the constant bickering over roles and missions. These arguments were vocal and severe, and the reason for this is clear—primary responsibility for a given task translated into force structure and budget share. These were battles the services could not afford to lose. All involved understood the weight of these issues, so Forrestal gathered the chiefs at Key West and Newport in a series of tense meetings designed to hammer out the details. The devil was in those details, and making decisions regarding them did not get easier after the law was passed.

In an attempt to quell disagreements, Forrestal designated primary versus collateral functions, but definitions were vague and subject to interpretation. Forrestal thought he had his chiefs on the same page regarding this subject, but events would show otherwise. The major arguments arose over strategic air warfare. The Air Force, and Forrestal for that matter, thought the issue was settled when that function was given to SAC. The Navy disagreed. Forrestal's plaintive sigh that the major question revolved around "what is to be the use, and who is to be user of air power?" was exactly on target. To be clear, this was not a question of airpower's importance, historical utility, or future growth; all the services recognized that airpower was the dominant force in the future wars that anyone in uniform thought might occur. All loved airpower; they loved it so much they wanted their own air arm to ensure they could achieve their military objectives. Questions therefore continually revolved around who would control those dominant air assets and against what objectives they would be directed.

The issues of strategic bombing and who would conduct it spilled over into the area of war plans. Military planners knew the methodologies needed to prepare for future war, but the aftermath of World War II left them in a quandary. Atomic weapons had put matters onto a new plane. Yet President Truman was reticent to address the matter. One historian has termed Truman's foreign policy "vague and inchoate" in the postwar period; he did not know what he wanted.[90] As a consequence, planners had little guidance from the White House on what major threats should concern them or what US goals were in the event of war. It was not even clear whether atomic bombs would be available in sufficient numbers or if they would be authorized for

---

[90] Leffler, "Emergence of an American Grand Strategy," 71–72.

use.[91] As a consequence, military planners *assumed* answers to those questions. The Air Force, SAC, and the joint planners identified the Soviet Union as the main adversary and Britain as the chief ally. They further assumed atomic weapons would be used from the outset of a general war, and the targets for those bombs would be the Soviet industrial infrastructure and its cities. Even given the US monopoly of atomic weapons, planners were pessimistic regarding the outcome of war and believed the Soviets would have little difficulty in overrunning continental Europe. The few and ill-equipped ground divisions opposing them would serve only as speed bumps in the Soviet dash to the English Channel. US war plans therefore assumed an atomic air offensive conducted by SAC would serve as the West's equalizer.

The US Navy's role in these plans was a subject of contention. Early iterations relegated the Navy to the traditional maritime roles of sea control and blockade. By the time of *Bushwhacker* in early 1948, naval airpower was accepted as playing a role in an air campaign against the Soviet Union, but the precise nature of that role was undetermined. By the end of 1949, war plan *Crasspiece* would include a strategic strike role for the Navy's aircraft. This episode, resented by the Air Force, was a crisis-in-waiting that had been brewing since the Key West talks, and it would lead to the mess detailed in the next chapter.

The slow path to an accepted and viable war plan took on increased urgency in mid 1948 when the Soviets blockaded West Berlin. This was a serious provocation, and the United States had a weak hand to play. The secrecy surrounding the atomic energy program continued to hamper SAC's planning efforts. There was but a pitifully small military force in Germany itself. Gen Curtis LeMay, the USAFE commander, later stated ruefully that there was not one American soldier between his headquarters at Wiesbaden and the Soviet border. The war plans were not adequate, and the forces were not available to conduct a serious defense if the Soviets did elect to escalate matters. Even so, SAC formalized its rotation schedule to Europe, and by the end of 1948, three groups were continually deployed there. The 3rd Air Division was established in Britain to handle this semipermanent SAC presence. Of importance, elements of SAC's 56th Fighter Group were also deployed to Britain in July, the first jet fighters (F-80s) to cross the ocean. The wondrous airlift was to be the salvation of Berlin—this

---

[91] Not until September 1948 would Truman endorse the use of atomic weapons, which he did in NSC-30, 10 September 1948, in US Department of State, *FRUS, 1948*, vol. I, 628.

was airpower backed by airpower—and the Air Force basked in the glow of a major foreign policy success. But this positive outcome could not hide other problems.

In the midst of the Berlin crisis the JCS wanted to look more closely into the affairs of SAC—the organization that was to spearhead any offensive action the United States would take. Their concern led Vandenberg to conduct his own investigation. What he saw angered him. SAC was not ready for war. There were some reasons for this failure—demobilization and constrained budgets—that were endemic throughout the Air Force, but the onus of responsibility fell on the SAC commander. Aircraft in-commission rates throughout 1947 and 1948 had hovered around 50 percent, and this became embarrassingly apparent in May 1947 when Kenney ordered a maximum-effort training exercise to "bomb" New York City. There were supposed to be 180 aircraft participating in the simulated attack, but only 101 actually arrived over the city. This was a sad situation, so in August SAC tried again, against Chicago, but the performance was even worse.[92] During the Berlin crisis the situation became more precarious. Gen George Kenney had been in charge since February 1946—he had had over two years to straighten things out. It was clear to Vandenberg that drastic action was needed.

Throughout these events were the usual threads that have continued to reappear in this story. The mission of strategic bombing, ever more critical in the atomic era, continued to be trumpeted by airmen as their raison d'être. Initially, they were bolstered by the fact that atomic bombs were so large and heavy only aircraft like the B-29 could carry them. But by 1948 airmen were beginning to realize they would not be able to maintain a monopoly on atomic delivery indefinitely. As one anonymous Air Staff officer wrote, SAC did not have a divine right to be the sole proprietor of the atomic bomb: "If the Greyhound Bus Company can demonstrate a capability of delivering bombs better than any other agency, that company will get the job, irrespective of any Key West or Newport agreements."[93] The recognition of this statement's brutal accuracy no doubt gave airmen additional strength as they fought the battles over unification, roles and missions, and war plans.

---

[92] *SAC History—1947*, vol. 1, 185–86.
[93] Little and Bowen, *History of the Air Force Atomic Energy Program*, vol. 2, 152.

One glaring revelation of the war-planning experience was the overriding importance of intelligence and its role in air targeting. As was painfully discovered during World War II, economic and industrial intelligence of a potential adversary was critical to planning an effective strategic air campaign. Yet American intelligence regarding the Soviet Union was inadequate. The apparatus built during the war to study the German and Japanese economic and military infrastructures would have to be recreated. Throughout the period covered in this chapter, intelligence regarding the Soviet Union was so poor as to make a viable targeting plan impossible. It was not coincidental that early war plans either avoided this subject altogether or merely provided a list of major Soviet cities slated for attack. Although the destructive power of atomic weapons might have encouraged air planners to depreciate the need for pinpoint targeting, this was a subterfuge, and airmen knew it. The surprise was that SAC could extol the decisiveness of atomic air attack without ever having to give detailed information on what those attacks would hit and what would be the effect of the hitting.

Leadership continued to be decisive in every endeavor. Carl Spaatz saw the AAF through the rocky years following VJ-Day and then on to unification. Keeping things together while his service disintegrated around him and the budget was slashed was a major challenge. His successor, Hoyt Vandenberg, was confronted with an even greater challenge—the Berlin crisis—almost as soon as he moved into his new office. Despite some minor missteps, the Berlin airlift was overall a ringing success. The commander in Germany, Curtis LeMay, was an outstanding officer and commander, but Vandenberg realized that a special expertise was required to run such a huge air transport operation.[94] Vandenberg's designation of William Tunner as airlift commander was the obvious and correct step.

Regarding SAC, the leadership issue was even more important. George Kenney had been one of the best air commanders in World War II. He had fought a brilliant air war in a distant theater with scant resources. He expected to return from the Pacific and command the AAF and the new Air Force. That was not to be, but Kenney accepted these disappointments with grace. His designation as the first SAC commander was weighty enough—as we have seen, the entire US military establishment viewed SAC as the tip of the spear in any future

---

[94] For an excellent biography of Tunner, see Slayton, *Master of the Air*.

conflict. But Kenney was not up to the task. Perhaps he was, as some suggested, too "political" and had his eye on greater goals; perhaps he was worn out by the long war he had already fought.[95] In any event, poor leadership put his command in a downward spiral too perilous to ignore when the Berlin crisis hit. Not only did he not wield a strong enough hand, he allowed his deputy, Clements McMullen, to institute a counterproductive cross-training program. To be clear, the motives of McMullen and Kenney were not base. Both men were dealt a weak hand with the demobilization and cutbacks that hit the Air Force and SAC. The belief that economy was necessary and the command needed to do more with less was a realistic response to the problems encountered. Recall that before World War II it was not unusual for pilots to double as navigators or bombardiers. LeMay himself was an outstanding and largely self-taught navigator at a time when the Air Corps did not train crew members for that specific position.[96] McMullen was merely attempting to institutionalize a practice that he and countless others had experienced as young officers before the war.[97] But now, the complexity of modern aircraft and related technology made such cross-training notions unworkable. At the same time Kenney was relieved, McMullen was replaced by Maj Gen Thomas S. Power.[98]

Vandenberg saw the need for change and took the necessary steps. LeMay later stated that when the chief gave him SAC, his orders were simple and direct: get the command ready to fight. There were no details provided on how to make that happen. Vandenberg did, however, give him a caution: experience demonstrated that a new unit generally performed poorly in its first fight. That could no longer be

---

[95] In March 1943, Kenney had visited Senator Arthur Vandenberg and other Republican Party leaders in Washington to discuss possible plans for a presidential candidacy for General MacArthur. The senator was the uncle of Gen Hoyt Vandenberg, and the two men were very close; undoubtedly, the latter knew of Kenney's political dalliance. Arthur H. Vandenberg personal diaries, vol. 15, 33, Arthur H. Vandenberg papers, Bentley Library, Ann Arbor, MI; and A. Vandenberg to MacArthur, letters, 17 August and 16 September 1943, RG 10, Box 1, MacArthur Archives, Norfolk, VA.

[96] LeMay, interview, 17 November 1976, 15–17. The Air Corps did not train officers for the navigator crew position until 1940. Before that time all flying officers were pilots and were expected to understand how to navigate over land and water. As aircraft like the B-17 developed long-range capabilities, this "additional duty" mentality came to an end. For the story, see Wright, *Most Probable Position*, chap. 7.

[97] McMullen went on to command the Air Materiel Area Depot at San Antonio, TX. A SAC maintenance commander at nearby Biggs AFB was having difficulty obtaining sufficient spare parts for his aircraft. He went to McMullen, who was extremely helpful—a class act. Montgomery, interview, 28–30 June 1983, 139–40. Montgomery would later become the SAC chief of staff.

[98] Power had flown B-24s in North Africa and Italy during the war, and then transitioned into B-29s and flew as part of the XXI Bomber Command out of Guam. Following the war he worked on the Air Staff, participated in the Crossroads atomic tests in 1946, and was slated to become the air attaché to Britain when LeMay tabbed him to be his deputy.

allowed to happen; SAC must be ready at the outbreak of war, not the following week.[99] SAC must be put on a perpetual war footing. Paradoxically, it could be argued that Kenney had put message ahead of mission—he strove so hard to sell SAC to politicians and the public that he neglected to see to the actual capabilities of his command. LeMay would not make that mistake.

---

[99] LeMay, interview, 17 November 1976, 32.

Chapter 5

Expansion and Adversity

Curtis LeMay rivals Billy Mitchell both in terms of importance and controversial careers. Born and raised in Columbus, Ohio, LeMay earned his commission through the Reserve Officer Training Corps in 1928 while working toward an engineering degree at Ohio State University. He won his wings the following year, and, although beginning as a pursuit pilot, in 1936 he moved to bombardment. LeMay arrived at the 2nd Bomb Group about the same time as the new YB-17s and over the next decade became known as one of the best navigators and pilots in the Air Corps. In 1937 he located the battleship *Utah* in exercises off California and "bombed" it with water bombs, despite receiving the wrong coordinates from the Navy.[1] The following year, he navigated B-17s 600 miles out to sea to intercept the ocean liner *Rex*, illustrating airpower's ability to defend American coasts from a seaborne invasion. In 1938 LeMay led B-17s to South America to display airpower's range and its role in hemisphere defense. War brought rapid promotion.

LeMay began the war as a group commander in the Eighth Air Force, but in 18 months he progressed from lieutenant colonel to major general and was an air division commander. He led from the front while also earning a reputation as an innovative tactician and problem solver, so when Hap Arnold had difficulty with the B-29 program, he chose LeMay to spur the program and then take over B-29 activities in India. Although these operations were not successful and eventually were halted due to excessive distances and logistical problems, LeMay's energy and ability continued to impress Arnold. In December 1944, the chief selected him to take over as commander of the XXI Bomber Command in the Mariana Islands. From there, the conclusive bombing assault against the Japanese home islands was planned and conducted.

Not long after taking over in the Marianas, LeMay took the risky and controversial step of abandoning the long-held American doctrine of high-altitude, daylight precision bombing; instead, he stripped his planes of armor and guns, loaded them with incendiaries, and sent

[1] LeMay, interview, 17 November 1976, 92–95.

them against Japanese cities at night and at low level. As we saw, this proved remarkably successful. Returning to the States, LeMay served two years as the head of the AAF's R&D effort and in October 1947 was named USAFE commander. He was there during the early months of the Berlin crisis, and on an inspection visit to Berlin, Vandenberg was impressed by his ability to get things done. When the chief needed a new leader at SAC, LeMay was the obvious choice; he possessed an indomitable will and an unshakeable faith in the efficacy of strategic airpower.

LeMay's personality was the subject of frequent caricature. He was unsophisticated, taciturn, tactless, hard working, and courageous. He led his bomb group on the Schweinfurt-Regensburg mission of August 1943, and while SAC commander stated that if his men went to war, he would be in the first plane. At the same time, he was a good family man and a doting father. He was sincerely concerned about his troops and labored to improve their food, housing, and recreation facilities. In the austere areas where many SAC bases were sited, this was important. In one letter LeMay noted that "pay alone is not a primary incentive." He wrote that "there must be a vital concern throughout SAC" for "individual consideration and firm personal guidance for our airmen."[2] In another letter, he wrote that "junior and senior officers who cannot or will not recognize the requirements to provide incentives other than pay for personnel under their command will not be promoted to higher grade."[3]

LeMay believed people wanted to work hard but needed incentives and leadership as well as recreation to recharge their batteries. For his part, he loved guns, hunting, fishing, and working on cars. He wanted all SAC bases to have an auto hobby shop in case there were others like him who found relaxation in overhauling a car engine.[4] He also pushed hard for better housing. Although hundreds of air bases had been built during the war, these temporary facilities were of substandard construction. LeMay devised a scheme to have a SAC Housing Association borrow money and then lease land to air bases so they could erect family housing units.[5] Although the plan fell through, it

---

[2] LeMay to O'Donnell, letter, 9 February 1949, in *SAC History—1949*, vol. 2, exhibit 20.

[3] LeMay to Vandenberg, letter, 9 February 1949, in *SAC History—1949*, vol. 2, exhibit 21.

[4] For the best biography of LeMay to date, see Coffey, *Iron Eagle*. For his autobiography, see LeMay with Kantor, *Mission with LeMay*.

[5] *SAC History—1949*, vol. 1, 252–58. Eventually, LeMay sat down with Nebraska senator Kenneth S. Wherry and asked for help. Wherry was sympathetic and pushed through legislation, patterned on the SAC Housing Association idea, which allowed government subsidies for base housing. The family units subsequently built were referred to as "Wherry Housing."

alerted politicians in Washington to the plight of SAC airmen while also sending a strong message through the command that LeMay was serious about improving conditions. Open-bay barracks built for enlisted troops by the Army's Corps of Engineers were to him an outdated concept; he wanted airmen in dormitories—two to a room—so they would have a better lifestyle. The Army objected, so LeMay had them built by local contractors. He had a group of wives select colors, drapes, and furniture to make the dorms more livable.[6] Although LeMay was known as tough and uncompromising, those who knew him best said he had a soft heart. He seldom became visibly angry or raised his voice. He cared about people and their welfare—but the mission came first. One of his comments regarding someone who was relieved because of an unfortunate accident was typical: "I can't tell the difference between unlucky and unskilled because the results are the same."[7] Above all, he demanded results, and unlike his predecessor, he had no innate prejudice against nonflying officers; in fact, when he became chief of staff in 1961, he selected William F. McKee as his vice—the first nonrated full general in Air Force history. McKee was an outstanding officer, and that is why he was promoted.

LeMay believed in education, and as warfare—especially air warfare—became more complex, the entire Air Force needed to be better educated to deal with that complexity. He wanted his officers and enlisted personnel to attend the military schools, and he also favored sending select individuals to civilian colleges to receive graduate degrees.[8] Yet he was emphatic that having brilliant people around him was not the key to success: "I'd much rather operate with a group of average individuals that were [*sic*] highly motivated." He expected his people to work hard and to operate as part of a team: "With this sort of a set-up you can build an organization, not around any one individual, but around a whole team that will function and continue to function even though you lose some members."[9] He practiced what he preached.

LeMay used his staff efficiently and effectively. He seldom gave detailed directives but provided subordinates the authority to use their judgment. The operations analysis chief at SAC watched LeMay operate for nine years and concluded his management style worked.

---

[6] LeMay, interview, 17 November 1976, 168–70; and Coffey, *Iron Eagle*, 295–96.
[7] Carlton, interview, 30 September 1980, 79.
[8] LeMay, interview, March 1965, 14.
[9] Ibid., 12.

> LeMay's reliance on the people he selected for senior positions [allowed] him
> time to be available on short notice. By concentrating on basic strategies and
> major decisions, while depending on his staff to formulate them, he escaped
> the trap of a bulging schedule that would have made mature planning diffi-
> cult. As a result, he was able to stay in complete control of SAC's operations,
> while being one of the most available persons in the headquarters.[10]

The stories told of LeMay and quotes attributed to him are legion. Although most are apocryphal, they were widely circulated and added to his mystique. He once entered a hangar and found it guarded only by an airman with a ham sandwich. He drove through a gate at one SAC base without stopping; the gate guard pulled out his sidearm and shot at the car. LeMay slammed on the brakes, got out, and berated the cop—for missing. One day he grew suspicious of a telephone re-pairman in his office; he pulled out his .45 and held the man prisoner until the air police arrived. At one of his bases an air policeman found an intruder in the nuclear weapons storage area, ordered the intruder to halt, and then fired a warning shot. When the individual kept run-ning, he shot and killed the man. The wing commander called LeMay and asked for guidance on how to handle the situation. LeMay told him to make the sky cop pay for the bullet he wasted on the warning shot.[11] He would fly into a base unannounced and declare to the wing commander that we were going to war: launch the force—with weap-ons. He would then watch for an hour or two to see how things were progressing before cancelling the alert. When asked whom he favored in the upcoming Army-Navy football game, he growled, "I hope they both lose." His cigar, both lit and unlit, became his trademark. (LeMay had Bell's palsy, a malady that affects the facial muscles, making it dif-ficult to keep the mouth from sagging. He usually had a cigar in his mouth to help strengthen those muscles.) While the general was standing next to a bomber being refueled, a maintenance officer asked him to extinguish his stogie before it blew up the entire base. LeMay's reply: it wouldn't dare. When someone called him a tough guy, he retorted that he didn't mind: he found that in his business it was the tough guys who led the survivors. He would need to be tough to deal with the many challenges facing his command.

---

[10] Zimmerman, *Insider at SAC*, 34.
[11] Montgomery, interview, 30 April–1 May 1984, 99.

Reforging the Weapon

One LeMay legend concerns "the attack on Dayton." After talking to his commanders and staff, he realized that they "weren't worth a damn." Unfortunately, they did not realize how bad they were, so he decided to show them. He announced an alert—a maximum effort of all SAC bombers to carry out a simulated attack on Dayton, Ohio. The strike would be made from high altitude, at night in lousy weather, using radar bombing techniques. According to LeMay, not one aircraft completed the mission as briefed.[12] The SAC history is not quite that damning, but it notes that the results of the mock attack were poor. For example, of 15 aircraft scheduled in one B-36 bomb group, six aborted and three others failed to "drop" over the target due to radar malfunctions. The story was the same in several other groups, and in still others aircraft that made it to the target were unable to return to their home airfields and had to divert elsewhere. Targeting accuracy on bomb drops was appalling, with an average miss distance of two miles.[13] LeMay had made his point.

The general then began to strip down the command and remake it. The three numbered air forces were reshuffled. This had been needed for some time: it made no sense to have a bomb wing at MacDill AFB in Florida assigned to the Fifteenth Air Force, headquartered in California. The air forces also had been organized along functional lines: the Eighth had mostly B-50s, while the Fifteenth flew largely B-29s; the Second Air Force contained all reconnaissance assets. LeMay made all three composite units with a mix of very heavy bombers (the new B-36s coming on line), mediums (B-29s and B-50s), a reconnaissance wing, and fighter escorts. This commonsense reorganization saved money, cut communication and travel time, and allowed for better combat training.

At the base level, the so-called Hobson plan was by this time fully implemented across the Air Force. Instead of the standard group designation, a wing now became the parent organization on base with two groups under it: an operational group of bombers, reconnaissance, fighters, or some mix thereof and an air base group consisting of maintenance, supply, administrative, and financial staff. The wing commander, a full colonel, was now in command of all units needed

---

[12] LeMay, interview, 9 March 1971, 37; and LeMay with Kantor, *Mission with LeMay*, 432–33.

[13] *SAC History—1950*, vol. 1, 76; and Clark to 7BW, letter, 17 January 1949, in *SAC History—1950*, vol. 4, exhibit 3. Dayton had not been used by SAC as a target previously, making it an honest test for bomber crews.

to carry out the assigned mission.[14] At the same time, the Air Force was introducing a new management system entailing comptrollers assigned to each command to help systematize financial planning and budgeting matters. Right behind these individuals would be computers; the Air Force pushed for their inclusion long before the other services.[15] These initiatives were not LeMay's doing, but he embraced them because they appealed to his sense of command responsibility and sound management.

Personnel issues remained: when Air Force headquarters imposed new cuts, LeMay wrote in exasperation that the efficiencies his reorganization was providing "will be accomplished only in time to be cancelled out by the cuts your office proposes."[16] In truth, the cuts and personnel shortages were a specialization concern. The aggregate numbers of personnel at SAC were close to the authorized strength. Although not at full manning, the debilitating era of units with less than half their complements was becoming a bad memory. Yet a lack of specialized people for radar, electronics, and engine maintenance remained problematic. In late 1949, for example, persistent B-29 engine problems caused most to be grounded until spare parts could be obtained and repairs made. Similarly, the B-36 was experiencing the typical troubles of any new aircraft: engines, exhaust systems, radars, defrosting systems, and fuel leaks.[17] A "maintenance control" system was installed at base level that centralized flight maintenance functions for better efficiency and permitted a crew chief and a limited number of mechanics to work on a single aircraft—they became the "owners" of the plane and were expected to know and understand all of its individual quirks and problems, thereby forestalling difficulties.

Vandenberg continued to prod LeMay, writing in September 1948 that he hoped the deficiencies noted in the Lindbergh report would be quickly addressed.[18] After the first of the year, Vandenberg sent Lindbergh back on another inspection trip. His report was better than the previous one but not by much. He began by stating, "The actual striking power of our Air Force is much lower than its numerical strength and material quality indicate." Lindbergh cited inadequate training and "diversion from the primary mission." He

---

[14] These organizational/administrative changes are covered in the SAC histories for 1948–50.

[15] These items are noted in the official history, but for insight from the man who pushed them, see Rawlings, *Born to Fly*, chaps. 6 and 7.

[16] LeMay to Norstad, letter, 28 May 1949, in *SAC History—1949*, vol. 2, exhibits not numbered.

[17] *SAC History—1949*, vol. 1, 252–58.

[18] Vandenberg to LeMay, letter, 21 September 1948, LeMay papers, LOC, box 61.

noted examples of poor flying: "I was present on two occasions when a B-29 squadron from England turned back to its home base rather than land under instrument conditions, which were above normal minimums in the first instance and bordering on VFR [visual flight rules] below 3,000 feet in the second instance. The GCA [ground controlled approach] radar was operating." Many B-29 crew members were "seriously concerned" because of the high accident rates in their group and inexperience of some pilots. Inadequate housing conditions remained a trouble spot, but he noted that LeMay was working on this problem.[19] Overall, SAC still had a long way to go.

LeMay could understand these types of problems and knew that hard work, more training, and better managerial skills could handle them soon enough. Other matters were more serious and dumbfounded him. In November 1948 he wrote to Vandenberg that two dispersal bases he visited were in shocking condition and "without even primitive operational facilities such as suitable control towers, radio aids, night lighting, crash and fire equipment, etc. As we are responsible for dropping the atomic bomb, I maintain that to be unable to dispatch aircraft into and out of these fields at night during marginal weather is ridiculous." He argued, "We must get top priority in filling the gaps in our atomic program."[20] It was a great help when Vandenberg put SAC and its combat efficiency at the top of his agenda, but it did not happen immediately. Not until October 1949 did the chief of staff direct that "first priority to those units comprising the Strategic Striking Force would be provided."[21] This move was long overdue.

For some time, airmen on the Military Liaison Committee and the Armed Forces Special Weapons Project had been complaining that the Air Force was not taking its atomic responsibilities seriously. In January 1948, Maj Gen William Kepner said the atomic energy program in the Air Force was "infirm." He urged a servicewide education program so airmen would understand the importance of the atomic mission. He also called for immediate action to "enunciate a policy giving atomic warfare an overriding priority."[22] Two months later, a board chaired by Gen Joseph McNarney issued a report on the subject almost brutal in its starkness. It stated that the Air Force "has not established complete strategic and operational plans for carrying out

[19] Lindbergh to Vandenberg, letter, 14 February 1949, Vandenberg papers, LOC, box 32.
[20] Little and Bowen, *History of the Air Force Atomic Energy Program*, vol. 2, 508.
[21] *SAC History—1949*, vol. 1, 20.
[22] Little and Bowen, *History of the Air Force Atomic Energy Program*, vol. 2, 152–53.

its mission of strategic atomic air warfare." The service needed to define its primary atomic mission and make clear what forces, training, equipment, logistics support, and basing were required to carry out that mission. Taking a swipe at leadership, McNarney stated, "This can be done adequately only by the top USAF planning and intelligence staffs, with assistance as required from Air University, SAC, AMC [Air Materiel Command], the Special Weapons Group, and others as may be necessary. It is not a committee job, not a job to be deposited in any other extracurricular staff agency." He reiterated that point: "atomic warfare must become the business of the Air Staff and the Command, not relegated to one agency such as the Special Weapons Group."[23] Regrettably, this report hit just as the Berlin crisis began to unfold, which was soon followed by the relief of Kenney. As a consequence, matters were still allowed to drift.

The following year another study, this one chaired by the vice-chief, General Fairchild, arrived at a similar conclusion: the central nature of atomic matters, and by extension SAC, to the Air Force mission.[24] It was soon after this report that Vandenberg issued his statement announcing SAC was the service's top priority. This was welcome news to LeMay and his command, but a pronouncement was only the first step.

What concerned LeMay most, and in fairness was a problem recognized by his predecessors, was that of accuracy. Crew bomb scores were inadequate and had to be improved. In a letter from General Fairchild to Kenney in mid 1948, the vice-chief had hit this point hard, noting that Airmen had become complacent about accuracy. Strategic bombing was all about putting bombs on target, but too many Airmen were reliant on atomic weapons to solve the problem for them. Fairchild argued that the paucity of atomic weapons meant a "shot-gun fashion" approach to bombing, as had been the case with ordinary bombs, would no longer work. Instead, commanders needed to think in terms of having a rifle with one cartridge and very few men; accuracy with that cartridge—the atomic bomb—was paramount. Fairchild concluded forcefully that "single bomb precision will be the measure of merit of bombing accuracy."[25]

LeMay agreed and was given a boost when deployments to Europe eased as the Berlin crisis ended. Instead of three bomb wings rotating

---

[23] Ibid., 155–57.
[24] Ibid., 162–63.
[25] Fairchild to Kenney, letter, 12 July 1948, in *SAC History—1948*, vol. 5, exhibit 127.

to Germany and Britain, only two were required. He requested that this lightened schedule be maintained while SAC transitioned to B-36s.[26] In addition, Arctic exercises and deployments were scaled back while the Berlin airlift was in progress and were not reinstated at its conclusion—the realization that such operations were far more difficult than anticipated was dawning on air leaders. Mapping projects also were curtailed, as were antisubmarine drills and sea searches.[27] All of this meant that SAC could begin focusing on its primary mission, which to LeMay was bombing accurately in simulated wartime conditions. This meant that exercise targets were changed frequently, as were aim points, altitudes, and run-in headings, to prevent crews becoming too familiar with training routines and thereby gaining inflated bomb scores. At the same time, crews used detailed radar surveys of US cities as training guides.[28] LeMay recalled these surveys as being extremely important:

> The first thing we did was pick out Baltimore (the city most like European cities) and God, I don't know how many thousands of pictures (scope pictures) we had from all directions and all altitudes and angles of Baltimore. Then you start making these plates for the trainer. You take a photograph and try to make out what the reflection is going to be like from the photographs and make a plate and compare it with the actual scope photo . . . and they kept getting better and better, so the plates were pretty good. We made a plate for all of our targets based on the photography we had or whatever information we had. Then they could make runs on their targets. Every crew had thousands and thousands of runs on his target with the information that we had, and we had a lot of photography. The Germans had photographed Russia pretty well up to Moscow, and we had all of that.[29]

In addition, radar bomb-scoring (RBS) detachments were deployed throughout the United States using sophisticated wind-measuring instruments and radar to determine the accuracy of simulated bomb drops. The use of RBS units increased dramatically under LeMay: in 1946 SAC logged 888 radar bomb runs; in 1950 that number leapt to 43,722.[30] These radar specialists also realized they could do more than measure results; they could assist a crew's bombing effort.

---

[26] LeMay to Norstad, letter, 8 March 1949, in *SAC History—1949*, vol. 3, exhibit 83.

[27] The comments of one squadron commander were apposite: "It seemed to our crews that the main objective of aerial warfare is to destroy the submarine at its source, i.e., in port, manufacturing bases, dens, and by blocking harbor entrances." *SAC History—1948*, vol. 1, 294.

[28] *SAC History—1950*, vol. 1, 88–96; and Garland to LeMay, letter, 2 March 1949, in *SAC History—1950*, exhibit 1.

[29] LeMay, interview, 4 June 1984, 12.

[30] "Radar Bomb Scoring Activities in Strategic Air Command: Origins and Growth Through 1951," SAC historical study, 13 May 1952, AFHRA, file K416.01-59, 9–11.

During the Korean War these teams deployed to Korea to aid B-29s on their bombing missions.[31]

A "gross error board" was established to review the problems of bombing inaccuracy and recommend corrective action. Operational readiness tests had been instituted in early 1948, but LeMay refocused them to emphasize flying, radar bombing, the in-commission rate of aircraft, and the ability to sustain a maximum effort over a period of several days. This was the birth of the dreaded ORI—the operational readiness inspections in which teams would fly into a SAC base unannounced and tell the wing or air division commander to assume war had broken out and to execute the unit's part of the war plan.[32] LeMay expected every wing to score at least 90 percent on these ORIs—in 1949 only three did so, while six others rated fair, and two were deficient. Work needed to be done. In addition, the bombing competition held in June 1948 was institutionalized and held annually. Crews from each bomb group would drop a series of simulated bombs from 25,000 feet using radar.[33] The winning crews returned home as heroes. Rivalry between the wings grew, and so did morale.

Undoubtedly, equipment problems were partly to blame for the poor bomb scores endemic throughout SAC, and LeMay directed his operations analysis division to look into the problem. As during the war, these mathematically minded problem solvers studied the situation thoroughly before concluding that radar equipment currently used was deficient; although newer versions were getting better, truly effective radars were still in the future. As a result, "we must continue to think in terms of personnel and techniques . . . and improvement henceforth will result mainly from exploitation of and concentration on many details at crew, command, and headquarters level." The main culprit, according to analysts, was consistency. There were too many techniques and procedures being utilized by crews and instructors— SAC needed to standardize its methods.[34] This would become a theme for the command in the years ahead.

The most significant initiative to improve SAC bombing accuracy was the Lead Crew School. LeMay had instituted such programs while a commander during World War II and decided to replicate the

---

[31] Ibid.

[32] The tone and drama of an ORI is well captured in the popular 1963 film, *A Gathering of Eagles.*

[33] *SAC History—1950*, vol. 1, 98–105.

[34] Dwyer to Zimmerman, memorandum, 30 September 1949, in *SAC History—1950*, vol. 4, exhibit 5. Note that the operations research (OR) of World War II was now operations analysis.

practice in SAC. While a division commander in England, he had noted how the crews never knew what target they were going to strike until the morning briefing. Afterwards they would scramble to prepare for the mission. The navigators and bombardiers needed more time. He began pulling certain crews aside and had them devote their entire preflight time to studying the target, its topography, landmarks, and distinguishing characteristics. That way, if weather was marginal over the target, these select crews would be better able to pick out their aiming points and targets. His technique worked; his division achieved greater accuracy, and soon the other air divisions adopted the same procedure.[35]

In June 1949 LeMay established SAC's Lead Crew School at Walker AFB, formerly Roswell Army Air Field, in New Mexico. There crews trained together in a standardized and uniform pattern. Each wing sent three crews to each class, where most training was in the air, although classroom academics were included. The school got off to a rocky start: half of the first class did not even graduate. Problems noted were poor aircraft maintenance on the planes—especially the radars—and crew inexperience. Although wings had been told to send their best crews, some commanders were not yet convinced of the school's utility; they sent people who were available and not necessarily crack troops. That attitude soon changed. By the time the Lead School had moved to MacDill AFB in January 1950, it was already establishing a reputation.[36] Each class performed progressively better, and after eight cycles, bomb scores had improved by over 50 percent. The intent was for these crews to return to their units and instruct the other crews on what they had learned, slowly but noticeably improving the performance of SAC.[37]

In December 1949, LeMay pushed through another radical idea—spot promotions. He met with Generals Idwal H. Edwards (deputy chief of staff for personnel) and Vandenberg, convincing them to allow him to promote lead crew members temporarily "on the spot" to the next grade. Winning bomb competition crews would receive promotions as well. The intent was to improve morale, give all a heightened sense of purpose and competition, and confirm that SAC was the premier organization in the Air Force. LeMay recognized this

---

[35] LeMay, interview, March 1965, 9–16.

[36] *SAC History—1949*, vol. 1, 133–38.

[37] *SAC History—1950*, vol. 1, 106–27. The best drop score from the eighth Lead School class was 1,650 feet—about the same as the Bikini miss in April 1946. Clearly, SAC still had a way to go.

would cause irritation within the service, so he made it clear that spot promotions would be based on merit and *continued* outstanding performance: "I intend to make an example of the first officer I find who has relaxed now that he has made temporary captain as a crew member." If a crew failed a check flight, the entire crew would lose their spot promotions. The first year LeMay promoted 237 officers. In 1950 he asked for and received permission to spot-promote higher grade officers as well.[38]

Yet, other factors outside of SAC remained sources of angst. In one of the many stories told of LeMay, during a briefing a young captain referred to the Soviets as "enemies." The general allegedly interrupted him and said, "Young man, the Soviets are our adversaries; the Navy is our enemy." He had some history for believing so.[39]

The Revolt of the Admirals

Disagreement over roles and missions erupted into one of the nastiest interservice fights in American history. The accords reached at Key West and Newport were quickly revealed as inadequate. The issue, as Secretary Forrestal had feared, concerned the function of strategic bombing. Although the Navy had that task only as a collateral function, it laid plans for building a "supercarrier" designed to carry multiengine bombers. These aircraft were to be used, among other things, to deliver atomic weapons.

The supercarrier had been under discussion in the JCS for some time. Forrestal agreed the Navy could build one such ship, but not an entire class, and then only with JCS concurrence.[40] Chief of naval operations, ADM Louis Denfeld, ignored Forrestal's qualifications and announced the carrier had been authorized. Spaatz, who had been at Key West when Forrestal expressed his views, angrily protested Denfeld's statement, so Forrestal referred the matter to the JCS. Denfeld and Gen Omar Bradley, the Army chief of staff, approved the ship, but Vandenberg, now chief, disagreed stating, "I have not felt, nor do I now feel, that I can give my approval to the 65,000-ton carrier

---

[38] *SAC History—1949*, vol. 1, 16. For a good discussion of the spot promotion system and its importance as a symbol of SAC culture, see Dealile, "SAC Mentality," 217–22 (unpub.).

[39] LeMay once commented, "I spent 80 percent of my time fighting the Navy [during World War II], and 20 percent of my time fighting the Japs." He had major fights with the Navy over supplies and targeting during the war. LeMay, interview, 16 November 1972, 19.

[40] Millis and Duffield, *Forrestal Diaries*, 393, 467; and "Press Release for Secretary Forrestal," 26 March 1948, in "Public Statements by the Secretaries of Defense" microfilm collection, UPA, reel 1.

project."[41] Congress, unaware of Forrestal's earlier comments or the dissents from Spaatz and Vandenberg, assumed all was well and approved funds for the ship.

The matter was not closed; the Navy established a secret office on its Pentagon staff, OP-23, to lobby behind the scenes for the supercarrier. Secretary of the Navy John L. Sullivan was not told about this office, which one observer stated was up to "dirty business," and when he found out about its existence ordered it disbanded.[42] The Air Force had its own consultants looking at the issue and preparing arguments against the ship's construction. On 18 April 1949, the keel of the USS *United States* was laid, and it appeared the Navy had won. But Forrestal had resigned the previous month, and his successor was Louis Johnson, an aggressive and politically oriented businessman. Upon taking office, Johnson declared he had no preconceived notions regarding the supercarrier, but the dissension it was causing was a concern. He asked the JCS to review the issue once again and report back to him.[43]

Denfeld responded that the new carrier's enhanced size and flush-top construction (there would be no "island" on the edge) allowed increased capability. Yes, the *United States* would be able to operate heavier, multiengine aircraft that could employ "more complex armaments"—atomic weapons—but it could also carry a larger number of smaller aircraft. The new carrier was an evolutionary step allowing greater air operations in support of the fleet.[44]

Vandenberg argued the ship was simply unnecessary and a waste of money—total cost of the carrier, its aircraft, and defensive screen would be $1.265 billion—8 percent of the entire annual defense budget. He also argued the ship was highly vulnerable and the Navy was "putting all of its eggs in one fragile basket." He referred to the agreements of the previous year—the Air Force was responsible for strategic bombing; let the Navy tend to sea control, antisubmarine warfare, and mine laying.[45]

These arguments had become standard fare. The surprise came from Bradley who now changed his opinion, agreeing with the Air

[41] Vandenberg to Forrestal, memorandum, 26 May 1949, Vandenberg papers, LOC, box 52.

[42] Vincent Davis, *Admirals Lobby*, 288–89; and Hammond, *Super Carriers and B–36 Bombers*, 39.

[43] Allen and Shannon, *Truman Merry-Go-Round*, 446; and "Mr. Secretary Johnson," *Newsweek*, 25 July 1949, 19.

[44] Denfeld to Johnson, memorandum, 22 April 1949, Vandenberg papers, LOC, box 52. The *United States* would be 158 feet longer and 77 feet wider than the largest existing carrier at the time, the *Midway*.

[45] "Supercarrier Study," 28 March 1949, Vandenberg papers, LOC, box 97; and Vandenberg to Johnson, memorandum, 23 April 1949, Vandenberg papers, LOC, box 52.

Force: "The Navy's mission as agreed to by the Joint Chiefs was to conduct naval campaigns designed primarily to protect lines of communication leading to important sources of raw materials and to areas of projected military operations." The supercarrier, added Bradley, was being built for strategic air operations, and that was not the Navy's primary function. The *United States* was too expensive.[46] Gen Dwight Eisenhower, now serving as chief of staff to the commander in chief, agreed with Bradley. Although he, too, had originally favored construction of the *United States*, he now changed his mind. Money was crucial, and the Navy's argument was illogical.[47]

Johnson then conferred with Congress and spoke with President Truman, who concurred with his plans and on 23 April announced the cancellation of the *United States*. The Navy and its supporters were outraged, and Secretary Sullivan, out of town when the announcement was made, resigned in protest. Soon after, rumors began circulating that SAC's new bomber, the Consolidated-Vultee (Convair) B-36, was not only a poor design not living up to expectations, but also there were unanswered questions regarding its contract. Clearly, the bomber was being built in lieu of the supercarrier to conduct the atomic mission without Navy support. Newspaper columnist Hanson Baldwin—a Naval Academy graduate—wrote a piece hinting of fraudulent airplane contracts and "financial high jinks."[48] Such rumors became serious enough that the House Armed Services Committee, chaired by Carl Vinson, called for hearings on the matter.

Hearings began on 9 August 1949, and the first speaker was Cong. James E. Van Zandt, who was also a commander in the Naval Reserve. Van Zandt reiterated all the rumors of fraud and misdoings he had heard and which had been circulating for weeks. Referring to an anonymous document, he said reports had reached him of 55 allegations of wrongdoing, some linking Air Force secretary Symington and Defense secretary Johnson with Floyd Odlum, president of Convair—favors given in return for contracts. Van Zandt claimed his anonymous document also noted four aircraft contracts had been cancelled to funnel more money toward Convair to buy more B-36s. Finally, he claimed plans were afoot for Symington to resign

---

[46] Bradley to Johnson, memorandum, 22 April 1949, Vandenberg papers, LOC, box 52.

[47] Hammond, *Super Carriers and B–36 Bombers*, 28.

[48] Hanson W. Baldwin, "War Plane Orders Face Examination by Congressmen," *New York Times*, 24 May 1949, 1; and Baldwin, "Inquiry on the B-36 Bomber," *New York Times*, 21 July 1949, 3.

from office and take over this expanded corporation. He wanted a full investigation.[49]

The hearings that followed were a fiasco. In response to the bar-room gossip of Van Zandt, House committee staffers conducted their own investigation and found nothing amiss. The Air Force sent a number of witnesses to the stand to defend the B-36 and its procure-ment details. General Kenney, who by then was commander of Air University, testified he was in charge of procurement at Wright Field in 1941, when a solicitation was put out for a bomber that could fly 10,000 miles and carry a 10,000-pound payload. There were four pro-posals, and of those, the Consolidated entry (the company had not yet merged with Vultee) was the best; he recommended the design to General Arnold, and the development contract was let. He left soon after for another assignment and was not involved with the B-36 again until he was SAC commander in 1946. When briefed on the status of the program at that time, he was "not happy with the infor-mation that I got." The B-36 was not living up to expectations; there were problems with its engines and propellers, and its range was not what had been hoped. Kenney suggested to Spaatz that the AAF re-consider its decision on the plane.

Much was made by the Navy of this disapproval, seeming to indi-cate the operational commander in charge of the new aircraft did not want it; therefore, some type of fraud must have been involved in its continued development. Not so, said Kenney. Convair put new en-gines on the aircraft, as well as new props; difficulties with the land-ing gear and flaps were corrected; the range was increased. By June 1947, Kenney decided that "the trouble that I had not liked had been cured. The airplane had astonished me." The B-36 could now climb to 40,000 feet—it was alone up there and could not be intercepted by any known aircraft. He then read into the testimony a letter he had sent to Secretary Symington on 18 June 1948 that reiterated these facts.[50] When asked if pressure had been put on him to support the airplane, he scoffed, "Nobody could sell me a bomber except the bomber." Congressman Van Zandt continued to push him on whether or not there were aircraft out there—like the Navy's Banshee jet fighter—that could intercept the B-36, but Kenney remained firm. He

---

[49] US Congress, *Hearings before the House Armed Services Committee: Investigation of the B-36 Bomber Program*, 13–15. Contents of the "anonymous document" are found on pp. 528–33.

[50] Meeting notes from a board reviewing the B-36 program that was held on 24 June 1948 confirmed the reversal in Kenney's stance. "Record of B-36 Procurement, 11 April 1941–1 May 1949," Lt Gen Kenneth B. Wolfe papers, AFHRA, file 168.7030-10, 17/7.

said simply he would take as many B-36s as Congress would give him. Given that all knew of the general's rough handling by the Air Force, his unmitigated support for the service and the plane was compelling.[51]

General LeMay followed and testified that on 3 January 1949 he had briefed the Air Force Senior Officers Board and asked for two additional groups and more aircraft for each group—72 more planes. That indicated his support for the bomber. The following month he briefed the board again and recommended the cancellation of the B-54—a reengined version of the B-50, which was itself an updated B-29. He said the B-36 "was the best possible airplane that we could procure." He, too, was pressed on the charges of fraud and collusion in the production contract but retorted characteristically, "I expect that if I am called upon to fight I will order my crews out in those airplanes, and I expect to be in the first one myself." When pushed on the Navy's new fighter and similar developments in Britain or the Soviet Union, LeMay responded in form: "It's my business to know these things. I know of no night fighter that could be brought against us at the present time that would be at all effective." Although Kenney had testified the B-36 would be employed solely as a night bomber, LeMay disagreed—he expected there would be instances when he would use the aircraft in daylight. In conclusion he stated categorically, "I have been an advocate of the B-36 ever since I heard about it."[52]

General Vandenberg and Secretary Symington were equally forceful in their testimonies, Vandenberg stating that LeMay knew more about strategic bombing than anyone in the world; if he said the B-36 would do the job, then it would.[53] Of importance, the JCS submitted a statement to Chairman Vinson that was not read into testimony but which had a powerful impact on the committee. The chiefs wrote that "in the initial phases of a war, the greatest possible advantage will accrue to the United States through the prompt launching of a strategic bombing offensive against the enemy's war-making potential." The statement noted that exhaustive studies had been conducted on this issue, and concluded: "The Joint Chiefs of Staff separately and jointly are of the firm opinion that the concept of strategic bombing, and the extent of its employment as now planned, are sound."[54]

---

[51] US Congress, *Hearings before the House Armed Services Committee: Investigation of the B-36 Bomber Program*, 115–39.

[52] Ibid., 139–63. Recall LeMay had been deputy chief of staff for R&D from 1945 to 1947.

[53] Ibid., 165–205.

[54] Kenneth Condit, *History of the Joint Chiefs of Staff*, vol. 2, 328.

Arguments made by the airmen and joint chiefs were so convincing the House realized the Navy's entire case depended upon Van Zandt's anonymous document. Demands were made to identify the nameless accuser. The committee council threatened to resign if that were not done. Vinson knew the author, so he called Cedric Worth to the stand. Worth was a Hollywood scriptwriter and Naval Reserve officer who held a Top Secret clearance as an aide to Assistant Secretary of the Navy Dan A. Kimball. When asked if he knew who authored the document charging the Air Force with criminal malfeasance, Worth admitted he wrote it himself, but conceded he had no proof any of it was true.[55] Secretary Kimball, who did not know of Worth's activities, was concerned about the authorship of the damning document and asked Worth to look into it. Worth did not admit he had written it himself. The situation was becoming a burlesque, and after hostile questioning, Worth admitted it was all just a "tragic mistake."[56]

Worth's testimony was a showstopper. The Navy and Van Zandt were humiliated, and Vinson told the admirals privately that evening he was going to bring the hearings to a close. Initially, he had intended to discuss the broader issue of unification and the Navy's role in future war, but Worth's testimony had forced his hand. Several admirals protested, but Vinson told them he was ending the hearings—they would have to wait until the following year when he would hold different hearings on unification and the Navy. The political climate was too charged with fraud and scandal to proceed.[57] The hearings closed on 25 August with a remarkable statement by Chairman Vinson: "There has not been, in the judgment of the committee, not one iota, not one scintilla, of evidence offered thus far in these hearings that would support charges or insinuations that collusion, fraud, corruption, influence, or favoritism played any part whatsoever in the procurement of the B-36 bomber."[58]

[55] The Air Force's Office of Special Investigations had determined the author of the document was Cedric Worth by matching the document to his typewriter. Symington passed that information on to Chairman Vinson. Hagerty, *Air Force Office of Special Investigations*, 60–61.

[56] US Congress, *Hearings before the House Armed Services Committee: Investigation of the B-36 Bomber Program*, 610–11. Worth described himself as a newsman, Hollywood scenario writer, Naval Reserve officer, and freelance writer. "Author of Letter Describes Career," *New York Times*, 25 August 1949, 5.

[57] "Notes on meeting with representative of Navy League in SECNAV's office," 11 January 1950, 3–4, copy of transcript received from US Naval Institute. Matthews met with the Navy League representatives to discuss the relief of Admiral Denfeld, and, in the course of the discussion, he referred to the "cowardly anonymous attack" made by Cedric Worth with the connivance of several Navy members.

[58] US Congress, *Hearings before the House Armed Services Committee: Investigation of the B-36 Bomber Program*, 654.

It was a clear victory for the Air Force, but the matter was not over. Although Vinson had said there would be further hearings, those would be postponed, perhaps indefinitely. Because of the Cedric Worth fiasco, the new Navy secretary, Francis Matthews, called for an internal investigation to discover if Worth had received help from the Navy staff in composing his fiction. As it turned out, he had received a great deal of help.[59] This damning investigation prompted Matthews and Denfeld to agree that further hearings would not be in the Navy's best interests. They would not get off so easily.

CAPT John C. Crommelin was disturbed over unification and what he saw as unequal treatment of the Navy, so he then leaked a classified document to the press, revealing widespread discontent within his service. He stated that it was "necessary to the interests of national security" that he make the report public so there could be an airing of the issues.[60] Denfeld was reluctant to open barely closed wounds, but his staff was adamant the Navy press on. They wanted new hearings to be used as a platform to debate defense priorities.[61]

Vinson rescheduled hearings for 5 October 1949. ADM Arthur Radford, commander of the Pacific Fleet, and CAPT Arleigh Burke, former head of OP-23, helped prepare the Navy's case before Congress.[62] Their arguments fell into three main categories: (1) the concept of an atomic strike by Strategic Air Command was a poor strategy, (2) the B-36—even if legally procured—was still a substandard weapon that could not carry out the atomic strike even if a good idea, and (3) the Navy was being treated as an unequal partner in the Defense Department.

Navy witnesses said the Air Force was attempting to beguile the American people with promises of a "cheap victory." Atomic bombing would not work because the B-36 was an inferior aircraft and would not be able to penetrate Soviet defenses. Moreover, such an atomic blitz was immoral and unworthy of America—even though the Navy was eager to participate in it. In an attempt to turn the tables on the Air Force, Radford argued it was the airmen who were putting all their eggs in one basket—the B-36—and other important missions

[59] Green, "Stuart Symington and the B-36," chap. 13 (unpub.); "House to Fight Air Force Slash," *Aviation Week*, 5 September 1949, 16; and Hammond, *Super Carriers and B-36 Bombers*, 40–41.

[60] Hanson W. Baldwin, "Danger in Defense Row," *New York Times*, 15 September 1949, 13; and "Navy Inquiry," *Aviation Week*, 19 September 1949, 16.

[61] "Notes on Meeting with Navy League and SECNAV," 4–6.

[62] Potter, *Nimitz*, 540.

of tactical air support and airlift were being slighted.[63] As for unifica-tion, the admirals claimed their budget was cut too drastically and they were threatened with impotency. Cancellation of the *United States* was proof the Army and Air Force were ganging up on them and trying to destroy them. Denfeld, the final Navy witness, was par-ticularly vocal about all of this.

The CNO began by claiming apprehension was felt in the Navy due to the trend "to arrest and diminish" its capabilities. The problem stemmed from reductions to the fleet resulting from "arbitrary deci-sions imposed without consultation and without understanding." As for supercarriers versus bombers, Denfeld claimed the air offensive "is not solely a function of the United States Air Force." He thought the Navy should have a voice in deciding whether the B-36 should be procured at all. He stated categorically that "projection of our armed strength overseas and hence keeping the war from our homeland is a Navy task." As for the *United States*, its cancellation was "neither in accord with the spirit nor the concept of unification." He concluded by proclaiming contradictorily that he "supported the principle that each service within budgetary limitations be permitted to design and develop its own weapons."[64]

General Bradley was aghast by this "Revolt of the Admirals" and later wrote, "Never in our military history had there been anything comparable—not even the Billy Mitchell rebellion of the 1920s, a complete breakdown in discipline occurred. Neither Matthews nor Denfeld could control his subordinates." Bradley lambasted Denfeld for letting "his admirals run amok. It was utterly disgraceful." He was especially irritated with the CNO for deliberately misrepresenting US war plans and atomic bomb tests to attack the Air Force.[65]

Vandenberg realized the Navy's position was untenable and that Denfeld and his admirals were attempting to defend the indefensible. The shadow of the B-36 hearings and the Navy's subsequent inquiry

---

[63] US Congress, *Hearings before the House Armed Services Committee on the National Defense Program—Unification and Strategy*, 46–52. One Navy witness, an aeronautical engineer, stated authoritatively that it was impossible for the B-36 to fly 10,000 miles at 40,000 feet. Instead, it would fly most of the mission at 23,000 feet, where its losses to enemy defenses would be "catastrophic." Just as he finished, an officer handed a tele-gram to Vandenberg, who in turn handed it to Vinson. It seems a B-36 had just landed at Spokane, WA, after having flown from Texas to Guam with a 10,000-lb. bomb load, dropped it, and then flown back to the States—a total of 10,000 miles, all at an altitude of 40,000 feet. Ibid., 164–65; and Sessums, interview, 25–28 July 1977 and 26–31 August 1978, 541–42.

[64] US Congress, *Hearings before the House Armed Services Committee on the National Defense Program—Unification and Strategy*, 350–61.

[65] Omar Bradley and Blair, *General's Life*, 488, 507–10. Several times during his testimony Denfeld re-ferred to a Top Secret report that examined the capability of the Air Force to carry out the war plan—when asked for details he coyly responded that he was not allowed to comment further due to classification issues.

hung over all, and the chief knew he held the upper hand. As a result, he began by describing the organization of the Joint Chiefs of Staff, charged by law with developing war plans. They were assisted by a Joint Staff, consisting of equal numbers of officers from the three services. At that time the Joint Staff was headed by an admiral. The chiefs were advised by civilian agencies led by distinguished scientists. All these groups had a hand in devising the current US war plan—and this was the *national* war plan, not the Air Force plan. That plan called for an atomic air offensive to be carried out by Strategic Air Command. In its war-fighting role, SAC worked for the JCS, not the Air Force, and its targets were selected by the Joint Staff. It was not the intent of the atomic air campaign to end the war; only surface forces could do that. Instead, the purpose of the air offensive was to serve as an equalizer to the millions of Soviet troops that greatly outnumbered our own forces. He asked if there was a better alternative: "Is it proposed that we build and maintain a standing Army capable of meeting the masses of an enemy army on the ground in equal man-to-man, body-to-body, gun-to-gun combat?"

No, the B-36 was not a perfect aircraft, but it was the best heavy bomber in the world. It had already flown 10,000 miles, dropped a 10,000-pound bomb, and returned to base, most of the trip at an altitude of 40,000 feet. As to contentions the bomber could be intercepted and shot down, Vandenberg said the bomber would get through. Regarding the claim the bomber would need escort, as had the B-17s, B-24s, and B-29s in World War II, the chief replied that SAC had its own fleet of fighter escorts to accompany the bombers partially on their way, but the distances involved were so great that escort to and from the target was infeasible; carrier-based aircraft would be even less useful. The bomber would get through.

As for the overemphasis on bombardment charged by Radford, Vandenberg gave statistics. There were 48 combat groups in the Air Force, but only four were equipped with the B-36. If the service were allowed to expand to 70 groups—its goal for the past five years—there would still be only four B-36 groups. When all aircraft (including the reserves) available at the start of a war were counted, the B-36 comprised only 3 percent of the total.

Referring to the *United States*, Vandenberg argued that the ship was simply not needed for the Navy's primary functions. Funds were too scarce to buy weapons not in support of the approved war plan. That was what unification was supposedly all about—eliminating redundancy and wasteful overlap. The Air Force had been given strategic air warfare as a primary function by the secretary of defense, and that decision was ratified by the president. SAC existed to carry out that function. Let them do their job.[66] It was a clinching argument. One observer noted wryly that "What strength there was in the Admirals' case was there by mistake."[67] The Air Force had won its brief in Congress and in the court of public opinion.

As a result of the hearings, relations between the Air Force and the Navy were strained for years. SAC got its B-36s, and the Navy lost a few admirals. Denfeld was fired immediately after his appearance before the House.[68] Navy secretary Matthews knew something was amiss when Denfeld refused to show him his testimony in advance, although the admiral had promised he would do so. Denfeld later said he was sorry for breaking his promise, but he was determined to make his case despite its violation of norms. He said his subordinates thought he was too soft; he had to show them he was "hard-boiled." Matthews later claimed he had already decided he could not live with Denfeld; his testimony to Congress was the last straw: "I could not administer the office with a CNO I could not trust. There are not two policies in the Navy; there is only one policy."[69] In his letter to President Truman detailing his reasons for firing his top officer, Matthews wrote, "Very soon after I assumed office, it became clear to me that there was definite resistance on the part of some naval officers to accepting unification of the Armed Services, notwithstanding the fact that it was established by law." As for the specific incident resulting in Denfeld's relief, the secretary stated, "A military establishment is not a political democracy. Integrity of command is indispensible at all times. There can be no twilight zone in the measure of loyalty to superiors and respect for authority existing between various official ranks. Inability to conform to such requirements for military stability would disqualify any of us for positions subordinate to the Commander in Chief."[70] It was a devastating indictment.

Some members of Congress were concerned that Denfeld was fired for speaking his mind and Matthews was guilty of imposing a gag order on naval officers testifying before Congress. The JCS looked

---

[66] See US Congress, *Hearings before the House Armed Services Committee on the National Defense Program—Unification and Strategy*, 451–69, for Vandenberg's testimony.

[67] "State of the Unification," *Economist*, 893–94.

[68] For the Navy's side of this sorry episode, see Barlow, *Revolt of the Admirals*.

[69] "Notes on Meeting with Navy League and SECNAV," 8–10.

[70] Matthews to Truman, letter, 2 October 1949, copy provided by the US Naval Institute.

into this matter but concluded, "The right of free speech, the necessity for witnesses to testify without fear of reprisal or intimidation, and the desire for fair play must be balanced against the requirements of responsibility and loyalty to constituted authority, particularly so in the case of the Armed Forces." Denfeld had gone too far in arguing his case, in direct contradiction of the known policies and beliefs of his service secretary. Matthews was well within his rights to fire him.[71]

Evaluating the Atomic Air Offensive

Behind the scenes of this spectacle, events of greater import were taking place. Secretary Forrestal was still worried over the events of the Berlin crisis. He therefore asked the joint chiefs to look into the atomic air offensive that was the key element of the national war plan. A report in December 1948 gave positive news: "It is estimated that the destruction of the first 70 objectives will reduce the total industrial output [by] more than 50 percent." It continued that strikes against the Soviet's oil facilities "would practically destroy the offensive capabilities of the USSR and seriously cripple its defensive capabilities." It noted the Soviet's rudimentary defensive radar system was in the process of being upgraded; even so, based on tests with the RAF's new interceptor, even a B-29 could penetrate Soviet airspace and a Vampire (British jet fighter) would get only one pass at the bomber—in good weather. If the weather were poor, they would not intercept the bomber at all on its inbound run.[72] The Air Force had conducted similar tests and obtained the same results, causing Secretary Johnson to conclude: "It appears that our bombers can fly over this country at 30,000 feet and above with practically no danger of intercept. It also appears that they can fly over England at above 30,000 feet with little danger of intercept. To my mind it follows that we can do the same over the USSR."[73]

Soon after, the chiefs decided to look at the matter again and appointed two separate groups to report back to them. The first, appointed in February 1949, was a board of officers chaired by Lt Gen Hubert R. Harmon, USAF.[74] In gathering data, Harmon's team visited

---

[71] Harmon to Landauer, letter, 19 April 1950, Harmon papers, AFA, A4, B10.

[72] JCS 1952/1, "Evaluation of Current Strategic Air Offensive Plans," 21 December 1948, in Ross and Rosenberg, *America's Plans for War against the Soviet Union*, vol. 9.

[73] Johnson to Kenney, letter, 8 May 1948, in *SAC History—1948*, vol. 5, exhibit 148.

[74] Harmon was the Air Force representative to the United Nations and because of his light work schedule was often given such tasks by the JCS.

SAC headquarters in Omaha and asked for briefings on targeting plans, aircraft availability, crew training, and performance. LeMay was irritated by this intrusiveness and called the Pentagon to complain, but Vandenberg responded by rebuking LeMay for his attitude and making it clear he expected unqualified support to be given Harmon's team, writing, "We cannot afford to be hypersensitive when we are questioned about our capabilities."[75]

LeMay was sensitive for good reason. On 12 May 1949, the Harmon Board submitted its report, *Evaluation of Effect on Soviet War Effort Resulting from the Strategic Air Offensive*. The report was not a ringing endorsement of airpower.

It began by making two assumptions: First, the Air Force could implement the war plan (*Trojan*) as directed; that is, it could fly all of its missions and deliver atomic weapons on the designated targets. Second, the accuracy figures specified in *Trojan*—a circular error probable of 3,000 feet—would be achieved. These were not trivial assumptions, because they ignored the effectiveness of Soviet air defenses (which were largely unknown) while also granting accuracy in delivering atomic weapons that had not yet been demonstrated in war. Nonetheless, the board saw its task as evaluating whether or not the strategic air offensive—if conducted as planned—would bring about the defeat of the Soviet Union.

Harmon and his colleagues concluded that the atomic offensive "would probably affect the war effort, and produce psychological effects upon the Soviet will to wage war." For air advocates, this was an unusually weak beginning. Although the effects on the Soviet war effort appeared significant—30 to 40 percent of Soviet industrial production would be neutralized—this loss would not be permanent. The length of time industrial capacity was reduced would depend upon Soviet recuperative powers (which were unknown) and the ability of the United States to follow up with more air strikes, both atomic and conventional. The board did note, however, that certain key industries, like petroleum, would be particularly hard hit.[76]

Soviet casualties would amount to 2.7 million dead and another 4 million wounded, "depending upon the effectiveness of Soviet passive defense measures." Physical destruction would be massive in

---

[75] Vandenberg to LeMay, letter, 15 February 1949, Vandenberg papers, LOC, box 45.
[76] The Harmon Report can be found in Ross and Rosenberg, *America's Plans for War against the Soviet Union*, vol. 11. This volume is not paginated; however, the pages on the original document are usually legible. The conclusions of the report, which are given first, are on pp. 3–6 of the original.

targeted cities, and living conditions for survivors would be "vastly complicated." Considering that the Soviet Union had suffered over 20 million deaths in World War II, had much of its territory overrun, and still gone on to victory, the statistics regarding an atomic air offensive were not remarkable.

Another disappointment for Air Force expectations came in the section dealing with psychological effects. The board maintained the atomic offensive "would not, per se, bring about capitulation, destroy the roots of Communism, or critically weaken the power of Soviet leadership to dominate the people." Indeed, "atomic bombing would validate Soviet propaganda against foreign powers, stimulate resentment against the United States, unify these people, and increase their will to fight." Regarding the effect of atomic strikes on Soviet military forces, the board asserted what war plans had assumed: despite the air offensive, Soviet forces would overrun most of Europe, the Middle East, and the Far East. However—a glimmer of optimism here—the Soviet offensive would gradually run out of steam due to the severe disruption of its industry, especially petroleum, to their rear.[77]

This was a serious blow to the Air Force, SAC, and the foundation upon which their doctrine and force structure was based. Vandenberg was livid. He protested the report's findings and submitted several changes to correct what he termed its "unwarranted conclusions." For example, he wanted to add that "Soviet recuperability would be vastly complicated by the great extent of the damage obtained within such a short time and by the destruction of industrial capacity vital to recuperation efforts." He also wanted to strengthen the paragraphs concerning the psychological effects on the Soviet population.[78] Admiral Denfeld would have none of it. He was delighted with the Harmon Board's conclusions and thought they were quite logical and fair—after all, the chairman was a senior Air Force officer. (It was the Harmon Report that Denfeld was probably alluding to during his testimony before Congress in October 1949.) In the end, the report was submitted with only minor changes made by the joint chiefs. Vandenberg submitted a dissenting opinion to the secretary of defense.

Omar Bradley, who was then Army chief of staff, wrote in his memoirs: "The air-power zealots were shocked and stunned by the report and felt betrayed by their own, Hubert Harmon. Vandenberg

---

[77] Ibid.
[78] Ibid. Vandenberg's memo is dated 8 July 1949, and its pages in the original, reproduced in Ross and Rosenberg, are 279–83.

mounted a vigorous effort to have the report suppressed or altered to eliminate its pessimistic tone. Denfeld gleefully seized upon the report."[79] Hanson Baldwin of the *New York Times* wrote that "considerable pressure" had been put on Harmon to change his views, but he had refused.[80] Harmon vehemently denied this, stating "whoever said that, lied." He went on, "at no time before, during, or after the preparation of the committee's report did any officer offer any approach to, or solution of, the problem before the committee."[81]

The final agency tasked by the joint chiefs to examine the capabilities of airpower in conjunction with the war plans was conducted by the Weapons Systems Evaluation Group (WSEG).[82] The group reported its findings in January 1950 and it, too, was critical of Air Force capabilities. The report began by stating bluntly that "logistical deficiencies and expected bomber attrition rates preclude an offensive on the scale contemplated in OFFTACKLE." (*Offtackle* was the successor to *Trojan*.) The war plan called for 220 atomic bombs to be dropped on 104 targets. The WSEG estimated that 70–85 percent of the attacking aircraft would indeed get through and hit their targets, but the losses could be as high as 30–50 percent, and these would be especially heavy in the medium bomber force of B-29s and B-50s staging out of the United Kingdom. Somewhat paradoxically, however, the group then admitted they had little information on Soviet air defenses. There were "grave deficiencies" in our intelligence capabilities regarding the Soviet Union, and these deficiencies must be addressed.[83]

It is not clear why these different committees tasked to study the effects of the atomic air offensive produced such divergent viewpoints. The Air Force and SAC were certainly put on notice they needed to focus more directly on the atomic mission—a decision they had already embraced. In truth, the Harmon Report, its Joint Staff predecessor, the WSEG study, or even the congressional hearings had little effect on the US defense posture. President Truman and Congress had turned their attention to rebuilding the domestic

---

[79] Omar Bradley and Blair, *General's Life*, 501.

[80] Hanson W. Baldwin, "Secret Report Backs Navy," *New York Times*, 14 October 1949, 3.

[81] Hanson W. Baldwin, "The Reply to the Navy," *New York Times*, 19 October 1949, 13.

[82] For the background to this group and an administrative history, see John Ponturo, "Analytical Support for the Joint Chiefs of Staff: The WSEG Experience, 1948–1976," Study S-507. Washington, DC: Institute for Defense Analyses, July 1976.

[83] WSEG, "Weapons Systems Evaluation Group Report No. 1," 8 February 1950, in Ross and Rosenberg, *America's Plans for War against the Soviet Union*, vol. 13, 158–93. Vandenberg had earlier protested that Soviet air defenses were not as robust as claimed, but the Joint Intelligence Committee responded lamely that so little was known about the subject they could not comment on it one way or the other. Kenneth Condit, *History of the Joint Chiefs of Staff*, vol. 2, 308–10.

economy in the wake of the Great Depression and World War II. They did not wish to be distracted by a budget fight between the military services, despite the importance the services gave to those issues.

Budget Battles

Besides the deep-seated antipathy between the services, the Revolt of the Admirals was a symptom of budget drought of the postwar era. Had more funds been available, it is possible the Air Force and the Navy could have worked out their differences; the American way of war is characterized by redundancy. The United States has always preferred to throw money—and technology—at its military problems rather than rely on the blood of its forces. As a result, it has tended to avoid questions of overlap between services and roles/functions, and for the past six decades has willingly supported two land armies and four air forces simply because it can. This presents a potential adversary with overwhelming problems: if it had to face only an extremely powerful army, navy, or air force, it might be able to adapt. But an adversary must face a nation that has vested its treasure in building the best services in the world, as well as being a world leader in space. Such a profligate posture only works in times of either economic abundance or an unusual fondness for the military among the populace. In the aftermath of World War II, dollars were so scarce real sacrifices had to be made by the military services. Their task was to ensure the sacrifices were visited on their brethren.

The Air Force thought it had some momentum in this fight. In mid 1947 the president had appointed an air policy commission headed by Thomas K. Finletter.[84] Secretary Symington and Generals Spaatz and Vandenberg testified before the commission and were vocal about their needs. Vandenberg, for example, called for 131 groups—70 active duty and the others in reserve. The 70 groups would consist of 21 heavy bomber groups, 22 fighter groups, and the rest attack, reconnaissance, and transport aircraft. The Air Force needed 3,200 aircraft per year to maintain those 70 groups.[85] At that time it was trying, unsuccessfully, to maintain 55 groups. His testimony came as a

---

[84] For an excellent overview of the Finletter Commission, see Wilson, "History of President Truman's Air Policy Commission and its Influence on Air Policy, 1947–1949," (unpub.).

[85] *Gen H. S. Vandenberg, Testimony before the President's Air Policy Commission, 26 November 1947*, vol. 6, 2518–53, located in Fairchild Library, Maxwell AFB, AL.

shock, and one news report called it "an astonishing break with military policy" because it was so candid about the sorry state of affairs.[86]

The Finletter Commission interviewed 202 witnesses and in its final report called for a national security built around the air arm. Airpower was necessary not just to defend the United States, but must also be capable of "dealing a crushing counter offensive blow on the aggressor." The report stated that to do this, the Air Force needed 70 groups consisting of 12,400 modern aircraft, 700 of which should be atomic-capable heavy bombers.[87] This was welcome news, and it was enhanced two months later when the House released its own findings on the issue of the nation's airpower. The Hinshaw-Brewster Report similarly extolled the dominance of airpower in national defense, and it too called for an Air Force of 70 groups.[88]

Although heartening, these reports changed little. Calls for an expanded Air Force were made while the defense budget was decreasing. Any buildup in air could only be gained by cuts to the Army and the Navy. Secretary Forrestal asked President Truman for an increased defense budget but was rebuffed. Instead, the president wanted all to think in terms of efficiency and cutting costs, not raising them. To ensure the chiefs heard his meaning, he sent each a letter stating, "There are still some of you who are thinking of representing the interests and objectives of your individual service rather than of interpreting the broad national program and its requirements to your subordinates and to the Congress."[89] He was insistent the chiefs hold the defense budget to $15 billion. This was glum news to all, and to the Airmen especially, because if they were to build to 70 groups as the Air Policy Commission and Congress suggested, they would need the lion's share of the funds—$7 billion.[90] Indeed, when the chiefs put forth their minimum requirements, the total was $30 billion.[91] All pleas were futile; the president would not budge. Over the next several months there was endless, bitter debate among the chiefs as to whose ox was going to be gored. General Eisenhower was recalled to

[86] "Security vs. Budget," *Aviation Week*, 8 December 1947, 7, 11–13.

[87] Finletter, *Survival in the Air Age*, 8–12, 25–28.

[88] "Report of the Congressional Aviation Policy Board," *Air Force*, April 1948, 12–15, 38–39; and "Air Force of 35,000 Planes is Urged," *U.S. Air Services*, March 1948, 14–17.

[89] Truman to Forrestal and Truman to Vandenberg, memoranda, 13 May 1948, both in Vandenberg papers, LOC, box 40.

[90] US Congress, *Hearings before the Senate Appropriations Committee on the National Military Establishment Appropriations Bill for 1950*, 80–90.

[91] Millis and Duffield, *Forrestal Diaries*, 502–5.

duty but had little real power. He could merely suggest to the services what they should do, he could not compel.

These financial contests lasted throughout 1948 and 1949, and the Revolt of the Admirals heightened tension. Not surprisingly, the biggest fights were between the Air Force and the Navy over whether it was more prudent to buy more bombers or more aircraft carriers. In March 1949, for instance, the Air Force called for expansion to the congressionally mandated 70 groups, but the Navy thought 48 groups were sufficient. What was interesting about this impasse was that the number of strategic bombing groups would have remained the same in either scheme; the Navy deleted the tactical groups: six medium bomb groups, four light bomb groups, five fighter, four airlift, and three reconnaissance groups.[92] (Recall that the Navy claimed in congressional hearings the Air Force focused too heavily on strategic bombing and ignored tactical airpower.) As for aircraft carriers, the Navy wanted nine; the Air Force responded they only needed escort carriers for their primary functions of antisubmarine warfare and mine laying.[93] Throughout all of this, Generals Eisenhower and Bradley tended to side with the airmen, but this only made the Navy more paranoid.

To further indicate the entrenched positions of all, in late 1948 Congress had defied the president and added an extra $615 million to the defense budget, earmarked for the Air Force. The bill passed 306–1. Truman vetoed it. Congress overrode the veto. Truman impounded the funds, stating that such excess funding was "inconsistent with a realistic and balanced security program."[94] It was a depressing situation; worse, the international situation did not seem to be improving, even though the Berlin crisis had ended favorably. This continuous problem with funding was one reason why SAC was chronically unable to expand its capabilities.

Intelligence and Joe 1

Reports from spies and émigrés were of some use in keeping tabs on the Soviet atomic program, but more was needed. Reliance on the

---

[92] Smith to Vandenberg, letter, 5 April 1949, Vandenberg papers, LOC, box 41; and US Congress, *Hearings before the Senate Appropriations Committee on the National Military Establishment Appropriations Bill for 1950*, 228, 240.

[93] Vandenberg to Johnson, memorandum, 10 August 1949, Vandenberg papers, LOC, box 41. For an overview of this period, see Kolodziej, *Uncommon Defense and Congress*, chaps. 2 and 3.

[94] Truman to Johnson, letter, 8 November 1949, Vandenberg papers, LOC, box 40.

British for intelligence sources was no longer feasible, and American capabilities needed to be upgraded. In testifying before Congress, Vandenberg, then director of central intelligence, summed the issue:

> The United States should not . . . find itself . . . developing its plans and policies on the basis of intelligence collected, compiled, and intercepted by some foreign government. . . . The United States should never again have to go hat in hand, begging any foreign government for the eyes—the foreign intelligence—with which to see. We should be self-sufficient.[95]

Vandenberg's experiences in G-2 and the Central Intelligence Group would prove of importance in his tenure as chief of staff. As he said in April 1947, "In my opinion, a strong intelligence system is equally if not more essential in peace than in war."[96] The air intelligence division shared this belief in staying abreast of potential threats and tried to examine the Soviet air defense system and air force. It was known they had no strategic bombing force during the war, but the Soviets had interned several B-29s that made emergency landings in eastern Siberia after missions against Japan. They reverse-engineered these B-29s and revealed their version, the TU-4, in August 1947.[97] The other main task of air intelligence—and for that matter several other intelligence agencies—was monitoring the Soviet atomic energy program.

It was not clear where the Soviets stood in atomic research, but it was obvious they were working feverishly to develop a bomb. Various agencies had projected when "Red Atom Day" would occur, and these predictions ranged anywhere from five to 20 years in the future. In July 1947, for example, the Joint Intelligence Committee had suggested the Soviets would be unable to achieve results for 10 to 15 years. The AAF dissented, arguing that if the Soviets followed the same steps as the United States they could have a bomb by 1952; moreover, information already made public regarding the atomic bomb would shorten the Soviet effort, allowing them to build a bomb as early as 1949. Given the closed nature of Soviet society and the lack of hard intelligence, all predictions were little more than guesswork.[98]

---

[95] US Congress, *Hearings before the Senate Armed Service Committee on the National Defense Establishment (Unification of the Armed Services)*, 491–94.

[96] Christensen, "Assessment of General Hoyt S. Vandenberg's Accomplishments as Director of Central Intelligence," 754.

[97] Aronsen, "Seeing Red," 116–17.

[98] "The Capabilities of the USSR in Regard to Atomic Weapons," JIC report 395/1, 8 July 1947, in "JCS Strategic Issues," reel 1; Richelson, *Spying on the Bomb*, 76–77; and Ziegler, "Intelligence Assessments of Soviet Atomic Capability," 10–17.

Before the first US device was detonated, Maj Gen Leslie Groves considered the problem of detection. He was looking ahead to when the US monopoly in atomic weapons would give way to proliferation. How would the United States determine when the Soviets had joined the atomic club? More importantly, how could the type, nature, and size of the blast be ascertained?

Throughout 1946 and 1947 the Atomic Energy Commission and the AAF/Air Force studied the problem of detection. Underwater seismic sensors were installed at various locations in the Atlantic and Pacific Oceans, but these would only work if an atomic bomb were detonated in the water. A total of 16 different technologies were studied, but the most promising was air sampling. Four squadrons of WB-29s were modified with an air scoop containing a sensitive filter system, and these aircraft made daily flights worldwide. The filters were changed during flight and the used filters placed in lead containers. Upon landing they were tested with Geiger counters for evidence of radioactive elements—elements that could only result from an atomic detonation. A careful study of the residue would also reveal the materials used in the bomb, the intensity of radioactivity, its yield, efficiency, and other parameters. This air sampling system was checked out in July 1948, when the United States conducted a series of atomic detonations at Eniwetok Atoll in the Pacific. Blast data was collected by several Air Force aircraft as the radioactive debris cloud drifted across the globe. The filters were duly collected, tested, and analyzed. The system worked, and David Lilienthal, head of the AEC, confided in his diary that the results were "quite remarkable and beyond our expectations."[99]

On the morning of 3 September 1949, an Air Force WB-29 registered unusual radioactivity on a flight over the Pacific. A normal count was below 50 hits per minute, but the sampling aircraft was recording over 1,000 counts per minute. The filters were collected and rushed to a laboratory in Berkeley, California, for study. Scientists concluded an atomic device of around 20 kilotons—a plutonium bomb like that used at Nagasaki—had been detonated in Russia during late August. Because Defense Secretary Louis Johnson was still skeptical, a panel of scientists convened in Washington to review the data. They confirmed the Berkeley findings, and Vandenberg for-

---

[99] Richelson, *Spying on the Bomb*, 82–88; Bukharin, "US Atomic Energy Intelligence against the Soviet Target," 655–67; "Report of Operation FITZWILLIAM," 1948, AFHRA, file 168.04-17; and Lilienthal, *Journals of David Lilienthal*, vol. 2, 384.

warded this information to Johnson and President Truman with a cover letter stating, "I believe an atomic bomb has been detonated over the Asiatic land mass during the period 26 August 1949 to 29 August 1949. . . . Conclusions by our scientists based on physical and radio-chemical analyses of collected data have been confirmed by scientists of the AEC, United Kingdom, and Office of Naval Research."[100] Two days later Truman announced to the American public that the Russians had exploded an atomic device, to become known as Joe 1 in honor of the Soviet dictator. The global situation was changing yet again.

Summary

Building SAC into an effective and efficient war-fighting arm was to be LeMay's greatest accomplishment. One well-known story of how he demonstrated his command's poor state of readiness concerned the "bombing raid" on Dayton, Ohio, that did not go off well. He then set about to retrain SAC. Using the authority delegated to him by Vandenberg, LeMay built new bases, facilities, and training programs; he began a lead crew school to promote standardized training and procedures. Through discipline he eventually transformed his command into one of the most effective military units in the world. Much more work was needed, but SAC was on a track toward success. It is important to note that rumblings were heard within the Air Force from early 1948 onwards that it was not taking atomic matters seriously enough. Several high-ranking airmen complained that SAC and its mission were not enjoying a suitable priority. They were correct, and the dismal state of the command became apparent during the Berlin crisis of 1948 that led to the relief of George Kenney and his replacement by Curtis LeMay. Even so, events moved slowly. It was only the successive events of Berlin, the Revolt of the Admirals, and Joe 1 that finally prodded Air Force leadership to refocus emphasis on its premier combat command. To be sure, endemic budget constraints contributed to this malaise, but other factors were at play.

LeMay remained as SAC commander for nearly nine years, an unusually long time for one person to remain in the same position. The

---

[100] Hewlett and Duncan, *History of the Atomic Energy Commission*, vol. 2, 362–66; and Richelson, *Spying on the Bomb*, 89–91.

extended tenure gave him the opportunity to make deep, long-lasting changes. Curtis LeMay became the face, the persona, and the soul of Strategic Air Command. In October 1951 he received his fourth star at the age of 44—the second youngest full general in American history (behind U. S. Grant who had been a few months younger)—and he would serve in that rank longer than anyone else (14 years).

LeMay recognized instinctively that accuracy lay at the core of strategic bombing—even with atomic weapons. He worked to improve accuracy by instituting a lead crew program and stressing the importance of consistency, repetition, and relentless training. One study by a SAC staffer looked at this matter and noted there were a number of key factors governing bombing accuracy. The first of those was planning: "a mission is made or broken in the planning stage." Detailed and meticulous preparation was essential: problems must be identified and solutions devised before an aircraft ever leaves the ground. Tactics and procedures were important: speed, altitude, run-in heading, navigation, and targeting details, such as the proper use of radar and the selection of the appropriate aim point. Training and more training—especially using realistic scenarios simulating wartime conditions—was essential. Target intelligence—both in the general sense of knowing what targets to hit, but also how exactly to hit them—was a factor identified and confronted late in the war. It was just as valid in the atomic age. Technology, in the form of a superior and accurate bombsight, was also necessary. At the speed and altitude flown by bombers, a poor bombsight would induce errors for even an outstanding bombardier. Most important was the influence of leadership. A good leader knew his business, and that included an intimate knowledge and understanding of all facets of the strategic bombardment mission: "a consistently good bombing organization has never been observed without this quality in the commander . . . of the detailed knowledge of the entire bombing problem."[101] LeMay understood this, and he selected subordinate commanders who also did. It was standard for wing commanders and their staffs to visit Offutt and brief their part in the emergency war plan to LeMay personally. In one instance he noticed that the staff did all the briefing while the commander watched. When LeMay asked him a question, the colonel had difficulty pronouncing the Russian locations properly. LeMay stopped the briefing: "I want you to go home and come back in one

---

[101] "Evaluation of Bombing Systems by SAC," [1955], AFHRA, file 416.04-10, 3–21.

week. The commanding officer is going to brief. He's going to learn the names of every target. You are going to know what it's all about. You are going to know everything about this. You are going to be prepared to answer every question I have."[102] He was not angry or nasty; he never raised his voice, but his insistence on professionalism was clear. This emphasis on training, standardization, and detail bore fruit. Following the Dayton attack in January 1949, similar assaults were launched on other cities over the next two years.

The complexity of the radar targeting problem was enormous; yet, accuracy steadily improved. To give an example: one exercise involved "bombing" an airfield near Springfield, Missouri. Crews were given targeting information the day before, and the information was scanty and incomplete—17-year old photographs of the city. The location of the airfield was not exactly known, so the crews were required to study the old photos, estimate what the prominent features would look like on a radar scope, and plan their mission on that information. When it was realized that such a problem would not be much different than that encountered by bomber crews penetrating the Soviet Union and using photos found in German archives at the end of World War II, one could understand the difficulties LeMay's command was confronting. Even so, the SAC crews attacked the Springfield airfield with "excellent results."[103]

Besides chronic personnel and maintenance issues, other problems arose. The roles and missions debate had not gone away, and it erupted into a startling display of insubordination and bad faith in mid 1949. Naval officers believed the Air Force message: strategic bombing with atomic weapons was the future of war. They felt, however, that they were being left behind. In their testimony before Congress, the admirals did not speak of the need for naval aviation to be used in a conventional war against an opponent with no navy and a limited air force—like North Korea. They believed their institutional survival depended on a share of the "atomic pie." The Key West and Newport agreements precluded such a move, and the Navy was desperate to find a way out of that box canyon. Regrettably, they chose a path that did them disservice. The smear campaign against the secretaries of Defense and the Air Force as well as the chief of staff and other airmen, was orchestrated from the highest levels of the Navy

[102] Gunderson, interview, 22–23 October 1987, 34.
[103] Ibid., 27–34.

staff. Although the resultant hearings totally exonerated the Air Force and cast shame on the Navy, some zealots within the sea service were not yet finished. Further hearings revealed the unhappiness within the fleet because sailors did not enjoy the same status and primacy they felt was their right. They had grown used to a president who had been a former assistant secretary of the Navy, a defense secretary who had been the Navy secretary during the war, and a chief of staff to the president who was an admiral. This did not strike the Navy hierarchy as biased in their favor; yet, they reacted violently to a new president, a new defense secretary, and a new JCS chairman who had an Army background. The admirals saw no inconsistency in their stance.

In one sense, the long-term result of the revolt was minimal. The Navy eventually got its big-deck carriers, and nuclear weapons went to sea. The Air Force bought its "Peacemakers," while at the same time recognizing their limitations—air leaders were quietly pinning their hopes on the all-jet B-47 and B-52. A few sailors were reassigned or nudged into retirement, and Admiral Denfeld was fired; but two key figures behind the action, Admiral Radford and Captain Burke, were hailed as heroes within their service and went on to wear four stars. The biggest loser was national security. The smears by uniformed officers against their civilian superiors were a serious blot on the US military tradition. Worse, the Revolt of the Admirals caused a lingering ill will and distrust within the services—the baleful maladies that unification of the armed forces was designed to correct.

The Air Force won a tactical victory in this fight but realized it was just a delaying action. Atomic tests had been carried out in 1948 at Eniwetok Atoll in the Pacific. The results of Sandstone were of enormous significance because they demonstrated that atomic bombs could be built one-third the size and weight of Fat Man devices while also using less uranium/plutonium. SAC would not have a monopoly on delivery much longer.[104] This was understood during the B-36 hearings. The Air Force therefore pinned its arguments to the war plan and the functions documents agreed to at Key West and Newport. Airmen repeated the mantra of "strategic bombing is *our* function" and "the national war plans specify a strategic bombing offensive as the main element of a US response." But these arguments lost cogency when atomic bombs dropped in size and weight to the point that

---

[104] Defense Nuclear Agency, "Operation SANDSTONE, 1948," 19 December 1948, 17–21; and Little and Bowen, *History of the Air Force Atomic Energy Program*, vol. 2, chap. 16.

small aircraft—carrier-based aircraft—could carry them. With a rapidly growing atomic stockpile of weapons, it sounded childish for airmen to claim that only SAC should deliver those weapons. By the end of 1949, war plan *Crasspiece* projected the employment of naval aviation in the atomic offensive.

Once again it should be stressed that the groups studying this matter were largely unaware of the limitations imposed by the small number of atomic bombs then on hand. The size of the atomic stockpile was an extremely well-guarded secret in the years immediately following the war. It is likely only a handful of people in the AAF knew how many bombs existed—only nine weapons in the entire US atomic inventory in June 1946; 13 one year later and 50 at the outbreak of the Berlin crisis in June 1948.[105] Sandstone, but especially Joe 1, would initiate a growth spurt in the stockpile that would continue for more than a decade. Since 1946 the joint chiefs had predicated their requests for atomic bomb production based on AEC capabilities; after Sandstone and Joe 1, they based their requests on war plan requirements. Actually, this result was not foregone.

In May 1950, Senator Brien McMahon asked the joint chiefs if they were satisfied with the amount being spent on atomic weapons. The chiefs responded lamely that they were "unable to make a categorical answer." This precipitated a pointed reply from McMahon: "Frankly, I cannot bring myself to accept the implication that on a question of military policy which all would agree is vitally significant—and which, in my personal judgment, is uniquely significant—the responsible military authorities of the United States are in a state of indecision."[106] The chiefs were clearly ambivalent about a critical issue, and it is not altogether clear why. The month after McMahon's letter, events in Asia would clarify the matter for everyone once and for all.

One other example of leadership needs to be mentioned. Lt Gen Hubert Harmon had been tabbed by the joint chiefs in early 1949 to chair the board examining SAC's ability to carry out the war plan. Although an Air Force officer, he presented a remarkably candid assessment that was much contested and resented by SAC and Vandenberg. Yet, only a few months later Vandenberg needed someone as his

---

[105] Rosenberg, "US Nuclear Stockpile," 26. The Mk. IV bomb began entering service in late 1948 and had a yield of 18–49 kilotons.

[106] McMahon to Johnson, letter, 10 March 1950; Bradley to Johnson, letter, 26 April 1950; Johnson to McMahon, letter, 5 May 1950; and McMahon to Johnson, letter, 6 May 1950, all in AFHRA, file 143.519-5.

special assistant for air academy matters. The subject of an Air Force academy was increasingly being studied, and chances for the establishment of such a school looked bright, but the chief knew such a task would require intelligence, tact, and moral courage. The politics involved in such an assignment were huge—merely choosing the site for such an academy was fraught with pitfalls. Vandenberg wanted someone he could trust to give him honest advice and to make decisions based on merit; he needed someone impervious to political influence. He chose Harmon, the man who had defied him a few months earlier. The incident said much regarding the matters of honor and integrity.

Besides the subject of leadership, mission and message dominated this chapter. The mission of strategic bombing remained the polestar for the Air Force, and it was very effective at spreading this message far and wide. In some cases, it perhaps went too far, and as during the interwar period, airmen oversold their capabilities. The Harmon Report and the WSEG study revealed serious problems in SAC's ability to carry out the war plan. Although Harmon's group assumed away the matter of actually conducting an air offensive as planned, the WSEG did not; it feared SAC losses would be prohibitive. The broader question was of greater concern. Both groups believed even an atomic offensive that was tactically successful would still be of marginal strategic success. Airmen believed that in an era of tightened defense budgets, there was little alternative. Vandenberg's comments before Congress that a war plan based on man-to-man and gun-to-gun fighting was insane struck a chord in most. Unless the administration dramatically expanded the defense budget—and attempts by Congress to do so were met with a spirited White House riposte—there was little logic to do anything but rely on airpower.

The detonation of the Soviet atomic bomb in August 1949, years ahead of most estimates, focused everyone's mind on the great transcendent threat. The monopoly was gone, and the country—but especially the Air Force and SAC— must address the threat to the east with renewed vigor. There would be little time to do so before other events intruded.

The Men and Machines That Built Strategic Air Command

Graduating class outside the Air Corps Tactical School, Building 800 (now Headquarters, Air University), at Maxwell Field (now Maxwell AFB), Alabama, in the 1930s.

Brig Gen William "Billy" Mitchell, considered by many the father of the modern Air Force.

The Boeing P-26A "Peashooter" was the US Army Air Corps' first all-metal monoplane fighter in regular service and could fly much faster in level flight than the older wood and fabric biplane fighters.

Col Edgar S. Gorrell became the first US military man to produce a comprehensive and detailed plan for strategic bombing in 1917.

The most notable contribution of the Martin MB-2/NBS-1 was the ship bombing trials in 1921. Flying out of Langley Field, Virginia, under the command of Brig Gen Billy Mitchell, the Martin Bombers sank a submarine, destroyer, cruiser, and battleship and proved the worth of aerial bombardment.

The Martin B-10's all-metal monoplane construction, along with its closed cockpits, rotating gun turrets, retractable landing gear, internal bomb bay, and full engine cowlings, outperformed contemporary pursuit planes and set the standard for bomber designs worldwide for decades.

The Consolidated B-24 Liberator, faster and with a longer range and heavier bomb load than the Boeing B-17 Flying Fortress, was used by all US services and several allies in every theater of operations during WWII.

The B-17 was primarily employed by the USAAF in the daylight precision strategic bombing campaign of WW II against German industrial and military targets. Airmen preferred it over the more modern and faster B-24 for its survivability and airworthiness.

The Fulda rail yard was an important transshipment point in the German rail system that was virtually destroyed by Eighth Air Force bombers.

Brig Gen Kenneth N. Walker, a coauthor of the air campaign strategy used to defeat Germany in WWII, received the Medal of Honor for his actions during a fatal B-17 Flying Fortress mission over the Japanese stronghold of Rabaul, New Britain, on 5 January 1943.

Gen Laurence S. Kuter served on the faculty of the Air Corps Tactical School from 1935 to 1939. A staunch strategic bombardment advocate, he was one of four officers tasked to write AWPD-1 in 1941.

As assistant chief of staff for war plans of the newly created Air Staff in Washington, then Maj Hal George headed a board of officers who prepared the plan for the air war against Germany. He later directed Air Transport Command throughout much of WWII.

Lt Gen Frank M. Andrews was the first air officer to serve as a deputy chief of staff on the Army's general staff. In early 1943, he succeeded Gen Dwight Eisenhower as commander of all US troops in the European theater of operations.

American B-24 Liberators bomb a rail yard in Germany during WWII.

Col Paul W. Tibbets Jr. (center) and the crew of the *Enola Gay* that delivered the first atomic bomb on Hiroshima, Japan.

The Enola Gay, a specially modified B-29 Superfortress named for the pilot's mother, dropped the atomic bomb "Little Boy" on Hiroshima 6 August 1945.

"Fat Man" was the code name assigned to the atomic bomb dropped 9 August 1945 on Nagasaki, leading to the Japanese surrender six days later.

Gen George C. Marshall was known as America's foremost soldier during WWII, serving as Army chief of staff from 1939 to 1945. He was named secretary of state in 1947 and formulated the "Marshall Plan" to rebuild war-torn Europe. In 1950 he became secretary of defense.

Gen George C. Kenney is best known as the commander of Allied Air Forces in the Southwest Pacific Area (SWPA) from August 1942 until 1945. He was appointed the first commander of Strategic Air Command in March 1946.

Commander of Eighth Air Force and later of US Strategic Air Forces Europe in WWII, Gen Carl "Tooey" Spaatz became the first US Air Force chief of staff.

Maj Gen Leslie Groves, director of the Manhattan Project, and physicist Robert Oppenheimer inspect the site of the Trinity test in September 1945.

Operation Crossroads Baker was the second in a series of detonations on Bikini Atoll in mid 1946 to test the effects of atomic weapons on ships.

Boeing's B-50 Superfortress strategic bomber was a post-WWII revision of the B-29 Superfortress, fitted with more powerful Pratt & Whitney engines and among the last piston-driven bombers leading to the jet age.

Douglas C-54 Skymasters, the military version of the DC-4 airliner, were the workhorses of the Berlin airlift, which broke the Soviet blockade after more than 10 months of round-the-clock operations.

Gen Hoyt S. Vandenberg was commanding general of the Ninth Air Force during WWII and served as the second CSAF from 1948 to 1953.

Lt Gen William H. Tunner used his expertise in large-scale military airlift operations in Air Transport Command (ATC) during WWII, commanding The Hump
operation, and later in Military Air Transport Service (MATS), directing the Berlin
airlift.

As Roosevelt's vice president, Harry S. Truman was kept ignorant of the development of the atomic bomb that he would later order dropped on Hiroshima and
Nagasaki, Japan.

FADM Ernest King, Secretary of the Navy James V. Forrestal, and FADM Chester Nimitz (l. to r.) confer at the Navy Department in late 1945.

Thomas K. Finletter, second secretary of the Air Force (April 1950–January 1953), previously served on the five-man commission that inquired into all phases of aviation and drafted the national air policy report.

As chairman of the House Armed Services Committee for much of his 51 years in Congress, Carl Vinson helped shape the US military through WWII and into the Cold War. *Photo courtesy of Ed Jackson, Carl Vinson Institute of Government (retired).*

The largest piston-driven warplane ever built, the B-36 Peacemaker was obsolescent from the outset in a world of supersonic jet interceptors, but it remained the only aircraft capable of delivering the full arsenal of US nuclear weapons until replaced by the B-52 Stratofortress in 1955.

Lt Gen Curtis LeMay, constantly an enigma and, to some, a pariah, nevertheless guided Strategic Air Command through the darkest days of the Cold War and established its legacy.

Gen Joseph McNarney, an airman, served as commanding general of US Forces in the European theater in WWII and later as the military governor of Allied-occupied Germany.

General of the Army Omar Bradley was one of only eight Americans to wear five stars and served as the first chairman of the Joint Chiefs of Staff.

Lt Gen Hubert Harmon commanded Thirteenth Air Force in the South Pacific during WWII and became the first superintendent of the US Air Force Academy in 1954.

The first secretary of the newly independent US Air Force, Stuart Symington (left), confers with its first chief of staff, Gen Carl "Tooey" Spaatz.

Artist's conception of the USS *United States* (CVA-58), first of four proposed "supercarriers," which was never completed due to limited funds and opposition from the Army and Air Force, ultimately leading to the "Revolt of the Admirals."

The venerable Boeing B-29 Superfortresses of the 98th Bombardment Group were recalled to service in Korea in 1950–53.

J. Robert Oppenheimer (right) with his successor at the Los Alamos National Laboratory, Norris Bradbury, in 1964.

The North American F-86 Sabre was America's first swept-wing fighter, built to counter the similarly designed Soviet MiG-15 in high-speed dogfights during the Korean War.

Dr. Lawrence Livermore (left) with Dr. Edward Teller, then director of the Livermore National Laboratory.

Lt Gen George Stratemeyer was the WWII chief of the Air Staff and Far East Air Forces (FEAF) commander during the first year of the Korean War.

Gen Emmett E. "Rosie" O'Donnell Jr. led the first B-29 Superfortress attack against Tokyo during WWII and served as commander of the FEAF Bomber Command at the beginning of the Korean War.

Soviet-built MiG-15s, such as this one provided by a North Korean defector, presented a major challenge to US air forces over Korea.

Gen Otto P. Weyland served as commander of Far East Air Forces during the Korean War and, later, of Tactical Air Command.

Atlas ICBMs, first launched in November 1958, formed one leg of the nuclear triad and vastly reduced attack warning time.

SAC's B-52s were on constant alert, either in the air or on the tarmac, throughout the Cold War.

B-47s often used jet-assisted takeoff (JATO) bottles, which were jettisoned once in the air.

The Distant Early Warning (DEW) Line was a first line of defense against Soviet bombers.

A YRB-36 carries a YF-84F in a trapeze during Project FICON to develop "parasite" fighters which would allow US bombers to penetrate Soviet air defenses.

Hungarian-born mathematician, aerospace engineer, and physicist Theodore von Kármán is credited with much of the research that enabled supersonic and hypersonic flight.

The McDonnell XF-85 Goblin, the smallest jet fighter ever built, was designed to fit entirely inside the bomb bay of a B-36, allowing the heavy bomber to carry its own fighter escort.

The Mark 7 "Thor" was the first tactical nuclear bomb adopted by US armed forces and was to be delivered using the toss method with the help of the low-altitude bombing system (LABS).

Gen Lauris Norstad was appointed commander of US Air Forces Europe in November 1951, and in 1956 was elevated to the position of Supreme Allied Commander Europe—the first airman to hold that job.

The length and depth of Paul H. Nitze's government service are best summed up in the title of his memoir, *From Hiroshima to Glasnost*.

The North American B-45 Tornado was the first USAF operational jet bomber and first multi-jet engine bomber to be refueled in mid-air. Although rapidly succeeded by the B-47 Stratojet, RB-45s served in Strategic Air Command through 1959.

Gen Curtis LeMay set the standards for SAC before moving on to ultimately become Air Force chief of staff.

SAC crew runs toward aircraft in a ready-alert launch.

Gen Thomas S. Power was LeMay's protégé and successor as CINCSAC in 1957.

Chapter 6

Nuclear Weapons, Custody, and the Korean War

The detonation of Joe 1 focused the minds of America's leaders. The monopoly of atomic weapons was gone. The Soviets were believed to have the beginnings of an atomic arsenal—the JCS suggested they could have 30 bombs by the end of 1950, and in the event of war, they would definitely use them.[1] Military leaders called for an immediate increase in the US arsenal. Air defense was hitherto largely ignored, but Vandenberg wrote a sobering memo to Secretary Symington in April 1950 noting that it was a weak point: there were only eight and two-thirds fighter wings, augmented by Air National Guard units, for the defense of the United States, and only two of those wings had an all-weather capability. At least 12 more fighter wings were needed. There were a mere 28 basic radars and seven control radars available in CONUS, and those were of marginal utility. At least 109 basic radars and 11 control radars were needed for an effective defense.[2]

War plans, until then virtually an intellectual exercise given the paucity of worthwhile intelligence on the Soviet Union, took on immediacy. Strangely, however, President Truman continued to maintain that a sound economy was the nation's first line of defense and resisted attempts to raise the budget; indeed, in his annual budget message in January 1950, he claimed that fiscal efficiency efforts would allow continued *reductions* in defense.[3] Defense Secretary Louis Johnson agreed wholeheartedly with this reasoning, believing efficiency and cutting fat would allow necessary military initiatives to be funded.[4] There was, however, one issue causing a great deal of discussion behind closed doors that all knew would cost money.

The theory behind thermonuclear detonation had been discussed in the 1920s when one scientist described the sun as a continuous series of explosions caused by the conversion of hydrogen into helium. These

---

[1] Kenneth Condit, *The Joint Chiefs of Staff and National Policy*, vol. 2, *1947–1949*, 521. The chiefs made this projection in comments on a revision of the *Offtackle* plan.

[2] Vandenberg to Symington, memorandum, 11 April 1950, DDQI, 1976, document 242B.

[3] Truman, *Public Papers of the Presidents, 1950*, 46–53.

[4] Johnson's biographer argues that the defense secretary sought to out-cut the president regarding the budget. McFarland and Roll, *Louis Johnson and the Arming of America*, 196–204.

explosions resulted not from the splitting of atoms but from the *fusion* of atomic nuclei. Only extremely high temperatures and pressures could induce fusion, however; normal explosives could not generate those conditions. The atom bomb changed the debate. Scientists now speculated that the force of a fission explosion might be enough to cause the fusion of hydrogen atoms—an atomic bomb could be used as a trigger to generate a thermonuclear detonation. Were this to occur, a hydrogen bomb could generate thousands of times more energy than an atom bomb. Scientists at Los Alamos during World War II were aware of these theories, but their focus was on accomplishing the first step—producing a fission atomic bomb. Nonetheless, studies were carried out and discussions continued among atomic scientists.[5] Not all of them liked the idea of thermonuclear weapons.

J. Robert Oppenheimer was known to be an opponent of thermonuclear development. He and others who had worked on the Manhattan Project developed moral scruples and began to regret their wartime research. Oppenheimer wrote in March 1948, "In some sort of crude sense which no vulgarity, no humor, no over-statement can quite extinguish, the physicists have known sin; and this is a knowledge that they cannot lose."[6] Not all felt similarly. Harold Agnew, a director at the New Mexico lab, described his coworkers in negative terms: "There were remnants of this feeling that we shouldn't pursue these endeavors. I was not in sympathy with these individuals; in fact, I thought they were nuts . . . they even got into religious matters. They would quote the Bible. I thought they were quite off their rockers, frankly."[7]

In October 1949 the General Advisory Committee to the AEC unanimously opposed thermonuclear development. The committee doubted a fusion weapon was technically feasible but also expressed moral objections: "We base our recommendations on our belief that the extreme dangers to mankind inherent in the proposal wholly outweigh any military advantage that could come from this development." The group concluded that employment of a hydrogen bomb would be tantamount to genocide; therefore, it should never even be built.[8]

David Lilienthal, head of the AEC, likewise opposed thermonuclear research because he too thought it would be a weapon of

---

[5] For background, see Rhodes, *Dark Sun*, passim; and Teller, *Memoirs*, chaps. 24–27.
[6] Oppenheimer, "Physics in the Contemporary World," 66.
[7] Blumberg and Owens, *Energy and Conflict*, 240.
[8] General Advisory Committee to Lilienthal, letter, 30 October 1949, in US Department of State, *FRUS, 1949*, vol. 1, 569–73.

mass destruction. He argued that testing such a device could release large amounts of radioactivity into the atmosphere, polluting the world.[9] He also contended that beginning such development would lead to an arms race with the Soviets. Lilienthal was so opposed to the new bomb that when Louis W. Alvarez, a leading physicist at Los Alamos who favored thermonuclear experimentation, came to argue the point with him, Lilienthal turned his back on Alvarez and refused to discuss the matter. Lilienthal's negative views were shared by AEC commissioners Henry Smythe and Sumner Pike.

The other two AEC commissioners disagreed. Gordon Dean feared that failure of the United States to pursue a hydrogen bomb would leave the Soviets with a monopoly—he had no doubt they were already working on such a device.[10] Lewis Strauss was more emphatic, arguing the hydrogen bomb was technically feasible and all talk of moral scruples was absurd. The Soviets had no such reservations and would forge ahead on the bomb. If they were to gain such a weapon first, "I am unable to see any satisfaction in that prospect." As for the pollution fear raised by Lilienthal, Strauss scoffed that it would take hundreds of detonations to release the pollution claimed. Finally, he argued that failure by the United States to undertake thermonuclear development would be seen by the Soviets as a trick and would thus gain no positive results.[11]

Air Force leaders strongly supported thermonuclear development. Soon after Joe I, Edward Teller, a leading physicist later known as "the father of the hydrogen bomb," raised the subject with Maj Gen Roscoe Wilson, deputy head of the AFSWP, who then briefed Vandenberg on Teller's ideas. Vandenberg was impressed and that very afternoon discussed the matter with the joint chiefs. The following day he met with the Joint Committee on Atomic Energy and mentioned the matter to the senators and congressmen as well. The committee chair, Senator Brien McMahon, was as enthusiastic about the prospects of the new weapon as was Vandenberg and wrote a strong letter to President Truman advocating thermonuclear development.[12]

Surprisingly, the other chiefs were not sold on the new weapon. It was initially believed a hydrogen bomb would be huge—weighing up

---

[9] US Atomic Energy Commission, *In the Matter of J. Robert Oppenheimer*, 682 (hereafter: *Oppenheimer Hearings*); and Lilienthal to Truman, memorandum, 9 November 1949, in *FRUS, 1949*, vol. 1, 576–85.

[10] See views of Gordon Dean in Lilienthal to Truman, memorandum, in *FRUS, 1949*, vol. 1, 583–84.

[11] Strauss to Truman, letter, 25 November 1949, in *FRUS, 1949*, vol. 1, 596–99.

[12] *Oppenheimer Hearings*, 127, 682–83; McMahon to Truman, letter, 21 November 1949, in *FRUS, 1949*, vol. 1, 588–95; and Rhodes, *Dark Sun*, 387–88.

to 50,000 lbs. A device that large could be carried by a B-36 and the new B-52 jet bomber then under development, but it would be far too heavy for tactical applications or for employment by carrier-based aircraft. The Sandstone tests of mid 1948 had revolutionized atomic bomb design, making tactical atomic weapons possible—the Army was even planning on atomic artillery rounds.[13] Now it appeared a nuclear weapon was in the offing that would crowd out fission bombs—the Army and Navy would once again be shut out, and the Air Force would regain its monopoly.

Vandenberg understood these fears and argued that in a war with the Soviet Union, there would be so many targets to be struck that a vastly expanded stockpile—especially one containing such powerful nuclear weapons—would be essential. Moreover, given the enormous power of fusion weapons, they would make far more efficient use of the scarce fissionable material available. The result was a 63-percent increase in the number of bombs in the stockpile and a 75-percent increase in the total yield of the bombs.[14] The chiefs were still not keen but also understood the dangers of deferring thermonuclear development in the face of probable Soviet exploitation of the new technology. In November they went on record stating that a Soviet monopoly in nuclear weaponry would be "intolerable." They reiterated this stance two months later, calling for development of a hydrogen bomb.[15]

Significantly, in October 1949 the treason of Klaus Fuchs came to light. Fuchs, a Canadian physicist, had worked at Los Alamos during the war and been involved in deliberations regarding a thermonuclear bomb. In January 1950 he was arrested in Britain as a Soviet spy. Although American intelligence officials were unable to interrogate Fuchs and discover the depth of his betrayal, it seemed obvious the information he had passed on to Moscow would give the Soviets a head start.[16] In a note to the joint chiefs, Admiral Sherman noted the arrest of Fuchs

---

[13] Rhodes, *Dark Sun*, 320; Wilson, interview, 1–2 December 1983; and Norris, Cochran, and Arkin, "History of the Nuclear Stockpile," 106–9.

[14] Vandenberg to JCS, memorandum, 11 March 1950; JCS 1823/1, "Military Considerations on Delivery of More Powerful Atomic Bombs," 13 June 1948, in Ross and Rosenberg, *America's Plans for War against the Soviet Union*, vol. 9.

[15] JCS to Johnson, memorandum, 23 November 1949, in *FRUS, 1949*, vol. 1, 595–96; and JCS to Johnson, memorandum, 13 January 1950, in *FRUS, 1950*, vol. 1, 503–11.

[16] Johnson to Truman, memorandum, 24 February 1950, in *FRUS, 1950*, vol. 1, 538–39; Lamphere and Shachtman, *FBI-KGB Wars*, 185–88; Rearden, *History of the Office of the Secretary of Defense*, vol. 1, 454; and Hirsch and Matthews, "H-Bomb," 23–30, argue that Fuchs was irrelevant because his information was outdated and wrong; however, even if that were true, no one knew that in early 1950 when the H-bomb decision was made.

and how this negatively impacted US security, writing that estimates of the Soviet stockpile "will be materially revised upward."[17]

Truman then appointed a panel consisting of Johnson, Lilienthal, and Secretary of State Dean Acheson to look into the matter of nuclear research. Johnson supported the hydrogen bomb, while Lilienthal was opposed; Acheson had not yet disclosed his opinion. He listened attentively to both men but was unconvinced by the arguments of Lilienthal, asking, "How can you persuade a paranoid adversary to disarm by example?"[18] He opted for development of the bomb. The three men went to the president on January 31 and presented their split decision. Lilienthal tried to explain his misgivings, but Truman cut him short, saying people had predicted the end of the world when he supported Greece in 1948. Nothing happened then, and he was certain things would be all right now as well. He then asked a simple question: "Can the Russians do it?" Everyone agreed they could. "In that case, we have no choice. We'll go ahead."[19] (It was later discovered that the Soviets had launched their own thermonuclear program 18 months earlier.[20]) Lilienthal resigned over this decision. His successor at the AEC, Gordon Dean, supported nuclear development. Dwight Eisenhower looked back on this event when president and argued, "If the Soviets had beaten us to the hydrogen bomb, Soviet power would today be on the march in every quarter of the globe."[21] The thermonuclear program was to be an outstanding success; the first hydrogen device was detonated in November 1952. SAC would soon get nuclear weapons that would dwarf everything in their existing arsenal.

Despite the president's commitment on the hydrogen bomb, Soviet aggressiveness in Berlin and Eastern Europe, and the detonation of Joe I, the budget process for FY 1951 was a depressing repeat of the previous two years. Funds remained in short supply, so the Air Force and the Navy continued to haggle over the relative merits of bombers and aircraft carriers. Secretary Johnson labored to keep his headstrong chiefs under control, and Eisenhower remained on duty as

[17] Sherman to JCS, memorandum, 1 December 1949, in "Records of the JCS, Part 2: 1945–1953: The United States," UPA, 1980, reel 2.

[18] Isaacson and Thomas, *Wise Men*, 487.

[19] David Lilienthal, "Special Report to the President," 31 January 1950, in *FRUS, 1950*, vol. 1, 513–23; Lilienthal, *Journals of David Lilienthal*, vol. 2, 632–33; Rearden, *History of the Office of the Secretary of Defense*. vol. 1, 453; and Bernstein, "Truman and the H-Bomb," 12–18.

[20] Sakharov, *Memoirs*, 94. Sakharov, the leading nuclear physicist in the Soviet Union and designer of its hydrogen bomb, stated that his team was directed by the Council of Ministers and the Party Central Committee in June 1948 to begin working on a thermonuclear weapon immediately.

[21] Hewlett and Duncan, *History of the Atomic Energy Commission*, vol. 2, 369–409. The Soviets exploded a hydrogen device on 22 November 1955.

temporary chief of staff to the president. All the chiefs were frustrated. The Air Force was still limited to 48 groups, and there was little hope for improvement. Secretary Stuart Symington resigned to protest the continued budget constraints.[22] Congress was quiescent; it recognized that more dollars would be needed for the new North Atlantic Treaty Organization as well as for the military assistance program designed to help allies get back on their feet militarily. There was also the added cost for thermonuclear development. All of those initiatives would cost a great deal of money, but no one seemed willing to appropriate it. One Washington reporter was puzzled by what he termed a "curious euphoria" that seemed to be gripping Congress and the Truman administration in the early months of 1950.[23] The much-pared FY 1951 defense budget passed the House in June—only a few days before North Korean forces exploded across the 38th Parallel.

The Outbreak of War

The cause of the Korean War dates from World War II, when Churchill, Roosevelt, and Chiang Kai-shek discussed the peninsula's postwar status at the Cairo conference in December 1943. The three leaders concluded that upon Japanese withdrawal, a period of trusteeship would precede Korean independence. Stalin agreed at Yalta in February 1945.[24] It would not be that easy. When Japan surrendered, Soviet troops moved into the northern portion of Korea and imposed a government under Kim Il Sung. To the south, US forces arrived and installed someone friendly to their interests—Syngman Rhee. Attempts at negotiating a unification scheme between the two sides came to naught. Secretary of State George Marshall decided to turn the matter over to the new United Nations, and in November 1947 that organization assumed responsibility for Korean unification.

The UN sent a commission to North Korea, but Kim Il Sung's government would not acknowledge its authority and refused the commissioners entry. The UN called for elections anyway. When the north refused to participate, elections were held in the south on 10 May 1948, and Rhee won. Ignoring reality, the UN promptly declared

---

[22] Symington would return to politics as chairman of the National Security Resources Board and then the Reconstruction Finance Corporation. In 1952 he was elected to the Senate from Missouri. Symington, interview, 2 May and 12 December 1978, 83.

[23] Parrish, *Behind the Sheltering Bomb*, 324. The reporter was Joseph Alsop.

[24] *FRUS: The Conferences at Cairo and Tehran*, 376, 448–49.

Rhee the president of Korea. In response, Kim Il Sung held his own "elections" in the north, which he of course won, and declared himself president of all Korea. In late 1948 the Soviet Union withdrew its occupation forces from the north, and several months later the United States withdrew from the south. This did not solve the problem—Korea was still divided, and diplomacy had failed.[25]

The United States appeared to be intent on washing its hands of Korea. In March 1949, Gen Douglas MacArthur, the Far East commander, stated in an interview that his "line of defense" included the Philippines and Japan—he did not mention South Korea.[26] Secretary of State Acheson said much the same thing nearly a year later in a speech before the National Press Club in Washington, stating, "The [US] defensive perimeter runs from the Ryukyus to the Philippine Islands."[27] Explicitly excluded from American interests were Korea and Formosa. If deterrence had been US policy, the statements by MacArthur and Acheson rendered it void; the communist governments in North Korea and China received a clear signal regarding US interests.

In March 1949 Kim Il Sung went to Moscow and proposed to Stalin an invasion of the south with the intent of unifying Korea under his leadership. Stalin said no. In September Kim again asked Stalin for his blessing; once again, Stalin refused. In January 1950, Stalin changed his mind and gave Kim the go-ahead and reaffirmed this decision in March. Kim then visited Beijing and asked for the approval of Mao Tse-tung. Not wishing to contradict Stalin, Mao gave reluctant approval to the North Korean invasion. Stalin made it clear that if the United States intervened, it would be up to the Chinese to intercede on North Korea's behalf. However, if the United States attacked China, Moscow would come to its aid.[28]

North Korea attacked across the 38th Parallel on 25 June 1950, catching the United States and South Korea by surprise. Defense Secretary Johnson and Gen Omar Bradley had left the Far East to return to Washington only the day before and obviously had no inkling of the invasion. The CIA, increasingly suspicious of the Soviet Union and its

---

[25] For the events in Korea before June 1950, see Gordenker, *United Nations and the Peaceful Unification of Korea*; Iriye, *Cold War in Asia*; and Buhite, *Soviet-American Relations in Asia, 1945–1954*.

[26] Schnabel and Watson, *Joint Chiefs of Staff and National Policy*, vol. 3, 38.

[27] Dean Acheson, speech before the National Press Club, 12 January 1950, in US Department of State, *American Foreign Policy, 1950–1955*, vol. 2, 2310–22. The quote is on pp. 2317–18. Formosa was the name then used for the island of Taiwan. The Ryukus are an island chain south of the Japanese home islands, the largest of which is Okinawa.

[28] Stueck, "Korean War," 266–74; and Jin, "Birth of the People's Republic of China and the Road to the Korean War," 240.

intentions, thought Moscow might attempt to use force to achieve its goal of world communism, but analysts continued to view Europe as the main danger area. Asia, but especially Korea, was ignored as a potential flash point. MacArthur was also caught unaware.[29] Obviously, the CIA had blundered badly, and the director of central intelligence was soon fired and replaced by Gen Walter Bedell Smith.

President Truman called his chief advisors together at Blair House— the White House was undergoing remodeling, so the Trumans were living across the street. Secretary of State Acheson opened the discussion with two suggestions: the United States furnish arms and equipment to the Republic of Korea (ROK), and American personnel in Korea be evacuated. He also recommended that the Seventh Fleet be moved to the Straits of Formosa to protect the island (where the Nationalist government of Chiang Kai-shek was located) from the mainland. Acheson feared that the Korean attack might be the first step in a communist Asian offensive. Bradley, chairman of the JCS, recommended that US air and naval forces attack the North Korean aggressors and help shore up ROK morale. He did not yet advise the use of American ground troops.[30]

Although bellicose, the chiefs and Secretary Johnson were leery of a war in Asia. Vandenberg, for example, was confident airpower could blunt the attacks, but feared the Soviet reaction. When Truman asked if Soviet air bases in the area could be "knocked out," Vandenberg said they could, but it would take time and involve the use of atomic weapons. The subject was not pursued. After listening to the discussion, Truman announced the following decisions:

1. General MacArthur was to send supplies to the ROK.

2. A survey team was to be sent to Korea to assess the situation.

3. The Seventh Fleet would take up a position between Formosa and the mainland.

4. The Air Force should make plans to "wipe out" Soviet air bases in the Far East but limit its actions at present to supporting the evacuation of American personnel.

5. All should consider where the Soviets might strike next.

---

[29] CIA study, "Estimates of the Effects of the Soviet Possession of the Atomic Bomb upon the Security of the United States," 6 April 1950, in "CIA Reports, 1946–1976" collection, UPA, 1980, reel 3. MacArthur's staff admitted among themselves they had been caught by surprise. Maj Gen Earle E. Partridge, diary, 26 June 1950, AFHRA, file 168.7014-1.

[30] This account is from notes taken by Philip Jessup, in *FRUS, 1950*, vol. 7, 156–61.

Vandenberg then asked the president if aircraft could attack North Korean tanks if necessary and was told yes.[31] Bradley said later the shadow of the late 1930s hung over the discussions that evening. All remembered how the policy of appeasement had encouraged aggression by Germany and Japan; they did not want that to happen again.[32]

The air commanders in the Far East were Lt Gen George E. Stratemeyer, head of Far East Air Forces (FEAF), and Maj Gen Earle E. "Pat" Partridge, commander of the Fifth Air Force. "Strat" was a West Point classmate of Eisenhower and Bradley (class of 1915) and during World War II served on the Air Staff and in the India-Burma Theater and then China. After the war he led Air Defense Command before moving to Tokyo and becoming commander of FEAF. Partridge was West Point Class of 1924. A fighter pilot early in his career, he transitioned to bombers and finished the war as commander of Eighth Air Force. After a stint on the Air Staff, he took over Fifth Air Force in October 1948.[33] The mission of the Fifth was the air defense of Japan. Its pilots—flying obsolescent P-51s, F-82s (the twin Mustang), and F-80s—were trained for interceptor duties, not close air support. Stratemeyer himself admitted FEAF was "totally inadequate for anything other than a limited air defense of Japan, Okinawa, and the Philippine Islands." His aircraft did not practice gunnery, there were no forward air controllers, and there was no joint training with the Army. MacArthur's ground forces were also trained and equipped for occupation duties—they were not expecting to engage in major ground operations and had little knowledge of air support procedures.[34] As for air strength, FEAF consisted of 1,172 aircraft, but only 533 of those were in operational units. The majority of those (365) consisted of obsolescent F-80 jet fighters. FEAF also had 22 B-29s based on Guam.[35] It would need reinforcements.

At the time of the North Korean invasion, Partridge was acting commander because Stratemeyer was out of town. Upon hearing of the invasion, Partridge directed the deployment of fighter bombers to cover the evacuation, and the first wing arrived in South Korea the

---

[31] Ibid.

[32] Omar Bradley, "U.S. Military Policy: 1950," 143–54.

[33] FEAF consisted of three numbered air forces: 5AF, headquartered at Yakota AB in Japan; 20AF, based at Kadena AB on Okinawa; and 13AF, located at Clark AB in the Philippines.

[34] Futrell, *United States Air Force in Korea*, 58; Lt Gen Edward Almond, "United Nations Operations in Korea," speech to the Air University, 8 October 1951, AFHRA, file K239.716250; and Timberlake, interview, May 1965, 17–18. Almond was commander of X Corps in Korea, and Timberlake was deputy commander of 5AF.

[35] Futrell, *United States Air Force in Korea*, 58.

following day. Almost immediately, F-82s ran into North Korean air-craft but turned away, not certain if they were authorized to fight. This lack of aggressiveness irked Vandenberg, who cabled Partridge to take action: "No interference with your mission will be tolerated."[36]

On the evening of 26 June the president and his advisors met again at Blair House. Truman directed Vandenberg to take whatever ac-tions were necessary to stem the invasion, although when asked if that meant going north of the 38th Parallel, the president said, "not yet." Gen J. Lawton Collins, the Army chief of staff, said the ROK army was in disarray and its chief "has no fight left in him."[37] Ameri-can troops would be necessary to stem the tide. The JCS then autho-rized MacArthur to attack all North Korean forces south of the 38th. Partridge later recalled that MacArthur was "astonished" by the di-rective and stated, "I don't believe it; I can't understand." He had been told explicitly that South Korea was not his concern, and there were no contingency plans for such a fight.[38]

The following day the UN Security Council branded the North Koreans as aggressors and pledged military support for the ROK. This surprising development occurred only because the Soviet Union was boycotting the proceedings and thus unable to veto the resolu-tion. Nonetheless, aid provided by other countries would be slow to arrive, and in the meantime the situation on the ground looked grim. Seoul had been overrun, and the remnants of ROK military forces streamed south. Truman authorized the deployment of a regimental combat team from Japan, to be followed by two divisions. The Air Force was simultaneously authorized to begin hitting targets in North Korea—although Vandenberg was warned to keep his aircraft away from the Manchurian and Soviet borders.[39]

On 3 July, Vandenberg ordered two SAC B-29 groups to Japan (the 22nd and 92nd) to join the 19th Bomb Wing already deployed to Okinawa. Two more B-29 bomb groups, the 98th and 307th, would soon follow, and an RB-29 reconnaissance squadron as well. All of these units were placed under the command of Stratemeyer at FEAF, but Maj Gen Emmett "Rosie" O'Donnell, commander of

---

[36] Maj Gen Earle E. Partridge, diary, 26 June 1950, AFHRA, file 168.7014-1; and O'Donnell to LeMay, letter, 10 July 1950, LeMay papers, LOC, box 65.

[37] *FRUS, 1950*, vol. 7, 179. Actually, MacArthur ordered air strikes north of the 38th Parallel on 29 June—the day before receiving authorization from Washington. Schnabel and Watson, *Joint Chiefs of Staff and National Policy*, vol. 3, 110.

[38] Partridge, interview, 16 February 1977, 39; Almond, "United Nations Operations in Korea," speech to the Air University, 8 October 1951; and Partridge, diary, 26 June 1950.

[39] *FRUS, 1950*, vol. 7, 217.

SAC's Fifteenth Air Force, was dispatched to the theater to head the newly formed FEAF Bomber Command (Provisional) that would consist of SAC units deployed to the theater. In truth, LeMay was not pleased with these events; he believed the dispatch of bomber groups to Asia—even though consisting of his least-capable air-craft—was a needless distraction from the primary goal of deterring a major war with the Soviets. He later commented, "I didn't want too many splinters to be whittled off the stick which we might have to wield."[40] In this initial surge, all the bombers sent were B-29s, but only nine of them had been Saddletree modified—those aircraft remained on Guam.[41]

At the same time, Vandenberg sought to deploy two more SAC bomb groups to England. He, like most American political and military leaders, believed the Korean assault was a feint to draw attention away from Europe. A CIA report concluded the Soviets seemed to be preparing for hostilities, although it was unclear whether they were exercising simple prudence, they were expecting to intervene in Korea, or they had designs on Europe.[42] Vandenberg wanted to take no chances, hence his desire to put more firepower in England. As noted, SAC bomb groups had been deploying to Europe since 1946, and the pace of those moves increased sharply during the Berlin crisis. After the blockade ended, SAC cut back its rotation schedule from three groups to two, but now the bomber presence would be boosted. During the Berlin crisis the bombers sent to England had not been atomic capable, but this time they would be. Given the political implications of such a move, the RAF stalled its approval until it could consult with Prime Minister Clement Attlee. Initially, the British were reluctant to agree to the deployment for fear the Soviets would see it as an "unfriendly act," but they soon concurred, and B-50s from the 93rd and 97th Bomb Wings began to move east. Attlee stressed, however, that the deployments must look "normal" and not be billed as a show of strength.[43] Mark IV atomic bomb casings, with their explosive

---

[40] LeMay and Kantor, *Mission with LeMay*, 458.

[41] Crane, *American Airpower Strategy in Korea*, 70. Ten aircraft were scheduled for the deployment, but the lead B-29 containing the wing commander, Brig Gen Robert F. Travis, crashed on takeoff from Fairfield-Suisun AFB on 5 August 1950. Travis was killed in the crash, and the atomic bomb on board (minus the core) was destroyed. Farmer, "Korea and the A-Bomb," 41–42.

[42] CIA, "Intelligence Memorandum No. 3232-SRC," 25 August 1950, DDQI, 1981, document 141A.

[43] Johnson to Vandenberg, message, 9 July 1950, Johnson to Norstad, message, 10 July 1950, and LeMay to Norstad, message, 10 July 1950, all in Vandenberg papers, LOC, box 56; and Young, "No Blank Cheque," 1447–49. For a review of the diplomatic documents themselves, which are often fascinating, see *FRUS, 1951*, vol. 1, 802–901.

charges and wiring but minus their atomic cores, accompanied the bombers—which were Saddletree modified—and SAC crews conducted loading exercises while in Britain. Initially, the bases in England lacked adequate security, bothering LeMay and Leon Johnson, the 3rd Air Division commander, but British paratroopers were eventually detailed to guard the bases, and perimeter fences were also built. A fighter group was deployed from CONUS to provide air cover.[44]

Within five days of receiving deployment orders, the B-29s sent to Japan were flying combat missions in Korea. This impressive response was a tribute to the rigorous training emphasized by LeMay. He had stressed that SAC's mission involved global deployment and operations, and he meant to ensure the command could do so. Mobility plans and exercises had noted the importance of deploying with spare parts, engines, equipment, and whatever else would be necessary to begin flying—LeMay wanted to rely as little as possible on resources located at the forward bases where his units would be deployed. Aluminum bins were fitted into the bomb bays to carry tools and spare parts, so the bombers arrived in the Far East crammed with equipment rather than ordnance. SAC plans called for units to take enough material with them to sustain operations for 30 days. Even so, there were shortages, such as adequate maps of Korea. In addition, Yakota Air Base soon became overcrowded, and crews were living in tents.[45]

Vandenberg wired to Stratemeyer that he did not want to presume to suggest specific targets for the SAC bombers, but "it is axiomatic that tactical operations on the battlefield cannot be fully effective unless there is a simultaneous interdiction and destruction of sources behind the battlefield."[46] O'Donnell also understood. The day he arrived in Tokyo he briefed MacArthur on his command's capabilities and suggested a "fire job" (incendiary attacks) on North Korean industrial centers. O'Donnell argued that the bombing of airfields, tanks, bridges, and "Koreans on bicycles" was useless; he wanted to go after "sources of substance." MacArthur denied the use of incendiaries and ordered O'Donnell to use only high-explosive bombs. Sensing MacArthur would soon change his mind—which he did—

---

[44] Moody, *Building a Strategic Air Force*, 344–45.

[45] "The Deployment of Strategic Air Command Units to the Far East, July–August 1950," SAC historical study, 1 December 1950, AFHRA, file 416.01-9, 7–8.

[46] Vandenberg to Stratemeyer, message, 3 July 1950, Vandenberg papers, LOC, box 86; Lt Gen George E. Stratemeyer, diary, 4 July 1950, AFHRA, file 7018-16, 51–52. This diary was edited and published by William T. Y'Blood as *Three Wars of Lt. Gen. George E. Stratemeyer*. Future references will give the date of the diary entry and the page number in Y'Blood.

O'Donnell ordered 3,000 tons of incendiary bombs shipped to the Far East.[47] On 11 July O'Donnell listed Bomber Command's prime missions, which included "destroying the enemy communication system" north of the Han River to the Manchurian border; destroying North Korea's industrial targets, fuel storage facilities, supply depots, and other military targets; destroying enemy air installations; and operating south of the 38th Parallel as directed. Bomber Command would not attack urban areas except when hitting the military targets noted above.[48] Reality on the ground soon intruded.

The first major B-29 strike took place on 13 July when 50 bombers attacked the port of Wonsan, North Korea. Despite doctrinal beliefs of airmen regarding the use of bombers, the situation on the ground demanded flexibility. By 11 July, Bomber Command's priority was close air support and isolation of the battlefield. As during World War II, the situation in Korea dictated bombers be used in a tactical role—US and ROK ground forces were in perilous straits. B-29s were diverted to tactical support of the beleaguered 24th Division. On 16 August, 98 B-29s dropped 859 tons of bombs on an area near Weagan in North Korea where it was believed enemy troops were massing. This was SAC's first massive close air support mission of the war and the biggest use of strategic bombers in a tactical role since Normandy. Unfortunately, post-strike reconnaissance could not confirm that any enemy troops were actually located in the area that had been bombed! The airmen were irked, and although ground commanders hailed the psychological effect of the bombing on American morale, even MacArthur admitted the uselessness of saturation bombing on suspected troop concentrations. On 3 August, Bomber Command used three of its bomb groups to conduct interdiction and strategic attack missions, while the other two groups would be available for ground support.[49] The latter missions were enormously gratifying to the ground commanders, and Maj Gen William F. Dean, commander of the 24th Division, stated appreciatively that "without this continuing air effort it is doubtful if the courageous combat soldiers, spread thinly along the line, could have withstood the onslaught of the vastly numerically superior

---

[47] O'Donnell to LeMay, letter, 11 July 1950, LeMay papers, LOC, box 65; Stratemeyer diary, 11 July 1950, 66–67.

[48] "Far East Bomber Command Provisional, 4 July–31 October 1950," vol. 4, Bk. 1, SAC historical study, AFHRA, file K713.01-8, 2–4.

[49] Futrell, *United States Air Force in Korea*, 94, 128; and Lloyd, *Cold War Legacy*, 153.

enemy."[50] By the end of the first month of operations, Bomber Command had dropped over seven tons of bombs, 55 percent of which were in close support. The command lost seven men killed in action.[51]

There were missteps. On 27 July a B-29 scheduled to drop its bombs on Pyongyang inadvertently flew into Soviet territory near Darien—the plane was 200 miles off course. It was intercepted by Soviet fighters but, amazingly, was merely escorted back to the border. On two other occasions, in September and again in November, B-29s became lost and dropped their bombs on Chinese territory at Antung.[52] These incidents, which could have had severe diplomatic repercussions, were glossed over at the time with no ill effects other than causing Stratemeyer, O'Donnell, and the crews involved some acute embarrassment.

To get a better handle on the situation, Vandenberg and Collins flew to Tokyo to meet with MacArthur in mid July. Collins later reported that the general was confident and poised—he was already planning an amphibious assault to crush the enemy. Vandenberg asked if he thought the Chinese might intervene, and, if so, would he need to move into Manchuria. MacArthur responded he could effectively choke off the Korean Peninsula from Russian or Chinese interference: "I see here a unique use for the atomic bomb—to strike a blocking blow—which would require a six-month repair job. Sweeten up my B-29 force—(we'll give them back)—perhaps by a rotational feature, and we can isolate the Korean Peninsula."[53] Whether atomic bombs would be authorized or not, he liked the job O'Donnell was doing with the B-29s.

The amphibious assault intimated by MacArthur was the masterstroke of Inchon that began on 15 September 1950—one of the most tactically decisive operations in modern history. The North Koreans were indeed crushed and sent fleeing north. On 27 September, President Truman gave MacArthur new orders. His objective was "the destruction of the North Korean Armed Forces." To attain this destruction, "you are authorized to conduct military operations, including amphibious and airborne landings or ground operations north of the

---

[50] Futrell, *United States Air Force in Korea*, 97.

[51] "Report of First Month of Operations FEAF Bomber Command," 13 August 1950, in "Deployment to the Far East" study, exhibit 40.

[52] Stratemeyer, diary, 27 July 1950, 85; 27 September 1950, 206; and 14 November 1950, 280–82.

[53] Memo to General Bolte, including transcript of conversation between Generals MacArthur, Vandenberg, and Collins, 17 July 1950, DDQI, 1976, 243A; Stratemeyer, diary, 14 July 1950, 71–74; and Collins, *War in Peacetime*, 81–83.

38th Parallel." The general's new mission was not merely to repel the invaders but to occupy the entire country.[54] It was a momentous decision soon shown to be a miscalculation.

Bomber Command's missions of interdiction and destruction of North Korean industry were high priority. There were five major industrial centers in North Korea: Wonsan, home to large oil refineries; Pyongyang, the capital and a major arsenal and arms producer; Hungnam, containing chemical and explosive plants; Chongjin, which had two large harbors and was a major rail center; and Rashin, also a center of major marshaling yards as well as oil storage facilities. There were also a number of smelting plants on the west coast and major hydroelectric plants situated along the Yalu River. These hydroelectric plants produced over 300,000 kilowatts of power, more than half of which went to Manchuria.[55] Altogether, Bomber Command intelligence planners came up with 18 targets of strategic importance. These were thoroughly saturated by the B-29s, and by mid October, O'Donnell issued a new mission directive—Bomber Command would only strike North Korean targets "which have a bearing on the tactical situation." The focus was to be on interdiction targets (enemy airfields, rail lines, highways, and marshaling yards), close air support, reconnaissance, and leaflet drops. O'Donnell also stipulated that targets within 50 miles of the Manchurian border would be attacked only with the specific approval of the FEAF commander and, even then, only under visual bombing conditions with positive identification.[56]

By September's end the only major target not seriously attacked, Rashin, was placed off limits by Washington because it was too near the Soviet border. B-29 losses throughout these operations were light.[57] On 4 November incendiaries were dropped on Chongjin—MacArthur had changed his mind regarding their use after Chinese forces were reported in Korea. By the end of 1950 it was apparent the strategic air campaign was over—17 of 18 major targets designated had been heavily struck; 70 percent of the rail and armaments factories in Pyongyang were destroyed, as well as 85 percent of the chemical

[54] Schnabel and Watson, *Joint Chiefs of Staff and National Policy*, vol. 3, 230. As early as 1 September, President Truman had committed himself to the unification of Korea. Of interest, on 22 September, Bradley was promoted to five stars; the following day George Marshall was named secretary of defense, replacing Louis Johnson.

[55] Futrell, *United States Air Force in Korea*, 184.

[56] "Far East Bomber Command Provisional, 4 July–31 October 1950," 4.

[57] Ibid., 35; and Futrell, *United States Air Force in Korea*, 192–93.

plants at Hungnam and 95 percent of the oil refineries at Wonsan.[58] These strikes amounted to barely 2.5 percent of all bomber sorties flown, yet produced disproportionate results. Upon completion of the strategic campaign, two B-29 wings returned to the States. In January 1951, O'Donnell departed as well. SAC continued to rotate B-29 wings through FEAF—the average deployment was four to six months. This meant Bomber Command maintained an average strength of 99 B-29s for the remainder of the war.[59]

Throughout October 1950, there were muted reports of Chinese units operating in North Korea, but the CIA, State Department, and MacArthur's own intelligence division discounted those reports. Everyone's focus was so firmly on Moscow and Soviet intentions that the motives and fears of the Chinese were discounted. Nonetheless, MacArthur was directed to use only ROK forces near the Chinese border to avoid provoking Beijing. Ominously, on 1 November the first Soviet-made MiG-15 jet fighter appeared over North Korea. The MiG-15 was a surprise to American intelligence. Small, light, fast, and agile, the Fagot was superior to anything the US Air Force had in-theater. The F-80 and F-84 were no match for the new MiG. North American F-86 Sabres would prove superior, but they would not be deployed into Korea until December and would never arrive in large numbers.

On 2 November, Stratemeyer asked MacArthur if his aircraft could cross the Yalu River to attack Chinese MiG bases. The Chinese had nearly 300 aircraft, and, if allowed to fly south unimpeded, they could seriously disrupt UN ground operations. It was better to destroy the nests of these aircraft as soon as possible to remove the threat. MacArthur agreed and pressed the JCS for approval. Initially, Vandenberg favored the idea, but after discussing it with Air Force secretary Thomas Finletter—Symington's replacement—decided against a widening of the war.[60] A few days later MacArthur directed air attacks against the Yalu River bridges—strikes the Chinese expected and feared.[61] When word reached Washington, the response was immediate—cancel the strikes. MacArthur was outraged and wired Washington that his command was threatened with destruction if the bridges were not

[58] Crane, *American Airpower Strategy in Korea*, 41.

[59] Futrell, *United States Air Force in Korea*, 195; and Moody, *Building a Strategic Air Force*, 396–97.

[60] Stratemeyer diary, 2 November, 1950, 252–53; Partridge diary, 2 November 1950; and *FRUS, 1950*, vol. 7, 1076–77.

[61] Zhang, *Mao's Military Romanticism*, 90.

dropped. This was a surprise to the joint chiefs, so after discussing the matter with Truman, MacArthur was told the bridges could be hit—but only if attacking aircraft did not violate Chinese airspace in doing so.[62] The United States was trying, belatedly, to deescalate the scope of military operations, but it was too late.

On 25 November 1950, Chinese forces hit the unprepared UN troops like a bulldozer and sent them flooding back south. It looked like the events of June and July were being replayed. Evacuation plans considered using the umbrella of atomic bombs if necessary. Stratemeyer called for more aircraft, both bombers and fighters—he was worried about Japan being attacked as well. SAC was placed on worldwide full alert.[63] The FEAF commander wanted two more groups of bombers sent over, and they should be equipped with atomic weapons. Vandenberg answered that he should prepare for their use and recommend appropriate targets. Stratemeyer provided the following suggestions: Antung, Mukden, Peking, Tientsin, Shanghai, and Nanking. He added that if the United States were soon involved "in the big one," he also would want to strike Vladivostok, Khabarovsk, and Kirin in the Soviet Union.[64]

On 3 December, Vandenberg told his JCS colleagues that China should be punished and called for bombing targets in Manchuria; a limited series of attacks involving two B-29 groups would not jeopardize Europe.[65] At the same time, LeMay was alerted and told to be ready. The SAC commander responded that if given the order to deploy, he would personally depart for the Far East.[66] Three days later the joint chiefs sent a warning to all commanders: "The JCS consider that the current situation in Korea has greatly increased the possibility of general war. Commanders addressed should take such action as is feasible to increase readiness without creating [an] atmosphere of alarm."[67] Concern was heightened when intelligence showed that the Russians were withdrawing personnel from Mukden—apparently in anticipation of atomic strikes. The CIA reported that both China and the Soviet Union seemed willing "to risk a showdown with the West

---

[62] Vandenberg to Stratemeyer, message, 6 November 1950, Vandenberg papers, LOC, box 86; and Schnabel and Watson, *Joint Chiefs of Staff and National Policy*, vol. 3, 290–94.

[63] Vandenberg to Stratemeyer, message, 30 November 1950, Vandenberg papers, LOC, 86.

[64] Stratemeyer to Vandenberg, message, 30 November 1950, and Vandenberg to Stratemeyer, message, 15 December 1950, both in Vandenberg papers, LOC, box 86; and Stratemeyer diary, 1 December 1950, 316–22.

[65] *FRUS, 1950*, vol. 7, 1330.

[66] LeMay to Vandenberg, message, 2 December 1950, LeMay papers, LOC, box 196.

[67] JCS to LeMay, message, 6 December 1950, LeMay papers, LOC, box 197.

at an early date." When President Truman was asked at a press conference if atomic weapons would be used to halt the destruction of UN forces in Korea, he replied the US response would include "every weapon that we have."[68] The world seemed on the precipice of another world war.

Fortunately, the situation calmed quickly, and the following month Vandenberg returned to Tokyo to assess the situation. He wanted LeMay to accompany him to meet with SAC personnel and discuss possible contingencies, but Secretary Acheson vetoed the idea. LeMay was "Mr. Atom Bomb," and his presence in Korea would "excite people unduly."[69] Maintaining a balance between signaling a strong warning regarding deterrence without alarming allies—and Congress—of a possible widening of the war was extremely difficult.

Custody of Atomic Weapons

As the world seemed to be lurching closer to another major war in late 1950, the issue of atomic weapons custody came to the fore. It had been a contentious matter for years. The Manhattan District had control over the design, manufacture, storage, and custody of atomic weapons, with Maj Gen Leslie Groves reporting to the Army chief of staff and the secretary of war, and they to the president. Civilian control over atomic weapons was assured by the president and secretary of war. In the aftermath of World War II, Congress, which had been kept largely in the dark regarding atomic matters, asserted itself. The Atomic Energy Act transferred control to the Atomic Energy Commission, whose chairman, David Lilienthal, was a ferocious defender of his turf. The military was shut out of the picture to a great extent.[70] As we have seen, the AAF—and later the Air Force—which had been pushed aside by Groves had even less input under the AEC.

The Military Liaison Committee, initially chaired by Lt Gen Lewis Brereton with Groves as a member, attempted to intrude itself into atomic affairs, but Lilienthal resisted such efforts. The key issue remained custody, and throughout 1947 the military lobbied unsuccessfully to

---

[68] Bradley and Blair, *General's Life*, 582; Truman, *Public Papers of the Presidents, 1950*, 727; and Hewlett and Duncan, *History of the Atomic Energy Commission*, vol. 2, 533.

[69] *FRUS: 1951*, vol. 7, 67–68; and Acheson, memorandum for the record, 12 January 1951, in "Official Conversations with Dean Acheson, 1949–1953" collection, UPA, 1980, reel 5.

[70] One senator thought Lilienthal a pacifist at best and a communist at worst, thus delaying his confirmation until April 1947. Rearden, *History of the Office of the Secretary of Defense*, vol. 1, 42.

obtain control over the weapons themselves. The MLC's argument was that "launch of an attack with atomic bombs under existing conditions would require a complicated procedure involving the dual responsibility of the Atomic Energy Commission and the Armed Forces."[71] The AEC responded that not only did the military have insufficient technical competence to handle and maintain the weapons, but uniformed custody would undermine civilian control. The MLC countered that until the AEC took over, the military *was* in control; obviously it had the technical competence necessary, and the AEC argument was specious. Moreover, a November 1947 exercise with the Eighth Air Force demonstrated that although the AEC was responsible for custody, it was unable to provide the logistical support needed to perform that duty. Exercise Ajax, the first such loading attempt, highlighted the problems of dual control: The initial assembly of the bombs was carried out at Sandia by AEC personnel. These components were then ferried by the 509th to Wendover Field, 100 miles west of Salt Lake City, where the assembly process continued under AFSWP personnel. This cumbersome and time-consuming process did not even utilize fissile material.[72] This was clearly inadequate, and even the AEC realized it.

The civilian control issue was a bit thornier, but the fact that only the president could authorize the use of atomic bombs seemed to relieve concern—at least to the military. The crux of the military argument, as articulated in both September and December 1947, was that in the event of war current procedures were inadequate to assemble bombs in a timely manner, move them out of storage to the required airfields, and then actually transfer control to waiting aircrews: "The armed forces must have the authority to place the forces and weapons at their disposal in strategically sound locations . . . readily available for instant use." The military warned that the Pearl Harbor attack had been facilitated by a lack of cooperation and centralization—such conditions must not be allowed to recur.[73] General Groves, in a strong letter to General Bradley, reiterated these points: "The atomic bomb will never be a truly military weapon until it is turned over to the military for custody and stockpiling. The Armed Forces should make a prompt, firm and continuous issue of this point until it is properly

---

[71] Ibid., 427.
[72] Defense Threat Reduction Agency, *Defense's Nuclear Agency*, 49–50.
[73] MLC to AEC, letter, 12 December 1947, "Records of JCS, Strategic Issues" collection, reel 1.

settled."[74] The scarcity of assembly teams, bomb commanders, and weaponeers—to say nothing of the disappointingly small size of the stockpile itself—tended to bear out such arguments.

The AEC rejected these contentions, and General Brereton appealed to Secretary Forrestal, who in turn asked the JCS for their opinion. Their reply was as expected: "neither prompt nor effective employment of atomic weapons could be assured unless the National Military Establishment was responsible for their custody."[75] The head of the AFSWP, Maj Gen K. D. Nichols, concurred and thought it "entirely impractical and dangerous to national security for the AEC rather than the military to have custody of weapons."[76] The three service secretaries agreed with these opinions in a note of March 1948.

William F. Carpenter succeeded Brereton as head of the MLC in February and took the matter forward. Carpenter was more conciliatory than Brereton, but it made no difference; relations between the AEF and MLC remained strained.[77] On 14 June, Carpenter wrote Lilienthal restating the views of his organization, the services, and the secretary of defense that custody should be transferred to the military—the same arguments made previously. Carpenter also contended it was essential to have a clear chain of command between the president and the "basic units which will be called upon to fight." Whenever a division of responsibility occurred, there was room for "failure." This failure was not necessarily the result of irresponsibility or willful neglect but simply "confusion or lack of full understanding as to what must be done and by whom." Because of the secrecy of the atomic energy program, the "users" of atomic weapons were unprepared for their duties in the event of an emergency:

> The user must know what the weapons look like, how to handle them, their state of readiness, and the extent to which minor alterations or repairs may be made without impairing their effectiveness. And he must have the confidence which comes only from complete familiarity with both components and test equipment so that he can be completely certain that they will operate effectively.[78]

Such an organization could not be created overnight. More to the point, "recent international developments have thrown into sharp relief

---

[74] Groves to Bradley, letter, 28 February 1948, ibid.

[75] Little and Bowen, *History of the Air Force Atomic Energy Program*, vol. 2, 71. The National Military Establishment was not renamed Department of Defense until 1949.

[76] Nichols, *Road to Trinity*, 245.

[77] "Notes on a History of the Military Liaison Committee for the Period 1946–1948," n.d. but presumably around 1950, AFHRA, file 143.5191.

[78] MLC to AEC, letter, 14 June 1948, AFHRA, file 143.5191.

the need for developing and putting into effect the arrangements outlined above to provide for the care, handling and transportation of those atomic weapons which will be utilized in the event of war or other emergency."[79] It was a good letter, but Lilienthal and the other commissioners were unmoved.

In late June, as the Berlin crisis was breaking into the open, the matter went to the president. Truman met with Forrestal and members of the AEC and MLC on July 21 and, after listening to the opposing viewpoints, ruled in favor of the AEC. Privately, however, he told Forrestal the issue was too hot politically for him to decide otherwise; change would have to wait until after the November elections.[80] Even so, in September, Truman directed a review of all procedures for the emergency transfer of atomic weapons, while also ordering the AFSWP to take steps to train the personnel required to assume custody in the event he should so direct.[81]

Exercises were conducted in December 1948 to test hand-over procedures. Atomic cores were transported from Los Alamos to nearby Kirtland AFB. At the moment of transfer, dummy cores were substituted. Things went smoothly, but more such exercises were needed.[82] Bomb assembly and transfer were simply too slow. The Air Force complained to the JCS that its short-term goal was to deliver 25 bombs per day and then accelerate that rate to 100 bombs per day. Ultimately, the goal was "the simultaneous delivery of the entire stockpile." The JCS concurred with this plan and directed the AFSWP to train the teams necessary to make such an assembly rate possible. The intent was to reach this target by April 1950.[83]

As the new Mark IV atomic bombs were produced—the designs emerging from the successful Sandstone tests of July 1948—assembly time was cut in half. In addition, SAC began conversion of C-97 aircraft to become mobile atomic bomb assembly facilities. These aircraft, code-named Chickenpox, were designed to speed the atomic bomb delivery process. Eventually, three such aircraft were built.[84]

---

[79] Ibid.

[80] George Elsey, MFR, n.d., DDQI, retrospective collection, 304A. Elsey was a civilian aide to President Truman and was present at the meeting on 21 July. See also, Millis and Duffield, *Forrestal Diaries*, 460–61.

[81] Little and Bowen, *History of the Air Force Atomic Energy Program*, vol. 2, 71–73; and Forrestal to Symington, letter, 28 July 1948, AFHRA, file 143.5191.

[82] Little and Bowen, *History of the Air Force Atomic Energy Program*, vol. 2, 109; and Nichols, *Road to Trinity*, 268.

[83] Ibid., 372–75. The JCS stated they needed 400 bombs to carry out the war plan; they would soon reach that total and then quickly surpass it.

[84] Ibid., 405–15.

War in Korea put matters on a different plane. This was a shooting war, and Chinese intervention and talk of World War III versus both China and the Soviet Union tended to focus the mind. In March 1950, President Truman had already authorized transfer of nonnuclear components to the Air Force and the Navy. The growing competence of the services to handle and secure these items was by that point undoubted. In addition, the move was justified as a way of taking some of the administrative burden off the AEC. Nuclear components were retained by the AEC, and this calmed fears regarding civilian control. In truth, Chairman Gordon Dean (Lilienthal's successor) was not pleased with the transfer. He was even less happy when the components were moved and he was not informed until afterward.[85] In July 1950 atomic bomb components, less the fissionable cores, were deployed to both Britain and Okinawa.[86] There matters stood for a year.

In early 1951 Vandenberg continued to fret about the custody issue. In a letter to LeMay he stated, "I agree with you as to the confusion that a major attack against Washington would produce with respect to orders that should emanate from the seat of Government. However, under existing law, authority to initiate the atomic offensive cannot be formally delegated either to field agencies of the Atomic Energy Commission or major commands of the Air Force."[87] In March 1951, Vandenberg wrote the president asking for the transfer of nuclear cores to the Air Force. There was evidence Soviet troops were massing near the Yalu River and Soviet submarines were gathered near Vladivostok. Some feared the Soviets were about to attack and push the United Nations out of both Korea and Japan. Dean immediately protested the Air Force request, using the standard arguments regarding civilian control of atomic energy.[88]

On 6 April, Vandenberg and Dean went to the White House. The AEC chairman arrived to discover that Truman had already decided to sign the memo prepared by the Air Force chief. The president explained his reasoning, but then added that the decision to actually employ the weapons would remain his; he also indicated the AEC and the State Department would play a role in an employment decision.

---

[85] Hewlett and Duncan, *History of the Atomic Energy Commission*, vol. 2, 537–38.

[86] Rearden, *History of the Office of the Secretary of Defense*, vol. 1, 432; and Nichols, 280.

[87] Rhodes, *Dark Sun*, 452.

[88] Significantly, while this crisis was brewing, a letter GEN Douglas MacArthur had written to Cong. Joseph Martin highly critical of administration policy was made public. Truman was infuriated and seriously considered relieving MacArthur. The issue of transferring nuclear weapons was therefore unfortunately tied up with the matter of the loose cannon in Tokyo. For a good discussion, see Anders, "Atomic Bomb and the Korean War," 1–6.

Nine atomic bombs, with their nuclear cores, were transferred to the Air Force and deployed to Okinawa. This was a momentous decision. For the first time the custody of atomic weapons had passed from the hands of the AEC to the Air Force and Strategic Air Command. Dean later commented that the president's decision "marked the end of the Commission's civilian responsibility over a portion of our war reserve."[89] He was correct.

The transfer of custody continued apace, and eventually the AEC became irrelevant in this matter. Nuclear weapons were deployed to the Pacific for use by SAC bombers should the need arise. In mid 1952, FEAF pushed hard to obtain a nuclear capability and nuclear weapons custody for its fighter-bombers. Gen Otto P. Weyland wrote Washington that in the event of Soviet attack, SAC's bombers were too far distant; if FEAF were to be saved, it needed its own nuclear force—just as tactical air forces in Europe had a similar deterrent force independent of SAC. He agreed SAC should have full control of the strategic deterrent, but FEAF should be provided with the "necessary capability of performing its theater air force mission." Weyland continued that FEAF was outnumbered "four to one" by the Russians and the Chinese—nuclear weapons would be his equalizer. General Twining, then acting chief while Vandenberg was in the hospital, agreed, arranging the transfer of atomic-capable fighters to the Far East. By the end of 1953, FEAF had 50 F-84Gs based in Japan capable of delivering nuclear weapons; the bombs themselves remained on Guam.[90] The custody fight that opened the atomic door to SAC soon opened it to the theaters as well.

Maj Gen Thomas S. Power, LeMay's deputy at SAC, was dispatched to Tokyo at the same time to meet with Gen Matthew D. Ridgway, MacArthur's replacement as UN commander in Korea, to discuss plans for the employment of the atomic bombs should they be necessary. Under the arrangements worked out in Washington, the B-29s would remain under the control of FEAF while engaged in conventional operations but under SAC control if the war went atomic. This arrangement, which came to be termed "phonetic command" because the liaison office was code-named X-ray, was instituted to ensure "SAC forces would never be isolated from the direct command of the CINCSAC." The intent of the phonetic commands—subsequently

[89] Hewlett and Duncan, *History of the Atomic Energy Commission*, vol. 2, 539; Anders, *Forging the Atomic Shield*, 137–38; JCS to Marshall, memorandum, 23 May 1951, DDQI, 1976, 248A; and Doris M. Condit, *History of the Office of the Secretary of Defense*, vol. 2, 464–67.

[90] James T. Kenney, "History of the Far East Air Forces Participation in the Atomic Energy Program, 1 July 1953–30 June 1954," FEAF Historical study, n.d., AFHRA, file K720.04-10, 2–8.

established in Europe (Zebra), Northeast Command (Oboe), Alaska (Victor), and the Middle East (Yoke)—was to provide atomic expertise and staffing to the theater commanders.[91]

Stalemate in Korea

By the fall of 1951 the situation in Korea had stabilized. General MacArthur's erratic behavior, embarrassing public pronouncements, and obvious disagreement with President Truman's objectives and war strategy led to his relief in April 1951. After a brief flurry of outrage, fanned by the press, Senate hearings were held to discuss the conduct of the war. As Congress and the public became educated on what was taking place half a world away, they realized the problems with MacArthur's assertion that there was "no substitute for victory." Vandenberg's testimony was important because he realized, as did those listening, that any expansion of the war to include China or Russia would fall most heavily on the Air Force. The conflict occurring in Asia was only a part of the global contest between democracy and communism. Europe was the vital region to be watched, and a major war in Asia would distract America from that region. The Air Force had global responsibilities; MacArthur did not. The general in Tokyo did not understand. Vandenberg testified that 80 percent of the Air Force's tactical strength and 25 percent of its strategic forces were tied up in Korea. Attempting to take on the full might of China, and perhaps even Russia, was too much. When asked what could be done to better prepare the Air Force for such responsibilities, Vandenberg stated—as he had for the three previous years—that even though the Air Force was in the process of finally building from its postwar doldrums, the new goal of 95 groups was still inadequate. Moreover, given Soviet atomic capabilities, a "Manhattan Project" for air defense was now necessary to guard against a potential air attack. In an earlier briefing to the joint chiefs, Vandenberg had declared that a Soviet bomber could penetrate US airspace, fly to any location and drop its bombs, and never be intercepted by a single aircraft.[92] In a remarkably frank comment before the Senate, the chief stated,

---

[91] "Phonetic Commands, May 1951–June 1959," SAC Historical Study no. 77, n.d., AFHRA, file K416.01-77, 1–3.

[92] Vandenberg to JCS, memorandum, 16 November 1950, Fairchild papers, LOC, box 1. Earlier that year Vandenberg had written Secretary Symington that the Air Force "cannot complete the entire strategic air offensive called for in the current emergency war plan" and it could not "provide the air defense for the United States and Alaska commensurate with the maximum risk we can afford to take." Vandenberg to Symington, letter, 11 April 1950, DDQI, 1976, 242B.

The fact is that the United States is operating a shoestring air force in view of its global responsibilities . . . we cannot afford to peck at the periphery . . . While we can lay the industrial potential of Russia today waste [*sic*], in my opinion, or we can lay the Manchurian countryside waste, as well as the principal cities of China, we cannot do both, again because we are trying to operate a $20-million business with about $20,000.[93]

The Air Force would continue to build and prepare for a major war with Russia and China, but in the meantime it would need to fight the "police action" in Korea.

The new UN commander in Korea, Gen Matthew Ridgway, was an obedient subordinate. There would be no more pontifical pronouncements emanating from Tokyo and no calls on the enemy to surrender before it was destroyed. For the next two years the opposing forces dug in roughly along the original demarcation line and fought a brutal war of attrition. In many ways it resembled the First World War more than it did the Second. The primary roles of airpower were twofold: to maintain air superiority over the peninsula and to fly close air support and interdiction sorties against Chinese/North Korean supply lines. There were few strategic targets left to strike in North Korea, so the mission of SAC's B-29s was a continual and relentless pounding of tactical targets.

The air superiority battle was of great significance. General Stratemeyer had stressed its necessity early in the conflict, but not everyone understood its ramifications. The Chinese periodically attempted to build airfields in North Korea; it was crucial these airfields be kept out of commission, and the B-29s played a major role in this effort. Reconnaissance aircraft would watch these airfields closely, and if it looked as if they were near to becoming operational, the B-29s would be sent to hit them. If these airfields became operational, the Chinese aircraft based there would be able not only to attack UN ground forces to the south but also to extend the range of the MiGs. This in turn would make it more costly, if not impossible, for UN aircraft, including the B-29s, to carry out their wide-ranging interdiction missions across Korea. Military operations, as bloody as they were, would have been far worse. The Chinese understood the stakes and attempted to extend an air umbrella south to protect these bases. The air battles in "MiG Alley"—the name given to the aerial battlespace in northwest

---

[93] US Congress, *Hearings before the Senate Armed Services and Foreign Relations Committees on the Military Situation in the Far East*, 1379. Vandenberg's entire testimony is contained in pp. 1375–1508.

Korea—were important because if the Chinese won there, they would be able to build those airfields.

Airmen believed air superiority was the decisive factor in preventing UN defeat; without it, the Eighth Army would have been pushed off the peninsula. Too often this was overlooked by those who saw the MiG Alley air battles as glamorous but of little real importance. This was shortsighted: the numerically superior foe, operating on shorter supply lines, was virtually prohibited from traveling in daylight, while UN forces had complete freedom of operation. The battle for MiG Alley was as important as the 1940 Battle of Britain: it ensured the UN would not lose. By mid 1951 the Chinese gave up on attempts to defend the bases; at the end of the war there were 34 airfields in North Korea—none of them operational.[94]

For the B-29s, the issue was more difficult. SAC knew the Superforts were increasingly obsolete—hence the concerted moves within the command to replace them. The new jet bombers were not yet available, however. Moreover, in keeping with the focus on nuclear deterrence and the protection of Europe, even B-36s and B-50s were held back from Korea. At one point, Stratemeyer had suggested to LeMay the use of B-36s, flying nonstop from CONUS to strike targets in North Korea, but the SAC commander refused, citing logistics difficulties.[95] The result was the continued use of B-29s, long past their prime, that were inadequate in the face of MiG-15s. SAC's 27th Fighter Escort Group was deployed to Korea to escort the B-29s, but its F-84Es were diverted to fly ground attack missions. LeMay was concerned about this situation and wrote Stratemeyer for an explanation. He was told the 27th was based in Japan and therefore did not have the range to fly escort over Korea. Airfields in South Korea were scarce, and those available had runways too short to accommodate heavily laden F-84s. This explanation hardly seemed convincing, and the unit redeployed back to CONUS soon thereafter. Even so, several SAC fighter wings rotated to the Far East during the war, but most were retained in Japan to sit alert as interceptors for the Japanese air defense mission.[96]

---

[94] Futrell, *United States Air Force in Korea*, 312, 682.

[95] Stratemeyer to LeMay, letter, 6 February 1951, and LeMay to Stratemeyer, letter, 6 March 1951, both in Twining papers, LOC, box 54.

[96] LeMay to Stratemeyer, letter, 30 March 1951, and Stratemeyer to LeMay, letter, 14 April 1951, both in "Development of Fighter-Escort in Strategic Air Command Through 1951," SAC Historical study, 1 June 1952, AFHRA, file K416.01-29, exhibits 33 and 38. See also Lloyd, *Cold War Legacy*, 157–61.

The escort solution was the F-86 Sabre, a terrific air-superiority fighter. USAF pilots were also far better than their Chinese adversaries— the F-86 racked up an 8-to-1 kill ratio over the MiGs during the war—but there were far too few of these jets available. In June 1951, for example, the Chinese had 445 MiG-15s stationed at airfields just north of the Yalu; FEAF could counter with only 89 Sabres. By October the number of MiGs had increased to over 500, while the complement of F-86s remained below 100. Indeed, the Fifth Air Force commander messaged Vandenberg that due to maintenance and supply difficulties, on any given day his command could muster on average only 40 Sabres.[97]

The Chinese also began using ground control intercept radars to direct the MiGs. These new radars were not jammable by SAC aircraft then in-theater.[98] As a result of their numerical superiority, combined with the new radars, when the MiGs attacked in force—it was not unusual for the Chinese to launch "trains" of up to 90 aircraft— the escorts were quickly overwhelmed. Vandenberg decided to send 75 more of the precious F-86s to the theater in late October 1951, but the following month the casualty toll was too much: five B-29s had been shot down in October, and four more had been damaged beyond repair. Brig Gen Joe Kelly of Bomber Command stopped most B-29 daylight missions into North Korea unless they were escorted by F-86s.[99] For the last two years of the war, B-29s were either escorted on daylight missions or flew in the dark. Fortunately, SHORAN, an electronic navigation and bombing aid, was added to the B-29s, allowing them to achieve a commendable accuracy.[100] Even so, the night was no sanctuary. Soviet-supplied searchlights and radar-controlled AAA—located on both sides of the Yalu River—took their toll on the bombers for the remainder of the war. Various tactics and solutions were used: B-26s accompanied the B-29s to suppress the searchlights—at least those on the Korean side of the Yalu—and the Superforts flew in small cells, both to limit time over the target and also to

---

[97] Crane, *American Airpower Strategy in Korea*, 85.

[98] Lloyd, *Cold War Legacy*, 181.

[99] Futrell, *United States Air Force in Korea*, 403–16. Everyone wanted the F-86s coming off the assembly line, and many went to Europe or Air Defense Command instead of FEAF. Eventually, around 150 Sabres would be deployed to Korea, but that was still less than one-third the number of MiG-15s arrayed against them.

[100] Far East Air Forces Bomber Command Provisional, "Narrative History: 1 July Thru 31 December 1951," AFHRA, file K713.01-20, 77–78, 163–98. SHORAN (SHOrt RAnge Navigation) was a navigation/bombing system consisting of at least two ground stations transmitting range and azimuth data to suitably equipped aircraft. Navigators could interpret the station signals to triangulate their positions. It was an accurate system that produced a CEP of around 500 feet. The only SHORAN sets in-theater initially were installed in B-26s; they were quickly transferred to the B-29s.

combine their electronic defenses. Radar-equipped night fighters also accompanied the B-29s. These techniques worked. Bomber Command believed its losses would have been triple what they were without such help.[101]

In early 1952, the joint chiefs asked Vandenberg for more options in the air war in Korea. He wrote Lt Gen Otto P. Weyland, the new FEAF commander, and suggested he consider targeting the 11 hydro-electric power plants along the Yalu River. Because of their location, as well as the major impact they would have on China itself, these targets had been struck early in the war but had been off limits since. In April 1952, Weyland went to Ridgway seeking approval, but the UN commander refused; he hoped the peace negotiations would finally bear results and did not want them disrupted.[102] When Ridgway was replaced by GEN Mark Clark in May 1952, he too was eager to try something new. The plants were hit by B-29s and fighter-bombers on 23 and 27 June. The strikes were successful, blacking out all of North Korea for two weeks, reducing power to 10 percent of its former capacity for the remainder of the war, and reducing the electricity to Manchuria by 23 percent.[103] Unfortunately, the international uproar following these "escalatory" strikes blunted much of their impact. Defense secretary Robert Lovett was forced to announce that UN policy had not changed and this was not a widening of the war—thereby sending mixed signals to China as to what exactly was the purpose of the air strikes.[104] In a caustic comment reflecting the irritation of many in uniform regarding the mixed signals, Brig Gen Don Z. Zimmerman, FEAF's director of plans, muttered, "Don't employ airpower so the enemy will get mad and won't sign the armistice."[105] The armistice was not signed anyway, so more steps needed to be taken.

Weyland and Clark nominated other strategic targets: the oil refineries and storage depots at Rashin near the Soviet border that had previously been off limits, the North Korean capital of Pyongyang, and the earthen dam system that kept the rivers of the north in check. These strikes were approved by Washington, which in turn notified

---

[101] Futrell, *United States Air Force in Korea*, 527–28, 614–16.

[102] Vandenberg to JCS, memorandum, 1 May 1952, in "Records of the JCS: The Far East" collection, UPA, 1979, reel 10; *FRUS, 1952–1954*, vol. 15, 52–54, 130; and Schnabel and Watson, *Joint Chiefs of Staff and National Policy*, vol. 3, 843–47.

[103] Futrell, *United States Air Force in Korea*, 483–89.

[104] *FRUS, 1952–1954*, vol. 15, 352–54.

[105] Futrell, *United States Air Force in Korea*, 435.

the allies in advance.[106] The capital was hit in August and the oil refineries in September. On all of these strikes, B-29s were used along with Air Force and Navy fighter-bombers. Tactically successful, the air strikes nonetheless failed to move the negotiations forward.[107]

November 1952 saw the election of a new president, Dwight Eisenhower, who had campaigned on a pledge to bring the war to a close. Upon taking office he directed the JCS to give him some options—there were no limits to what they could propose. On 19 May 1953, the joint chiefs presented their proposal, which stated in part:

> It is the view of the Joint Chiefs of Staff that the necessary air, naval, and ground operations, including extensive strategical and tactical use of atomic bombs, be undertaken so as to obtain maximum surprise and maximum impact on the enemy, both militarily and psychologically. If undertaken piecemeal—for example, starting with a naval blockade, followed by gradually increasing air operations, and finally followed later by ground operations—we would minimize the chance of success of the course of action outlined.[108]

Two days later the new secretary of state, John Foster Dulles, met with Prime Minister Jawaharlal Nehru of India and implied strongly that American patience had reached an end. It has long been assumed Dulles warned Nehru that if China did not modify its position at the peace talks, then an air attack on Manchuria, to include atomic bombs, would be the next step.[109] This message was reportedly passed to Beijing. At the same time, more atomic bombs were moved to Okinawa in case they were needed. It appears the Chinese took these veiled threats seriously. Ever since the president-elect had visited the war zone in December 1952, the Chinese expected a major escalation of the conflict, to include the use of nuclear weapons. In January 1953 they began a vast construction program to build tunnels, trenches, and hardened bunkers to protect their troops and supplies. At one point over 500,000 soldiers and workers were engaged in these projects.[110]

In May 1953 the air war took another escalatory step when the dam and dike system of North Korea was attacked with devastating

---

[106] Vandenberg to JCS, memorandum, 10 August 1952, in "Reports of the JCS: The Far East" collection, reel 10. In an occurrence all too infrequent during the Korean War, the Rashin mission displayed highly successful joint cooperation: the B-29s were ably escorted by carrier-based Navy jets.

[107] For a good discussion of the strategic missions flown by the B-29s in 1952–53, see Crane, *American Airpower Strategy in Korea*, 118–25.

[108] *FRUS, 1952–1954*, vol. 15, 1062. Contrast these comments to the "gradual escalation" policy carried out little more than a decade later in Vietnam.

[109] Ibid., 1069. For a review of the incident, see Keefer, "President Eisenhower and the End of the Korean War," 267–89; and Dingman, "Atomic Diplomacy during the Korean War," 50–91.

[110] Zhang, *Mao's Military Romanticism*, 238.

results. Thousands of acres of rice fields were flooded, and roads and rail lines were similarly washed away. Entire villages were inundated. The American position was hardening, and Vandenberg, soon to retire, told an audience at the Air War College that the United States should blockade the Chinese coast, break its rail lines, mine its rivers, and destroy those industrial installations that were contributing to her war-making capacity. He suggested an atomic strike on Mukden.[111]

On 27 July 1953, an armistice agreement was signed. There is no formal peace treaty—to this day—and both sides remain heavily armed astride a demilitarized zone roughly in the same location as the original 38th parallel demarcation line established in 1945.

Summary

The Berlin crisis followed by the surprise detonation of the Soviet atomic bomb caused deep soul-searching in late 1949 and early 1950. For SAC it meant an increased priority while also adding impetus to LeMay's reforms. The command rose to the occasion with a flurry of exercises and programs to ensure it was deserving of such priority.

The detonation of Joe I led to calls for a dramatically expanded atomic weapons stockpile. In addition, the question of whether physicists should be directed to explore the hydrogen bomb was brought to the fore. Opinion was divided among the scientific community, although not among the military. Although the Navy and Army were initially reticent to embrace the new weapon because it threatened to grant more power to the Air Force due to its presumed huge size, resistance quickly crumbled. All in uniform recognized that failure to proceed with thermonuclear experimentation would leave the field open to the Soviets. When President Truman asked the simple but vital question of whether or not the Soviets would be able to build such a bomb, even David Lilienthal, who was adamantly opposed to the new bomb, was forced to admit they could. Such a situation was "intolerable"—the term used by the JCS. The hydrogen bomb promised to be a thousand times more powerful than the atomic bomb—for the Soviets to build such a doomsday weapon and enjoy a monopoly

---

[111] Gen H. S. Vandenberg, speech to the Air War College, 6 May 1953, AFHRA, file K239.716253-126. Vandenberg was dying of cancer and knew it. He would retire in June and die the following April. The JCS and Air Force leaders had discussed the use of atomic weapons throughout the war, and the opinions of the participants often changed. In the early months of the war, for example, Vandenberg, LeMay, and O'Donnell all agreed that given the dearth of suitable strategic targets in North Korea, it would be counterproductive to use atomic bombs on tactical objectives. Crane, *American Airpower Strategy in Korea*, 57–58.

was unacceptable. As we now know, the Soviets went through no such soul-searching: they initiated work on the hydrogen bomb in mid 1948—before they had even detonated Joe 1.

Six months after the decision to begin thermonuclear research, the suspicions of the "cold warriors" regarding the Soviets seemed confirmed when their proxies in North Korea launched an invasion across the 38th Parallel. The attack was totally unexpected. Deterrence failed, partly because the United States had not communicated clearly to the communists that such an attack would not be allowed to stand. Indeed, a speech by Secretary of State Dean Acheson in March 1950 stated explicitly that Korea fell outside America's sphere of influence. The commander in the Far East, Gen Douglas MacArthur, had not been told to protect that nation. North Korean leaders, and their supporters in Moscow and Beijing, interpreted such signals to mean that the United States would stand aside if force were used to unify the peninsula. Both sides misinterpreted and misunderstood—with tragic results.

Given the nonchalance shown by American leaders toward South Korean security in early 1950, it was astonishing—no doubt to the communists as well as to the American people—that President Truman reacted so quickly and forcefully. Still, it was a near-run thing. The poorly trained and equipped ROK forces were quickly swept aside. American reinforcements arriving from Japan were equally unprepared. As US and ROK forces fled south, finally stopping to dig in at the tip of the peninsula near Pusan, it was airpower that saved the day. Tactical aircraft, but also SAC B-29s, were used in a relentless pounding of North Korean forces and their overstretched supply lines. The enemy was already spent when MacArthur launched his stunning assault at Inchon. As quickly as the North Koreans had moved south, they now retreated north. At this point American and UN leaders made another serious miscalculation: they directed MacArthur to move north of the 38th Parallel, pursue and destroy the remnants of the North Korean forces, and occupy the entire peninsula. Korea would be unified after all.

Ignoring signals from Beijing and intelligence reports on the ground that indicated an increasing number of Chinese forces in North Korea, MacArthur's armies moved blissfully forward, dangerously separated and vulnerable. The Chinese struck in late November, and once again the battle surged south. This was a "new war" against a powerful and dangerous enemy. Talk of world war emerged once again, along with discussion of the use of atomic weapons, much like the height of the Berlin crisis two years earlier.

At this point the enduring and vexing issue of atomic weapons custody once again rose to prominence. The Air Force was in the forefront of the custody battle, but the Navy was vitally interested in the matter as well. Although the AEC fought a determined rear-guard action for two years, the military persisted in its arguments that national security demanded control by the military. These arguments, which had been used for four years, took on cogency with the war in Korea. The stakes were too high to permit confusion in the event a major war with China or the Soviet Union was imminent. In April 1951, President Truman finally agreed to the logic of his military advisors and transferred control of atomic weapons to Strategic Air Command. Soon thereafter atomic weapons were deployed both to Europe and the Pacific, where they have remained for the last six decades.

Although fear of major war quickly abated and peace negotiations began in Korea, it became obvious the war would not end soon. Peace talks dragged on for two more years, and so did the war. The situation would be repeated in Vietnam during the following decade.

Although SAC's B-29s were designed for strategic bombing and few such targets existed in Korea, they nevertheless provided extended and important service throughout the war. The true industrial base for North Korea was in Russia and China—areas off limits to the Superfortresses. In addition, some of the seemingly most lucrative targets within North Korea itself, such as oil refineries and electric generating plants, were considered politically sensitive and therefore also off limits for most of the war. Consequently, the B-29s flew tactical support missions.

Initially, five bomb groups were deployed to the Far East—based in Japan, Okinawa, and Guam—but this number dropped to three groups by 1951. Rosie O'Donnell, one of LeMay's top operational subordinates, was the first commander of FEAF Bomber Command. Upon his departure in January 1951 to resume his position at Fifteenth Air Force, a series of commanders rotated through Tokyo to gain experience in a combat environment.

The bombers, generally a force of around 100 aircraft along with reconnaissance planes and a wing of fighters, flew until the end of the war. Altogether, Bomber Command logged over 21,000 sorties and dropped nearly 160,000 tons of bombs. Most of these targets, around 80 percent (16,000 sorties), were interdiction targets—railroads, bridges, road junctions, and the like. Another 1,400 sorties were flown against industrial areas, 1,250 versus airfields, and 2,700 in support of UN ground forces. Over three years of combat, Bomber Command lost 24 aircraft to enemy action, with many others sustaining damage; 627 aircrew members were lost.[112] The bomber war had been fought by the B-29, but when the war ended, the aging piston-driven veteran was quickly phased out. The last B-29 left the inventory in November 1954.[113]

Far East Air Forces Bomber Command was deactivated in July 1954 and its units returned to SAC. LeMay's forces had proved their mettle. The first commander of SAC, Gen George Kenney, had made a trip to the Far East in the fall of 1950, before the Chinese intervention, and reported to Vandenberg that airmen needed to be careful about learning the wrong lessons from Korea: "We have no guarantee that our next opponent will know so little of the art of war and will be so inflexible and stupid as the North Koreans."[114] The accuracy of these words would be demonstrated the following month when the Chinese, who had also been given scant credibility as a military force, launched a massive attack that not only caught UN ground troops by surprise but also inflicted severe damage. The MiG-15, also a surprise to US intelligence, was far better than anticipated, and only the F-86 was comparable. The aging B-29s were shown to be seriously obsolescent and with little defense against this threat. New and better bombers would be necessary if the enemy were the Soviet Union.

The issue of bomber escort arose as it had in World War II. SAC had several wings of escort fighters and wanted to exercise these units in Korea, but for various reasons that did not often happen, and the deployed F-84 wings flew ground support or sat alert in Japan. Nonetheless, escort missions were flown by SAC as well as FEAF fighters; however, the exact purpose of fighter escort arose anew. In a stunning decision, one FEAF fighter wing commander told his charges that their mission was to "bring the bombers home." He was irritated by the adulation and medals being extended to those fighter pilots who shot down MiGs. This was misplaced praise; rather, he wanted "awards and decorations for the successful completion of the mission itself, the safe return of all escorted bombers." In a concluding state-

---

[112] Moody, *Building a Strategic Air Force*, 397; and Lloyd, *Cold War Legacy*, 186.

[113] Lloyd, *Cold War Legacy*, 190. B-29s converted for refueling and reconnaissance remained active for several more years.

[114] Kenney to Vandenberg, letter, 5 October 1950, AFHRA, file 168.041-1.

ment reminiscent of similar arguments made at the Tactical School in the 1930s and the Eighth Air Force during World War II, the colonel concluded, "The escort fighter should regard his aircraft as additional guns or defensive artillery to prevent attacks upon the bomber."[115] Lessons are learned in any conflict, but it is important to ensure they are the correct lessons.

Although one hesitates to claim any silver linings emerging from the black clouds of a war that cost so many lives, it is nonetheless true that great numbers of SAC crew members gained invaluable combat experience, as did their commanders. By the middle of 1953 and the armistice, SAC was organizationally and administratively sound and battle hardened. It would move on to its acme as the dominant force in American military policy.

---

[115] "Fighter-Escort" study, 312.

Chapter 7

The Technological Imperative

A theme of this study is that airpower and technology are inextricably linked. Hap Arnold believed this and through the interwar years had maintained close contact with engineers, scientists, and industrialists. During the war he strengthened and broadened those relationships, believing airpower would evolve and become dominant through technological advance. As the war ended, Arnold looked to the future.

Theodore von Kármán, a brilliant Caltech scientist whom Arnold had met in the 1930s, was a world leader in aeronautical research. Arnold was especially drawn to him because the team he gathered at Caltech was not just interested in theory but pushed for *applications* to their research.[1] In August 1944, Arnold met with von Kármán at LaGuardia Field in New York. The scientist climbed into the general's staff car, the driver was dismissed, and the two men talked. Arnold got straight to the point: he wanted von Kármán to assemble a group of scientists to "work out a blueprint for air research for the next twenty, thirty, perhaps fifty years." The team would have Arnold's full backing, and all doors would be open to them. Von Kármán was impressed by the offer but especially by Arnold's vision. He agreed.[2]

Von Kármán's Scientific Advisory Group (SAG), which consisted of 33 scientists from academia and industry, spent months meeting with captured German scientists while also visiting their secret laboratories as they were liberated. All of this was a treasure trove. On 23 July 1945, von Kármán updated Arnold on the SAG's findings. He made several points: aircraft would soon move beyond the speed of sound and be able to deliver ordnance at great distances; "small amounts of explosive material will cause destruction over areas of several square miles"; air defenses would be bolstered by radar-controlled missiles; speed, produced by jet propulsion or rocket power, would be essential to penetrate these new defenses; "perfect communication" was in the offing; the problems of weather would soon be overcome; and "fully airborne task forces" delivered from the air could strike distant points.[3]

---

[1] Daso, *Architects of American Air Supremacy*, chap. 4.
[2] Ibid., 125–27.
[3] The interim report, "Where We Stand," is reproduced in Daso, appendix B.

The 12-volume study, titled *Toward New Horizons*, reached Arnold's desk on 15 December and was accompanied by a summary volume, *Science: The Key to Air Supremacy*. The report was breathtaking in its vision and scope. Airmen had never done anything like it, and it would serve as a blueprint for Air Force R&D for decades. The SAG focused on unmanned aircraft, rocketry, navigation and communications systems, air transport, all-weather operations, precision weaponry, and atomic weapons. In addition, von Kármán offered observations on the nature of science and its relationship to air leaders. He pushed for major R&D laboratories, the most advanced equipment, education of airmen in the importance of technology via the "infiltration of scientific thought," and a "global strategy for the application of novel equipment." R&D was crucial. Von Kármán wanted 25 to 33 percent of the Air Force budget devoted to it. In a resonant passage, the report stated, "The men in charge of the future Air Forces should always remember that problems never have final or universal solutions, and only a constant inquisitive attitude toward science and a ceaseless and swift adaptation to new developments can maintain the security of this nation through world air supremacy."[4]

In 1947, Carl Spaatz formed the Scientific Advisory Board to institutionalize von Kármán's beliefs, but *Toward New Horizons* was a unique effort. The Air Force updated the report every decade or so, but those efforts relied on internal assets and had a more specific focus, such as the problems of space exploration or the future of Air Force laboratories.[5] Nonetheless, the germ of the overarching idea—that technology and the Air Force were integrally linked—was firmly established.

Unfortunately, demobilization hit the aircraft industry as hard as it did the military. The US aircraft industry was the largest in the world in 1944, but three years later it had plummeted to 44th place; employment in that sector dropped from over two million to fewer than 200,000 during the same period. Industry giants like Curtiss-Wright, Martin, Republic, North American, and Convair would either go out of business or be absorbed by other companies in the years ahead.[6] The Air Force understood the crucial role played by the aircraft industry—airpower is defined by this relationship in ways that sea and ground power are not. Air

---

[4] Daso, *Architects of American Air Supremacy*, 322. *Science: The Key to Air Supremacy* is reproduced in Daso, appendix C. The SAG did not address the issue of space exploration or satellite development but did discuss ballistic missiles. Another shortcoming of the study was its failure to discuss electronic warfare.

[5] Gorn, *Harnessing the Genie*, 4–9.

[6] Converse, *History of Acquisition in the Department of Defense*, vol. 1, *Rearming for the Cold War, 1945–1960*, 262.

leaders therefore tried to spread around the available contract funds to several companies to keep their factories and workforces busy.[7] Even so, problems were major, and airmen had their own concerns.

The challenge was in finding top officers, who were more inclined to operations, with the vision and insight to seek out and embrace the advanced technologies so vital to airpower's success. As one historian noted, "The spirit had been strong, but the flesh, in the form of a technically trained officer cadre, had been weak."[8] Fortunately, enough such officers existed, and Air Force leaders were wise enough to nurture and groom them. Curtis LeMay was the first deputy chief of staff for R&D, and this experience was formative for him. He later stated, "There weren't many plans laid. . . . We just threw our money into basic tools because we had nothing."[9] Budget constraints combined with demobilization were debilitating, but things still needed to get done. Regarding the technology itself, the most obvious need rested with aircraft. From the beginning of World War II, airmen recognized the importance of speed, range, carrying capacity, and accuracy. If the mission of airpower was strategic bombardment, then outstanding bombers were essential. This required that programs be instituted early in the war to fill this need.

Building the Bombers

The workhorse bombers of World War II had their origins before the war. The B-17, B-24, and B-29 were all developed—and the first two flown—before Pearl Harbor. Range and payload were the basic characteristics of a bomber. A plane can only carry so much, whether ordnance or fuel. To reach long distances, the bomb load must be reduced; carrying a heavy bomb load meant a shorter range. Airmen and engineers realized this: their goal was to design and build aircraft that could carry several tons of bombs *and* fly several thousand miles. The B-17 and B-24 were good, but the Air Corps wanted more.

In April 1934 the Air Corps solicited bids for a very heavy long-range bomber. Boeing responded with its Model 294, which first flew

---

[7] Converse argues that performance and Air Force requirements were the primary considerations, but airmen were not blind to the problem of sustaining the industrial basis. In 1948 General Vandenberg agreed to purchase 10 DC-6s and another 10 Constellations in an effort to "tide over" the Douglas and Lockheed companies that were enduring difficult times. Ibid., 272–73, 276–9.

[8] Little, "Organizing for Strategic Planning," 74.

[9] LeMay, interview, 9 March 1971, 5.

on 15 October 1937 and was designated the XB-15. It was the largest and heaviest airplane built in the United States up to that time: its wingspan was 149 feet versus 104 for the B-17. It was 20 feet longer, with a gross weight was over 70,000 pounds—more than double that of the Fortress. The problem with the plane was its lack of engine power: its four motors, each producing 1,000 horsepower, were not big enough. One Boeing expert summed the XB-15's problem nicely: "It provided an example of a typical situation, where a promising new design was handicapped by lack of the bigger power plants necessary to develop its full potential."[10] Only one prototype was built, and it was later converted to a cargo plane. The knowledge gained from the experience was, however, useful in the B-29 program.

An Air Corps solicitation in February 1935 resulted in another behemoth. Douglas submitted a four-engine design to be designated the XB-19. The aircraft, significantly larger even than the XB-15, encountered serious delays and did not make its maiden flight until 27 June 1941, three years behind schedule. From the beginning, the Air Corps made it clear this was an experimental contract only—no large orders would follow. This fact, combined with a shortage of funds and significant technical problems, caused the lengthy delay. Still, it was an impressive aircraft, although, like the XB-15 it suffered from a lack of engine power. The maximum speed for the Douglas was a meager 204 mph. Upon receiving new engines in 1943, the speed climbed to 265, but that was still far too anemic. Like the XB-15, the XB-19 was used as a transport during the war, and, also like the Boeing, its development produced useful information on the construction of very large aircraft.[11]

In April 1941, the Air Corps circulated another bomber proposal, this one for an aircraft that could carry 10,000 pounds of bombs for 5,000 miles and then return to its base. The bomber should be able to reach 35,000 feet and have an airspeed of between 240 and 300 mph. Four companies submitted bids, and the winner was announced on 16 October: Consolidated's Model 37—which was to become the B-36.[12]

Development was slow, largely because Consolidated was busy producing the 18,000 B-24 Liberators needed for the war. The program had a low priority, and the aircraft did not roll out until 8 September 1945; its first flight was 11 months later.

[10] Bowers, *Boeing Aircraft since 1916*, 199–201; and "Chronological Record of the XB-15," 19 November 1957, AFHRA, file K110.7002-3B.

[11] Francillon, *McDonnell Douglas Aircraft since 1920*, vol. 1, 307–8.

[12] The other three companies were Boeing, Douglas, and Northrop.

As we saw, the big plane had numerous teething troubles, and at one point General Kenney recommended the program be cancelled. Lt Gen Nathan F. Twining at Air Materiel Command disagreed, arguing that all new aircraft had problems, and those of the B-36 were not severe enough to warrant cancellation. General Spaatz concurred, and the program continued. Six times the B-36 program was reviewed, and each time air leaders decided the plane, despite its problems, was superior to its competitors, the YB-49 and B-54.[13] Kenney changed his mind as the difficulties experienced by the B-36 were gradually solved.

Even so, it was a rocky road, and budget stringency meant that the Air Force goal of 70 groups, 21 of which would have consisted of bombers, was stalled at 48 groups. In the smaller plan, the bomber force was hit hard: there would be only 14 groups, four of which would be equipped with B-36s. Getting even this number into the inventory was problematic. A host of problems cropped up with fuel leaks, propeller vibrations, the radar gun system, engines, and other difficulties. None of these was unusual for a complex new aircraft, but the B-36 was ever in the limelight—partly because of its incredible size and partly because of the Navy's public attacks. In truth, the aircraft was not living up to expectations.

Although it routinely demonstrated that it could carry a huge load over a long distance, making flights of over 8,000 miles while carrying 10,000 pounds of bombs half that distance, its speed and altitude capability were inadequate. In October 1948, Convair suggested adding four jet engines to the six conventional pusher props already installed.[14] The jets would be mounted two to a nacelle on each wing. The new design, the B-36D, made its first flight in March 1949.[15] It was this aircraft that LeMay and Vandenberg hailed as a success at the congressional hearings during the "Revolt of the Admirals."[16] The D model could cruise at 406 mph, had a service ceiling of 44,000 feet, and could carry a 10,000 lb. atom bomb for 5,000 miles, drop it, and

---

[13] Congressional staffers conducted an investigation of the B-36 procurement history in conjunction with the hearings held by the House in 1949. This report was published separately as US Congress, *Hearings before the House Armed Services Committee on the Investigation of the B-36 Bomber Program*, H. R. 234, 81st Cong., 2nd sess., 1950, 1–34.

[14] Consolidated Aircraft Corporation merged with Vultee Aircraft in 1943 to form Convair.

[15] Pyeatt and Jenkins, *Cold War Peacemaker*, 76–79.

[16] There was much discussion at the Senior Officers Board comparing the B-36 to the B-50 and B-54, with LeMay favoring the B-36, saying the new jet pods would increase the speed, altitude, range, and bomb load. "Report of Senior Officers Board Convened to Consider the Modification Program and R&D Program for the USAF," 21 February 1949, AFHRA, file 168.15-10, 13.

return home. Later models had a payload of 86,000 lbs. and could easily haul the initial hydrogen bombs that weighed 42,000 lbs. Sixteen 20 mm cannons provided defensive firepower. The unaugmented crew consisted of 15: eight officers and seven enlisted. Training missions often lasted 40 hours, requiring an augmented crew of up to 28.[17]

Despite the hype, the B-36 was recognized as an interim bomber. One SAC senior engineer said simply, "I was fascinated by the B-36, but it was obsolete before it was built, and we all knew it."[18] LeMay later concurred with that view, noting, "Sure, we got the thing flying and going . . . [but] we had more trouble than we should have had on a normal airplane due to the basic design and to the overall job that the Convair people did."[19] Newer jet fighters, like the F-86 and the MiG-15, would be able to reach the altitude of a cruising B-36 and get a good shot at it; the next generation, like the F-100 or MiG-17, would have had their way with it.[20] The maintenance problems plaguing the bomber never went away, and the SAC history noted ruefully that "by early 1950 it was vividly clear that the B-36 had not approached the anticipated and desired level of operational reliability." An "operational engineering section" was established to focus on B-36 maintenance problems. This helped, but the aircraft was still a chore to keep combat ready.[21] Eventually, 11 SAC wings would be equipped with the Peacemakers—both the bomber and reconnaissance versions—but as the jet-powered B-52 began entering the inventory in 1956, the older bombers were retired.[22] The last B-36J had its final flight in February 1959. A total of 385 of these giants were built, nearly a third of which were reconnaissance aircraft.[23] None ever dropped a bomb in anger.

LeMay appreciated the B-36 and its payload capability, but he also knew the bomber was a stopgap. When the Chinese intervened in Korea and there was serious talk of war with both the Soviet Union and China, he wrote, "In view of the rapidly deteriorating international

---

[17] The B-36's record bomb load of 92,100 lbs. was dropped on 30 June 1948. Jacobsen and Deaver, *Convair B-36*, 10.

[18] Wilson, interview, 1–2 December 1983, 112.

[19] LeMay, interview, 16 November 1972, 37. LeMay thought Convair's management team was not as effective and efficient as Boeing's, and this had much to do with the B-36's problems.

[20] Jacobsen and Deaver, *Convair B-36*, 255–56.

[21] *SAC History—1952*, vol. 1, 76–82.

[22] One B-36 was converted into a cargo aircraft, the XC-99, and another was used as a test bed for a nuclear-powered aircraft—a chimera that the Air Force chased for over a decade. For the latter, see R. D. Little, "Nuclear Propulsion for Manned Aircraft," USAF Historical Division Liaison study, April 1963, AFHRA, file K168.01-11; and Vincent Cortright, "Dream of Atomic-Powered Flight," 30–36, 69.

[23] The RB-36 was an impressive reconnaissance asset because its size accommodated several large cameras and other sensors. Altitude limitations spelled its doom; when the U-2 was developed, which could fly above 70,000 feet, the RB-36 became redundant.

situation we must have a bomber with substantially higher performance characteristics than the B-36." He knew this would be the B-52, and he pushed hard for its procurement: "I consider the development and production of the B-52 aircraft of vital concern to the national security."[24]

The AAF had issued a contract to Boeing in June 1946 to explore jet propulsion in a bomber. The company's first effort employed a turboprop design—jet engines powering a conventional propeller. The plane fell short on performance parameters, so Boeing substituted pure jets—eight of them in four pairs—and a swept-wing design. The Air Force approved and ordered two prototypes; the first was rolled out in November 1951.[25]

LeMay liked the aircraft immediately and saw it as the best alternative for replacing the B-36. When the Korean War broke out, he asked for acceleration of the B-52 program and for Air Force headquarters to make it a top priority.[26] As the development program continued, LeMay watched it closely. He did not like the tandem cockpit configuration initially proposed and directed Boeing to redesign the aircraft to feature conventional side-by-side seating for pilot and copilot. His reasoning was sound: crew coordination and cross-checking would be significantly improved with the traditional configuration. Cost also became a concern. LeMay was bothered by this, but analysts showed him that the B-52 could carry the new hydrogen bombs—which weighed 42,000 lbs.—whereas the B-47 (a medium jet bomber also built by Boeing, discussed below) could not. Moreover, the B-52 would be able to deliver significantly more conventional bombs than the Stratojet, which meant that in the long run, the B-52 would be more economical in carrying out a sustained bombing campaign.[27]

The first flight of the new bomber was 15 April 1952, and its performance pleased everyone. Although not as large as the Peacemaker, the B-52 was a big aircraft: 152 feet long, 48 feet high, and a wingspan of 185 feet. A number of different models were produced over the years, but the H model (which emerged in 1961) had a maximum takeoff weight of 488,000 lbs., a maximum speed of 650 mph, and a service ceiling of 50,000 feet. Its bomb load was enormous: internally

---

[24] "Strategic Air Command Requirements for Long-Range Strategic Strike Force, 1950–1952," 6 April 1955, SAC historical study, AFHRA, file K416.04-4, 2.

[25] "The B-52: Background and Early Development, 1946–1954," SAC historical study, 1956, AFHRA, file K416.01-60, 3–15.

[26] LeMay to Vandenberg, letter, 12 September 1950, in "B-52," SAC historical study, exhibit 4.

[27] "B-52," SAC historical study, 31–42.

and externally it could carry up to 70,000 lbs. in various configurations. In addition, the B-52 could carry air-launched cruise missiles,
like the Hound Dog, as well as the Quail decoy missile, designed to
mimic the B-52 and thus confuse enemy radar.[28] The first operational
bombers, B models, entered service in late 1954. C models, which
were heavier, a tad faster, and carried a bigger bomb load, began entering SAC in mid 1956. Eventually, over 744 of the bombers would
be built, 68 of which are still in active service nearly 60 years later.[29]

Those were the heavyweights. SAC also developed and operated a
number of medium bombers. The very heavy bomber of World War
II, the B-29, was downgraded to a medium bomber when the B-36
arrived on the scene. As we saw, it was the obsolescing Superfortress
that fought in Korea. All of these aircraft had been built during World
War II; some had been put into storage and then brought back out
and refurbished when needed for combat.

As early as 1944 the AAF realized the B-29 could be improved and
began working on a version incorporating more-powerful engines.
This aircraft, the B-29D, flew in May 1945, and the AAF planned to
buy 200. After the war ended, procurement was cut to 60. By the end
of 1945 the aircraft's designation was changed to the B-50. One historian claimed the change was "an outright ruse to win appropriations
for the procurement of an aeroplane that by its designation appeared
to be merely a late version of an existing model that was being cancelled wholesale."[30] That is plausible because the size of the bomber
remained roughly the same—an identical wingspan and length—but
the more-powerful engines induced handling problems, so the tail
height was increased by three feet. Superficially, the aircraft looked
the same, although a close observer would have noticed the larger
fairing on the engines and the taller tail. There were other small
changes, such as a different aluminum alloy that gave greater strength
at less weight, reversible propellers, better windows with a built-in
deicing feature, and hydraulic boost for the rudder, among others.
The Air Force claimed there was only 25 percent similarity between
the B-29 and the B-50, hence the new designation. The performance
of the B-50 was appreciably better: it had a higher max takeoff weight
(173,000 lbs. vs. 140,000 lbs.), faster speed (385 vs. 365), higher ceiling

---

[28] Bowers, *Boeing Aircraft since 1916*, 337–47.

[29] The definitive history of all B-52 models and variants is in Knaack, *Encyclopedia of U.S. Air Force Aircraft and Missile Systems*, vol. 2, 205–94.

[30] Bowers, *Boeing Aircraft since 1916*, 398.

(37,000' vs. 31,800'), and longer range (5,830 mi. vs. 4,650 mi.). Both bombers could carry 20,000 lbs. of bombs internally, although the B-50 was equipped to carry an additional 8,000 lbs. externally.[31]

The B-50 was an interim bomber. It provided excellent service and was a proven design, but the much anticipated arrival of the jet-powered Boeing B-47 would quickly drive it out of service. While 371 B-50s were built, most were retired in 1956, although 136 were converted into tankers for Tactical Air Command, ensuring them another decade of service.[32]

The AAF issued a proposal for a medium-range jet bomber in 1943. The Boeing design appearing the following September was unexceptional, but intelligence data gathered on jet and aerodynamic experimentation garnered from the Germans enabled a redesign. The swept-wing XB-47's maiden flight was in December 1947, but delays ensued—Boeing blamed the Air Force for introducing too many design changes, and the Air Force countered with charges of poor management. LeMay was unhappy, regardless of who was at fault, and commented bitterly that the program was a year behind schedule, and the way things were going, the B-47 would "become available for the Air Force devoid of the equipment which makes a plane a bomber."[33]

The Stratojet was worth the wait. One of the most beautiful bombers ever built, the B-47 was sleek, fast, and agile. Unusually, the pilots sat in tandem, like a two-seat fighter plane, rather than next to one another. One bomb delivery maneuver, the "low altitude bombing system," entailed a Stratojet streaking in at low altitude, pulling up sharply into a 45-degree climb, releasing its nuclear bomb, completing a half roll, and then aileron rolling upright—an Immelmann aerobatic maneuver.[34] Some pilots said the B-47 handled like a fighter plane, although that had its downside. One wing commander admitted, "The plane is in a category all of itself. And it has become apparent that all pilots cannot fly it. . . . It is just too much airplane for some."[35]

The jet was so aerodynamically smooth that pilots had difficulty getting it slowed down for approach and landing, and once it was on

[31] Ibid., 282, 300.

[32] There was a version of the B-50, termed the B-54, which employed variable discharge turbine (VDT) engines, an unsuccessful exhaust-driven supercharger design. The Air Force held much hope for this technology, but it eventually proved a failure. In 1949 the Senior Officers Board discussed the VDT and B-54 at length. "Report of Senior Officers Convened to Consider the Production and the Research and Development Program for the USAF," 21 February 1949, AFHRA, file 168.15-10, 13–20.

[33] SAC History—1951, vol. 2, 57.

[34] Lloyd, Boeing's B-47 Stratojet, 72.

[35] SAC History—1951, vol. 2, 121. Top speed of the B-47 was over 600 mph.

the ground it was hard to stop, putting excess pressure on the braking system. Boeing therefore incorporated an aviation first—drag chutes, which the pilot could deploy to help the plane decelerate. Despite its six jet engines, a fully loaded B-47 needed a great deal of runway for takeoff. That problem was solved by incorporating jet-assisted takeoff (JATO) bottles—small rocket engines attached to the fuselage for takeoff. These 18 bottles, later increased to 33, provided extra thrust to get the bomber airborne; after liftoff the JATO bottles were jettisoned, and the ground crew drove out to retrieve the canisters. In addition, water/alcohol injection was used on the engines to boost power temporarily on takeoff.[36] LeMay liked the design, calling it a "workhorse bomber" that would replace the B-29s and B-50s in the inventory. He appreciated its speed and altitude capability, noting it provided the flexibility to penetrate either high or low, depending on the threat.[37]

The B-47 was the first bomber designated as a "weapon system," acknowledging its sophistication and complexity. Nonetheless, it had problems: in 1951 the Air Force took delivery of 204 B-47Bs, and not one of them was suitable for combat. Costly upgrade and retrofit programs were funded to correct myriad problems. The first B-47s were not declared operational until October 1952 and were not deployed overseas until mid 1953.[38] Specific problem areas included the tail gun turret, which proved to be a headache. Another new innovation, ejection seats for the crew, also proved troublesome.[39] Given its 600-mph speed and altitude capability of 33,000 feet, an RB-47 reconnaissance model was developed that proved successful. These aircraft made numerous flights over Soviet and Chinese territory during the Cold War, each mission individually approved by the White House. Despite the plane's capabilities, these were extremely risky missions, especially after the new MiG-17 came on the scene. Eventually, seven RB-47s would be shot down by the communists.[40]

Over 2,000 Stratojets were built—290 of which were reconnaissance versions—with the last delivered in 1957; the B-47 left the inventory in early 1966. The E model was especially capable and had a 25,000 lb. payload with an unrefueled combat radius of 2,000 miles.

---

[36] *SAC History—1951*, vol. 2, 30–73. Theodore von Kármán had developed the JATO bottles.

[37] "Report of Senior Officers Board Convened to Consider the Production Program and Research and Development Program for the USAF," 8 March 1949, AFHRA, file 168.15-10, 456.

[38] *SAC History—1953*, vol. 5, 18–21.

[39] Lloyd, *Boeing's B-47 Stratojet*, 62.

[40] Ibid., 172–73, 181.

It could carry several types of conventional or nuclear bombs, including the Mk. 36, a 17,000 lb. bomb with a force of 24 megatons.[41] Like its predecessor medium bombers, the B-47 would need help getting to and from its targets, and therein lies a tale.[42]

The Challenge of Range

Alexander de Seversky was a fighter pilot and ace in the Russian navy during World War I—despite having lost a leg during a crash. Seversky claimed the loss of his leg made him a better pilot because it forced him to use his head to stay out of trouble. After the Russian Revolution, Seversky became an American citizen and put his head to work as an aeronautical engineer. He recalled one mission during the war when he had playfully reached up and grabbed the trailing radio antenna of a bomber he was escorting. It gave him an idea: what if the wire were a hose that could pass gasoline from one plane to another, thus extending its range? Escort fighters could then accompany the bombers to their targets. His first US patent was for an air refueling device sold to the Army Air Service. In June 1923 a DH-4 biplane used Seversky's invention to refuel another DH-4 in flight. A few months later the same plane flew from Suma, Washington, to San Diego using four in-flight refuelings, quadrupling its range.[43]

In January 1929 a C-2A Ford Tri-Motor named *Question Mark* took off from San Diego on New Year's Day to see how long it could stay aloft. Two Douglas C-1 transports were converted into "tankers" by installing hoses to pass gas to *Question Mark*. The first refueling occurred over the Rose Bowl game and continued for the next six days, during which the C-1s passed nearly 5,700 gallons of gas and oil, as well as food, spare parts, and mail.[44] Of the *Question Mark's* five-man crew, three would later rise to high rank: Carl Spaatz, Ira Eaker, and Pete Quesada. They and the other two crewmen were awarded Distinguished Flying Crosses. Although the flight seemed to

---

[41] Knaack, *Encyclopedia of U.S. Air Force Aircraft and Missile Systems*, vol.vol. 2, 155–57; and Dill, "Doomsday Armada," 14.

[42] In addition to the bombers discussed above, others seeing limited operational service were the North American B-45, Martin B-57, and Douglas B-66. There were also a number of experimental bombers: XB-35/YB-49 (the "flying wings"), XB-42, XB-43, XB-46, XB-49, and XB-51. For details, see Knaack, *Encyclopedia of U.S. Air Force Aircraft and Missile Systems*, vol. 2.

[43] Meilinger, "Alexander P. de Seversky and American Airpower," in Meilinger, *Paths of Heaven*, 242–43; and Smith, *Seventy-Five Years of Inflight Refueling*, 1–3.

[44] Parton, "*Air Force Spoken Here*," 70–76.

portend an aeronautical revolution, such was not the case. The military saw no practical application for the capability. That view would eventually change.

World War II demonstrated the need for range. Although B-17s and B-24s could reach Berlin from England and Italy, ranges in the Pacific theater were extreme. Tankers would have been useful. Although experiments were done in April 1943 using a B-24 as a tanker with a B-17 as a receiver, the procedures were too complex to employ the system on a major scale. Air leaders decided to wait for the liberation of bases nearer to Japan that could house longer-range B-29s. Air refueling could also have extended the range of escort fighters—the mission Seversky had conceived in 1917. The lack of escort early in the war led to catastrophe at places like Schweinfurt, when the bombers went in alone. The problem was acute, and the solution as we saw was the unglamorous drop tank. Air refueling was not considered for fighter escort, perhaps because of the sheer scale of the problem—by mid 1944 there were over 5,000 US fighter aircraft in Europe. At a time when factories were straining to produce aircraft to supply a global war, building hundreds of tankers was unthinkable. The issue of air refueling lay dormant until the Cold War, when its advantages were reexamined.

The United States and its allies were outnumbered three to one on the ground in Europe. SAC would be the equalizer. But Moscow was a long way from the United States—5,000 miles; how would the bombers reach their targets and return? One solution was cruise control—using fuel leaning and precise airspeed for better efficiency and longer range. The results were surprising: a B-29 from the 509th used such methods to fly 5,767 miles while carrying a 10,300 lb. bomb load half that distance. This was impressive, but still not good enough.[45] A Heavy Bombardment Committee met in September 1947 to discuss the problem. Very-long-range aircraft like the B-36 were one answer, but even the sleek B-47, then in the development stage, was only a medium bomber. Air refueling was the obvious solution.[46]

The Air Force looked first at the old "grab and drag" method employed during the 1920s in which both tanker and receiver aircraft trailed lines. The receiver's line ended in a grapnel, which, when the lines were crossed, enabled the receiver to grasp the tanker's line and

---

[45] *SAC History—1948*, vol. 1, 280.

[46] Julian, "Origins of Air Refueling in the United States Air Force," in Neufeld, *Technology and the Air Force*, 87–88.

its attached refueling hose and reel it in. This system, updated by the British after World War II, was cumbersome, time consuming, difficult, and somewhat hazardous, but it worked.[47]

On 30 June 1948, SAC stood up its first air refueling squadron at Davis-Monthan AFB, Arizona, and in December a B-50 flew nonstop for 10,000 miles. This Queen Bee exercise gave airmen the idea of an around-the-world flight using aerial refueling. In early 1949 there were only two refueling squadrons in SAC, attached to the 43rd and 509th Bomb Wings. By year-end there was increased talk of a global flight, so training accelerated. One staffer noted, however, "It is imperative that such a flight not be initiated until every part of the entire mission is carefully planned in detail, thoroughly flight-tested, and double-checked."[48] Planners presented LeMay with a mission concept envisioning six B-50s departing the United States at 24-hour intervals and heading east. There would be four air refueling locations: the Azores, Saudi Arabia, the Philippines, and Hawaii. At each point two tankers would fill one aircraft. LeMay liked the overall scheme but changed the plan to one aircraft rather than six. On 19 January the idea was briefed to Vandenberg and Secretary Symington, and they approved. When they asked the odds of a B-50 actually making it all the way, they were told about 25 percent.[49]

SAC planners were pessimistic due to the rudimentary state of air refueling at the time. The two tanker squadrons were just learning this challenging procedure, and the flight would require eight successful fuel transfers. Training continued, and on 25 February 1949, a B-50 from the 43rd Bomb Wing named *Global Queen* took off from Carswell AFB, Texas, headed east. Sixteen hours later it landed in the Azores with engine trouble. The following morning *Lucky Lady II* launched to try its luck. The aircraft encountered bad weather, and there were minor mishaps with engine cooling flaps, propeller deicers, and the like, but for the most part the epic journey was uneventful. *Lucky Lady II* touched down at 0931 local time, 2 March, at Carswell. The crew was greeted by Secretary Symington and Generals Vandenberg and LeMay. The SAC commander stressed the flight's importance:

---

[47] *SAC History—1949*, vol. 1, 84. The definitive history of the British system was written by one of its designers. Perhaps for that reason, he scarcely even mentions the probe system developed by Boeing! Tanner, *History of Air-To-Air Refueling*.

[48] Irvine to LeMay, letter, 17 November 1948, in *SAC History—1950*, vol.vol. 6, exhibit 5.

[49] *SAC History—1950*, vol. 6, 65–66. The plan called for five backup aircraft to stand ready at Carswell, which was a good idea. When *Global Queen* failed, it was *Lucky Lady II*'s chance. If she were forced to land somewhere, the next aircraft would take off and try to make it.

"This means that we can now deliver an atomic bomb to any place in the world that requires an atomic bomb."[50]

Over the next several years the number of aircraft modified to use the looped-hose system multiplied. The plan was to have all six medium bomb wings in SAC equipped with an air refueling capability over 18 months. Planners soon realized, however, that this system had severe limitations: it could not be used by aircraft flying over 190 knots or by fighter aircraft. In a conference held at Air Materiel Command in February 1949, the Air Force asked for new ideas.

An alternative was the "probe and drogue" system involving a hose reeled out from the tanker with an attached basket shaped like a huge shuttlecock. The receiver aircraft was equipped with a probe that plugged into the basket. This system worked well for smaller aircraft, but large planes were difficult to maneuver while trying to plug a basket.[51] In addition, the amount of fuel transferred by this method was limited, approximately 250 gallons per minute. At that rate it would take over an hour to top off a bomber. There were other problems: frequent failure, oscillation and whipping of the hose, fuel leaks, and inadequate lighting for night operations.[52] Nonetheless, the system was useful for fighters. In September 1950 an F-84E flew nonstop from England to Maine—a 10-hour flight that was a transatlantic first for a jet fighter.[53] During the Korean War a squadron of KB-29s deployed to Japan to test the system in combat with jet fighters. The world's first combat air refueling took place on 6 July 1951. Vandenberg had expressed concern to Weyland that increased enemy air activity might threaten FEAF's airfields in South Korea, so the Air Force tested air refueling for jet fighters in the event the F-84s had to redeploy to Japan.[54] FEAF, and TAC, were well pleased with the realization of how air refueling could impact fighter operations. In 1952 tankers began escorting and refueling fighter squadrons across both the Atlantic and the Pacific. In July, Operation Fox Peter I deployed

---

[50] Ibid., 65–75. The crew of the *Lucky Lady II* received Distinguished Flying Crosses, but like the tanker pilots who had made the 1929 *Question Mark* flight a reality, the tanker crews who enabled the 1949 circumnavigation were not rewarded and their names not recorded in the SAC history.

[51] *SAC History—1950*, 91; and Adams to Cabell, letter, 24 January 1950, in *SAC History—1950*, vol. 2, exhibit 1. The probe-and-drogue method is still in use today for US Navy/Marine Corps aircraft and helicopters. KC-135s can be modified on the ground to use the probe-and-drogue system. The KC-10 and the new Boeing tanker under development can use either method on the same flight.

[52] Austin to Cabell, letter, 24 January 1950.

[53] *SAC History—1952*, vol. 1, 225–30. This system was invaluable for deploying fighter wings overseas during an emergency—it would ordinarily take several weeks to disassemble a fighter unit, put its aircraft on ships to be moved overseas, and then reassemble the aircraft after unloading.

[54] Vandenberg to Weyland, letter, 17 January 1952, in *SAC History—1952*, vol.vol. 4, chap. 3, exhibit 28.

the 31st Fighter Wing to Japan: 58 F-84Gs, led and periodically refueled by KB-29s, flew from Turner AFB in Georgia to Japan. It would be the first of many such deployments.[55]

The limitations of the probe-and-drogue system for large aircraft led to the flying boom. By 1950 Boeing had perfected a system using a boom extending down and telescoping out from the rear of a tanker. A boom operator, sitting in the old tail gunner's position, could actually "fly" the boom, which was equipped with small wings termed *ruddervators*. The receiver maneuvered behind the tanker and flew formation; the boomer would then fly his boom into the receiver aircraft's receptacle. The boom system transferred fuel at 600 gallons per minute—more than twice that of the probe and drogue.[56] The first boom-equipped KB-29P was delivered to SAC's 97th Air Refueling Squadron at Biggs AFB, Texas, on 1 September 1950.

Over the next several years the number of tankers in SAC exploded—by the end of 1954, there were 683 tankers in 32 squadrons.[57] With the move toward an all-jet bomber force, however, even the boomed KB-29s and KC-97s were inadequate. Piston-driven tankers could not keep up with jet bombers, nor could they reach their altitude when loaded with fuel. As a result, B-47s had to descend and slow down to rendezvous with the tankers. What ensued became almost comical. As the B-47 took on gas and grew heavier, its stall speed increased, which meant it had to accelerate not to fall out of the sky. This in turn required both the tanker and the bomber to go into a descent to pick up speed to stay above a stall. Eventually, both aircraft would then go into a climb. As the airspeed slowly bled off, another descent was necessary. This porpoise maneuver, while connected, required inordinate skill for both the tanker and bomber pilots. Moreover, once the refueling was accomplished, the B-47 had to climb back to cruising altitude and accelerate—a process that consumed 25 percent more fuel than if the refueling had occurred at the bomber's altitude and cruising speed.[58] The Air Force needed a jet tanker, and the solution was the KC-135, born in 1955.

The KC-135 provided a quantum jump in capability over the KB-29. It could carry 31,200 gallons of fuel while also hauling 40 tons of cargo or 160 passengers. The jet tanker could offload six times as much fuel

[55] Smith, *Seventy-Five Years of Inflight Refueling*, 34–38. Eventually, TAC gained its own tanker force of KB-50s.
[56] Ibid., 26–27.
[57] Ibid., 31.
[58] *SAC History—1952*, vol. 1, 182–201; and Zimmerman, *Insider at SAC*, 63.

as the KB-29 and twice that of the KB-97, and because it had twice the range of the KB-97, one KC-135 could take the place of three or more piston-driven tankers. Moreover, the Stratotanker could do so at the same speed and altitude as the B-47 and B-52.[59] SAC embraced the KC-135 and purchased 732, while also buying 744 B-52s. These aircraft were to become a team over the next several decades.

During the latter half of the 1950s, SAC and its nuclear weapons dominated the military structure. But what of the thousands of fighter planes in the Air Force inventory? TAC went heavily into the nuclear delivery role in the 1950s, and pilots trained to deliver nuclear weapons as much as they trained for close air support.[60] As the fighters took on the nuclear role, they needed air refueling to extend their range so they could reach targets in Eastern Europe. The issue of tankers refueling fighters was contentious because SAC wanted the tankers for its bombers. LeMay asserted, "The demand for tanker aircraft by bombardment units of this command and by other commands [FEAF and USAFE] precluded any such arrangement."[61] Nonetheless, SAC began transferring some of its older KB-29s and B-50s to TAC, which eventually acquired its own tanker force.[62] When these aircraft were retired due to age during the Vietnam War, SAC assumed responsibility for air refueling of all TAC aircraft, as well as cargo planes, aircraft of the Navy and allies, and of course its own bombers. Fighter-bombers like the F-4 and F-105 bore the brunt of the air war against North Vietnam; tankers turned tactical fighters into strategic bombers.

The Penetration Problem

Range was crucial, but it was not the only problem. The B-17s and B-24s had been able to reach targets in Germany; enemy interceptors, both to and from the target, were the next concern. As we saw, escort was essential, but designing and building small, agile fighters with the

---

[59] "Capabilities and Features of the KC-135 Tanker-Transport," 10 September 1958, AFHRA, file K416.861-1, 6–11.

[60] In early 1954 General Twining, then chief of staff, stated it was his goal for all tactical fighters and bombers to be capable of delivering nuclear weapons. Converse, *History of Acquisition in the Department of Defense*, vol. 1, 460.

[61] *SAC History—1952*, vol. 1, 106.

[62] LeMay to Power, letter, 3 May 1960, AFHRA, file K416.01-21. LeMay was vice-chief of staff at this point, and Power was CINCSAC. The demise of the B-36, which was most in need of escort, meant that SAC was able to disband its fighter escort wings, lessening the need for its KB-29s.

requisite range was a technological challenge. The amazing P-51 solved the problem during the war, but the concern reemerged afterward.

When SAC was formed in 1946, planners assumed escort would be necessary for the B-29s going against the Soviet Union. SAC therefore included escort wings in its numbered air forces. Originally, it was to have 12 fighter wings, but that number dropped quickly. In mid 1946 only one wing was operational (and two others on paper); by late 1947 there were five; a year later it was down to two and in 1951 back up to seven. Some of these deployed for the Korean War, although they were not often used in their primary mission.[63]

Surprisingly, although tens of thousands of fighters existed at the end of the war, they were almost immediately scrapped, and it proved difficult to equip SAC with serviceable P-47s and P-51s. Even these proved inadequate—they had neither the range nor the performance to successfully escort the B-29s. F-82 Twin Mustangs also proved unsatisfactory. The introduction of jet-propelled F-80s was an advance, but they were obsolescing quickly, and the Korean War soon demonstrated their inadequacy. In April 1950 LeMay admitted that SAC had no long-range escort capability.[64] F-84s were to be the best-available answer, and SAC was equipped with these jets by 1952. In truth, the Thunderjets were not up to the task either. Because targets in the Soviet Union were even farther away than had been German factories, the issue of sufficient range for escort reappeared. SAC began to experiment.

First, air refueling was used to extend the range of the F-84s, and this helped somewhat but not enough to allow escort of the bomber force into and out of Russia. The arrival of high-flying and faster jet bombers added another layer of complexity to an already thorny problem. Although the F-84 had the speed to keep up with the B-50 and the B-36, it lacked the range and altitude capability to accompany B-47s. Moreover, the appearance of Soviet fighters like the MiG-15 made the F-84s outmatched. A study conducted by SAC in February 1951 revealed that "neither current escort fighters nor programmed escort fighters have a capability of adequately defending bombers"; therefore, the bomber force would "suffer an unacceptable loss rate during daylight conditions over enemy territory defended by interceptors."[65]

---

[63] "Development of Fighter-Escort in Strategic Air Command through 1951," SAC historical study, 1 June 1952, AFHRA, file K416.01-29, 261.

[64] "Notes from Commanders Conference, Exercise DUALISM," 25–27 April 1950, AFHRA, file 168.15-10, 219.

[65] Boyd, "SAC Fighter Planes and Their Operations," 5.

SAC needed a high-performance escort fighter with a 3,000-mile range. McDonnell produced the XF-88 in mid 1950, which LeMay liked but the Air Force did not. Eventually, McDonnell added new engines, and the resulting F-101 was a great success. Ten wings of Voodoo fighters were programmed, but by 1956 and the imminent arrival of the B-52, SAC changed its mind. Money would be better spent on more bombers. After only a few weeks in SAC, the F-101s were transferred to Air Defense Command.[66]

Range remained an obstacle, and unusual—if not bizarre—solutions were offered to overcome it. In 1948 a parasite fighter, the XF-85 Goblin, was built to be carried inside the bomb bay of a B-36. The intent was for Peacemakers carrying F-85s to accompany the nuclear-toting bombers into enemy territory. If enemy interceptors appeared, the Goblins would be dropped out of the bombers (a B-36 could carry two) via a trapeze mechanism, ignite their engines, and maneuver to take on the attackers. At the conclusion of the dogfight, the F-85s would return to the B-36, reattach to the trapeze, and be lifted back into the bomb bay.[67] The F-85 flew four times, but reengaging the trapeze proved so difficult the project was dropped.

At the same time, SAC experimented with other ideas for its fighter force besides escort. The revolution in nuclear weapons design meant fighters could deliver them as well. In January 1953, SAC converted its F-84s to carry the new weapons and become part of the nuclear strike force. The problem of range remained, so one scheme involved mounting a trapeze bracket on the underside of a B-36. An F-84F would be attached to the trapeze (which was external and not in the bomb bay as with the XF-85) and would carry a nuclear weapon. Upon entering Soviet airspace, the fighter would detach and zoom off to drop its bomb. It would then return to its mother ship, reattach to the trapeze, and both would return home.[68] In a related concept, straight-wing F-84Es would attach themselves to the wingtips of a modified B-36. The fighters would then shut down their engines and be "towed" by the bomber to enemy airspace, where the faster and more-maneuverable fighters would restart their engines, detach, and fly on to drop their nuclear weapons. They would then reattach to the

---

[66] "Development of Fighter-Escort in Strategic Air Command through 1951," 284–86.

[67] Pyeatt and Jenkins, *Cold War Peacemaker*, 221–22; and Gudaitis, "It Seemed Like a Good Idea at the Time," 68.

[68] Pyeatt and Jenkins, *Cold War Peacemaker*, 222–24. The Republic F-84 came in different models; most were straight-wing designs termed the *Thunderjet*. The F-model had swept wings and was called the *Thunderstreak*. The RF-84F version was called *Thunderflash*.

B-36 for the ride home.[69] Another application of this concept used the F-84 as a reconnaissance aircraft to fly ahead of the bomber once inside Soviet airspace and locate suitable targets.[70]

These ideas went nowhere, but the fact they were even attempted illustrates the seriousness of the problem. The Korean War indicated once again that unescorted bombers would have difficulty penetrating even modest air defenses in daylight—and during the summer months northern Russia was always in daylight. Yet repeated attempts to build a suitable escort fighter were unsuccessful. Eventually, SAC gave up on the escort idea but was still reluctant to let go of its fighters. Perhaps the jets could assume a new mission as part of the nuclear strike force and either attack targets near the enemy border or be "carried" into enemy airspace for that mission. This proved infeasible, and the nuclear-capable fighters were eventually transferred to theater commanders.

Reconnaissance was also a requirement, so abortive attempts were made to convert the fighters for this mission. These ideas also foundered due to range and survivability problems in the face of superior Soviet interceptors. In 1958, SAC received two wings of F-86s, but these aircraft were sent to Spain and used for air base defense—another new mission. Finally, SAC gave up. It surrendered the fighter force, which had never been a high priority within the command, and gave its assets to other commands that could make better use of them. The constant changes in aircraft type, mission, movement to different air bases, and shortages of specialized jet mechanics and other maintenance personnel were revealed in the dismal combat-ready statistics of the jets throughout this period, as shown in the table below:

SAC fighter combat readiness

	1946	1947	1948	1949	1950	1951	1952	1953	1954	1955	1956	1957
Assigned Units	3	5	2	2	3	3	4	6	6	7	6	0
Combat Ready	0	0	2	2	2	0	1	4	0	2	3	0

Source: Robert J. Boyd, "SAC Fighter Planes and Their Operations," SAC Historical Study, 1988, 22.

---

[69] Ibid., 224–26; and Anderson, "Dangerous Experiments," 64–72. Initial tests were conducted on a modified B-29. After several dozen successful flights, the idea was abandoned when a coupled F-84 rolled over onto the bomber—both planes went down, and all crew members were killed.

[70] Power to LeMay, letter, 19 October 1949, in SAC History—1949, vol. 3, exhibit 111.

Only twice during this 12-year period were all of SAC's fighter wings combat ready, and during five years, none of the wings achieved this status.[71] Apart from this seeming neglect and confusion, the original problem remained: how would SAC's bombers penetrate enemy airspace to complete their mission?

Other solutions seemed to offer better results. SAC planned to build deployment bases on the periphery of the Soviet Union. Escort fighters would launch in the event of war, top off their tanks with air refueling once airborne, and then escort the bombers as far as possible into enemy territory before turning back—not unlike the situation during World War II.[72] This idea ran into difficulties.

The greatest utility of overseas bases is that they are near potential crisis areas. The greatest *limitation* of overseas bases is that they are near potential crisis areas. The issue is vulnerability. Initially, SAC hoped air bases in the Arctic would allow B-29 missions over the North Pole to become commonplace, but deployments from 1946 to 1948 demonstrated that such operations would be extremely difficult. A backup plan was for SAC aircraft to base at forward locations in Europe, the Middle East, and Asia—within unrefueled striking distance of their targets.[73] The B-29s and B-50s did not have intercontinental range, so such bases were essential. Political considerations made permanent bases problematic, so in 1946 SAC began bomb group rotations into Europe, usually billed as training exercises. After the Berlin crisis, SAC rotations continued, while billions of dollars worth of materiel was stockpiled in Europe (Project Seaweed) for a future emergency. With the detonation of the Soviet atomic bomb in August 1949, SAC realized such forward bases were becoming increasingly vulnerable. It therefore pushed for bases in Morocco—close enough to the Soviet Union to serve for staging but far enough back to allow some protection from an enemy strike.[74] The following year a construction program was launched to build four bases in French Morocco—the first was completed in 1951 at Sidi Slimane.

---

[71] Another part of the problem was the introduction of Air National Guard and Air Reserve wings into the SAC fighter force. Seldom were these units at full strength, thus adding to combat-readiness problems. Also illustrative, while SAC bombing competitions were held every year, only one fighter competition was ever conducted—and that not until 1956 when the fighters were on their way out of the command.

[72] One of the benefits of air refueling is that most aircraft can fly at a heavier weight than they can take off. Therefore, it is common for aircraft to take off with a reduced fuel load but heavy payload, climb to altitude, and then fill their tanks with an air refueling.

[73] For the story surrounding these early basing plans, see Converse, *Circling the Earth*.

[74] "Overseas Bases: A Military and Political Evaluation," AF History Division study, 2 April 1962, AFHRA, file K416.601-13, 2.

Three more bases were built in Spain.[75] These, along with airfields in England, Turkey, and Guam, would serve as bulwarks of an overseas basing system designed to outflank the Soviet Union. To be sure, numerous bases would also be built throughout Germany, Italy, France, and elsewhere for short-range fighter aircraft, but the bombing offensive was initially planned to rely on bases not so close to the front.

General LeMay recognized the vulnerability of overseas air bases and in January 1952 stated his goal "to launch our offensive from this continent."[76] That was not yet possible, so forward bases were essential. The matter came to a head in 1954 when a study by the California-based RAND think tank concluded that those bases were highly vulnerable to a Soviet first strike, especially if the Soviets employed nuclear weapons. The analysts examined the distances from allied bases to targets in the Soviet Union, to favorable entry points into enemy territory based on known air defenses, to allied sources of supply, and from enemy airfields to the SAC forward bases. They then compared the forward-basing scheme against a scenario relying on CONUS-based aircraft with intercontinental range. Realizing this would be impossible for the B-47—which was then becoming the SAC workhorse—they acknowledged that air refueling was necessary to get the bombers to forward bases, but these airfields would be used for staging purposes only. Permanent forward bases were likely to be primary targets for Soviet air strikes, but those same airfields would be at less risk if only in operation part-time. Their conclusion was stark: regarding the system of forward basing, "we can expect the majority of the force to suffer serious damage on the ground."[77] That sounded too much like what had happened at Pearl Harbor and Clark Field in 1941. RAND acknowledged that it was possible to limit damage through camouflage, hardening, and dispersal, but the results were less satisfactory than a US-based bomber force relying on air refueling and brief stops at staging bases in Europe and the Middle East. Strangely, Albert Wohlstetter and his RAND colleagues were lukewarm to the benefits of air refueling, citing its enormous cost versus a ground-based refueling system—320 percent more by their calculations. Nonetheless, they conceded it would be useful to have tankers available as a hedge against the loss of the refueling airfields overseas.[78]

---

[75] Schake, "Strategic Frontier," chap. 3 (unpub.).
[76] "Overseas Bases" study, 4.
[77] Wohlstetter et al., "Selection and Use of Strategic Air Bases," viii.
[78] Ibid., xv.

This report had a significant impact. In Exercise Full House that same year, SAC tried another scenario: overseas bases would be used for poststrike staging only. In other words, air refueling would allow the bomber force coming from CONUS to hit its targets; on the way back it would stop at bases in England, the Middle East, or Guam to refuel. The exercise was a success, and SAC made this poststrike profile its basic war plan, especially necessary for the B-47 (and later B-58) medium-range bombers.[79]

Within a year the Air Force had placed an order for its first KC-135 tanker, and within a decade it had bought over 700, of which some 400 are still in service. As SAC became more reliant on the long-range B-52, plans would change again. The new US strategy in the event of war was to launch the B-52 fleet from secure bases in CONUS—air refueling would get the strike aircraft to their targets and back. This in turn meant a major effort to build new air bases in northeast Canada, Newfoundland, and Greenland. The Northeast Command, until then a backwater, assumed new importance as SAC shifted its tanker forces in that direction. Eighth Air Force headquarters was moved to Westover AFB, Massachusetts, to oversee this refocus. The bombers would lift off from their bases and hit tankers flying out of Goose Bay, Thule, and other northern bases, fly to their targets in the Soviet Union, and hit the tankers again on their way home.[80]

The Importance of Electronic Warfare and Countermeasures

The need for aerial refueling, the problem of penetrating enemy airspace, the resultant inability to provide escort fighters, and the crucial issue of overseas air bases all increased the difficulty of carrying out the war plan. How would SAC fulfill its task of delivering a devastating bombing offensive? All the factors just noted chipped away at the problem but left unanswered the fundamental question of how, precisely, the bombers would reach targets deep in the Soviet Union, destroy them, and make their way back to safety.

The solution SAC finally adopted was to send in its bomber force without escort, employing instead electronic countermeasures (ECM), decoys, and deception to slip past Soviet defenses. Altitude

---

[79] "Overseas Bases" study, 5.
[80] *SAC History—1956*, vol. 2, 175–80.

was a temporary expedient. Before surface-to-air missiles (SAM), the main threat to aircraft was from interceptors and AAA. One of the major aspects of the B-36 debate with the Navy was whether the big bomber could get through; the Navy thought jet interceptors would be able to knock it down. Introduction of the B-47 and later the B-52 upped the altitude capability of the bombers while also increasing speed. It was believed that a 600-mph bomber at 40,000 feet would make it through. The epitome of this belief in altitude and speed emerged in the North American XB-70, developed as an effort to go in very high (70,000 feet) and very fast (Mach 3). Unfortunately, the deployment of high-altitude-capable SAMs, specifically the Soviet SA-2 system that shot down Francis Gary Powers's U-2 in May 1960, put an end to that idea. The reverse tactic was then suggested—bombers would go in at low altitude, barely above the tree tops, and hopefully *below* the capabilities of the Soviet SAMs and radar-guided AAA.[81] Sometimes, bombers, like the B-58 Hustler, would go in very fast (it had a top speed of Mach 2) and low; at other times, B-52s would go in low and slow, trusting their ECM gear for safety. SAC and Soviet air strategists and tacticians fought an ongoing and very complex cat-and-mouse game throughout the Cold War.

The "Wizard War" of World War II had seen a persistent and vigorous battle between electronic warfare (EW) specialists. The Germans jammed British radar and used navigation beams to guide their bombers to targets in England. The British countered with spoofing, bending, or jamming.[82] This seesaw battle lasted throughout the war. Japan was less advanced in this field than was Germany, so the bomber crews of the XXI Bomber Command were able to degrade the air defense radars of the Japanese. At least, they could eventually. Initially, B-29 radar operators "could turn on the machine" and that was it. LeMay recalls a professor visiting from MIT who "couldn't believe how poorly trained our people were." He started a radar school, and things improved rapidly. "Before the thing was over we were destroying inland targets . . . in the middle of a thunderstorm."[83] As for ECM, one electronic specialist claimed there were rooms full of jammers in the Marianas, but they were in storage because no one

[81] Project Long Range was conducted by SAC in 1957, testing the feasibility of B-36s penetrating at low altitude, around 500 feet, to stay below radar coverage. As they approached their targets, the bombers would ascend quickly to "medium altitude" to deliver their weapon. *SAC History—Jan–Jun 1957*, vol. 1, 73.

[82] For an excellent overview told by one of the major figures, see R. V. Jones, *Wizard War.*

[83] LeMay, interview, 4 June 1984, 6.

knew how to use them. Instead, chaff and rope were used. Fortunately, the flak was not nearly as severe as it had been over Germany.[84]

Most ECM operators were enlisted specialists, although one officer was allotted per group. When the war ended, demobilization decimated the electronic warfare field in the AAF. The chief of one ECM school noted that within weeks of V-J Day his school had no students and no instructors. Another electronics officer recalled, "We had no equipment, no aircraft installations, no training programs, no training aids, no doctrine, no research and development programs to speak of, and only a handful of RCM [radar countermeasures] officers to begin anything with."[85] SAC was especially hard hit. Electronic warfare was more vital to the attacking bomber forces of SAC than it was to anyone else. As the war had shown, an enemy would defend its territory and its most vital centers vigorously. Yet, as was the case with intelligence officers, there were virtually no EW experts within the AAF when the war began, and such individuals had to be brought into uniform from civilian life. When the war ended, these civilians left to pursue more lucrative careers in the burgeoning electronics field. Of the 5,600 EW specialists needed by the AAF, over 70 percent were mustered out by March 1946. Worse, SAC personnel policies ensured that such vital individuals were made to feel unwelcome. Maj Gen Clements McMullen, the vice-commander and chief of staff of SAC until September 1948, had little use for nonrated officers—which most EW specialists were—and he labored to push them out of his command. Although a SAC staff study of November 1947 stressed the need for EW personnel to ensure the safety of aircraft and crew in combat, McMullen was unmoved. By mid 1947 there were barely a dozen such officers left in SAC.[86]

Maj Gen Roger Ramey at Eighth Air Force wrote LeMay soon after he had taken over SAC detailing the problems with ECM—they needed far more personnel and equipment devoted to this area. Specifically, the B-29s needed jammers to counter Soviet radars; otherwise, SAC bombers would have little chance of penetrating enemy airspace.[87] Another report was even grimmer. The need for ECM was

---

[84] Ibid., 9. Chaff, code-named "window" during the war, had been developed in 1937, but fear that the Germans would copy it and use it against London in a renewed blitz delayed its employment until July 1943. For the story, see Webster and Frankland, *Strategic Air Offensive against Germany, 1939–1945*, vol. 1, 400–1. A related item used to confuse radar was "rope," strips of aluminum foil hundreds of feet long that could jam across a wide spectrum of frequencies.

[85] Kuehl, "Radar Eye Blinded," 43, 56 (unpub.).

[86] Ibid., 49–53, 63, 80.

[87] Ibid., 89.

of "desperate urgency"; otherwise, taking on Soviet radars would be "inordinately dangerous."[88] LeMay ordered his deputy to review the issue, but years of neglect meant it would take time before personnel were trained and equipment was produced to remedy the situation. The SAC history confesses that when LeMay assumed command, "the electronic countermeasures capability in SAC units was practically non-existent."[89]

In January 1951 an exercise to test the ECM capability of B-50s against an air defense threat was a near-total failure—the bombers reached the target (Abilene, TX) with barely half their required ECM gear still working—had it been actual combat, the attacking force would have been decimated.[90] The few dozen jammers that existed in SAC in 1949 were of World War II vintage; even those were not permanently installed on the aircraft. Instead, racks were built into the bombers, and if intelligence gathered for the mission to be flown indicated a threat, jammers would be installed. There was not enough room to install enough jammers to counter the entire frequency spectrum, so analysts would provide guidance on what threats the crew was likely to face, and the specific jammer needed was then loaded on board. Even so, the B-29 and B-50 were not programmed to carry an ECM operator. If jammers were installed, a gunner would stand down, the radio operator would become a gunner, and the ECM expert would sit in.[91]

When SAC sent its B-29s to war in Korea, they were unprepared for a serious ECM fight. FEAF had paid almost no attention to electronic warfare, and it is noteworthy that the Bomber Command history notes enthusiastically that "the efficiency of ECM analysis in the Far East in September [1951] was strengthened by the addition of another ECM officer." Now there were *two* such officers at headquarters![92] Fortunately, North Korean air defenses were of a primitive nature, so the B-29s met little opposition, at first. Although the B-29's ECM gear was of World War II vintage, the leftover Japanese radars used by the North Koreans were worse. That changed with the Chinese intervention and the arrival of MiG-15s and Soviet-

---

[88] Armstrong to Asst DCS/O for Programming, letter, 3 November 1948, in *SAC History—1951*, vol. 4, exhibit 6/40.

[89] *SAC History—1951*, vol. 1, 194.

[90] Kuehl, "Radar Eye Blinded," 117–18.

[91] *SAC History—1951*, vol. 1, 211.

[92] Far East Air Forces Bomber Command Provisional, "Narrative History: 1 July Thru 31 December 1951," AFHRA, file K713.01-20, 64, 77.

made radars. Now the B-29s would have to fight their way to the target and back. The dearth of suitable ECM personnel and gear was quickly felt and classically revealed when the ECM operator added to the B-29 was not even afforded a real crew position. He monitored his instruments sitting on the crew chemical toilet that included no seat belt, oxygen hookup, or intercom jack![93]

Tactics called for ECM-equipped RB-29s to accompany the bomb droppers and fly figure eights over the target area to help nullify enemy radar defenses. Even so, by mid 1951 the B-29s were in trouble. As we saw, for this and other reasons, the B-29s could barely survive in an environment including MiG-15s, radar-guided searchlights, and gun-laying radars supplied by the Soviets.[94] The bombers retreated to the relative safety of night and attempted to avoid whenever possible the areas near the Yalu River.

Fortunately, B-29 night bombing operations using SHORAN produced excellent results, although the gear interfered with the ECM jammers on board, reducing even further the bomber's defenses.[95] On the evening of 11 June 1951, the bombers ran into MiGs guided by ground sites using Russian gun-laying and searchlight radars. Two of the four bombers were shot down and the other two severely damaged. Making conditions worse was LeMay's decree that the latest ECM equipment could not be utilized by the B-29s in Korea. LeMay feared that using the full panoply of electronic systems would provide the Soviets and Chinese too much intelligence on American capabilities. He wanted to hold back information to protect SAC in the event "real war" broke out and the bombers had to go against the full might of Soviet or Chinese defenses. At the time of the Kwaksan mission just noted, the B-29s were not even allowed to employ chaff to confuse enemy radar. This device had been used by the RAF as early as 1943 and was hardly an innovation; yet crews were denied its use until September 1952.[96] Similarly, the latest jammers were not sent to the Far East. Partly, this was due to the lack of room and electrical power output of the B-29s—as noted, the ECM operator did not even rate a true crew member position. As had been the concern with chaff, LeMay did not want new jammers deployed in Korea for fear

[93] Kuehl, "Radar Eye Blinded," 127; *SAC History—1951*, vol. 1, 174. Not every B-29 carried an ECM operator when going into combat; usually, one such aircraft would accompany a bomber formation to provide protection.

[94] Lloyd, *Boeing's B-47 Stratojet*, 181–82.

[95] Kuehl, "Radar Eye Blinded," 137–38; and "Far East Bomber Command Provisional, 4 July–31 October 1950," vol. 4, book 1, SAC historical study, AFHRA, file K713.01-8 111.

[96] *SAC History—1951*, vol. 1, 132; and Kuehl, "Radar Eye Blinded," 142, 152.

they would reveal too much about SAC capabilities—capabilities he hoped would never be revealed, but certainly not until the opening days of World War III.[97]

Even so, the Korean War laboratory provided insights into Soviet and Chinese equipment and tactics, while also training and educating a new generation of SAC crew members on the importance of electronic warfare to a strategic bombing campaign. Obviously, SAC was surprised by the quality and capability of Soviet equipment. It had been customary to disparage Russian technology and assume it was a generation behind that made in America. The explosion of an atomic bomb years ahead of schedule and the appearance of the MiG-15 over North Korea quickly disabused American airmen of these notions. It was also not lost on LeMay and his command that just as SAC had held back some of its latest and best equipment so as not to tip its hand, so too were the Soviets holding back to mask their own capabilities.

By the end of the Korean War, LeMay believed ECM was as important as armament to the survivability of the SAC bomber force. During that period SAC's ECM budget quintupled.[98] Given the intractable problems of providing escort to the bombers, ECM would be a main weapon of defense. By the end of 1954, the B-36—but especially the RB-36—was fitted out with increasingly advanced ECM gear. The plane's size made the incorporation of extra equipment, antennae, and an additional ECM crew member a simple task.[99] One SAC wing commander later stated that the bomber's ECM was excellent: "With our broad jamming I don't think the Russian gun laying equipment could lay a glove on the B-36."[100] The B-47, on the other hand, was virtually defenseless when first built; it was thought the bomber's high speed and altitude capability would keep it safe. The emergence of the MiG-19 quickly put an end to such folly. Eventually, the Stratojet was equipped with an automatic jamming pod installed in the bomb bay; the EB-47s would then accompany the bombers to clear a path to the target and back. In later models two ECM operators would occupy the pod during flight.[101] The B-52 would be the first jet bomber designed and built with

[97] Kuehl, "Radar Eye Blinded," 160–61.
[98] SAC History—1951, vol. 1, 213.
[99] Pyeatt and Jenkins, Cold War Peacemaker, 125–26.
[100] Irvine, interview, 17 December 1970, 31.
[101] Lloyd, Boeing's B-47 Stratojet, 111.

ECM in mind from the outset—the crew position of electronic warfare officer, or EWO, was included from the beginning.[102]

Summary

Technology determined the capabilities and limitations of airpower. From 1903, when the Wright Brothers first flew, a number of technical challenges needed to be addressed: speed, payload, navigation and targeting accuracy, self-defense, safety/reliability, weather, and range. All were formidable challenges, and all were confronted by SAC in the decade following World War II. Many of these factors were interrelated: self-defense could be addressed by adding machine guns, but it was also a function of speed and altitude—which were affected by payload. Engineers and airmen worked these issues, designing and building aircraft and engines offering maximum performance. Usually, there had to be compromises. The B-36 had a massive payload capability and an impressive range and altitude reach, but it was ponderously slow. The medium bombers were simply that—medium bombers. One observer has argued the Air Force did not know what it wanted in the late 1940s, so the medium bombers were an attempt to cover several bets.[103] If true, it was a useful strategy. The medium bombers were important aspects of strategic airpower that could haul a significant bomb load over long distances—the B-29 and B-50 could easily carry four times the bomb load over three times the distance as could the B-17 and B-24. In the postwar era, however, such performance was not good enough.

The jet engine changed the parameters of the problem. Piston-driven bombers were too slow to stand much chance against Soviet MiGs that were 200 mph faster. Even the "six turning, four burning" hybrid B-36 was inadequate. The B-47 and B-52 were to be the technical solution to bomber vulnerability—at least they would provide *part* of the solution.[104]

Range remained fundamental. As the SAC chief of plans, Maj Gen John P. McConnell, noted dryly, "As long as the Soviet Union is the enemy and not Canada, range matters."[105] The distances to targets

---

[102] Kuehl, "Radar Eye Blinded," 207–19.

[103] Brown, "Flying Blind," 88–89 (unpub.).

[104] "The SAC Bombardment Training Program, 1946–1959," SAC historical study, 15 April 190, AFHRA, file K416.01-80, passim.

[105] Converse, *History of Acquisition in the Department of Defense*, vol. I, 480.

deep in Russia were simply too great without either forward basing or air refueling. Both would eventually be used—air bases in Europe, the Middle East, and the Pacific were built to serve as prestrike staging bases for bombers. This concept was similar to that used by the B-29s during World War II when they based in India and staged through China to hit targets in Japan. LeMay was leery of this concept—he had commanded the B-29s in India and understood the problems entailed. He was reluctant to rely on politically risky forward bases for the success of his mission. Changes of government could result in previous basing agreements going awry—this is what happened in Morocco, Libya, Saudi Arabia, France, Iceland, and elsewhere, and it remains a problem today.

Military risk was another matter. Even before the Berlin blockade, LeMay, who was then the USAFE commander, fretted over the vulnerability of his airfields to a Soviet surprise attack. His bases were devoid of hardening or even rudimentary camouflage. Air defenses were outdated or nonexistent. Staging bases were nonetheless built in Europe simply because they had to be. LeMay knew the danger and believed the solution was an intercontinental bomber flying from CONUS that did not rely on forward airfields. A RAND study of 1954 confirmed SAC fears, arguing that forward bases would be wiped out at the beginning of a nuclear war. One solution was to build bases forward, but not as forward as before—England, French Morocco, Spain, and Guam would be air bastions in the event of war. Even then, these bases would be used largely as poststrike recovery fields. This would help to ensure not only their survival—in an era limited by the number of nuclear weapons available it was supposed the Soviets would not waste ordnance on empty airfields—but also that of the aircraft. Instead, bombers would launch from CONUS, strike targets in the Soviet Union, and recover at forward fields.[106] After refueling they would return home to reload. This became the SAC plan that was enabled by air refueling. This plan soon changed.

The advent of nuclear-tipped ballistic missiles made even staging bases vulnerable. LeMay returned to his goal of relying on CONUS bases. The advent of the B-52 and KC-135 helped realize this goal. Even so, the threat of a Soviet missile first strike necessitated changes. In 1954 the Air Force proposed construction of a string of radar sites

---

[106] Despite their vulnerability, LeMay liked the idea of forward bases simply because they compounded the Soviets' targeting problems. LeMay, interview, 16 November 1972, 44.

in the Arctic stretching across Canada, the Aleutians, Greenland, and Iceland. This DEW (Distant Early Warning) Line, eventually consisting of nearly 100 sites, became operational in April 1957 and provided warning of a Soviet bomber attack. The advent of intercontinental ballistic missiles (ICBM) required a different response: a ballistic missile early warning system (BMEWS) was built in 1959 to give some warning (15 minutes) of a Soviet missile attack.[107] As we shall see, the threat of a Soviet missile strike led to SAC countermoves: dispersal and both ground and airborne alert programs. This entire subject illustrates the iterative nature of strategy—weapons or technologies generate new plans, which in turn result in enemy counters, leading to different plans and technologies, which then lead to more counters, ad infinitum—a never-ending cycle of actions and reactions.

Aerial refueling was attempted soon after World War I ended. By the end of the interwar period, systems were developed, especially in Britain, which would enable large aircraft to extend their range almost indefinitely. This system was not used during World War II, partly because Allied bombers were able to strike most targets in Germany. Air refueling would have been useful to enable fighter aircraft to escort the bombers, but the British system would not permit such operations. Moreover, the large number of escorts used on a given day—nearly a thousand—made the production of so many tankers impractical. The capability remained dormant until after hostilities ended. At that point the need for range greater than that during the war forced a reexamination of the air refueling issue.

The British system was workable, but in truth it had made little advance in two decades. A new idea was the probe-and-drogue system that obviated the use of trailing wires, cables, grapnels, and winches, but it also had problems. LeMay eventually insisted the boom method be used by SAC, and since SAC owned the tankers, all Air Force aircraft would use the boom. The wisdom of that decision is still debated; the US Navy, for example, uses the probe-and-drogue.[108] Nonetheless, in 1950 the decision to adopt the boom made sense; it permitted bombers to more easily refuel in the air and to do so quickly. As far as LeMay was concerned, that capability was primary because it helped assure the success of his primary mission.

---

[107] For the development of the DEW Line and BMEWS, see Schaffel, *Emerging Shield*, chaps. 8–10.

[108] As late as 2005, a high-level report argued that all Air Force aircraft should be reconfigured to use the probe-and-drogue method. Bolkcom and Klaus, "Air Force Refueling Methods."

Initially, B-29s were converted to tanker use, as were C-97s—a transport developed from the B-29. Hundreds were built for SAC and did yeoman service. The advent of the jet bombers indicated, however, that piston-driven tankers were inadequate. SAC conducted Project Power Flite in January 1957 to demonstrate the capability the new B-52 offered and why a jet tanker was essential. SAC sent three B-52s around the world with air refueling in 45 hours and 19 minutes. The aircraft, refueled by KC-97s, logged the first jet bomber circumnavigation. Upon landing, the lead pilot complained they could have done it five hours faster had they had jet tankers.[109] It was obvious to SAC that a jet tanker was essential, and in 1954 the Air Force solicited proposals for such an aircraft. Boeing was then testing a new prototype, the "Dash 80," which looked promising. Although Boeing lost the design competition to Lockheed, the Air Force nonetheless purchased some of the Dash 80s, soon designated the KC-135, while the Lockheed aircraft was being developed. The first KC-135 was accepted by the Air Force on 31 January 1957.[110] The aircraft was so successful, the Lockheed tanker was cancelled. Over 400 Stratotankers, several times modified, are still flying.

The issue of air refueling was bound up with the problem of penetration. Getting the bombers into Russia was only part of the problem; how would they survive once there? During World War II the Eighth Air Force had paid a heavy price for prewar myopia that argued escort fighters were technically infeasible and unnecessary. It was a huge error, and Curtis LeMay had been a witness to that poor decision. Fighter escort had saved the bomber offensive, and it seemed reasonable to assume escort would remain necessary. Yet the distances involved were so much greater that the development of a truly long-range escort fighter was simply impossible. Subterfuges such as parasite fighters were attempted. Today, such experiments appear silly, but at the time they were trying to address a real problem. Speed was also considered as a possible solution. During development of the B-47 there arose a typical discussion of trade-offs—speed versus range—to better enhance the prospects of penetrating enemy air defenses. A bombardment board, which included LeMay, opted for speed because tests indicated it would severely diminish the

---

[109] *SAC History—Jan–Jun 1957*, vol. 1, 85–88. Typically, all 27 of the B-52 crew members received Distinguished Flying Crosses from LeMay. The only reference to the tankers in the official history was the comment noted above that they were too slow.

[110] The KC-135 was not a derivative of the 707 airliner as is commonly thought; rather, both aircraft descended from the Dash 80.

chances of a Soviet interceptor getting a clear shot at the streaking bomber.[111] It appeared SAC did not take the fighter escort problem seriously—the combat-ready status of the fighter wings was poor throughout their decade of existence—but LeMay bristled at charges of neglect: "Let me ask you why you have a lack of interest in buying your wife a new mink coat every year?" To LeMay the issue was one of money and priorities. Yes, he thought it nice to have escort—as it would be nice for your wife to have a fur coat—but the command's priority was the bomber fleet, and that is where the money went.[112]

In the end, LeMay decided the bombers would need to go in alone. Speed and altitude adjustments would be important, and tactical experimentation would tinker endlessly with the best method and formation for surviving in enemy airspace—bad weather, night operations, and evasive tactics would all be used.[113] The rise of the surface-to-air missile spelled the end of high-altitude bomber penetration.

Electronic warfare would also be critical. EW emerged in World War II when radar, navigation beams, and jammers were used by all sides. At the end of the war, this area was particularly hard hit by demobilization. There had not been a career field for such specialists in the AAF; most personnel employed had been draftees or reservists. After V-J Day this expertise was allowed to atrophy. The Korean War demonstrated anew how important this arcane technology and expertise were to successful air operations. Fortunately for SAC, the North Koreans were similarly deficient in this field—the B-29s had a breathing space to catch up. It was not a moment too soon. The Chinese intervention introduced Soviet-made equipment of a far higher caliber than that of the North Koreans. SAC would scramble to match it.

The war reaffirmed the importance of command and leadership. Although initially remiss in understanding the need for electronic warfare and the specialists who would conduct it, SAC learned quickly. As explained above, survival in the face of high-grade Soviet defenses during a general war would demand a very robust EW and ECM capability. SAC actively supported EW because its senior leaders saw the need for it. The TAC community, on the other hand, did not—a lack of vision many pilots would rue dearly in Vietnam the following decade.

---

[111] Julian, "Origins of Air Refueling in the United States Air Force," 86.

[112] LeMay, interview, 16 November 1972, 38.

[113] George F. Lemmer, "The Air Force and the Concept of Deterrence, 1945–1950," USAF Historical Division Liaison study, June 1963, AFHRA, file K168.01-13, 19–20.

Guided missiles and rocketry were promising fields in the aftermath of the war. Although American scientists like Robert Goddard had been experimenting since the 1920s, it was the Germans who made the most significant strides during the war. The V-1 cruise missile and V-2 ballistic missile were meant by Hitler to be war-changing weapons. They almost were. Fortunately, they arrived too few and too late to make a difference in the war's outcome—even if they were a frightening new reality to the British population.

After the war, much of Germany's technology—and indeed many of its scientists, including Werner von Braun—were brought to the United States and hired to work in this field. LeMay had always been supportive of such research, dating back to his two years on the Air Staff when these research programs began. As SAC commander he specifically stated that he wanted guided missiles developed at the earliest possible date and incorporated into war plans. This was another way to extend the range of bomber aircraft—equip them with nuclear-tipped cruise missiles, like the Hound Dog that would eventually be carried by the B-52, that could clear a path for an attacking force or simply lengthen the bomber's reach by several hundred miles.[114]

There were other missile programs that SAC closely followed from 1950 onward. Rascal was an air-launched cruise missile that carried a nuclear warhead. Snark was a surface-to-surface missile with a range programmed to be anywhere from 1,500 to 5,500 miles. It had a Doppler and inertial guidance system and could carry a nuclear weapon. Navaho was a supersonic surface-to-surface missile with a 3,500-mile range; Brass Ring was a cruise missile to be carried by the B-47; and Atlas was an ICBM. These weapons were being developed by the Air Development Center at Wright AFB in Ohio, but SAC had a "gentleman's agreement" with the center that "no important decisions concerning these missiles would be made without some consideration being given to the Command's point of view."[115] To be clear, LeMay favored missile and rocket development, but as he often stated, his mission was nuclear war, not test and experimentation. He wanted proven, operational equipment in SAC, not prototypes. In one speech, LeMay referred to the "ardent proponents" of guided missiles and their claims, but these "enthusiasts" did not have the facts on their side: "I believe it would be courting disaster to decimate the conventional proven force and its follow-on of the true intercontinental supersonic manned bomber aircraft [B-70] before the missile system has proven a progressive replacement." Moreover, given their relative inaccuracy, he viewed ICBMs as predominantly area weapons—manned bombers would still be necessary and, indeed, must remain the backbone of the deterrent strike force.[116] Yet LeMay actively promoted missile development, and the most important of the missile programs would soon become an operational weapon in SAC—the Atlas ICBM.

Convair had been experimenting in the missile field since the war ended, but it was the Atlas that became its top priority. Unfortunately, due to severe budget constraints, the AAF had to cancel its ballistic missile program in 1947. The advent of the Korean War and increased funding resurrected the program through the auspices of the new Air Research and Development Command. Brig Gen Bernard A. Schriever was chosen to head the Atlas program—the most promising of the ballistic missiles on the design board—and have it operational in six years. The prospects for Atlas were boosted considerably in September 1955 when President Eisenhower made it one of his top military priorities. The leadership of Eisenhower and Schriever was crucial, and the Atlas first flew successfully on Kitty-hawk Day—17 December 1957.[117] SAC would be transformed by the development of ballistic missiles.

---

[116] *SAC History—Jan–Jun 1956*, vol. 1, 14.

[117] For the Atlas program, see Neufeld, *Ballistic Missiles in the United States Air Force, 1945–1960*, especially chaps. 3 and 4. See also Gantz, *United States Air Force Report on the Ballistic Missile*. The Atlas did not become an operational ICBM until 1959.

Chapter 8

Expansion, Intelligence, and Targeting in the Nuclear Age

On 31 January 1950, President Truman directed his National Security Council (NSC) to provide a thorough report—to include military, political, and economic factors—regarding the Soviet threat. Despite his continual calls for defense budget cuts, it is possible the president was beginning to worry the threat was greater than he had thought. His advisors warned him the Soviets were undoubtedly moving forward on nuclear research, and Kremlin motives and intentions were frequently discussed. On 8 February, for example, the director of the State Department's policy planning staff, Paul H. Nitze, submitted a report arguing the Soviets were guided by matters of expediency—not law or international norms. While probably not planning on launching an all-out war against the West, the Soviets were willing "to undertake a course of action, including a possible use of force in local areas, which might lead to an accidental outbreak of general military conflict." Nitze went on to warn that "the soft spots on its periphery" would be a primary area of Soviet-communist action.[1] These predictions were borne out by the events in Korea a few months later.

The report requested by the president, termed *NSC 68*, was submitted on 14 April 1950. It was an important document, and its drafting had caused heated debates between the State and Defense Departments. Defense Secretary Johnson was particularly irritable throughout the process and dissented from State's entire thrust because it called for a massive armament buildup that was at odds with his budget-cutting mentality. He eventually went along, simply because the joint chiefs unanimously favored the planned rearmament.[2] The document that emerged was stark. It began by asserting that the Soviet Union "is animated by a new fanatical faith, antithetical to our own, and seeks to impose its absolute authority over the rest of the world." The Russians might use force, or they might resort to "nonviolent methods in accordance with the dictates of expediency." The

---

[1] Paul H. Nitze, study, 8 February 1950, in *FRUS, 1950*, vol. 1, 145–47.
[2] McFarland and Roll, *Louis Johnson and the Arming of America*, 224–31.

document warned that postwar Soviet expansion into Eastern and Central Europe must not be allowed to continue—"any substantial further expansion of the area under the domination of the Kremlin would raise the possibility that no coalition adequate to confront the Kremlin with greater strength could be assembled." The Soviet menace threatened "not only this Republic but civilization itself."[3] Its military power was growing.

Echoing the national war plans, NSC 68 maintained that a Soviet attack would overrun most of Europe, occupy the oil-rich Middle East, and consolidate communist gains in the Far East. The Soviets would soon have the capability to launch air strikes with atomic weapons against Canada and the United States. Further, the Soviet Union had an atomic stockpile of 10–20 weapons that would grow to 25–45 in one year and increase to 200 by mid 1954. This date was significant: an attack with 100 atomic bombs would inflict serious damage on the United States, and a stockpile of 200 weapons would ensure half that number would actually hit the country. While the United States was disarming due to budget constraints, the Soviet Union was on a massive rearmament program—nearly 40 percent of its "gross available resources" was being directed to military purposes.[4] NSC 68 required that steps be taken to counter this growing threat.

The study gave lip service to the idea of abolishing atomic weapons, but in the absence of such elimination, "we have no alternative but to increase our atomic capability as rapidly as other considerations make appropriate." NSC 68 also argued it was "imperative to increase as rapidly as possible our general air, ground and sea strength and that of our allies to a point where we are militarily not so heavily dependent on atomic weapons. . . . Without superior aggregate military strength, in being and readily mobilizable, a policy of 'containment'—which is in effect a policy of calculated and gradual coercion—is no more than a policy of bluff."[5] It reiterated and clarified this position:

> In specific terms, it is not essential to match item for item with the Soviet Union, but to provide an adequate defense against air attack on the United States and Canada and an adequate defense against air attack on the United Kingdom and Western Europe, Alaska, the Western Pacific, Africa, and the

---

[3] "A Report to the President Pursuant to the President's Directive of January 31, 1950" [NSC 68], 14 April 1950, in FRUS, 1950, vol. 1, 234–38.

[4] Ibid., 249–57. Using this prediction, the NSC 68 referred to 1954 as "the year of maximum danger."

[5] Ibid., 253, 267.

Near and Middle East, and on the long lines of communication to these areas. Furthermore, it is mandatory that in building up our strength, we enlarge upon our technical superiority by an accelerated exploitation of the scientific potential of the United States and our allies.[6]

This was quite an agenda, and its expansive recommendations, in contrast to the stated budget policies of President Truman and Secretary Johnson, were controversial. Five days after receiving *NSC 68*, the president requested specific answers addressing what programs were to be expanded under the plan and how much it would cost. Privately, Paul Nitze, one of the report's authors, conceded that the suggested military buildup would cost $40 billion annually. Yet Johnson continued to assert that he saw no reason to raise the defense budget beyond $13 billion, and his proposal for FY 1951 was only $12.1 billion, an amount that would have cut the Air Force to 42 wings.[7] Maj Gen Truman H. Landon, who had been on the *NSC 68* committee, later said simply, "Mr. Johnson was doing his damnedest to cut the guts out of the Department of Defense."[8] The expansion advocated in *NSC 68* was still unapproved when the Korean War erupted on 25 June. It is questionable whether it ever would have been implemented had war not intervened, but the North Korean invasion was conclusive: President Truman then accepted, de facto, the major military buildup recommended in the report. On 19 July the defense budget leapt by 41.4 percent, and by September the joint chiefs proposed a budget of $260 billion over the next five years.[9] Johnson, still clinging to fiscal stringency, protested these figures as being unnecessary—he was fired the next day and replaced by retired general George C. Marshall.[10]

The impact of this buildup on the Air Force and SAC was dramatic. *NSC 68* suggested the Air Force grow from 48 to 70 wings. As a result of the Korean War, this proposed total rose to 95 wings by December 1950 and then 143 wings by the end of 1954.[11] The reality

---

[6] Ibid., 283.

[7] Doris Condit, *History of the Office of the Secretary of Defense*, vol. 2, 8; Poole, *Joint Chiefs of Staff and National Policy*, vol. 4, 14–15, 28–29; and Nitze, *From Hiroshima to Glasnost: At the Center of Decision—A Memoir*, 96.

[8] Landon, interview, 31 May–3 June 1977. The Navy often claimed Johnson was "pro–Air Force," but the facts show otherwise. This proposed budget would have gutted the Air Force and SAC.

[9] Poole, *Joint Chiefs of Staff and National Policy*, vol. 4, 225.

[10] Johnson had hung his hat on austerity and believed Truman would support him in this stance—it was a huge shock when the president fired him. Johnson's biographers provide a damning appraisal: "Johnson was driven by politics, power, and personal ambition but rarely by principle." McFarland and Roll, *Louis Johnson and the Arming of America*, 359.

[11] JCS to SECDEF, memorandum, 6 December 1950, in *FRUS, 1950*, vol. 1, 475–77.

was almost as impressive. Before the war, SAC contained 527 bombers, mostly medium-range B-29s and B-50s. The command also had 67 tankers, 161 escort fighters, and 80 reconnaissance aircraft. Overall, SAC had 71,490 officer, enlisted, and civilian personnel deployed to 17 bases—all in CONUS. By the end of 1953, it consisted of 170,982 personnel and had 762 bombers, half of which were B-47s. It also owned 502 tankers, 235 escort fighters, and 282 reconnaissance aircraft spread over 39 air bases—10 of which were overseas.[12] These numbers—personnel, wings, aircraft, and bases—would continue to increase over the next decade. The official JCS history notes that President Truman made a conscious decision as early as autumn 1951 to refocus the defense budget toward airpower. This massive Air Force and SAC buildup would presage the New Look strategy enacted by the Eisenhower administration two years later.[13]

This rapid expansion took time and effort to digest. SAC reorganized in 1951, first by taking some of the administrative load off its wing commanders. At each SAC base an "air base group commander" was appointed, who ran administrative activities. The wing commander retained control of the operational units, along with supply and maintenance. If the wing deployed, the wing commander led it, with the base commander remaining behind. At bases housing two bomb wings, an air division was established—under a brigadier general—to oversee matters. Although personnel manning increased, SAC relied heavily on Air National Guard and reserve assets—in 1951 there were over 4,000 reservists on duty in SAC, and its four fighter escort wings were all Guard units.[14] SAC was also given two new missions: aerial minelaying and antisubmarine warfare. As in World War II, the Navy had little interest in conducting such mundane missions. In the battle of the Atlantic, hundreds of B-24s had been diverted for Navy use to hunt German U-boats, and in the Pacific, B-29s sowed the vast majority of aerial mines. Now SAC was called upon to perform these maritime missions while the Navy moved vigorously into strategic bombing, one of its collateral functions.[15]

---

[12] John T. Bohn, "The Development of Strategic Air Command, 1946–1973," SAC historical study, 19 September 1974, 13, 33; and "SAC Statistical Data from 1946," SAC historical study, 8 September 1970, AFHRA, file K416.197-1, 4–20.

[13] Poole, *Joint Chiefs of Staff and National Policy*, vol. 4, 101.

[14] *SAC History—1951*, vol. 1, 4–11, 29–30. LeMay favored the reserve contingents over those of the Air National Guard because he believed the former were better trained and the latter were "too political." LeMay, interview, 14 September 1978, 5–7.

[15] *SAC History—Jan–Jun 1952*, vol. 2, 80.

Not surprisingly, a demand for specially trained mechanics and aircrew specialists was voiced immediately. These professionals seemed ever in short supply in SAC, but the rapid expansion meant more were needed. In fact, the number of personnel required was disproportional to the number of wings being formed—the increased complexity of modern aircraft and systems required greater numbers of electronic, radar, communications, and propulsion specialists per wing. As SAC moved into rocket and missile development, specialized requirements increased further. In late 1952, SAC recommended that Air Training Command begin an eight-week course in guided missile fundamentals. This was to be followed by longer, more-specialized courses for specific weapons systems—Snark, Matador, and others. SAC was anticipating the missile revolution, and its people needed to be educated.[16] Additional headquarters staffs also dictated a large number of trained financial and administrative personnel, usually enlisted. The increasing use of global communication networks, such as the Strategic Air Command Operations Control System, likewise called for a growing number of trained technicians.[17] LeMay, a life-long ham radio operator, understood the challenge and requirement of maintaining worldwide communications with far-flung units. The use of high-frequency (HF) radio employing ionospheric scattering techniques was the breakthrough that allowed the SAC commander to maintain global contact with his forces.[18]

More air bases were needed, and LeMay insisted that new facili-ties—not the ramshackle temporary buildings built during the war—be constructed to house the new units. As before, family housing was a priority item, as were dormitories—not open-bay barracks—for en-listed Airmen. LeMay worked his people hard, sometimes 80–90 hours per week. Although his own schedule was no lighter, he realized such pressure demanded compensation. In April 1951 the SAC commander wrote the vice-chief of staff arguing that necessities "were not limited to operational requirements but include items which affect the welfare and morale of the command. It is important that the permanent party personnel on these bases are adequately housed and that ample rec-reational facilities are made available."[19] When he did not get the answer he wanted fast enough, he wrote the Air Staff pointedly the following

---

[16] *SAC History—Jul–Dec 1952*, vol. 1, 30–35.
[17] *SAC History—Jan–Jun 1952*, vol. 1, 4–12, 22–23.
[18] Thompson, *Fifty-Year Role of the United States Air Force in Advancing Information Technology*, 57–59.
[19] LeMay to Twining, letter, 5 April 1951, in *SAC History—1951*, vol. 3, exhibit 47.

month: "Apparently I did not make my point. We need additional bases as permanent installations for the long-term needs for the good of the families."[20] Resources began flowing.

Requirements for war-fighting equipment were even more critical. The demand for bombers, due not only to *NSC 68* expansion but also to the needs of the Korean War, necessitated that dozens of B-29s be taken out of storage and refurbished. There were shortages everywhere—vehicles, tools, facilities, spare parts, even paper supplies.[21] SAC struggled to keep up. At the same time, LeMay insisted that high standards be rigorously maintained. The emphasis on integral crews—core units that flew together—remained. Inspections, in both frequency and stringency, continued. A shooting war in Asia reminded everyone of the command's motto, "War is our profession—peace is our product." SAC existed to deter war, but it must be ready to fight if deterrence failed. Security at SAC bases intensified dramatically, with armed guards at the gates, at the headquarters buildings, and on the flight line. The threat of sabotage, not just by isolated criminals but through organized military attacks overseas, was taken very seriously.[22]

Thoughts on Total War

Although a banality, it was nonetheless true that atomic and nuclear weapons put the matter of war planning and strategy on an entirely new plane. Airmen had long viewed strategic bombardment as a war-winning mission, but the power of atomic weapons—thousands of times more powerful than whole armadas of aircraft loaded with conventional bombs—necessitated new thought patterns. As we have seen, SAC, Air Force, and joint staff war planners all grappled with this issue. Given the demobilization and ongoing calls for budget stringency, political and military leaders realized, with few dissenters, that atomic weapons would have to be the equalizer for the United States and its allies. Yet they also understood that the atomic monopoly would not last forever. Some even considered whether it was prudent to strike while the United States still enjoyed its dominant position. Detonation of the Soviet atomic bomb in August 1949

---

[20] LeMay to Timberlake, letter, 25 May 1951, in *SAC History—1951*, vol. 3, exhibit 34.

[21] Thompson, *Fifty-Year Role of the United States Air Force in Advancing Information Technology*, 56–57.

[22] LeMay to Twining, letter, 10 May 1951, in *SAC History—1951*, vol. 4, exhibit 4/2.

made such musings more prevalent. Should not the United States launch a preventive war against the Soviet Union before it had a chance to build up its own stockpile of atomic and nuclear weapons?

As early as 1947, Gen George Kenney, then SAC commander, noted in a speech the overwhelming power of atomic weapons: "One hundred bombs will release more energy than all the TNT of all the belligerents in World War II and do it in one mission. . . . No nation, including our own, could survive such a blow." How best to defend against such a threat? In words not so subtle as to mask their meaning, Kenney then stated, "The advantage accruing to the aggressor who makes a surprise attack has become so great that it can almost be considered decisive. I believe this should be studied, analyzed, and discussed far more than we are doing today."[23] Three years later—while Air University commander and soon after the detonation of Joe 1—Kenney wrote Vandenberg expressing this idea once more.

Kenney had attended the Exercise Dualism commanders' conference in April 1950—a meeting of Air Force senior leaders. Vandenberg opened the meeting, followed by his intelligence chief. All of the major commanders spoke, outlining the mission and capabilities of their commands. When it was his turn, LeMay was frank; detonation of the Soviet atomic bomb had forced a reappraisal. He needed a much larger SAC with more personnel and aircraft to carry out the national war plan. During the discussions that followed, someone raised a question regarding "taking the first blow," because national policy was set against a preventive war. LeMay questioned that assertion. "I think we in the military ought to do something about educating the people that we do not have to take the first blow." After a pointed response from the audience, he clarified, "I didn't mean by that statement that we should go out and attack Russia tomorrow. I do mean that there are many ways of determining when you are going to be invaded. One is to wait until somebody hits you on the head with a ballbat [sic] and then determine whether he is mad at you; the other is to start to swing and hit when the blow lands. That is what I'm talking about."[24] Kenney was in the audience and concurred with LeMay's remarks,

[23] *SAC History—1947*, vol. 1, 139.
[24] "Notes on Commanders' Conference, Exercise DUALISM," 25–27 April 1950, AFHRA, file 168.15-10, 240. The terms *preventive* and *preemptive* were often used interchangeably at the time, but later observers defined *preventive war* as attacking an enemy not then an immediate threat but whose power was growing and would be a serious threat in the future. *Preemptive war* was striking an enemy who was an immediate threat and who was actually making preparations to attack you. The comment by LeMay suggested a preemptive strike. He would make similar statements throughout his career and afterwards, but was also keen to emphasize that the decision of *when* to strike was never his own but the president's.

writing Vandenberg that he was "worried about the time elapsing from the day that the whistle is blown before we can launch our first atomic strike." He feared that a surprise attack would so denude the United States of its war-making capability as to make an effective response impossible. He concluded, "It is going to be so difficult to shorten the time before we can start effective retaliation that this in itself constitutes another argument for reexamining our national attitude toward fighting what has been wrongly termed a preventive war. It would not be a preventive war, because we are already at war."[25] Vandenberg brushed off these ideas but recognized that Kenney was not the only one making such arguments.

The commandant of the Air War College, Brig Gen Orvil A. Anderson, was one of Kenney's subordinates who agreed with his boss and indeed had been an advocate of a preventive strike since the end of World War II. One Air Force general noted later that when he visited Maxwell AFB to lecture, he was struck by how the Air War College was little more than "a platform for Orvil Anderson" and his "preaching preemptive strikes and preventive war."[26] Indeed, Anderson's papers are full of lectures in which he addresses this topic from the AWC lectern.[27] Eventually, he went too far. In an assumed off-the-record interview with a local news reporter soon after the outbreak of the Korean War, Anderson called for preventive war against the Soviet Union. To his mind, the Kremlin was behind the North Korean invasion and needed to be severely punished. When this story hit the press, Vandenberg was irate. He rejected Anderson's explanations that he did not realize he would be quoted and that he was not feeling good that day anyway. Vandenberg relieved him.[28] It was one thing for Kenney and others to express their beliefs on this incendiary issue in private at a classified commanders' conference or in a personal letter to the chief, but public pronouncements were unacceptable—especially since General MacArthur was already beginning to strain the limits of propriety with his pronouncements from Tokyo not aligned with administration policy.

Such discussions were not confined to the Air Force. A Joint Intelligence Committee report of February 1950 stated, "A tremendous military advantage would be gained by the power that struck first"—

---

[25] Kenney to Vandenberg, letter, 29 April 1950, AFHRA, file 168.15-10.
[26] Wilson, interview, 1–2 December 1983, 121.
[27] See Anderson's papers, AFHRA file 168.7006-1, box 1.
[28] For an account of the incident, see Scrivner, "Pioneer into Space," chap. 11 (unpub).

the argument voiced by Kenney three years earlier.[29] That August, Navy Secretary Francis Matthews was both more pointed and public. During a speech in Boston, he specifically endorsed a policy of preventive war and stated that such an action would earn the United States the title of "the first aggressors for peace."[30] He was immediately rebuked by President Truman.

LeMay has often been accused of wanting to take matters into his own hands and launch such a strike, but there is no evidence of this; by their actions, civilian leaders demonstrated they dismissed such notions as well. By 1957 President Eisenhower had given SAC "predelegation" authority, which meant that in the event of a Soviet nuclear strike and severed communications with Washington, SAC could launch a retaliatory strike on its own authority. When asked about this, LeMay stated, "If I were on my own and half the country was [sic] destroyed and I could get no orders and so forth, I wasn't going to sit there fat, dumb, and happy and do nothing."[31] Clearly, the president did not expect him to, and LeMay was entrusted with such authority.

Elsewhere in the Air Force, the Air University was studying the matter in some depth. Project Control was a concept envisioning the attainment of air supremacy over the Soviet Union. Once this was attained, the United States would dictate to Kremlin leaders which actions were acceptable and which were not. Airpower, specifically SAC, would be used to enforce these dictates. "Air Persuasion" would evolve into "Air Pressure" and then into "Administration"—the possible occupation of key areas in the Soviet Union to ensure compliance. In 1954 this concept was briefed to the secretaries of defense and state as well as the director of the CIA. The chairman of the joint chiefs, ADM Arthur Radford, was very positive on the idea.[32]

Others were wrestling with such matters as well. After becoming president, Eisenhower directed a study of national security policy in a project termed Solarium. His civilian planners presented three options, one of which involved preventive war against the Soviet Union. It appears the president never seriously considered that option—during the Solarium briefing he commented acidly, "You can't have this kind of war. There just aren't enough bulldozers to scrape the bodies off the streets." Even so, Eisenhower relied firmly on SAC and its

---

[29] K. Condit, *History of the Joint Chiefs of Staff*, 516.

[30] Biddle, "Handling the Soviet Threat," 276.

[31] Herken, " 'Not Enough Bulldozers': Eisenhower and American Nuclear Weapons Policy," 85–89.

[32] Biddle, "Handling the Soviet Threat," 290–92.

nuclear capability, commenting in 1959 that he expected deterrence would remain successful, but in the event it failed, the job of SAC was to "hit the Russians as hard as we could." The Kremlin might start the war, but the United States would finish it.[33]

The Solarium project illustrates a postwar-era phenomenon of great importance—the rise of civilian academics as war strategists. World War II had demonstrated the utility and even necessity of not just scientists, but engineers, mathematicians, and political scientists being involved in military policy making. The operations research divisions existing at all major commands and combat units throughout the war provided invaluable assistance. Hap Arnold, for one, was sold on their importance, and one of his initiatives was to establish a think tank to assist the AAF—and soon the Air Force—to study particularly thorny problems. In March 1946 an AAF contract with Douglas Aircraft Corporation established Project RAND (a contraction for "research and development") to conduct "outside the box" thinking. The project's connection to Douglas soon raised eyebrows, so in 1948 RAND split off as a separate corporation and moved into offices in downtown Santa Monica, California. RAND became the prototype for the unprecedented involvement of civilian academics in military strategic thinking.

RAND's founders saw it as an adjunct to the Air Staff, "the part of the Air Force responsible for management and decision making." That was a heady self-assessment. Still, the self-confidence displayed by such an assertion was not unjustified. RAND developed what it called a "systems analysis" approach, which it argued "offered the promise of charting an analytical path through the Air Force's—and the nation's—difficult options in the postwar period."[34] The academics at RAND realized the rigorous mathematical approach used by OR during the war could only go so far—some problems were impervious to scientific precision. The hope was that "a wider framework of analysis with more variables and less reliable data" would be able to grapple with problems that did not lend themselves to OR-style precision. More cynically, as one historian subtly phrased it, systems analysis offered to "provide a veneer of scientific objectivity to what might otherwise be seen as a political decision."[35] A more positive view of systems analysis argued, "It borrowed and modified mathematical and physical methods when necessary and applied them to complex human-machine

[33] Herken, " 'Not Enough Bulldozers,' " 85–89.
[34] M. Collins, *Cold War Laboratory*, xiii–xiv.
[35] Ibid., xiv, 171.

problems. Typical methods included game theory, probability, and ap-plications of physical laws such as classical mechanics and electromag-netic theory for radar."[36] Over time, it was this second view of RAND's capabilities that became most accepted. Machines were built and oper-ated by humans; this social dimension of technology needed somehow to be taken into account. It took time.

RAND began by tackling key technological issues confronting the AAF, including some of the first work done on guided missiles. In addition, its "Strategic Bombing Systems Analysis" study of 1947 looked at attrition probabilities of enemy interceptors on bomber for-mations using various mission profiles. The analysis, which included stringing model airplanes from the ceiling and running them at each other on different headings and at differing altitudes, was amateur-ish.[37] Still, the approach was novel, and more importantly, RAND quickly developed more sophisticated techniques. As we saw earlier, Albert Wohlstetter's overseas basing study was a seminal work that had a major impact on SAC thinking.

SAC appreciated the quality of RAND analysis, just as previous bomb commanders had welcomed the assistance of operations analysts during World War II. Nonetheless, military veterans remained skeptical of civilian professors, most of whom had never worn a uniform, much less seen combat. In a response to one report, for example, Lt Col Jack Catton (later a full general) wrote Lt Gen Idwal H. Edwards that al-though one RAND report "provided some convincing answers," it must still be handled with extreme care. It was an "academic study," and he was reluctant to accept its conclusions which "are definitely limited in scope to a particular set of conditions and assumptions and should not be applied out of context." Catton feared that the knowledge base of the analysts was limited and dated: "it is therefore inevitable that such a study will be overtaken by events."[38] Gen Joseph McNarney, com-mander of Air Materiel Command, echoed these reservations, com-menting that the RAND analysts tended to "shoot from the blue." He and some other senior officers believed the RAND products were over-priced and provided marginal results.[39]

[36] S. Johnson, *United States Air Force and the Culture of Innovation*, 14.
[37] Ibid., 162–64.
[38] Catton to Edwards, letter, 2 May 1950, in *SAC History—1950*, vol. 4, exhibit 15.
[39] M. Collins, *Cold War Laboratory*, 190. Bernard Brodie exemplified the highly intelligent and self-important brand of analysts who populated RAND. Brodie had been a civilian naval analyst during the war and afterward wrote with insight about atomic weapons and their impact on war. When he attempted to lecture SAC and LeMay on what targets to hit in the Soviet Union, however, he was quickly brushed aside. For the pro-Brodie side of the story, see Steiner, *Bernard Brodie and the Foundations of American Nuclear Strategy*.

This negative opinion was reinforced in some quarters when the Santa Monica think tank released its long-range bomber study, three years in preparation, that concluded the B-52 was not a good idea. RAND disliked the high cost of the proposed aircraft and suggested a "budget bomber" that could be procured in greater numbers. George Kenney commented acerbically that RAND's "budget airplanes" represented a dangerous compromise of quality to obtain quantity—it sounded too much like the Army's decision to buy scores of mediocre B-18s rather than a modest number of B-17s prior to World War II. LeMay likewise rejected any suggestion of cancelling the B-52, for which he had high and, as would be proven, justifiably positive hopes, but he was intrigued by parts of the study. In a typically expressive comment, the SAC boss noted, "I am beginning to see that maybe we would be better off with just ninety-mile-an-hour boxcars but a hell of a lot of them all carrying RCM [radar countermeasures]."[40] His reaction was surprisingly accurate regarding the need for ECM.

RAND was not the only think tank composed of civilian academics studying military issues. Project Vista, an idea supported by the chief scientist of the Air Force (Louis Ridenour) and several civilian scientists, studied the possible utility of tactical nuclear weapons. This study, conducted during 1951 and 1952 on the campus of Caltech, rejected the SAC notion of future war—massive strikes telescoped in time against a myriad of Soviet high-value targets. Rather, Vista advocated a range of weapons "suitable for a multiplicity of military purposes." The study was dominated by J. Robert Oppenheimer, who, as we have seen, was firmly against large weapons and especially nuclear devices. The study called for a reduced emphasis on SAC and a concomitant buildup of tactical airpower capable of employing smaller nuclear weapons against tactical targets near the battle zone.[41] To many military leaders, this was another report conducted by academics with little understanding of war seeking to insert themselves into matters of strategy. As one would expect, LeMay and his staff at Offutt took a dim view of Vista. The struggle between the academics and the military would continue.

Over the next several decades, civilian analysts and university professors delved deeply into the esoteric world of nuclear strategy. This was partly because it appealed to their highly developed sense of

[40] M. Collins, *Cold War Laboratory*, 202, 207.
[41] Gilpin, *American Scientists and Nuclear Weapons Policy*, 114–31; Freedman, *Evolution of Nuclear Strategy*, 65; and Moody, *Building a Strategic Air Force*, 365–68.

pedantic argumentation but also because it was virtually impossible to prove them wrong. Nuclear theorists of the 1950s were in much the same position as airpower theorists had been between the world wars. There was little empirical evidence available upon which to base a doctrine—in the case of nuclear weapons, only two had ever been employed in anger. As a result, theories regarding nuclear strategy—like many airpower ideas of a generation earlier—were heavy on conjecture and speculation. For the same reason that there were few hard facts to support these theories, there was little evidence to deny them either. This was the golden age of the civilian strategists, who wrote many books and articles advancing theories on how a nuclear war might begin, end, or be avoided. In truth, not a great deal of expertise or a detailed understanding of military tactics or technology was needed to spin these concepts. One student of the genre notes with a delightful sense of caustic wit,

> Any reasonably intelligent undergraduate can learn the essentials of nuclear strategy in mere hours of instruction and study—or can become reasonably expert in the subject in a semester. Indeed, 93 minutes spent watching Stanley Kubrick's consummate film *Dr. Strangelove or: How I Learned to Stop Worrying and Love the Bomb* (1964) will teach attentive viewers much of what they need to know in order to understand the principal nuclear debates.[42]

Perhaps the subject of nuclear strategy is not that simple. Yet the core tenet of the discipline revolves around the matter of deterrence, and that is not a complicated subject. The trick was in building a military force to ensure any potential adversary would clearly understand that aggression would result in unacceptable damage—damage so severe it would render meaningless any possible gains hoped for by an attack. Terms such as *assured destruction* and *balance of terror* were merely fugal variations of the deterrence theme. Even so, SAC was responsible for fighting the nuclear war should deterrence fail.

The "New Look" and Tactical Nuclear Weapons

The rapid growth of the nuclear stockpile, combined with the dramatically smaller size of the devices, meant the Army and the Navy were able to develop their own special weapons. The Army, for example, sought to field an atomic artillery piece, prompting Senator Brien McMahon to inquire of Defense Secretary Marshall if it was

---

[42] Mueller, "Strategic Airpower and Nuclear Strategy," 280.

really feasible, "or does it basically reflect the Army's desire to get into the atomic act?"[43] As we saw, Air Force fighter aircraft like the F-84 were able to carry the smaller bombs as well. The Far East Air Forces commander pushed strongly for the deployment of nuclear weapons to his theater, under his control, for possible use in the event of war. The same was true in Europe. When Gen Dwight Eisenhower was appointed NATO's first Supreme Allied Commander Europe (SACEUR) in December 1951, he moved quickly to acquire his own nuclear weapons. Given his enormous prestige and fame, he had little difficulty securing such a capability.

By early 1952, the SACEUR had 80 nuclear weapons assigned to his command to be delivered by his air component, United States Air Forces Europe (USAFE).[44] The USAFE commander was Lt Gen Lauris Norstad, an outstanding airman who had worked with Eisenhower many times previously. The bomb carriers would be medium-range B-29s and B-50s, but also F-84s and Navy AJ-1s. All weapons would be in the 20-kiloton range.[45]

Joint war plans of the early 1950s, such as *Offtackle, Reaper,* and *Headstone,* continued to posit a war begun by a massive Soviet attack in Central Europe and the Middle East. The initial Western response would consist of a massive nuclear retaliatory strike, but, as previously, there would be a role for all the services, and the war would unfold like World War II, complete with a major amphibious assault to retake the continent. LeMay rejected these plans, arguing that "the primary task is the strategic offensive." He complained the United States was spending too much money on the Navy and the Army. "I don't know what the Army is going to do under *Offtackle*; they are going to start assembling a land army to do something. . . . It looks to me like a build-up for another Normandy invasion some place." He continued in the same tone, grumbling, "apparently we are going to fight World War II over again. I don't see how you can do it that way." He did not want to fight World War III in the same long and bloody fashion. In LeMay's view, the Air Force, and SAC, should get the lion's share of the defense budget, "but it won't do the job if 30 percent goes to air, 30 percent to Army, and 30

---

[43] McMahon to Marshall, letter, 2 May 1951, in "Records of the JCS, Part 2, 1946–52: Strategic Issues, Europe and NATO, Section I," microfilm collection, UPA, 1981, reel 3.

[44] Borgiasz, *Strategic Air Command*, 20.

[45] JCS to Eisenhower, memorandum, 18 January 1952, in "JCS Strategic Issues, Europe" collection, reel 3. In January 1953 all SAC fighter escort wings were converted to strategic fighter wings—the aircraft were capable of delivering nuclear weapons.

percent to Navy."[46] As we shall see, the SAC commander was correct in plumping for an asymmetrical defense budget, and such a policy decision was but a few years in the offing.

When Eisenhower took over as president in January 1953, he directed a "New Look" at defense policy and in October issued a national security statement. All talk of balanced forces was jettisoned, and Eisenhower instead called for major change:

> In specific situations where a warning appears desirable and feasible as an added deterrent, the United States should make clear to the USSR and Communist China, in general terms or with reference to specific areas as the situation requires, its intentions to react with military force against any aggression by Soviet bloc armed forces. . . . In the event of hostilities, the United States will consider nuclear weapons to be as available for use as other munitions.[47]

This was LeMay's argument, and now President Eisenhower was in agreement. He publicly acknowledged this by stating that "atomic weapons have virtually achieved conventional status within our armed services."[48] He reiterated this point the following year: "When these things are used on strictly military targets and for strictly military purposes, I see no reason why they shouldn't be used just exactly as you would use a bullet or anything else."[49] Field Marshal Bernard Montgomery, deputy SACEUR, echoed these sentiments: "I want to make it absolutely clear that we at SHAPE [Supreme Headquarters, Allied Powers Europe] are basing all our planning on using atomic and thermonuclear weapons in our defense. With us it is no longer: 'They may possibly be used'; it is very definitely: 'They will be used, if we are attacked.' "[50] Gordon Dean, chairman of the AEC, affirmed these sentiments when he gushed that his organization was working on a situation "where we will have atomic weapons in almost as complete a variety as conventional ones, and a situation where we can use them in the same way. This could include artillery shells, guided missiles, torpedoes, rockets and bombs for ground-support aircraft among others, and it would include big ones for big situations and little ones for little situations."[51]

Curtis LeMay believed similarly. In fact, throughout the Korean War he had advocated the use of atomic weapons simply because they

---

[46] "Notes on Commanders' Conference, Exercise DUALISM," 250.

[47] NSC 162/2, 20 October 1953, in FRUS, 1952–1954, vol. 2, 593.

[48] Gaddis, Long Peace: Inquiries in the History of the Cold War, 124.

[49] Freedman, Evolution of Nuclear Strategy, 73.

[50] Ibid., 79.

[51] "Science and the Citizen," Scientific American, November 1951, 32.

were more efficient and, to his mind, more humane in the long run. Years later he would rail at those who spoke of the moral implications of employing atomic bombs by noting that more people died in the firebombing of Tokyo than at either Hiroshima or Nagasaki. In Korea, all the major cities in the north were destroyed by B-29s using conventional bombs—but this took place over three years and involved the loss of dozens of aircraft and their crews. Atomic bombs could have done the job far more quickly and with less loss of life. Which was more humane?

The new secretary of state, John Foster Dulles, embraced the New Look and made several speeches over the next year supporting it. In one he referred to "massive retaliation" as the new American strategy; the phrase stuck. Eisenhower was clear on the priorities to implement this policy. When the Army chief of staff pushed for more funds for his service, the president exploded that "the only thing we fear is an atomic attack delivered by air on our cities." Building up the Army was senseless, and if Ike did that, "you would want to impeach me." The problem with the Army chief was, "he's talking theory—I'm trying to talk sound sense."[52] The Soviets did not fear a large US Army; they feared SAC. Massive retaliation would rely on the deterrent capability of nuclear-equipped bombers.

Such beliefs were reinforced when the Technological Capabilities Panel of the Science Advisory Committee delivered a report to the president. This panel, chaired by James R. Killian Jr., presented a stark appraisal of the Soviet threat. The report began by noting the Soviets could not mount a decisive air strike against the United States, but the United States *could* mount such an air attack "that would inflict massive damage and would probably be conclusive in a general war." This situation was expected to remain stable for the next five years. In 1960, however, trouble would begin as the Soviets would by then possess a "multimegaton capability," a huge nuclear stockpile, and a robust delivery capability. Without an adequate defensive capability, the United States would be "in danger of surprise attack and possible defeat." A large offensive and defensive buildup was necessary, including development of an operational ICBM and an expansion of Strategic Air Command "in sufficient numbers to permit its bombers to be airborne toward targets within the warning interval."[53] Specifically,

---

[52] "Diary entry by President's Press Secretary (Hagerty)," 1 February 1955, in *FRUS, 1955–1957*, vol. 19, 39.

[53] Report by the Technological Capabilities Panel of the Science Advisory Committee (Killian Panel), "Meeting the Threat of Surprise Attack," 14 February 1955, in *FRUS, 1955–1957*, vol. 19, 41–56.

the panel called for dispersal of SAC assets to satellite bases and a ground alert program. Airpower was ascendant.

For the Air Force and SAC, the results of the New Look were dramatic. Rather than a roughly balanced defense budget of one-third going to each service, airpower became dominant. Although overall defense funding dropped following the Korean War—like Truman, Eisenhower believed a sound economy was the primary factor in American security—the percentage devoted to the Air Force rose significantly to nearly 50 percent of the total, and this dominance would last for the rest of the decade, as shown in table 8-1. SAC would receive approximately one-third of the Air Force budget during this period, or around 17 percent of the entire defense budget.

Table 8-1. Department of Defense budget share and percentage of total (in billions of dollars)

Year	DOD Total	Air Force		Army		Navy & Marines	
1949	$14.0	$1.7	12.1%	$7.9	56.4%	$4.4	31.4%
1950	$13.4	$3.5	26.1%	$5.8	43.3%	$4.1	30.6%
1951	$20.9	$6.4	30.6%	$8.6	41.1%	$5.9	28.2%
1952	$40.6	$12.9	31.8%	$17.5	43.1%	$10.2	25.1%
1953	$43.2	$15.1	35.0%	$16.2	37.5%	$11.9	27.5%
1954	$39.9	$15.7	39.3%	$12.9	32.3%	$11.3	28.3%
1955	$35.0	$16.4	46.9%	$8.9	25.4%	$9.7	27.7%
1956	$35.2	$16.8	47.7%	$8.7	24.7%	$9.7	27.6%
1957	$37.8	$18.4	48.7%	$9.0	23.8%	$10.4	27.5%
1958	$38.4	$18.4	47.9%	$9.1	23.7%	$10.9	28.4%
1959	$40.3	$19.1	47.4%	$9.5	23.6%	$11.7	29.0%
1960	$40.1	$19.1	47.6%	$9.4	23.4%	$11.6	28.9%
Total	$398.8	$163.5	41.0%	$123.5	31.0%	$111.8	28.0%

Department of Defense, Annual Report of the Secretary of Defense (Washington, DC: GPO, annually 1949–1960); and Mollenhoff, Pentagon: Politics, Profits and Plunder, appendix A. Figures do not include OSD expenditures, which were generally less than 1 percent of the DoD budget; rounding errors apply.

As an increasing number of atomic weapons moved to the theaters to back up the new airpower strategy, the question of how to employ additional bombs arose. LeMay understood the decision to move the weapons overseas and employ them using tactical aircraft, but he argued that unity of command and economy of force dictated a central targeting authority. He wanted theater commanders to select the targets for the retardation mission—the effort to slow a Soviet ground offensive by striking its forces and their supply lines. They would forward them to the JCS, who would then pass them on to SAC for inclusion on the master target list—the JCS would prioritize the targets. LeMay wanted a SAC outpost deployed overseas to work with the theater staffs to facilitate target selection; these "deputy SAC commanders" were referred to as "phonetic commands."[54] This had occurred toward the end of the Korean War when Lieutenant General Power (termed *X-ray*) deployed to Guam when it appeared atomic weapons might be used. Power worked with Far East Command and the theater air commanders to plan for the eventuality of atomic strikes. In Europe the problem arose again; SACEUR wanted control over the nuclear weapons in his theater, but so did SAC.

The problem was redundancy. When SAC compared its war plan, which was approved by the JCS, with those of the theater commanders, also JCS approved, overlap was apparent. In the Far East, for example, SAC planners discovered duplication on 115 airfields and 40 complexes. Worse, they found triplication on 37 airfields and 7 complexes. In Europe the problem was similar: duplication on 121 airfields and 48 complexes, with triplication on 31 airfields. The planners at SAC, SACEUR, Far East Command, Pacific Command, and Atlantic Command had similar goals in many cases, reflected by the need to eliminate similar targets, but the result was waste. As the number of nuclear weapons available in the US stockpile proliferated, SAC conceded the desirability of some overlap to ensure key targets were neutralized, but there were limits. Moreover, sequencing was important—targets needed to be struck in the proper order so that blast effects or countermeasures did not interfere with other aircraft or missiles arriving at or near the same time.[55] Coordination was essential, and LeMay was vocal on the subject:

---

[54] "Phonetic Commands, May 1951–June 1959," SAC Historical Study no. 77, n.d., AFHRA, file K416.01-77, 1–3; Borgiasz, *Strategic Air Command*, 15, 123; and Moody, *Building a Strategic Air Force*, 365, 369.

[55] This entire argument was laid out in surprising detail before the Senate. US Congress, *Hearings before the Senate Armed Services Committee, Study of Airpower*, 84th Cong., 2nd sess., 1956, 167–73.

I hope that out of this will come one target list for the country. We should be able to take all the targets that all the commanders think are important and arrange them in some sort of a priority list—the first one will contribute the most to the winning of the war and on down the list. Then the JCS could assign to the various commands that have the capability for destroying these targets the chores of destroying them. Then I think we would have real coordination.[56]

The solution took time and individual effort. Larry Norstad, the USAFE commander, pushed Vandenberg to give him direct control of all nuclear weapons assigned to the theater. Vandenberg refused, arguing that he intended to keep command channels "absolutely clean"—he wanted strategic air operations to proceed from the JCS, to him, and thence to LeMay. A deputy SAC commander, termed *Zebra*, would be assigned to the SACEUR staff to ensure coordination. SACEUR's weapons were another matter and not under his or SAC's authority. On the other hand, the chief conceded it was not useful for SAC to get into "the real estate business" in Europe by assuming operational and administrative control of numerous air bases, which should remain largely under USAFE control.[57]

The compromise was the formation of the 7th Air Division, a SAC unit, along with Third Air Force, a USAFE unit. Aircraft delivering nuclear weapons in the 7th were controlled by SAC through *Zebra*, while USAFE aircraft ultimately were under the command of the theater commander. All bases were under USAFE for administrative purposes. Norstad was trusted by Eisenhower, as well as by those in Washington and Omaha, making this awkward system work.[58] In the agreement that Norstad hammered out between Eisenhower and LeMay, SACEUR would determine the military significance and priority of retardation targets; SAC would judge the technical and operational suitability of those targets and determine the appropriate weapons; and SACEUR would obtain the necessary approval for his targeting scheme from NATO and the JCS.[59] The chief planner at USAFE headquarters at the time later recalled that the war-planning process was "very complicated" because of security issues. He needed intelligence, often provided by NATO allies, but those allies were not allowed to know what it was for or why.[60] It would take several years before the process was streamlined to be less cumbersome.

---

[56] *SAC History—Jan-Jun 1957*, vol. 1, 50.

[57] Roman, "Curtis LeMay and the Origins of NATO Atomic Targeting," 60–61.

[58] Twigge and Scott, *Planning Armageddon: Britain, the United States and the Command of Nuclear Forces*, 34.

[59] Roman, "Curtis LeMay and the Origins of NATO Atomic Targeting," 61–68; and Jordan, *Norstad: Cold War NATO Supreme Commander: Airman, Strategist, Diplomat*, 81–83.

[60] Ellis, interview, 17–21 August 1987, 73.

To better organize the proliferation of nuclear weapons, the Air Force devised an intelligence objectives manual that divided Soviet targets into three categories—Bravo, Romeo, and Delta. Bravo targets were top priority for SAC and referred to Soviet long-range bombers, the air defense network, and its associated command and control system. Delta targets were Soviet industry and Communist Party facilities. Romeo meant retardation, and these targets were Soviet surface forces, both ground and sea, that needed to be blunted in the event of an attack into Central Europe. SAC was primarily concerned with Bravo and Delta targets, while theater commanders worried about Romeo and retardation. LeMay conceded the necessity of the retardation mission but hoped that some of those targets would include facilities and systems whose destruction would make the strategic air offensive easier.

LeMay's overriding concern was the Soviet air force—it had to be destroyed at the outset of war, both to prevent it from attacking the United States but also to render it unable to stop the SAC assault.[61] As for Delta targets, SAC increasingly focused on urban areas, which it viewed as centers of Soviet strength. Not only were they population centers, they also were loaded with war industries. As thermonuclear weapons increasingly joined the stockpile, it was apparent that a relatively small number of megaton-size bombs would obliterate Soviet cities and all they contained. A study conducted by the JCS in 1955 concluded that 77 percent of all Soviet military and industrial targets were within three miles of city centers across the country. Not only would Soviet industry and its war-making capability be destroyed by a SAC air offensive, it also would take Russia several years to recover from the strikes—if they could do so at all.[62]

Throughout this period the number of warheads in the US nuclear arsenal continued to grow, as did the number of targets in the Soviet Union that merited destruction. In 1956, the war plans listed nearly 3,000 separate targets in Russia. By 1959, SAC planners had listed and analyzed over 20,000 separate targets, and by 1963, they had settled on 8,400 as worthy of receiving the attention of a strategic bomber or ICBM.[63] Overarching all discussions of appropriate targets was the essential need for intelligence.

[61] *SAC History—Jan–Jun 1957*, vol. 1, 4. SAC targeting priorities were listed as the Soviet nuclear capability and its delivery forces; support "as feasible" of the Allied forces in Europe and other strategic areas; and third, Soviet "war sustaining resources."

[62] Borgiasz, *Strategic Air Command: Evolution and Consolidation of Nuclear Forces*, 124–26.

[63] Rosenberg, "U.S. Nuclear War Planning, 1945–1960," 49.

Intelligence and Targeting

The essential importance of intelligence to air strategy was recognized in World War I. As we have seen, strategic bombing of an enemy's vital centers did not require merely intelligence, but specific types of intelligence, along with a powerful analytical capability. Certainly, air planners needed knowledge of an enemy's air defense system, for example, but this type of operational, technical, and tactical intelligence was not different in kind from what military planners had always required. Air planners contemplating a strategic bombing campaign also needed detailed technical information on an adversary's economy and infrastructure. During World War II an entire apparatus was set up, shared by the AAF and British, which gathered and analyzed this new type of economic intelligence.

After the war, the focus shifted to a new adversary, while at the same time, the intelligence system so painfully built during the war was unceremoniously discarded. Yes, a CIA was established, but it had limited capabilities; it was totally caught by surprise not only by the Soviet atomic bomb detonation but also by the North Korean invasion and then the massive intervention by the Chinese a few months later. The Air Force, and SAC specifically, realized it would need to expand its own intelligence capabilities if it were to prepare for major war.[64] The early attempts at writing a joint war plan were troubling: *Pincher*, *Broiler*, and other plans demonstrated that little was known about the Soviet Union. It was no coincidence these early war plans merely listed a number of large cities as potential targets; that was as definitive as the planners could get. One intelligence officer at SAC later commented on this problem, noting ruefully that initially there was very little information available—planners had to rely on old data from the Germans, attaché reports, and whatever enlightenment they could glean from CIA studies.[65] These were slim pickings.

SAC's first effort to obtain direct information on the Soviet Union was the use of reconnaissance aircraft to monitor its air defense network. Although not easy, this task was the least challenging to explore. "Ferret" aircraft—B-17s loaded with electronic gear—flew along the Soviet borders hoping to generate a response. Usually, this resulted in the ferrets being "painted" by air defense radars. Electronic

[64] Capt Sander A. Laubenthal and John W. LeLand, "SAC Intelligence Collection during the Korean War," SAC historical study, n.d., AFHRA, file K416.601-12, 1–2.
[65] Smith, interview, 3–5 March 1983, 37–38.

experts could then analyze these signals and determine what type of radars the Soviets had and where they were located. Initially, it was apparent the Soviets were using British and American systems they had obtained via Lend-Lease during the war.[66] This gave SAC a clear insight into Soviet radar capabilities, although the Russians soon began to build their own systems.[67] By mid 1947 these flights had charted a chain of Soviet radars along its borders—except in the Arctic regions. During the Berlin crisis the following year, an electronic-intelligence B-29 flew along the corridors to and from the beleaguered city to monitor Soviet emissions. Although it was intercepted by Soviet fighters, no hostile action was involved.[68]

These ferret flights were of great importance and continued for years in both Europe and Asia. The data gathered helped to form an electronic order of battle regarding the Soviet air defenses—both capabilities and vulnerabilities.

SAC also needed information on Soviet targets inland. This was a more difficult task. Photo reconnaissance aircraft had been used during World War II, but this function suffered heavily in the budget cuts of the postwar era. By September 1947 only 24 such aircraft existed in the entire command. Once again, inadequacies discovered during the war-planning process would awaken air leaders. Maj Gen Pat Partridge, while serving on the Air Staff in 1948, wrote the head of Air Force intelligence, Maj Gen George C. McDonald, stating, "The scope of the reconnaissance needed to carry out atomic bomb attacks in Russia staggers my imagination."[69] He was justified in being staggered. Very few aerial photos existed of the Soviet Union, and most of those were captured German images taken during the war. Clearly, this was not good enough; such photos did not go beyond the Ural Mountains, for example. In 1950 General LeMay admitted that reconnaissance was "critical," but up to that point his command had been able to obtain very little targeting material. He added, "The reconnaissance force that we have simply will not provide that target interpretation in the time we have available. The first is totally inadequate to get the post-strike damage assessment photography which we need." He also

---

[66] For a personal account, see Hall and Laurie, *Early Cold War Overflights, 1950–1956*, vol. 1, 285–92. This is a rich source. Hall and Laurie sponsored a conference in 2001 on the subject, and for the first time, over a dozen participants told their stories of events that had previously been highly classified.

[67] Farquhar, *Need to Know: The Role of Air Force Reconnaissance in War Planning*, 40–41, 99–100.

[68] Ibid., 66–67, 107–9.

[69] Partridge to McDonald, memorandum, 31 January 1948, in Hall and Laurie, *Early Cold War Overflights*, vol. 2, document 3.

thought the problem would worsen when counter–air force operations were carried out against the Russian strike force. Intelligence was so lacking on the size and location of the Soviet air force that "it is not possible to estimate what we can do about it."[70]

The upshot of this need was the use of RB-29s equipped with long-focal-length cameras (at least 100 in.) flying along the Soviet borders and taking oblique-angle pictures into denied territory. Sometimes these missions would penetrate Soviet airspace for a better view. Such flights were dangerous and were accompanied by great diplomatic as well as personal risk to the aircrews. The Soviets often filed formal protests; on other occasions they simply shot the planes down. Between 1946 and 1961, the Soviets shot down 40 Air Force and Navy reconnaissance aircraft, with the loss of 169 crew members.[71]

The Korean War gave impetus to SAC reconnaissance efforts. When the war broke out, there was only one SAC reconnaissance unit in the Far East—it was there for a mapping mission. It stayed and was soon joined by others. FEAF's reconnaissance capabilities were similarly limited; one squadron of RF-80s based at Yakota and another squadron consisting of two RB-17s and four RC-45s located on Guam were all it could muster. Nonetheless, the aircraft available immediately began flying photo missions over Korea, both prestrike and poststrike, to measure the damage inflicted by the bomber attacks.[72] Targeting, as always, was crucial, but the intelligence assets on hand at the beginning of the war were virtually nonexistent. One of the first analysts to arrive in theater noted, "The only targeting materials US forces had were in some obsolete target folders we found in an old filing cabinet." This data had been compiled during World War II, while the topographic charts located were all in Japanese—also of vintage age.[73]

A major problem involved photo interpretation. There were few such analysts available—they, too, had been mustered out after World War II. Although the Army was dependent on photo reconnaissance to plan its operations, it had no one trained to interpret the photos produced by Air Force flights—it relied on airmen to do that task.[74]

---

[70] "Notes on Commanders Conference, Exercise DUALISM," 223–24, 227.

[71] Lashmar, *Spy Flights of the Cold War*, 211. For dozens of accounts from crews who flew a number of different overflight missions and were often fired upon, see Hall and Laurie, *Early Cold War Overflights*, vol. 1. At least 12 of the aircraft lost were SAC reconnaissance aircraft—six RB-29s, four RB-50s, and two RB-45s. Lloyd, *Cold War Legacy*, 226.

[72] Laubenthal and LeLand, "SAC Intelligence Collection during the Korean War," 4.

[73] Hardy and Hall, *Photographic Aerial Reconnaissance and Interpretation: Korea, 1950–1952*, 2.

[74] Dickens, "USAF Reconnaissance during the Korean War," 248.

This was a fine art. One participant during that period noted that "a lot of Chinese tombs were targeted as antiaircraft artillery sites until we finally got to know what the heck was going on there and what the structures and terrain looked like." He continued more hopefully, "You can see and analyze all activity on the ground, far more than just the initial target. Cameras with telephoto lenses permitted you to see every gun, tank, truck, and rickshaw, all occupied or unoccupied gun positions, each aircraft, where they were, what they are, their type, and even their alert status." Analysts could also examine the economic side of the problem, identifying various electrical power stations, steel mills, aluminum plants, "and even figure out their rate and level of production."[75] It was an invaluable, much-demanded skill limited to a handful of experts.

The safety of the B-29s, as well as other UN aircraft, during the war dictated an enhanced knowledge not only of Soviet capabilities but also those of the Chinese. Flights were soon proceeding along the borders of both countries. On 18 October 1950 a reconnaissance plane reported the presence of 75 to 100 aircraft parked at Antung Airfield on the Chinese side of the Yalu River. The next day they were gone.[76] Something was brewing, as soon confirmed by the arrival of a large number of jet aircraft in the theater.

The Air Force initially used RB-29s for such flights near the Yalu, but as with the bombers, the arrival of MiG-15s limited the use of these aircraft in daylight. Indeed, one historian argues that the presence of MiGs in early November 1950 led to the curtailment of reconnaissance flights over North Korea, and this in turn led to surprise when the Chinese attacked at the end of the month.[77] To fill the intelligence gap, RF-84s, RF-86s, and RB-45 jet bombers were employed for missions near and over the Chinese and Soviet borders.[78] The greater speed and altitude capability of these aircraft helped ensure their survivability while gathering information. It was aerial reconnaissance that discovered the Chinese were attempting to build bases in North Korea. Bombers were sent to disrupt this construction, and subsequent reconnaissance flights continued to monitor their progression. If more strikes were needed, they were scheduled.[79]

[75] Hall and Laurie, *Early Cold War Overflights*, vol.1, 323–24.
[76] Laubenthal and LeLand, "SAC Intelligence Collection during the Korean War," 5.
[77] Dickens, "USAF Reconnaissance during the Korean War," 243.
[78] Hall, "Clandestine Victory: Eisenhower and Overhead Reconnaissance in the Cold War," 121.
[79] Dickens, "USAF Reconnaissance during the Korean War," 245–46.

By the end of the war, reconnaissance versions of the new B-47 bombers were flying over Korea, Manchuria, and the Soviet Union.[80] Such flights, which would eventually include RB-57s and U-2s, would become more frequent. Of course, the Korean War was just one of the tasks requiring reconnaissance. For the next decade SAC aircraft, as well as those under the direction of the CIA and USAFE, would fly numerous missions near and over Soviet and Chinese territory to gather intelligence. In Asia, the Nationalist Chinese were also energetic in flying reconnaissance aircraft provided by the United States to fly dozens of missions over Chinese "denied territory."[81] In addition, the Royal Air Force received RB-45 jet reconnaissance aircraft in 1952, painted in British livery, which were flown over the Soviet Union.[82] By 1956, the CIA and not the military services were flying most of these classified reconnaissance missions. The shoot down of a U-2 in May 1960 would curtail these flights. The arrival of satellites would remove a huge burden from these vulnerable and overtaxed assets.[83]

The mechanics of translating raw intelligence into a coherent targeting plan was a major undertaking. By the Korean War, SAC had decided that, as in World War II Germany, the Soviet oil industry should be the main target system to be struck. The Joint Staff disagreed, arguing that the Soviet electrical system was more lucrative. Electricity was another major system air planners had considered during the war. Recall that AWPD-1 planners had accorded it top priority for the strategic bombing campaign. Because of its small and scattered nature, however, air commanders bypassed the power grid as a major target system. The Strategic Bombing Survey criticized that decision, contending the prewar planners had been correct in identifying it as a major bottleneck target whose destruction would have had disproportionately serious effects on the German war effort. A decade later the same arguments—pro and con—were being made again regarding the vulnerability and importance of the Soviet oil and electrical networks. LeMay took a practical view of the debate; World War II in Europe and the Pacific had demonstrated to him that it was fruitless to attempt to identify a single target system; destroying

---

[80] One such flight, on which one of the authors flew as a passenger, is recorded in Hardy and Hall, *Photographic Aerial Reconnaissance and Interpretation*, 75–88.

[81] Hall and Laurie, *Early Cold War Overflights*, vol. 1, 325–26, 329–30.

[82] Hall, "Clandestine Victory," 122; and Lloyd, *Cold War Legacy*, 188.

[83] Laurie, "The Invisible Hand of the New Look: Eisenhower and the CIA," 95–99. Flying a military reconnaissance aircraft over another country—even if unarmed—could be construed as an act of war. For this reason, President Eisenhower had all U-2 flights conducted by civilians under the auspices of the CIA. Using this scheme, the flights were merely considered "spying"—illegal but not as provocative as a military "act of war."

the German—and Soviet—industrial base meant "blasting it down, plant by plant."[84]

A member of the Air Staff's intelligence division gave a detailed picture to an Air War College audience in 1948 on how planners went about solving the targeting problem. Lt Col W. J. Smith began by recalling the proverbial tale of King Richard III, who was killed at the Battle of Bosworth when his horse was hobbled after losing a shoe— "for want of a nail" a kingdom was lost. The goal of the air planner was to discover the appropriate "nails" in an enemy nation that would have similarly major effects.[85] Recall that such an analogy was behind the Air Corps Tactical School's industrial web theory of the 1930s. The task of Smith's office, the Strategic Vulnerability Branch, was to gather and catalog the countless bits and pieces and attempt to form them into a coherent picture—he compared it to building a jigsaw puzzle. The result of this extensive collection of data was a "bombing encyclopedia" that contained a tabulation of individual installations in the target nation. This multivolume work—which grew daily— contained, for example, an entire book on the Russian aircraft industry, subdivided into airframe versus engine assembly plants. Each installation was entered alphabetically with location coordinates, floor space, capacity, number of workers employed, products produced, date information was gained, and other significant facts available.[86] According to Smith, a modern nation had at least 70,000 targets. The task of the air planner was to find the 700 "nails" that were the most vulnerable to attack while also providing the greatest payoff.[87]

The details of how this information transformed into a target plan were much like those employed by the AWPD-1 planners in 1941 and their counterparts at Eighth Air Force headquarters and other such agencies during the war. The enemy economy was viewed as a system; the goal was to find the critical nodes within that system which made the entire network function. In some cases, as with the petroleum industry, it would be necessary to hit the refineries themselves, but also the oil pumping stations. Again echoing the lessons learned from the war, Smith noted that stockpiles were crucial in this planning effort. The Soviets, for example, had extensive oil reserves, so even airstrikes

---

[84] Moody, *Building a Strategic Air Force*, 360–64; and Poole, *Joint Chiefs of Staff and National Policy*, vol. 4, 163–67.

[85] Lt Col W. J. Smith, "The Strategic Vulnerability of Russia," lecture to Air War College, 18 March 1948, AFHRA, file K239.716248-48, 3.

[86] For an example of one of these encyclopedias from April 1952, see AFHRA, file K142.6-1.

[87] Ibid., 4–5.

knocking out 80 percent of their oil production would have little short-term effect. Planners therefore had to query their superiors as to whether they expected the war to be short or long; if the latter, then taking out the refineries would still be a wise move.[88] The recuperation capability and excess capacity potential of each industry had to be factored in also. All of this required intelligence, and here the briefer admitted the limits of his branch's knowledge. They had useful information on "European Russia," some gained from German sources collected during the war, while other intelligence was derived from reconnaissance flights, and still more from Russian newspapers, "which if read critically" can provide much useful knowledge. Other sources used were even more vague—postcards, recollections from travelers, trade magazines, and scientific journals. Even so, activities taking place in "never-never land" (Siberia) were almost completely unknown. It was feared, however, that massive construction was going on there with the intention of making the Soviet Union impervious to anything less than a massive atomic attack.[89]

Other important points made by Colonel Smith regarded the importance of the Soviet "satellite countries" that supplied them with labor and resources while also serving as a huge buffer zone. He concluded by stressing the need for better intelligence and employing an analogy: a superbly trained and equipped air force without adequate intelligence is no better than a well-trained and muscular athlete who is blind.[90]

Two years later another member of the Air Staff intelligence division lectured at the Air War College and gave his view of the targeting problem. He noted that the purpose of any strategic bombing mission was to achieve the greatest effect at the least cost—cost being defined as the fewest bombs necessary to achieve the goals of the commander. This particular briefing attempted to drill down a bit deeper; the purpose of Richard Grassy's lecture was to discuss the principles of weapon selection and an estimate of force requirements. Using the example of a steel plant, it was necessary to know not just the facility's size and location, but also its internal makeup—the location of the blast furnaces, the open-hearth buildings, where the ingots were produced, and so forth. Obtaining such information was difficult but not impossible. "In many cases we have complete drawings of all the buildings within the plant,

---

[88] Ibid., 8–9.
[89] Ibid., 17–19.
[90] Ibid., 20.

complete schedules of the materials used in the construction and as much detail as we would have on any industrial plant in the US." This knowledge was often gained from engineering firms in the United States that had helped build the plants prior to World War II.[91] Once again, this was precisely the same process used before and during the late war to gain a picture of German industry. Even so, the briefer warned that factories were camouflaged and locations and maps deliberately falsified to throw off the targeteers.

As for weapons to be used, Grassy discussed both atomic and conventional weapons. This was interesting because it reaffirmed for the AWC audience that the atomic stockpile at the time was not large enough to cover all targets—a major conventional bombing campaign as in World War II would still be necessary. The blast damage results from the war relied totally upon conventional "blockbuster" bombs. Even so, the briefer admitted this was still not an exact science—"that measure of averaging is usually not sufficient, as there are many complicating factors such as the overlap of the effective area of one bomb and another, the orientation of the bomb with respect to the building structure" and the effect of near misses and bomb distribution.[92] In sum, such weaponeering and bomb damage assessment were as much an art as they were a science—a conclusion with which any Eighth or Twentieth Air Force planner from World War II would have agreed.

For SAC, this process was the full-time task of hundreds of individuals throughout the command. Despite the paucity of photographs, experts nonetheless produced radar images of what they expected targets to look like on a radar scope. This system was cross-checked by using photos of US cities that generated projected radar returns which were then compared to actual radar returns of those same cities.[93] Each folder contained all this information, as well as penetration points into Soviet airspace, air defenses en route, enemy airfields, the types and capabilities of any enemy fighters they might encounter, and the best way to get in and out of the target area. "Safe haven" areas were also designated where damaged aircraft could head and either crash land or bail out. These areas, generally sparsely populated, offered crews the best chance to survive until recovered by search and rescue forces.[94]

---

[91] Richard G. Grassy, "Principles of Weapons Selection & Estimate of Force Requirements," lecture to Air War College, 11 April 1950, AFHRA, file K239.716248, 4.

[92] Ibid., 7.

[93] Ratkovich, interview, 8–9 January, 55–57.

[94] Smith, interview, 3–5 March 1983, 59–60.

Reflecting his experiences during the war, LeMay instituted a program in which crews were assigned specific targets from the emergency war plan. They would study and memorize all information on this target in minute detail over a period of months and even years—if they ever had to actually launch during war, they would have run simulated attacks against that same target on hundreds of occasions already. Before a crew could be certified as combat ready, it would have to brief its mission in its entirety—routes, defenses, altitudes, airspeeds, and so forth—to the wing or air division commander.[95]

Summary

Contrary to some depictions, Curtis LeMay did not reject progressive or scientific thinking. Nor did he resent the introduction of civilian academics into what normally had been the military's preserve. Indeed, one historian refers to him as the "godfather of RAND" for his vigorous support of the new think tank when he served as deputy chief of staff for R&D. LeMay had worked with OR specialists in Europe and the Pacific and had often relied on their advice when devising tactics, formations, weapons, and strategy. It was LeMay who directed RAND to study ballistic missiles in 1946—he was concerned the Navy was moving ahead in this area and the AAF would be left behind.[96] He later stated that "no miracles came from RAND, but they did a number of useful things." His main complaint was that the analysts would "stray off into blind alleys and do things that had no relation to national defense." He wanted them to focus and stick to those issues where they were competent.[97]

LeMay was far more intelligent and thoughtful than most portraits paint him; he understood not only the details of technical and technological problems, but also their greater implications. He valued the inputs of civilian professors. One RAND analyst summed the issue nicely: total war as exemplified by nuclear war involved all elements of a society—it erased the easy categorization between military and civilian spheres. As a result, "The collapse of such distinctions signaled a situation in which all citizens and all knowledge were continually

---

[95] Ibid., 43–44.
[96] Abella, *Soldiers of Reason: The RAND Corporation and the Rise of American Enterprise*, 14–19.
[97] LeMay, interview, 9 March 1971, 20.

part of national defense."[98] War was increasingly an effort transcending narrow boundaries and the preserve of military professionals. LeMay understood that new reality.

Yet LeMay was ever cognizant of the fact that he, as the commander, was responsible for results. The ethereal and philosophical professors at RAND and elsewhere were able to provide some good ideas and at times some cogent analysis—but the buck stopped at SAC. It would be the agency going to war, and LeMay never forgot that. He studied the targeting problem extensively, as did his staff—it was one of the main functions of his operations analysis function. He trusted their analysis more than he did that of civilian think tanks. [99]

The nuclear war theorists used impeccable logic in devising their scenarios. They wrote with erudition and energy regarding deterrence, assured destruction, preemption, gradual escalation, and related concepts. But to LeMay, all such theories were of limited use. War had its own logic and its own rules, and they were in no way as predictable or systematic as civilian academics believed. If logic were the key to strategy, then the Japanese would never have been so foolish in 1941 as to attack the United States and Britain, whose combined strength and resources dwarfed their own.

The proliferation of nuclear weapons—resulting from new designs that made the weapons smaller and more powerful while using less fissionable material—revolutionized American military strategy and policy. All the services went nuclear. This in turn required a mechanism to coordinate the use of these numerous yet very powerful weapons. SAC pushed for overall control but was resisted. Ultimately, the theater commanders were given authority over the hundreds of nuclear weapons positioned in their areas. As always, the decision to actually employ those weapons rested solely with the president. As for targeting, SAC was able to convince the JCS that it was essential to have a rational and coordinated plan for the use of nuclear weapons—it was foolish to allow theater commanders, either on land or sea, to employ these weapons unilaterally, without considering the operations of the other services that would be dropping weapons in the same area. This drive toward centralization would continue, resulting in the single integrated operational plan—the SIOP—first approved in 1961.

---

[98] M. Collins, *Cold War Laboratory*, 131. Although some of the RAND analysts were political scientists—like Albert and Roberta Wohlstetter, Herman Kahn, Bernard Brodie, and Carl Builder—the vast majority were hard scientists or engineers: over 95 percent of them in 1951. Ibid., 140.

[99] Zimmerman, *Insider at SAC*, 55–56.

The growth of the stockpile and the buildup of nuclear-capable bombers in SAC were so dramatic as to allow unprecedented sharing of nuclear technology. Not just the Army and Navy were given nuclear devices, but President Eisenhower even provided them to allies. The Royal Air Force was slow to rebuild after World War II, and its inventory of Lancasters was obsolescing at an even faster rate than were the B-29s of SAC. There were plans to develop a number of "V Bombers," long-range jet aircraft that could reach targets in the Soviet Union, but these new planes were several years in the future. In the interim, B-29s were taken out of mothballs and provided to the RAF in June 1952; they were referred to as "Washingtons." The bomber was, in the phrase of Marshal of the Royal Air Force Sir John Slessor, "the great deterrent."[100] In January 1954, Eisenhower went a step further and told Prime Minister Winston Churchill that in the event of war, the United States would transfer nuclear weapons to the UK for use on RAF aircraft.[101] Things had come a very long way since the early postwar years when US laws and procedures denied even high-ranking officers access to atomic weapons and their secrets.

Unquestionably the Europeans and Eisenhower saw the nuclear deterrent, exemplified by the bombers of Strategic Air Command, as the most economical way of assuring Western security. Talk of abandoning continental Europe to a Soviet onslaught was dropped from war plans; instead, NATO adopted a "forward strategy" that hoped to stop a Soviet attack at the Rhine or preferably the Elbe River. This was a tall order, and to do so, nuclear weapons were essential. NATO had barely 10 divisions in place when the Korean War broke out; worse, of those, only the two US divisions were combat ready. At the Lisbon Conference in February 1952, NATO agreed to provide 89 2/3 divisions by M + 30 for defense against the Soviets. This was absurd, and all knew it; such a mass of troops simply did not exist. Massive retaliation was a calculated strategy of replacing ground forces with nuclear weapons.[102] In the evocative words of Carl Spaatz, airpower would negate the "wall of flesh" strategy that envisioned the West attempting to match the Soviets man-for-man across the central German plain.[103]

---

[100] Slessor, *Great Deterrent*, 24.

[101] Twigge and Scott, *Planning Armageddon*, 32, 101.

[102] Ibid., 148; and Poole, *Joint Chiefs of Staff and National Policy*, vol. 4, 185–87, 293.

[103] George F. Lemmer, "The Air Force and Strategic Deterrence, 1951–1960," SAC historical study, 1964, AFHRA, file K168.01-13, 4. It should also be noted that NATO defense hinged to a great extent on West Germany and whether France would acquiesce to its rearmament and entry into the alliance.

The US military buildup suggested by *NSC 68* in mid 1950 was not undertaken until events forced the issue; the outbreak of the Korean War initiated the expansion. Although the entire US military enjoyed a near-doubling in size during the war, its aftermath was even more dramatic for the Air Force. Significantly, it was President Truman who accepted the airmen's arguments and directed a defense budget heavily in favor of the Air Force. The New Look implemented by President Eisenhower, which saw the Air Force shooting for a goal of 143 wings, merely confirmed this trend. This priority meant airmen were garnering nearly half of the entire defense budget by the middle of the decade. This priority remained even when Eisenhower cut the defense budget in FY 1954 and slowed Air Force growth to 120 wings. This cut was vocally resisted by General Vandenberg, but the primacy of airpower in the national security strategy remained in place—in fact, the Air Force was soon allowed to expand to 137 wings.[104]

National war planning continued to rely on airpower to strike the initial, decisive blow. For a time—before the Soviets detonated their first atomic bomb and in the year or so thereafter—there was talk in some quarters of preventive war. In truth, it does not appear most American leaders ever seriously considered this option. As the Joint Chiefs of Staff stated when rejecting it, "The idea of deliberately starting a war would engender such public revulsion as to make the idea untenable."[105] Some within the Air Force, including Generals Kenney, LeMay, and Anderson, nonetheless suggested the notion be considered, but only Anderson made the mistake of voicing his opinion in public. He was immediately fired and retired. It should also be noted that throughout the Korean War, Curtis LeMay had advocated the use of atomic weapons because he believed they were more efficient and, to his mind, more humane in the long run.

Although many leaders besides LeMay, including President Eisenhower, would later state that nuclear weapons should be considered merely as just another tool in the military's arsenal, it was becoming increasingly apparent that was not the case. In the minds of more and more people worldwide, nuclear weapons were acquiring a paradoxically positive and negative mystique that has never really ended. The nuclear threshold has not been breached since 1945 by any nation, despite the proliferation of these weapons. Although countries have

---

[104] Vandenberg, who was known to be suffering from terminal cancer, retired in April 1953. For his last budget fight, see Meilinger, *Hoyt S. Vandenberg: The Life of a General*, 197–200.

[105] Twigge and Scott, *Planning Armageddon*, 31.

striven to develop and build a nuclear stockpile for prestige purposes or the belief it would offer greater security, the actual employment of such weapons has encountered an impassable psychological barrier that has not yet been ruptured in nearly seven decades.[106] It is one of the great paradoxes of modern air and space power that nuclear weapons are most useful when they are never used.

Table 8-2. US nuclear weapons stockpile

Year	Warheads	Year	Warheads	Year	Warheads
1945	2	1951	650	1957	5,400
1946	9	1952	1,000	1958	7,100
1947	13	1953	1,350	1959	12,000
1948	50	1954	1,750	1960	18,500
1949	250	1955	2,250	1961	23,000
1950	450	1956	3,250		

Cochran, Arkin, and Hoenig, *Nuclear Weapons Databook,* vol. 1, 15.

As had been the case since World War I, all talk of targeting and air strategy circled back to the matter of intelligence. Airpower provided the theoretical possibility of striking all targets within an enemy nation, but the number of possible targets exceeded the number of bombs and aircraft available to hit them. Although the US nuclear stockpile approached 23,000 warheads by the end of the Eisenhower presidency (see table 8-2)—some of them several megatons in size—SAC held that many of those would never be used or that they would be ineffective. A Soviet first strike would undoubtedly claim numerous aircraft and nuclear weapons storage facilities; Soviet air defenses would down scores more aircraft; and other weapons would either not detonate or would interfere with other warheads going off in the same vicinity. It was the SAC belief that the best defense was a good offense, and the more nuclear weapons available for use, the less likely they would ever be used.

Still, identifying, analyzing, cataloging, and targeting the tens of thousands of potential targets in the Soviet Union—and later China—

---

[106] For a discussion of this concept, see Tannenwald, *Nuclear Taboo.*

was a monumental feat. The techniques used to perform this vital function were quite similar to those created during World War II. SAC had its own OR division (later changed to Science and Research Division), and these civilian analysts were invaluable. They used methodologies similar to those of their forebearers; the enemy's economy was carefully studied to see what made it work. Then that network of systems was deconstructed—how could the economy and military infrastructure of the enemy be destroyed? Although some may have believed the size and destructive power of thermonuclear weapons had eliminated the need for precision employment, LeMay rejected such an idea. He insisted that planners specify pinpoint targets for their strikes, and he further demanded that his bomber crews work to increase their accuracy. He also insisted that the bomb groups themselves be involved in the targeting process. He recalled that during World War II the crews did not know their targets until the day of the mission, giving them little or no time to adequately prepare. He wanted his crews to know their targets well in advance so they could study and plan how best to penetrate to the targets and destroy them.[107] But how was SAC able to identify the thousands of targets it desired to hit?

First, targets and their priority were determined by the joint chiefs based on the recommendations of SAC, the theater commanders, and various intelligence agencies. The JCS would then dole out these targets to SAC and the theaters. The chiefs would at the same time specify the degree of assurance assigned to each target. For example, a target requiring a 90 percent guarantee of destruction would require more or larger-yield weapons assigned against it than a target needing only a 60 percent assurance. Similarly, a target might necessitate specific tactics or aircraft used to ensure a high level of confidence. These tactical and technical decisions were made by the operational commanders involved.[108] As noted, redundancy was advisable if the JCS required a very high level of assurance regarding a target's destruction. In other cases, LeMay labored to eliminate the danger of overlap and fratricide between targets through annual conferences held among all those participating in nuclear delivery.

To gather the necessary information on potential targets, ferret aircraft were initially used to fly along the Soviet borders to listen to

---

[107] LeMay, interview, 16 November 1972, 42.
[108] Smith, interview, 3–5 March 1983, 69–71, 114–17.

communications and track electronic emissions. This practice quickly revealed its limitations. Increasingly powerful cameras, using oblique configurations, were developed to peek more deeply into denied territory. Finally, the inadequacies of Soviet air defenses were exploited to permit overflights into Russian and Chinese airspace. This was a risky scheme, and Soviet air defenses improved rapidly to prevent such incursions. Dozens of US, British, and Nationalist Chinese reconnaissance aircraft were lost to Soviet air defenses and interceptors. By 1956 the United States had developed the U-2 high-altitude reconnaissance aircraft—essentially a powered glider—to fly above the range of Soviet aircraft and missiles. These aircraft, along with RB-45s, RB-47s, and RB-57s, produced an astonishing number of high-fidelity photographs of territory and targets never before seen, but over time they, too, became vulnerable. The downing of a U-2 over Soviet territory and the capture of its pilot in May 1960 were a diplomatic disaster for the United States. Eventually, satellites would fulfill the essential reconnaissance function—not just for the United States, but for the Soviets as well. Without such detailed intelligence sources, the SAC war plans were little more than guesswork.

Over it all stood Curtis LeMay. He pinned on his fourth star in 1951, one month prior to his 45th birthday. In 1955 he was retitled commander in chief, Strategic Air Command (CINCSAC). His relentless insistence on performance and professionalism put enormous pressure on his command and its personnel. He knew that, but he believed the stakes were too high to demand anything less. He remembered the two decades between the world wars when the Air Corps did not have the aircraft, personnel, organization, or training it needed. The result was an air arm that entered the war unprepared. He would not let that happen on his watch. He understood the burdens he imposed, and thus his spot promotion system, lead crews, and sustained emphasis on better housing and facilities helped to make it all bearable.

He performed his task well. By the end of his nine-year tenure at Offutt AFB in July 1957, SAC had developed into an organization of renowned professionalism and precision. It kept the peace because it trained so unremittingly for war.

Chapter 9

Retrospect and Epilogue

One of the most fundamental aspects of the strategic bombing story is the importance of mission and message. Airmen from World War I onward realized they needed to define themselves as unique. To justify an independent service—which in turn would permit equal funding, doctrinal formulation, and promotion/organizational opportunities—airmen needed to perform a unique mission. Strategic bombing, the ability to strike an enemy's vital centers at the outset of war, was that mission. There were dissenters within the Air Service and Air Corps, but unquestionably the followers of Billy Mitchell, and later Frank Andrews and Hap Arnold, held sway before and during World War II. Ground support was certainly not forgotten, as some would later claim; indeed, most of the AAF force structure was devoted to tactical airpower. Nonetheless, airmen viewed strategic bombing as the essential core mission of the service. The aftermath of the war that saw Strategic Air Command formed as the primary combat unit within the AAF and later the Air Force confirmed this long-standing inclination and belief.

This sense of mission and message was strongly resisted by the Army and Navy for their own institutional as well as doctrinal reasons. Change is often difficult, and adjusting to warfare in a new medium was not easy for either of the traditional services. What today would be termed "jointness" was not universally recognized for most of the period covered in this study, and it was not even seen as desirable by many officers. Coordination and cooperation had been the words used to describe those few times in American history when sailors and soldiers were required to work together. The advent of the airplane and, especially, a global war seemed compelling reasons to finally force jointness. They did not. Fortunately, the sheer overwhelming power of the United States during the war served to paper over numerous shortcomings. It must also be said that all interservice rivalry is not bad or self-serving. Competition is desirable among the services to ensure the best ideas are tested and subjected to an intellectual give and take. Competition is the American way. But it can go too far when the services dissemble or deliberately work at cross-purposes toward another service to further their own parochial ends—as the Navy did in slandering civilian and military leaders in 1949.

Jointness was and remains essential in achieving effective and efficient combat operations. Pearl Harbor was the epitome of generals and admirals not communicating effectively—and not developing a climate that allowed their staffs to do so either. These types of problems resurfaced in the Korean War. There was an enormous amount of mistrust and sometimes deliberate misunderstanding between the services regarding motives and purpose. Such a debilitating climate hurt the US war effort. Worse, similar problems resurfaced in Vietnam the following decade. In that war's aftermath, the services finally took small, hesitant steps toward jointness. Even today the last vestiges of interservice rivalry are not totally ended, and financial reasons are often the root of the problem. These disruptions arise most viciously during times of severe budget constraints. That was certainly the case in the late 1940s.

Education was a vital activity throughout this period. The mission of airpower had to be converted into a message, and that message needed to be taught to the airmen who would be charged with carrying it out. During the interwar years, the Air Corps Tactical School played this vital function, educating the generation of airmen who would lead the AAF during World War II. Virtually all of that war's senior air leaders had passed through Maxwell Field and been exposed to ideas on strategic airpower. In modern terms, the ACTS served as a combined Squadron Officers College, Air Command and Staff College, and Air War College—with a dash of weapons school thrown in for good measure. In the postwar era, the Air Force would found its own academy in Colorado as well as a series of schools designed to educate airmen on their profession throughout their careers. Specialized schools and classes were established as well for missiles and rocketry, nuclear physics, electronics, and a host of other disciplines. The Air Force formed its own graduate school—the Air Force Institute of Technology—to award technical degrees to selected airmen. Much later, it would set up the School of Advanced Airpower Studies (now School of Advanced Air and Space Studies) to educate future strategists. In addition, the Air Force sent an increasing number of officers to civilian graduate schools to earn degrees in a variety of fields simply to make them better-educated professionals. LeMay believed in education, although, as with all else, the SAC mission came first. He was more than willing to send his personnel off to school—as long as it did not interfere with completion of the command's mission of deterrence and war preparation.

The Air Force retained its interest in—some would claim fascination with—technology. The Scientific Advisory Board (SAB) established after World War II has continued in operation to the present day, although its fortunes and influence have fluctuated. The status of R&D was similarly recognized as vital throughout this early period of SAC's existence and would continue to be of critical importance in the decades ahead. The deputy chief of staff for research and development, the position suggested by the Spaatz Board in 1945 that was first held by Maj Gen Curtis LeMay, was disbanded when the Air Force became independent in 1947. The functions of R&D were then absorbed into the Air Materiel Command. As a result, some complained that the Air Force was not taking R&D seriously. The SAB argued this function should once again be broken off and made separate from the business of producing, modifying, and monitoring aircraft and systems already developed. One historian claims that matters seemed to languish because General Spaatz was less interested in R&D and technology in general than Arnold had been. The tenure of Hoyt Vandenberg as chief was therefore viewed as important because he had "a broader vision."[1]

Vandenberg looked into the matter. He directed Air University to conduct a study, while also asking old friend Jimmy Doolittle for his views. Both agreed R&D was being shortchanged. The chief then reorganized: a new Air Research and Development Command was formed, and the position of deputy chief of staff for R&D was reborn on the Air Staff.[2] At the same time, Vandenberg established the new position of chief scientist. The SAB was an essential body and well respected, but it was a committee—with all the inherent limitations of such a group—and operated on a part-time basis. Vandenberg wanted someone available full time who could react quickly to his queries. In January 1950 Dr. Louis Ridenour, a physicist trained at Caltech, was selected as the first chief scientist.[3]

Strategic Air Command benefitted greatly from these initiatives and strongly encouraged them. General LeMay had learned from his job in R&D the vital importance of technology to airpower. He had a deep interest in all things mechanical himself and played a direct role in monitoring the development of new innovations for SAC. His understanding of the broad range of technologies affecting his

---

[1] Day, *Lightning Rod: A History of the Air Force Chief Scientist's Office*, 19.
[2] S. Johnson, *United States Air Force and the Culture of Innovation*, chap. 2.
[3] For the creation of this position, see Day, *Lightning Rod*.

command was impressive: he knew the importance of jet propulsion, rockets, electronic warfare, aerodynamic advancement, global communications, rocketry, and, of course, atomic/nuclear weapons development. All of these fields advanced dramatically during his long tenure at Offutt. LeMay believed in technology, if only because he so well realized that the most-advanced aircraft and systems were essential to carry out his command's mission. His own words highlight this understanding:

> When I took over SAC, the first war plan called for shipping B-29s overseas. We depended on overseas bases. The B-50 gave us more range. Then tankers, the B-47, and the B-52 gave us still greater range. This changed the plan from one of fighting from bases overseas to primarily one of fighting from bases here at home. Improvements in radar were also very important, for they changed tactics. Missiles created changes in the targets assigned in war plans. Some changes in plans are due to new thinking and new tactics, but the bulk of the change is due to new equipment.[4]

His predecessor, George Kenney, also understood this fundamental reality and reportedly once commented, "Air power is like poker. A second-best hand is like none at all—it will cost you dough and win you nothing."[5] Like Kenney, LeMay wanted SAC to have the best hand.

To use another metaphor, intelligence and targeting were where the rubber met the road for SAC. The command's mission once war broke out was to use its aircraft to put bombs on specific targets in Soviet territory. This truism, that airpower was in essence targeting and that in turn was dependent on intelligence, was recognized as early as World War I. Throughout the interwar years the instructors at the ACTS labored to think this through—it was new territory in warfare. They studied economics and various branches of engineering and deduced that modern nations were dependent on their economic infrastructures. It was therefore incumbent on air planners to understand how those systems worked and then, more importantly, how to make them fail. It could be argued that not enough time and energy were spent on this crucial area between the wars. But given the dire fiscal straits in which the Air Corps found itself, something had to give. The ground war zealots who dominated the Army between the wars were loath to spend scarce dollars on an air arm, and the funds allocated were for the basics. Looking back it is easy to criticize airmen for not thinking through the problems of strategic

---

[4] LeMay, interview, January 1965, 8.
[5] Westenhoff, *Military Airpower*, 13.

bombing deeply enough and not conducting more experimentation and analysis. Yet funds were limited, and they had to make do with the small sums allotted to them.

War demonstrated that problems identified before the war, especially in this area of intelligence gathering, analysis, and targeting, were even greater than had been imagined. Entirely new organizations had to be established to address this shortfall, and by war's end the results were impressive. After VJ-Day, however, Congress slashed defense budgets, and these newly created intelligence functions were inevitably among the first to be chopped. Aircraft had to be procured, and aircrews had to be trained. Nonetheless, the problem was understood—the Operations Research units were retained, problems were contracted out to think tanks like RAND, and small staffs at SAC headquarters and its numbered air forces continued to work the issues. Eventually, they developed a "bomb encyclopedia" to catalog tens of thousands of potential targets in the Soviet Union and China, and techniques were developed and constantly refined to ensure those targets could be located and destroyed. The effort to produce radar pictures depicting targets in Soviet territory is an example of how hard work, inspiration, and creativity combined to address a thorny problem.

Leadership dominated all. Visionaries and practitioners were equally important in formulating and nurturing ideas about strategic bombing and then risking advancement in a ground-oriented Army to spread those ideas. A succession of true leaders arose—officers who, through their drive, courage, and ingenuity, turned ideas into hardware and into practice. Billy Mitchell, Ben Foulois, Frank Andrews, Hap Arnold, Carl Spaatz, and Hoyt Vandenberg played essential roles in this story. Leadership within SAC itself was no less vital.

Part of this leadership thread within SAC was the determination to instill a specific culture throughout the command, a culture that emphasized thoroughness and preparation. Curtis LeMay had always been famous for his insistence on rigorous, realistic training. As a commander in World War II, he had installed lead crew programs that rewarded the best airmen and gave them additional training and guidance; he then put them back in operational units in leadership positions to teach their colleagues. It was the same approach he took at SAC. Commanders would know their business, just as LeMay knew his. One of his wing commanders who was *not* an admirer nonetheless conceded this point eloquently:

LeMay knew his trade. This is something about him. He knew bombardment; he had learned it the hard way. He had done it personally; he knew what bombers could do, he knew how to navigate, he knew how to bomb, he knew how to fly, and he knew what he wanted of the people. He knew what to expect of the planes. He was a hardheaded bastard and insisted on getting it. He knew that you had to train people to do it. Those were his sterling qualities that really made him a great damn field commander. He knew what to expect, what to demand, and how to get it.[6]

LeMay also convinced Air Force headquarters to allow him to institute the spot promotion system. This was an unprecedented move. There had been brevet promotions in the past, but they were largely ceremonial and did not include an increase in pay or seniority. In SAC, the promotions were substantive—although dependent on continued high performance. LeMay's program was at the core of his belief that SAC had the most important military mission in the nation: it was responsible for the security, indeed the survival, of the United States. He believed that and wanted his personnel to believe it as well—from the senior general to the junior airman. Providing his troops with instant recognition was tangible proof that he and the Air Force were serious about the primacy of the SAC mission.

It is common to hear commanders aver that personnel are the key to success; yet their actions are not always consistent with such assertions. That was not the case with SAC. LeMay stated forcefully and often that personnel were the number one priority of the command. Testifying before the Senate in 1956, he began by emphasizing, "I consider the lack of skilled manpower to be my most critical deficiency."[7] He worried about this problem continuously. Yes, he rode his people hard and realized that at times this caused unhappiness and frustration, but he also labored to reward them. In the same testimony he argued that "pay alone will not solve the problem [of retention]. If we are going to retain the people, we must look after the family. At the present time we have some 82,000 families in SAC with only 16,842 appropriated and Wherry houses. That leaves 72,000 families to look for their own place to live. . . . Often this leads the airman to separation from the Air Force."[8] LeMay's efforts to correct the situation produced mixed results: personnel retention rates within the command were always troublesome—a product of constant stress—

---

[6] Combs, interview, 28–29 June 1982, 200.

[7] US Congress, *Hearings before the Senate Armed Services Committee on the Study of Airpower*, 84th Cong., 2nd sess., 67.

[8] Ibid., 81.

yet command performance remained exceptionally high.[9] The official history addressed this paradox in an unusually sensitive passage:

> The mental and emotional stress of life in SAC resulted in serious personnel problems which directly affected the command's mission. Both exasperation and pride were evident in the attitudes of SAC's officers and airmen. The exasperation resulted from the tensions of living under a state of constant alert and flying frequently long-range missions. Flying at all hours of the day or night and repeated absences from their families, ranging up to three months, further compounded this situation. It proved difficult to maintain a normal home life, and both the flyers and their families suffered. Under these circumstances, the equivalent of combat fatigue in peacetime was not an unusual phenomenon in SAC. . . . But over and above all . . . there existed a sense of dedication and mission among many of SAC's personnel—officers, airmen, and civilians—which caused them to carry out their tasks in spite of physical and mental hardships.[10]

This stress was why there was such a strong emphasis on housing and recreation facilities.

Professionalism and an emphasis on people were two aspects of the cultural change LeMay brought to SAC. Another aspect, and one closely related, was his insistence that the command consider itself on a perpetual war footing. From Hiroshima onward, Air Force leaders stressed that in the atomic age it was no longer possible to enjoy the time-honored American tradition of blissful unpreparedness for war followed by surprise, then setbacks, and finally the awakening of the sleeping giant who shakes off its slumber and slowly prepares to fight. The unpreparedness that he himself had faced as a group commander at the start of World War II, when he had no aircraft, no equipment, and no trained personnel, had impacted him profoundly. Good men had died because of such unpreparedness.[11] No more. The specter of an "atomic Pearl Harbor" was often cited to stress the importance of an Air Force in being, ready at the outset of hostilities to fight decisively. LeMay embraced this concept. He constantly told his command to act like they were already at war. He did not want competent performance to occur only weeks or months after war began; he wanted SAC ready immediately. When he took command, such ideas were fanciful. SAC had no such capability. But the new commander

---

[9] Enlisted retention rates, perhaps not surprisingly, were lowest among the skilled positions—individuals who had myriad opportunities outside the Air Force—such as jet engine mechanics and radar repair specialists. For detailed statistics, see *SAC History—Jul–Dec 1956*, vol. 1, 95–96.

[10] *SAC History—Jan–Jun 1957*, vol. 1, 35–36.

[11] LeMay, interview, 16 November 1972, 5–7.

began from his first days in office to inculcate that belief throughout the organization.

He began with the training already noted—his crews *would* be able to launch on time, find their targets anywhere in the world, and then destroy them. There was more to it than that. LeMay's emphasis on standardization and top performance was reflected in his operational readiness inspection mentality. Any SAC unit, at any time, could be visited by a team of inspectors and told to execute the war plan. No preparation. No warning. No chance to get things in order. Real war would come without such niceties, and LeMay was determined to ensure that his people would be ready if the unexpected occurred. Base security was similarly a legend around the Air Force. True, any operational airfield had gate guards and security, but SAC took things to an extreme level. Armed guards patrolled the flight line with trained dogs. Infiltration exercises were constantly run, as "aggressors" would attempt to enter SAC bases and "blow up" aircraft or facilities. They would leave written messages if they were successful: "At 0834 a bomb went off in this building and all its inhabitants were killed." LeMay wanted his personnel to *assume* they were targets—always—and they must therefore be ready.[12]

When the Soviets detonated their first atomic bomb, SAC took matters to a higher level. And when they went on a massive rearmament program and there was talk of a bomber gap and then a missile gap developing, LeMay stepped up preparations even more. Eventually, dispersal bases were built all over the country, and bombers and tankers would deploy there in small numbers to confuse and complicate a possible enemy attack. He also instituted the alert program. The advent of ballistic missiles meant that warning time would be measured in minutes not hours. Beginning in late 1956, SAC began testing the concept of bombers and tankers placed on continuous alert. The following year the alert program became routine, both in CONUS and overseas at bases like Sidi Slimane in French Morocco.[13] Initially, crew members would live together in the BOQ or dormitory; eventually SAC would build underground alert facilities near the flight line. If the klaxon sounded, crews would rush to their aircraft and launch. They had two minutes to start engines, five minutes

---

[12] This was another reason LeMay stressed the need for housing; he wanted his people, especially key personnel, to live on base where they would be more secure in the event of sabotage or a terrorist attack but also to be nearby in the event of a crisis.

[13] "Overseas Bases: A Military and Political Evaluation," SAC historical study, 2 April 1962, AFHRA, file K416.601-13, 6. The overseas alert missions were referred to as "Reflex" deployments.

to taxi, and 15 minutes to take off.[14] At some point, the crews were told it was simply an exercise and they could return to quarters. The crews never knew: sometimes they would be recalled as they started engines or while taxiing out; at other times they would launch, climb to altitude, refuel, and proceed toward their targets on the other side of the globe. LeMay's intention in all of this was not melodrama or some type of childish fascination with military discipline. Rather, it was part of his plan to develop within SAC a unique, definable, and recognizable military culture of seriousness and purpose. Over the four decades of its existence, this culture was sometimes derided by those in other Air Force commands who had no such immediacy in their mission. At times, even SAC personnel grew resentful and weary of the never-ending insistence on perfection and instantaneous response. But the culture nonetheless existed throughout the life of the command, and it was imposed by the iron will and determination of Curtis LeMay, Tom Power, John Ryan, and a host of other leaders who shared this belief. SAC veterans would claim that the culture of professionalism within the command was one of its greatest strengths, and the Air Force lost much when SAC and its distinctive ethos ended in June 1992.

It was true that LeMay relied on a coterie of officers, mostly combat veterans, who had served with him before. To him, this was common sense. His personnel chief was candid about this: "If we didn't know them, if nobody knew them who could vouch for them, they didn't come. And the people that LeMay didn't want to lose, he didn't lose. People that we wanted to get rid of, we got rid of."[15] To LeMay, this reliance on proven ability, reputation, and experience was important. He once noted,

> When I went into World War II, I didn't have any combat experience and I certainly didn't enjoy the process of getting it. It's something I wish we could avoid, if at all possible. It's not possible to avoid it. If we're successful in keeping out of a war, we're going to finally arrive at a point where no one in the military service has had combat experience. I hope we arrive at that point. If we do have to fight sometime, then we're going to have to depend on the training and background that we've given our leaders in the subjects of war, and I think our school system is set up to teach people to solve problems, and, after all, that's all war is—solving problems. If you've had experience in it, so much better.[16]

---

[14] See *SAC History—Jan–Jun 1957*, vol. 1, 131–54, for a discussion of the dispersal and alert programs.
[15] Russell, interview, June 1988, 57.
[16] LeMay, interview, March 1965, 16.

In LeMay's view, experience was the best teacher, even if, paradoxically, he sincerely hoped it was never again necessary to gain that experience. One SAC commander noted this problem of experience. He had made colonel at age 29 due to World War II—he then remained at that rank for the next 10 years. Because he had advanced so quickly, he was tested but inexperienced—he had not enjoyed a gradual and normal increase of responsibilities and rank during his career. He lacked "seasoning." He therefore recalled the annual commanders conferences led by LeMay as critical to his own development as a leader. LeMay and his staff, the "old heads," "taught us and talked to us" about management, leadership, and professionalism.[17] Professionalism throughout SAC would be the appropriate substitute for combat experience.

This professionalism was buttressed by a rock-like integrity that started at the top. One of SAC's problems in 1948 had been the tendency to bend the rules so units appeared more capable than they actually were. LeMay put a stop to that and was ruthless in rooting out commanders who continued to play games with readiness reporting. As one study of leadership in the early Air Force describes the SAC commander,

> General LeMay . . . would absolutely not tolerate this type of lack of integrity. A commander whose unit hadn't been scoring too well in the management control system and whose unit had failed in a readiness inspection, and whose record was proved clean by the inspector usually got help and a second chance; but God help the commander in whose unit false reporting and other hankypanky was found to exist.[18]

This assessment, written by one of LeMay's wing commanders, went on to say that his fellow commanders appreciated this type of example: it inspired them to a higher standard.

According to Bernard Brodie and other RAND analysts and academic biographers, Curtis LeMay was of limited intellectual ability and unable to grasp the measured nuances of their theories. Given his appearance and taciturn personality, it was easy for academicians to err by dismissing him as an intellectual lightweight. LeMay did not make small talk and did not speak merely to generate conversation,

---

[17] Martin, interview, February 1988, 43. Martin recalled LeMay's harping on adequate recreation facilities. When he took command of Loring AFB in Maine, he realized it was in the middle of nowhere—the nearest town, several miles away, contained 500 people. Martin then had his engineers build a 1,000-foot "mountain" on base; 200 inches of snow each year made this a formidable ski slope. He built a "chalet" that was decorated by his wife, and every weekend the base would turn out to ski Mt. Loring.

[18] Puryear, *Stars in Flight: A Study in Air Force Character and Leadership*, 234.

misleading some into thinking he had nothing on his mind. From LeMay's perspective, however, things looked far different. He had been to war and had led men in desperate battle. Those he trusted in his inner circle were fellow airmen and combat veterans and operators who shared a similar intellectual framework.[19] They were not stupid, simple-minded, or foolish. They were certainly not war lovers. Those who have served a career in uniform would no doubt argue the military is among the most conservative institutions when it comes to war fever or jingoism—those who have been to war understand the price and are therefore loathe to pay it. Moreover, LeMay's strong support throughout his tenure at SAC for the civilians who populated his operations analysis function illustrates that he believed in such expertise as a necessary adjunct to his command, but these analysts—*his* analysts—had worked with him for years and "lived" in SAC, flown in its aircraft, and dealt with its personnel. He trusted them. After he retired, LeMay expressed his deep-seated concerns with the defense academicians:

> Today's armchair strategists, glibly writing about military matters to a public avid for military news, can do incalculable harm. "Experts" in a field where they have no experience, they propose strategies based upon hopes and fears rather than upon facts and seasoned judgments.
>
> It never ceases to amaze me that so many intelligent people believe they can become expert in a field where they have had so little training or experience. . . . If the military professional, once retired, fails to defend his profession against charlatans and dilettantes, I believe he has failed in the final service he should perform for his country. . . . A lifetime of study and practice of the military art had not prepared me for the pretentious language of the new breed of military philosophers.[20]

Obviously, LeMay was impatient with the civilian scholars who had not worn a uniform yet presumed to discuss the details and complexities of war as if it were a game. Yes, he understood the value of such exercises to train the minds and test procedures, but he never forgot that such war games were simply that—games. He was the commander, the man responsible to the president and the American people to deter cataclysmic war or to win it if deterrence failed. Those academics who criticized him had no such responsibility.

---

[19] Significantly, the B-29 veterans of Pacific operations dominated this group. They held a far different view of war than did their European counterparts—small groups of bombers operating against area targets rather than the 1,000-plane missions against precision targets and involving swarms of escort fighters. I thank Dan Kuehl for this interesting insight.

[20] LeMay with Smith, *America Is in Danger*, xi–xiii.

Curtis E. LeMay was the perfect man for the job at that time. It is difficult to imagine anyone else taking hold of SAC as forcefully and imposing his will on a large bureaucracy. His name and image became synonymous with his command—a rare occurrence in the military, where leaders come and go fairly quickly and therefore are seldom able to put their stamp on an organization. LeMay certainly did, and this was because of several factors: he had a clear vision of what SAC was chartered to accomplish, and he was able to explain and internalize that vision to his subordinates. He was tireless in working toward his goals and expected all who worked for him to be just as dedicated. One of his more successful subordinates later stated that LeMay would probably define an outstanding officer "as one who worked harder and was more successful by virtue of hard work than his contemporaries."[21] LeMay would doubtless have described his own success in such terms.

Curtis E. LeMay left SAC in July 1957 to become the Air Force vice-chief of staff. The move was unexpected and not particularly to his liking—he hated Washington and the endless cocktail parties that conducting business there entailed. The chief of staff, Gen Nate Twining, had been tapped by President Eisenhower to move up to become chairman of the Joint Chiefs of Staff—the first airman to hold that august position. In his place, Gen Thomas D. White moved in to become the chief—he chose LeMay as his vice. White was an intellectual who had made his reputation as an attaché and staff officer. It is likely he selected LeMay for balance—the two could not have been more unalike. Yet they got along well and were a solid team for the next four years.

LeMay had been at SAC for nearly nine years and was reluctant to leave—he always felt as if there were more to do. In truth, he left SAC in excellent shape. The new CINCSAC was Gen Thomas S. Power, who had left SAC in 1954 to head Air Research and Development Command. He returned in July 1957 and would remain at Offutt for another seven years while continuing to move SAC forward in capability.

New aircraft like the B-58 Hustler would join the inventory; much later, so would the B-1 and FB-111. A new tanker, the KC-10, would also join the fleet in 1980. The venerable B-52 as well as the KC-135 would remain in service even at this writing, although much modified and reduced in numbers. In 1959 the Atlas ICBM became operational, and it was followed by the Minuteman series, giving SAC a

---

[21] Carlton, interview, 13–15 August 1979, 79.

secure and potent missile deterrent that formed one-third of the strategic triad. For several years after LeMay's departure, SAC would continue planning for Armageddon—World War III against the Soviets and possibly even the Red Chinese. Its planes and missiles would continue to sit alert—or in some instances fly alert. By July 1961 one-half of SAC was on nuclear alert at locations all over the world. Command and control would also change as "Looking Glass" aircraft containing the CINCSAC or his designated representative would begin flying in heavily modified C-135 aircraft in February 1961.[22]

Just prior to LeMay's departure from SAC, Offutt received a new "control facility"—a headquarters building consisting of three floors above ground and four more below. The lowest basement housed the storied command center where huge global maps and charts provided the location of every SAC aircraft, everywhere in the world, along with its combat status. From here the CINCSAC could monitor and control his global assets. LeMay had wanted such a facility ever since 1948—he had been forced to move his command into the old Martin aircraft plant at Offutt. Congress was not, however, conducive to spending the millions of dollars necessary for what it deemed a gold-plated headquarters building.[23] To LeMay, of course, it was not that—it was a largely invulnerable command post from which he or his replacement could direct a war in the event "the balloon went up." He later remarked that he never got anywhere with Congress until he submitted a request for a new "control facility." Every combat command needed one of those, and Washington finally agreed.

The core functions of Strategic Air Command continued with only slight change for more than three decades. SAC would remain the focus of nuclear deterrence and nuclear war fighting should deterrence fail. Soon after LeMay left SAC, the National Security Council delivered a report that resembled *NSC 68* in its Cold War rhetoric. According to "Deterrence and Survival in the Nuclear Age," the Soviet Union was implacably expansionist, and its "great efforts to build military power go beyond any concepts of Soviet defense." The report detailed the Soviet armament surge, noting that it possessed "a spectrum" of atomic and nuclear weapons and 1,500 medium-range bombers along with 3,000 more short-range bombers to deliver them. Russia had surpassed the United States in ICBM development. It also had extremely

---

[22] "Alert Operation in the Strategic Air Command, 1957–1991," SAC historical study, December 1991, 2–11.
[23] The new building opened in December 1956. *SAC History—Jan–Jun 1957*, vol. 1, 24.

formidable air defenses, 8,500 jet fighters, and 175 line divisions. This capability was sobering. The report was blunt in addressing how to counter this force: "The protection of the United States and its population rests, therefore, primarily upon the deterrence provided by SAC."[24] The report called for a Defense Department budget increase of 10 percent over the next five years. Specifically, it called for upgrades to SAC radars, full implementation of its nascent alert concept, surface-to-air missile defenses for SAC bases, dispersal of SAC aircraft, hardened shelters, hardened silos for the SAC ICBMs scheduled to come on line in two years, and the deployment of a ballistic missile warning system.[25] This was no doubt music to the ears of LeMay and Power. They would continue to view SAC as the tip of America's spear.

Since the end of World War II, US atomic/nuclear strategy and policy had been developed at three different levels. Overall planning guidance came from the president and the National Security Council; national war plans were developed by the Joint Chiefs of Staff. SAC—later the theater commands—was responsible for recommending specific targets to be vetted, approved, and prioritized by the JCS. SAC, its wings, and the theater staffs were responsible for operational planning and production of the emergency war plan (EWP). It was this EWP that SAC crew members studied, analyzed, and lived with during their tours in the command. Although the Army and Navy believed they were directly impacted by the nuclear targeting process, in truth the number of strategic warheads they controlled was small, so most planning remained with SAC. Even so, difficulties developed as the number of nuclear weapons proliferated and the services, plus the theaters, moved more deeply into the nuclear field—by 1960 the US arsenal contained over 18,000 warheads and was still growing.[26]

Significantly, the custody issue, which had caused so much turmoil and disagreement in the late 1940s and early 1950s, had become a minor factor by the end of the decade. President Eisenhower had worked both sides of that street and realized that the necessity for quick response in the event of a crisis meant the old arguments of "civilian control" were no longer valid. He was in control and that was enough. Initial custody by the AEC at a single location had given way to a number of nuclear stockpiles around the country and overseas.

---

[24] NSC 5724, "Deterrence and Survival in the Nuclear Age" (*Gaither Report*), 7 November 1957, in *FRUS, 1955–1957*, vol. 19, 639–42.

[25] Ibid., 643–47.

[26] Rosenberg, "U.S. Nuclear War Planning, 1945–1960," 35–41.

By the end of 1956 the "bombs on base" program had moved the weapons onto the airfields, where they were under the direct control of the SAC wing commander. The bombs were stored near the aircraft themselves, and those aircraft (and missiles) on alert contained live warheads.[27] The old bugaboo of wondering how long it would take to transfer and load nuclear weapons in the event of an emergency was solved. By the time Eisenhower left office, over 90 percent of all US nuclear weapons were under military control.[28]

The struggle over the control of nuclear targeting had also been heated. LeMay had often complained of the inefficiency, redundancy, and even danger of several different commands possessing nuclear weapons who intended to use them to fulfill their own war plans. Studies had demonstrated the large amount of overlap between these plans. LeMay argued that one central targeting plan was essential. He was content to let the JCS serve as the arbiter of all nuclear weapons decisions, but *some* centralized authority was mandatory.[29]

This situation was finally addressed in 1960 when Defense Secretary Thomas Gates directed the formation of the much needed Joint Strategic Target Planning Staff (JSTPS) to rationalize targeting. At one point hundreds of targets in Europe and the Pacific were either duplicated or triplicated on various target lists. The JSTPS, which reported directly to the JCS, was designed to correct such errors. The Navy strenuously resisted Gates' directive, but it was overridden. The head of the JSTPS was the CINCSAC, and his deputy was a naval officer; although the staff group was nominally joint, it was located at Offutt AFB and consisted largely of SAC personnel. The single integrated operational plan that this group developed included all the strategic targets listed by the Air Force, Navy, and Army; later it would incorporate NATO targeting priorities as well.[30] The first SIOP, in July 1961, listed some 3,200 targets to be struck by SAC bombers, Atlas ICBMs, and submarine-launched Polaris missiles—thousands more would be targeted by tactical aircraft. The number of targets and warheads assigned by the SIOP planners would increase during the years ahead—by 1980 the SIOP contained nearly 9,000 targets.[31]

---

[27] *SAC History—Jan–Jun 1957*, vol. 1, 49–53.

[28] Rosenberg, "U.S. Nuclear War Planning," 43.

[29] *SAC History—Jan–Jun 1957*, vol. 1, 50–52.

[30] Britain's Royal Air Force worked closely with SAC on targeting issues, as did the Royal Navy when it acquired nuclear-missile submarines. For an excellent overview, see Freedman, "British Nuclear Targeting," 109–26.

[31] Ball, "Development of the SIOP, 1960–1983," 57–62, 81; and Charles K. Hopkins, "Unclassified History of the Joint Strategic Planning Staff (JSTPS)," 26 June 1990, AFHRA, file TF5-2-67.

SAC reached its peak in terms of manpower and probably influence in 1962 following the Cuban missile crisis, during which it went on full alert worldwide. At that point it contained 282,723 personnel, 2,759 aircraft, and 57 air bases—43 in CONUS and 14 overseas. From that point on, the command would see its influence wane. The main reason for this denouement was undoubtedly the Vietnam War. Korea should have been a harbinger that the world was changing in ways that had little to do with the two superpowers, but neither the Air Force nor SAC saw it that way. The administration of John F. Kennedy and its embrace of a more-flexible response became, to some degree, a self-fulfilling prophecy. Within two years of this policy taking root, the United States was embroiled in a counterinsurgency against the Vietcong in Southeast Asia. Soon after, it was ensnared in a major conventional war with North Vietnamese military forces as well. This type of conflict was not conducive to the notion of massive retaliation, and most would argue that it did not even lend itself to a major strategic bombing campaign. LeMay disagreed, arguing as he had during the Korean War that a short but massive application of strategic airpower would have brought far more favorable conclusions in a much shorter period of time and at dramatically less cost in both blood and treasure. He was ignored and pushed into retirement by a defense secretary who thought his ideas were outdated.

During his reign as CINCSAC, followed by his tenure as vice-chief and then through the first half of his tour as chief of staff of the Air Force, LeMay saw the influence of the bomber command grow dramatically. It had garnered the most funds—nearly one-third of the Air Force budget—and the largest number of personnel. Its senior personnel populated the key leadership positions throughout the Air Force—heading not only most major commands but also most of the deputy chief of staff positions in the Pentagon. In October 1961, LeMay appointed Gen Walter "Cam" Sweeney—a career bomber pilot—to head Tactical Air Command. He later stated that he made the move because "TAC was behind the times."[32] Others referred to it as an attempt to "SACemcize" the command, and indeed the entire Air Force.[33] The fighter pilots bitterly resented the move.

Although he should have known better, LeMay did not view the installation of Sweeney at TAC as an insult or an attempt at humiliat-

---

[32] LeMay, interview, 17 November 1976, 133.
[33] Ratkovich, interview, 8–9 January 1985, 61.

ing the fighter command. He was primarily concerned with performance, and in his view, TAC was simply not up to snuff. As chief of staff it was his duty to remedy the situation.

This was not the first time he had acted in a way that he thought was eminently reasonable but that was construed as a deliberate insult. In July 1953 he had ordered an exercise: he wanted 400 SAC bombers to "attack" the United States unannounced to see if they could get through. The scheme entailed aircraft taking off at night from a number of different bases, proceeding at low level east and west, and flying several hundred miles out to sea. There they would turn around and streak back toward the United States—aiming for New York City; Washington, DC; and Los Alamos. Air Defense Command (ADC) was caught with its flaps down. SAC later claimed that only two of its aircraft were effectively intercepted and "shot down"—and one of those was lost after it had bombed its target. (One participant recalled that seven bombers were "lost.") The ADC commander, Gen Ben Chidlaw, was incensed by the surprise attack and called LeMay to protest, asking why he had not been warned as a courtesy. LeMay replied that he did not trust him not to tell his subordinates, thus ruining the value of the maneuver. Chidlaw then called Twining to complain; the chief simply told LeMay not to do it again.[34] Once more, the context is crucial. To LeMay, the mission of protecting the United States was not just primary, it was everything. He was unconcerned with the niceties of conventional behavior toward his colleagues and whether or not their pride was injured. He was interested solely in exercising his command and seeing if it could perform its primary mission on a no-notice basis. Others saw it differently and would not soon forget such treatment.

Vietnam was a turning point in US Air Force history. Certainly, the B-52s of SAC that were deployed to Guam and Thailand played a major role, as had the hundreds of KC-135s that proved indispensible to the American war effort. But the big bombers were largely relegated to close air support or the area bombing of "suspected enemy troop concentrations." It was not until the Linebacker II operations of December 1972 that the SAC heavies attacked Hanoi and Haiphong and braved the extreme air threat that the F-105s and F-4s of TAC had endured since 1965. The B-52s took heavy losses given the number

[34] For the two views of this incident, see Rosenberg, "'Smoking Radiating Ruin at the End of Two Hours,'" 24; and Montgomery, interview, 30 April–1 May 1984,184–85.

of sorties flown, but 15 bombers lost and five more heavily damaged paled in comparison to the more than 1,700 aircraft lost by tactical airmen to enemy fire. Valor and importance are not determined by the amount of blood spent, but it was nonetheless the case that tactical airpower and tactical airmen had borne the brunt of the combat burden in Vietnam, and in the aftermath of the war it was the fighter pilots who asserted themselves and took command of the Air Force. In 1968, Gen Bruce K. Holloway, a fighter pilot and ace during World War II, was named CINCSAC. In July 1982, Gen Charles A. Gabriel, a fighter pilot, became chief of staff—the first fighter pilot to hold that position since Hoyt Vandenberg. Seven more fighter pilots followed Gabriel into the position of chief. There has not been a bomber pilot as chief of staff since 1982.[35]

It also must be said that SAC's decline and fall was a product of its tremendous success. The nuclear-armed warriors of Armageddon were so professional, so accomplished, and so respected by adversaries in Moscow and Beijing, they had made war unthinkable. As the decades passed, the specter of nuclear war retreated. The superpowers learned to live with the awesome destructiveness at their disposal. They realized there could never be a winner if World War III broke out, either by design or by chance. As world political and military leaders came to accept that reality, they began to back away from the abyss—they began to disarm. Nuclear weapons and delivery systems did not disappear by any means and no doubt will remain with us indefinitely, but the immediacy of total war receded to the point where it was seldom given serious thought. In 1991, SAC changed its motto to "Peace . . . Is Our Profession," reflecting the reality that nuclear-tipped missiles and a relatively small number of manned bombers were adequate to ensure against inanity. SAC stood down from alert.

In late January 1957, not long before he left SAC to become vice-chief, LeMay gave a talk to the Air Force commanders' conference. He began by noting the recent memorandum from the secretary of defense clarifying the roles and missions of the services. By his interpretation, the memo suggested that the Army had acknowledged its primary responsibility for the close battle—100 miles deep on either side of the forward edge of the battle area. This was good news to LeMay because it signaled to him that the Army was prepared to

---

[35] For an insightful look at this tension between bomber and fighter pilots, see Worden, *Rise of the Fighter Generals.*

develop and procure short-range missiles to provide its own close air support, freeing the Air Force from this responsibility. Although this interpretation was not what the Army believed—or the rest of the national leadership either for that matter—LeMay then used his reading of the memo to speculate on its impact.

To LeMay, this allowed the Air Force to move more fully toward its primary responsibility—defense of the United States from Soviet attack and the concomitant requirement to launch a devastating nuclear strike against the Soviet Union in the event of war: "National policy dictates that the first objective of our air strength today must be deterrence. We deter through our capability to win. Not through our capability to win ground skirmishes, but to win the air power battle." The known Soviet buildup threatened this deterrence capability, which meant "we can no longer afford the luxury of devoting a substantial part of our offensive effort to campaigns other than the decisive air battle."[36] This was a belief LeMay had expressed as early as 1951, but now, he believed, conditions made his contention irrefutable. The new roles and missions clarification meant that TAC's traditional role was now overtaken by events: "It provides us with the long-awaited opportunity to lift from the neck of our tactical air forces the yoke which has tied them to old concepts of ground strategy. As we shake off the interdiction and close-support roles, SAC's mission becomes TAC's mission." LeMay continued that since the "distinction between SAC and TAC becomes purely arbitrary; we serve no purpose in retaining it." The Air Force was being presented with a great opportunity to "phase out of our inventory the carryover aircraft and equipment which we have inherited from those concepts. We can stop putting our money into short range, fair weather, vulnerable aircraft which serve to support ground forces rather than air power."

LeMay suggested the combination of SAC and TAC into a single, large command, "Air Offensive Command." He professed indifference as to whether TAC absorbed SAC or the other way around.

When SAC stood down in June 1992, its tanker assets were given to the new Air Mobility Command. The remaining B-1s and B-52s (and soon the stealthy B-2s) were transferred into another new command, Air Combat Command (ACC), which also contained all of the assets of the former Tactical Air Command. The new ACC would be

---

[36] Gen Curtis E. LeMay, "Address to Major USAF Commander's Conference," 28–30 January 1957, in *SAC History, Jul–Dec 1957*, vol. 2, exhibit 2.

centered at TAC's old headquarters building on Langley AFB in Virginia; the new ACC commander was the former TAC commander; and the new ACC patch was the old TAC patch with "Air Combat Command" substituted where "Tactical Air Command" had been printed.

LeMay was prescient in calling for a new command that grouped all Air Force combat aircraft under one head, but he would have been astounded at the details of the amalgamation that eventually took place less than two years after his death.

Appendix

The following tables show the SAC budget, personnel, and force structure between the years 1946 and 1960.

Number of SAC personnel and bases, 1946–1960

Year	Officers	Enlisted	Civilians	Total	Active Bases
1946	4,319	27,871	4,903	37,093	18 CONUS
1947	5,175	39,307	5,107	49,589	16 CONUS
1948	5,562	40,038	6,365	51,965	21 CONUS
1949	10,050	53,460	7,980	71,490	17 CONUS
1950	10,600	66,000	8,273	85,473	19 CONUS/1 OS
1951	19,747	113,224	11,554	144,525	22 CONUS/11 OS
1952	20,282	134,072	11,667	166,021	26 CONUS/10 OS
1953	19,994	138,782	12,256	170,982	29 CONUS/10 OS
1954	23,447	151,466	14,193	189,106	30 CONUS/11 OS
1955	26,180	151,595	18,222	195,997	37 CONUS/4 OS
1956	27,871	169,170	20,238	217,279	36 CONUS/19 OS
1957	29,946	174,030	20,038	224,014	38 CONUS/30 OS
1958	34,112	199,562	25,029	258,703	39 CONUS/25 OS
1959	36,435	199,970	26,204	262,609	40 CONUS/25 OS
1960	37,562	202,507	26,719	266,788	46 CONUS/20 OS

Source: Bohn, "Development of Strategic Air Command, 1946–1973."

Number of SAC Aircraft, 1946–1960

Year	Bombers	Tankers	Fighters	Reconnaissance
1946	148	--	85	31
1947	319	--	350	35
1948	556	--	212	58
1949	525	67	161	80
1950	520	126	167	112
1951	669	208	96	173
1952	857	318	230	193
1953	762	502	235	282
1954	1,082	683	411	410
1955	1,309	761	568	379
1956	1,650	824	336	327
1957	1,655	766	0	240
1958	1,769	962	54	195
1959	1,854	1,067	56	180
1960	1,735	1,094	0	113

Source: Bohn, "Development of Strategic Air Command."

SAC bombers by type, 1946–1960

Year	B-29	B-50	B-36	B-47	B-52	B-58	TOTAL
1946	148						148
1947	319						319
1948	486	35	35				556
1949	390	99	36				525
1950	286	196	38				520
1951	340	219	98	12			669
1952	417	224	154	62			857
1953	110	138	185	329			762
1954		78	209	795			1,082
1955			205	1,086	18		1,309
1956			247	1,306	97		1,650
1957			127	1,285	243		1,655
1958			22	1,367	380		1,769
1959				1,366	488		1,854
1960				1,178	538	19	1,735

Source: Bohn, "Development of Strategic Air Command, 1946–1973."

SAC tankers by type, 1949–1960

Year	KB-29	KC-97	KC-135	Total
1949	67			67
1950	126			126
1951	187	21		208
1952	179	139		318
1953	143	359		502
1954	91	592		683
1955	82	679		761
1956	74	750		824
1957		742	24	766
1958		780	182	962
1959		745	322	1,067
1960		689	405	1,094

Source: Bohn, "Development of Strategic Air Command, 1946–1973."

SAC fighters by type, 1946–1960

Year	P-51	P-80	F-82	F-84	F-86	Total
1946	85					85
1947	230	120				350
1948	131		81			212
1949			81		80	161
1950				167		167
1951				96		96
1952				230		230
1953				235		235
1954				411		411
1955				568		568
1956				336		336
1957						0
1958					54	54
1959					56	56
1960						0
Total	998	908	90			

Source: Bohn, "Development of Strategic Air Command, 1946–1973."

SAC reconnaissance aircraft by type, 1946–1960

Year	F-2/9/13	RB-17	RB-29	RB-45	RB-50	RB-36	RB-47	RB-57	RF-84	Total
1946	31									31
1947	35									35
1948		24	30	4						58
1949		18	62							80
1950			46	27	19	20				112
1951			30	38	40	65				173
1952			18	22	39	114				193
1953			8		38	137	99			282
1954					12	133	265			410
1955					12	133	234			379
1956						247[1]	254	16	57	(574)
1957						127[2]	216	24		(367)
1958							176	19		195
1959							174	6		180
1960							113			113
Total	998				908	90				

Source: Bohn, "Development of Strategic Air Command, 1946–1973."

---

[1] Aircraft designated as B/RB-36.
[2] Aircraft designated as B/RB-36.

Bibliography

Books and Articles

Abella, Alex. *Soldiers of Reason: The RAND Corporation and the Rise of American Enterprise*. New York: Harcourt, 2008.

Ader, Clément. *Military Aviation*. Edited and translated by Lee Kennett. Maxwell AFB, AL: Air University Press, 2003.

"Air Force of 35,000 Planes Is Urged." *U.S. Air Services*, March 1948, 14–17.

Air Ministry. *The Origins and Development of Operational Research in the Royal Air Force*. London: HMSO, 1963.

"Air Service, Air Force, and Air Power." *Aviation*, 25 April 1921, 522–23.

Albright, Joseph, and Marcia Kunstel. *Bombshell: The Secret Story of America's Unknown Atomic Spy Conspiracy*. New York: Times Books, 1997.

"Alert Operation in the Strategic Air Command, 1957–1991." SAC Historical Study, December 1991.

Allen, Robert S., and William V. Shannon. *The Truman Merry-Go-Round*. New York: Vanguard, 1950.

Anders, Roger M., ed. *Forging the Atomic Shield: Excerpts from the Office Diary of Gordon E. Dean*. Chapel Hill: University of North Carolina Press, 1987.

———. "The Atomic Bomb and the Korean War: Gordon Dean and the Issue of Civilian Control." *Military Affairs* 52 (January 1988): 1–6.

Anderson, C. E. "Dangerous Experiments: Wingtip Coupling at 15,000 Feet." *Flight Journal*, December 2000, 64–72.

The Army Almanac. Washington: GPO, 1950.

Arnold, Gen Henry H. *Global Mission*. New York: Harper, 1949.

Aronsen, Lawrence. "Seeing Red: US Air Force Assessments of the Soviet Union, 1945–1949." *Intelligence and National Security* 16 (Summer 2001): 103–32.

Asada, Sadao. "The Shock of the Atomic Bomb and Japan's Decision to Surrender—A Reconsideration." *Pacific Historical Review* 67, no. 4 (November 1998): 477–512.

Baer, George W. *One Hundred Years of Sea Power: The U.S. Navy, 1890–1990*. Stanford, CA: Stanford University Press, 1994.

Ball, Desmond. "The Development of the SIOP, 1960–1983." In *Strategic Nuclear Targeting*, edited by Ball and Jeffrey Richelson. Ithaca, NY: Cornell University Press, 1986.

Barlow, Jeffrey G. *Revolt of the Admirals: The Fight for Naval Aviation, 1945–1950*. Washington, DC: Naval History Center, 1994.

Beaumont, Roger. *Right Backed by Might: The International Air Force Concept*. Westport, CT: Praeger, 2001.

Behrman, Greg. *The Most Noble Adventure: The Marshall Plan and the Time When America Helped Save Europe*. New York: Free Press, 2007.

Berg, A. Scott. *Lindbergh*. New York: G. P. Putnam's Sons, 1998.

Bernstein, Barton J. "Truman and the H-Bomb." *Bulletin of the Atomic Scientists*, March 1984, 12–18.

Biddle, Tami Davis. "Handling the Soviet Threat: 'Project Control' and the Debate on American Strategy in the Early Cold War Years." *Journal of Strategy Studies* 12 (September 1989): 273–302.

———. *Rhetoric and Reality in Air Warfare: The Evolution of British and American Ideas about Strategic Bombing, 1914–1945*. Princeton, NJ: Princeton University Press, 2002.

Bland, Larry I., ed. *Papers of George Catlett Marshall*. Vol. 5, *The Finest Soldier, January 1, 1945–January 7, 1947*. Baltimore: Johns Hopkins University Press, 2003.

Blumberg, Stanley A., and Givinci Owens. *Energy and Conflict: The Life and Times of Edward Teller*. New York: Putnam's, 1976.

Bohn, John T. *The Development of Strategic Air Command, 1946–1971*. Offutt AFB, NE: HQ SAC, 1972.

Bolkcom, Christopher, and Jon D. Klaus. "Air Force Refueling Methods: Flying Boom versus Hose-and-Drogue." Congressional Research Service report, 11 May 2005.

Borgiasz, William S. *The Strategic Air Command: Evolution and Consolidation of Nuclear Forces, 1945–1955*. Westport, CT: Praeger, 1996.

Borowski, Harry R. *A Hollow Threat: Strategic Air Power and Containment before the Korean War*. Westport, CT: Greenwood Press, 1982.

Bowers, Peter M. *Boeing Aircraft since 1916*. London: Putnam, 1966.

Boyd, Robert J. "SAC Fighter Planes and their Operations," SAC Historical Study, 1988.

Bradley, David. *No Place to Hide*. Atlanta: Little, Brown, 1948.

Bradley, Gen Omar N. "U.S. Military Policy: 1950." *Reader's Digest*, October 1950, 143–54.

Bradley, Gen Omar N., with Clair Blair. *A General's Life*. New York: Simon & Schuster, 1983.

Buhite, Russell D. *Soviet-American Relations in Asia, 1945–1954*. Norman: University of Oklahoma Press, 1981.

Bukharin, Oleg. "US Atomic Energy Intelligence against the Soviet Target, 1945–1970." *Intelligence and National Security* 19 (Winter 2004): 655–79.

Byrd, Martha. *Chennault: Giving Wings to the Tiger*. Tuscaloosa: University of Alabama Press, 1988.

Campbell, Richard H. *The Silverplate Bombers: A History and Registry of the Enola Gay and Other B-29s Configured to Carry Atomic Bombs*. Jefferson, NC: McFarland, 2005.

Caraley, Demetrios. *The Politics of Military Unification*. New York: Columbia University Press, 1966.

Chapel, Charles E., ed. *Aircraft Power Plants*. New York: McGraw-Hill, 1948.

Chennault, Capt Claire. "Special Support for Bombardment." *U.S. Air Services*, January 1934, 18–21.

———. *Way of a Fighter*. New York: G. P. Putnam's Sons, 1949.

Childs, Marquis W. "The Battle of the Pentagon." *Harper's Magazine*, August 1949, 47–53.

Christensen, Charles R. "An Assessment of General Hoyt S. Vandenberg's Accomplishments as Director of Central Intelligence." *Intelligence and National Security* 11 (October 1996): 754–64.

"Chronology of Changes in Key West Agreements, April 1948–January 1958." JCS Historical Study, 7 February 1958.

"Chronology, Functions and Composition of the Joint Chiefs of Staff." JCS Historical Study, 1979.

Cline, Ray S., and Maurice Matloff. "Development of War Department Views on Unification." *Military Affairs* 13 (Summer 1949): 65–74.

Clodfelter, Mark A. "Molding Airpower Convictions: Development and Legacy of William Mitchell's Strategic Thought." In *The Paths of Heaven: The Evolution of Airpower Theory*, edited by Phillip S. Meilinger. Maxwell AFB, AL: Air University Press, 1997.

Cochran, Thomas B., William M. Arkin, and Milton M. Hoenig. *Nuclear Weapons Databook*. Vol. 1, *U.S. Nuclear Forces and Capabilities*. Cambridge, MA: Ballinger, 1984.

Coffey, Thomas M. *Hap: The Story of the U.S. Air Force and the Man Who Built It, General Henry H. "Hap" Arnold*. New York: Viking, 1982.

————. *Iron Eagle: The Turbulent Life of General Curtis LeMay*. New York: Crown, 1986.

Cole, Alfred C., et al., eds. *The Department of Defense: Documents on Establishment and Organization, 1944–1978*. Washington, DC: Secretary of Defense Historical Office, 1978.

Cole, Henry G. *The Road to Rainbow: Army Planning for Global War, 1934–1940*. Annapolis, MD: Naval Institute Press, 2003.

Collins, Gen J. Lawton. *War in Peacetime*. Boston: Houghton Mifflin, 1969.

Collins, Martin J. *Cold War Laboratory: RAND, the Air Force, and the American State, 1945–1950*. Washington, DC: Smithsonian Institution Press, 2002.

Commander, Joint Task Force–1. *Report on Atomic Bomb Tests Able and Baker (Operation CROSSROADS)*, 2 vols. Washington, DC: Department of the Navy, 15 November 1946.

Condit, Doris M. *History of the Office of the Secretary of Defense*. Vol. 2, *The Test of War, 1950–1953*. Washington, DC: Office of the Secretary of Defense, 1988.

Condit, Kenneth W. *The Joint Chiefs of Staff and National Policy*. Vol. 2, *1947–1949*. Washington, DC: Office of Joint History, 1978.

Converse, Elliott V., III. *Circling the Earth: United States Plans for a Postwar Overseas Military Base System, 1942–1948*. Maxwell AFB, AL: Air University Press, 2005.

————. *History of Acquisition in the Department of Defense*. Vol. 1, *Into the Cold War*. Washington, DC: Department of Defense Historical Office, 2012.

Cooke, Ronald C., and Roy C. Nesbitt. *Target: Hitler's Oil; Allied Attacks on German Oil Supplies, 1939–1945*. London: William Kimber, 1985.

Coox, Alvin D. "The *Enola Gay* and Japan's Struggle to Surrender." *Journal of American–East Asian Relations* 4, no. 2 (Summer 1995): 161–67.

Copp, DeWitt S. *A Few Great Captains: The Men and Events That Shaped the Development of U.S. Air Power*. New York: Doubleday, 1980.

————. "Frank M. Andrews: Marshall's Airman." In *Makers of the United States Air Force*, edited by John L. Frisbee. Washington, DC: Office of Air Force History, 1987.

Cortright, Vincent. "Dream of Atomic-Powered Flight." *Aviation History*, March 1995, 30–36, 69.

Cox, Sebastian, ed. *The Strategic Air War against Germany, 1939–1945*. London: Frank Cass, 1998.

Crane, Conrad C. *American Airpower Strategy in Korea, 1950–1953*. Lawrence: University Press of Kansas, 2000.

Craven, Wesley Frank, and James Lea Cate, eds. *The Army Air Forces in World War II*. 7 vols. Chicago: University of Chicago Press, 1948–58.

Daniels, Gordon, ed. *A Guide to the Reports of the United States Strategic Bombing Survey*. London: Royal Historical Society, 1981.

Daso, Dik A. *Architects of American Air Supremacy: Gen Hap Arnold and Dr. Theodore von Kármán*. Maxwell AFB, AL: Air University Press, 1997.

Davis, Richard G. *Carl A. Spaatz and the Air War in Europe*. Washington, DC: Smithsonian Institution Press, 1992.

Davis, Vernon E. *The History of the Joint Chiefs of Staff in World War II, Organizational Development*. Washington, DC: Office of Joint History, 1972.

Davis, Vincent. *The Admirals Lobby*. Chapel Hill: University of North Carolina Press, 1967.

Day, Dwayne A. *Lightning Rod: A History of the Air Force Chief Scientist's Office*. Washington, DC: USAF Chief Scientist's Office, 2000.

Defense Threat Reduction Agency. *Defense's Nuclear Agency, 1947–1997*. Washington, DC: Department of Defense, 2002.

De Seversky, Alexander P. *Air Power: Key to Survival*. New York: Simon & Schuster, 1950.

———. "My Thoughts on the War." *Popular Aviation*, April 1940, 18–19, 86–88.

———. "Ordeal of American Air Power." *American Mercury*, July 1941, 7–14, 127.

———. *Victory through Air Power*. New York: Simon & Schuster 1942.

D'Este, Carlo. *Decision in Normandy*. New York: E. P. Dutton, 1983.

Dickens, Samuel T. "USAF Reconnaissance during the Korean War." In *Coalition Air Warfare in the Korean War, 1950–1953*, edited by Jacob Neufeld and George M. Watson Jr. Washington, DC: Air Force History and Museums Program, 2005.

Dill, Peter. "The Doomsday Armada." *Airpower*, January 1992, 10–19, 46–55.

Dingman, Roger. "Atomic Diplomacy during the Korean War." *International Security* 13 (Winter 1988/89): 50–91.

Doolittle, Gen James H., with Carroll V. Glines. *I Could Never Be So Lucky Again: An Autobiography*. New York: Bantam, 1991.

Ehlers, Robert S., Jr. *Targeting the Reich: Air Intelligence and the Allied Bombing Campaigns*. Lawrence: University Press of Kansas, 2009.

"The Emperor's Rescript." *Current History*, September 1945, 191–92.

Faber, Peter R. "Interwar U.S. Army Aviation and the Air Corps Tactical School: Incubator of American Airpower." In *The Paths of Heaven: The Evolution of Airpower Theory*, edited by Phillip S. Meilinger. Maxwell AFB, AL: Air University Press, 1997.

Farmer, James H. "Korea and the A-Bomb." *Flight Journal*, December 2010, 40–46.

Farquhar, John T. *A Need to Know: The Role of Air Force Reconnaissance in War Planning, 1945–1953*. Maxwell AFB, AL: Air University Press, 2001.

Finletter, Thomas K. (chairman). *Survival in the Air Age*. Washington, DC: GPO, 1948.

Finney, Robert T. "History of the Air Corps Tactical School, 1920–1940." Air Force Historical Study no. 100, 1955; reprinted by the Air Force History and Museums Program, 1998.

Foulois, Maj Gen Benjamin D., with Carroll V. Glines. *From the Wright Brothers to the Astronauts: The Memoirs of Major General Benjamin D. Foulois*. New York: McGraw-Hill, 1960.

Francillon, René J. *McDonnell Douglas Aircraft since 1920*, Vol. 1. Annapolis, MD: Naval Institute Press, 1988.

Freedman, Lawrence. "British Nuclear Targeting." In *Strategic Nuclear Targeting*, edited by Desmond Ball and Jeffrey Richelson. Ithaca, NY: Cornell University Press, 1986.

———. *The Evolution of Nuclear Strategy*, 3rd ed. New York: Macmillan, 2003.

Freeman, Roger A., and David Osborne. *The B-17 Flying Fortress Story*. London: Arms and Armour, 1998.

Futrell, Robert Frank. *Ideas, Concepts, Doctrine: Basic Thinking in the United States Air Force, 1907–1964*. 2 vols. Maxwell AFB, AL: Aerospace Studies Institute, 1971. (Republished by Air University Press in 1989.)

———. *The United States Air Force in Korea, 1950–1953*. Rev. ed. Washington, DC: Office of Air Force History, 1984.

Gaddis, John Lewis. *The Long Peace: Inquiries in the History of the Cold War*. New York: Oxford University Press, 1987.

Gabel, Christopher R. *The U.S. Army GHQ Maneuvers of 1941*. Washington, DC: Center of Military History, 1991.

Gantz, Lt Col Kenneth F., ed. *The United States Air Force Report on the Ballistic Missile*. Garden City, NY: Doubleday, 1958.

Gaston, James C. *Planning the American Air War: Four Men and Nine Days in 1941*. Washington, DC: National Defense University Press, 1982.

Gentile, Gian P. *How Effective Is Strategic Bombing?* New York: New York University Press, 2001.

Giangreco, D. M. "Casualty Projections for the U.S. Invasions of Japan, 1945–1946: Planning and Policy Implications." *Journal of Military History* 61 (July 1997): 521–82.

Gibson, James M. *Nuclear Weapons of the United States*. Atglen, PA: Schiffer, 1996.

Gilpin, Robert. *American Scientists and Nuclear Weapons Policy*. Princeton, NJ: Princeton University Press, 1962.

Goldberg, Alfred, ed. *A History of the United States Air Force, 1907–1957*. Princeton, NJ: Van Nostrand, 1957.

Goodrich, Leland M. *The United Nations*. New York: Thomas Y. Crowell, 1959.

Goralski, Robert, and Russell W. Freeburg. *Oil and War: How the Deadly Struggle for Fuel in World War II Meant Victory or Defeat*. New York: Morrow, 1987.

Gordenker, Leon. *The United Nations and the Peaceful Unification of Korea*. The Hague: Martinus, 1959.

Gorn, Michael H. *Harnessing the Genie: Science and Technology Forecasting for the Air Force, 1944–1986*. Washington, DC: Office of Air Force History, 1988.

Greer, Thomas H. "The Development of Air Doctrine in the Army Air Arm, 1917–1941." Air Force Historical Study no. 89, 1955; reprinted by the Air Force History Office in 1985.

Griffith, Thomas E., Jr. *MacArthur's Airman: General George C. Kenney and the War in the Southwest Pacific*. Lawrence: University Press of Kansas, 1998.

Gudaitis, Frank. "It Seemed Like a Good Idea at the Time." *Aviation History*, March 2011, 68.

Hagerty, Col Edward J. *Air Force Office of Special Investigations, 1948 to 2000*. Washington, DC: Department of the Air Force, 2001.

Hall, R. Cargill. "Clandestine Victory: Eisenhower and Overhead Reconnaissance in the Cold War." In *Forging the Shield: Eisenhower and National Security for the 21st Century*, edited by Dennis E. Showalter. Chicago: Imprint Publications, 2005.

Hall, R. Cargill, and Clayton D. Laurie, eds. *Early Cold War Over-flights, 1950–1956.* 2 vols. Washington, DC: National Reconnaissance Office, 2003.

Hammond, Paul Y. *Super Carriers and B-36 Bombers.* Indianapolis: Bobbs-Merrill, 1963.

Hansell, Maj Gen Haywood S., Jr. *The Air Plan That Defeated Hitler.* Atlanta: Higgins-McArthur, 1972.

———. *Strategic Air War against Japan.* Maxwell AFB, AL: Air University Press, 1980.

Hardy, Ben, and Duane Hall. *Photographic Aerial Reconnaissance and Interpretation: Korea, 1950–1952.* Manhattan, KS: Sunflower University Press, 2004.

Herken, Gregg. *The Winning Weapon: The Atomic Bomb in the Cold War, 1945–1950.* New York: Knopf, 1980.

———. "'Not Enough Bulldozers': Eisenhower and American Nuclear Weapons Policy, 1953–1961." In *Forging the Shield: Eisenhower and National Strategy for the 21st Century,* edited by Dennis E. Showalter. Chicago: Imprint Publications, 2005.

Hewlett, Richard G., and Oscar E. Anderson Jr. *The History of the United States Atomic Energy Commission.* Vol. 1, *The New World, 1939–1946.* University Park: Pennsylvania State University Press, 1962.

Hewlett, Richard G., and Francis Duncan. *The History of the Atomic Energy Commission.* Vol. 2, *Atomic Shield.* University Park: Pennsylvania State University Press, 1969.

Hinsley, F. H., et al., eds. *British Intelligence in the Second World War.* 5 vols. London: HMSO, 1970–90.

Hirsch, Daniel, and William G. Matthews. "The H-Bomb: Who Really Gave Away the Secret?" *Bulletin of the Atomic Scientists,* January/February 1990, 23–30.

"History of the Organization and Operations of the Committee of Operations Analysts (COA)," 29 November 1945, AFHRA, file 118.01.

Holley, Irving B., Jr. *Buying Aircraft: Matériel Procurement in the Army Air Forces.* Washington, DC: Office of the Chief of Military History, 1964.

———. "General Carl Spaatz and the Art of Command." In *Air Leadership,* edited by Wayne Thompson. Washington, DC: Air Force History Office, 1986.

Hooker, Nancy H., ed. *The Moffat Papers: Selections from the Diplomatic Journals of Jay Pierrepont Moffat, 1919–1943*. Cambridge, MA: Harvard University Press, 1956.

"House to Fight Air Force Slash." *Aviation Week*, 5 September 1949, 16.

Howard, Vaughan, and Chase C. Mooney. "Development of Administrative Planning and Control in the AAF." Air Force Historical Study no. 28, 1946.

Hurley, Alfred F. *Billy Mitchell: Crusader for Air Power*. New York: Franklin Watts, 1964.

Huston, John W. *American Airpower Comes of Age: General Henry H. "Hap" Arnold's World War II Diaries*. 2 vols. Maxwell AFB, AL: Air University Press, 2002.

Huzar, Elias. *The Purse and the Sword: Control of the Army by Congress through Military Appropriations, 1933–1950*. Ithaca, NY: Cornell University Press, 1950.

Iriye, Akira. *The Cold War in Asia*. Englewood Cliffs, NJ: Prentice-Hall, 1974.

Isaacson, Walter, and Evan Thomas. *The Wise Men: Six Friends and the World They Made*. New York: Simon & Schuster, 1986.

Jacobsen, Meyers K., and Scott Deaver. *Convair B-36: A Comprehensive History of America's "Big Stick."* Atglen, PA: Schiffer, 1997.

James, Dorris Clayton. *The Years of MacArthur*. Vol. 2, *1941–1945*. Boston: Houghton Mifflin, 1975.

Jin, Niu. "The Birth of the People's Republic of China and the Road to the Korean War." In *The Cambridge History of the Cold War*. Vol. 1, *Origins*, edited by Melvyn P. Leffler and Odd Arne Westad. New York: Cambridge University Press, 2010.

Johnson, David E. *Fast Tanks and Heavy Bombers: Innovation in the U.S. Army, 1917–1945*. Ithaca, NY: Cornell University Press, 1998.

Johnson, Stephen B. *The United States Air Force and the Culture of Innovation, 1945–1965*. Washington, DC: Air Force History and Museums Program, 2002.

Jones, B. I., and Chauncey L. Sanders. "Personnel Problems Related to AAF Commissioned Officers, 1939–1945," Air Force Historical Study no. 11, 1951.

Jones, Howard. *"A New Kind of War": America's Global Strategy and the Truman Doctrine in Greece*. New York: Oxford University Press, 1989.

Jones, R. V. *The Wizard War*. New York: Coward, McCann, 1978.

Jones, Vincent C. *United States Army in World War II: Special Studies: Manhattan: The Army and the Atomic Bomb*. Washington, DC: Center of Military History, 1985.

Jordan, Robert S. *Norstad: Cold War NATO Supreme Commander— Airman, Strategist, Diplomat*. London: Macmillan, 2000.

Julian, Thomas A. "The Origins of Air Refueling in the United States Air Force." In *Technology and the Air Force: A Retrospective Assessment*, edited by Jacob Neufeld, George M. Watson Jr., and David Chenoweth. Washington, DC: Air Force History and Museums Program, 1997.

Keefer, Edward C. "President Eisenhower and the End of the Korean War." *Diplomatic History* 10 (Summer 1986): 267–89.

Kelsey, Benjamin S. *The Dragon's Teeth? The Creation of United States Air Power for World War II*. Washington, DC: Smithsonian Institution Press, 1982.

Kennedy, Paul. *The Parliament of Man: The Past, Present, and Future of the United Nations*. New York: Random House, 2006.

Kintner, William R. *Forging a New Sword: A Study of the Department of Defense*. New York: Harper, 1958.

Klein, Burton H. *Germany's Economic Preparations for War*. Cambridge, MA: Harvard University Press, 1959.

Knaack, Marcelle Size. *Encyclopedia of U.S. Air Force Aircraft and Missile Systems*, Vol. 2, *Post–World War II Bombers, 1945–1973*. Washington, DC: Office of Air Force History, 1988.

Kolodziej, Edward A. *The Uncommon Defense and Congress, 1945–1963*. Columbus: Ohio State University Press, 1966.

Kreis, John F., ed. *Piercing the Fog: Intelligence and Army Air Forces Operations in World War II*. Washington, DC: Air Force History and Museums Program, 1996.

"Lack of Strategic Plan Hampers Development of U.S. Air Power." *Aviation Week*, 1 March 1948, 11–12.

Lamphere, Robert J., and Tom Shachtman. *The FBI-KGB Wars: A Special Agent's Story*. New York: Random House, 1986.

Lashmar, Paul. *Spy Flights of the Cold War*. Annapolis, MD: Naval Institute Press, 1996.

Launius, Roger D., ed. *Innovation and the Development of Flight*. College Station: Texas A&M University Press, 1999.

Laurie, Clayton D. "The Invisible Hand of the New Look: Eisenhower and the CIA." In *Forging the Shield: Eisenhower and National Se-*

curity for the 21st Century, edited by Dennis E. Showalter. Chicago: Imprint Publications, 2005.

Leffler, Melvyn P. "The Emergence of an American Grand Strategy, 1945–1952." In *The Cambridge History of the Cold War*. Vol. 1, *Origins*, edited by Leffler and Odd Arne Westad. New York: Cambridge University Press, 2010.

LeMay, Gen Curtis E., with MacKinlay Kantor. *Mission with LeMay*. Garden City, NY: Doubleday, 1965.

LeMay, Gen Curtis E., with Maj Gen Dale O. Smith. *America Is in Danger*. New York: Funk & Wagnalls, 1968.

Lilienthal, David. *The Journals of David Lilienthal*. Vol. 2, *The Atomic Energy Years, 1945–1950*. New York: Harper & Row, 1964.

Little, Robert D. "Organizing for Strategic Planning, 1945–1950." Air Force Historical study, 1964.

Little, R. D., and Lee Bowen. *A History of the Air Force Atomic Energy Program, 1943–1953*. 5 vols. Washington, DC: Air Force History and Museums Program, 1959.

Lloyd, Alwyn T. *A Cold War Legacy: A Tribute to Strategic Air Command, 1946–1992*. Missoula, MT: Pictorial Histories Publishing, 1999.

———. *Boeing's B-47 Stratojet*. North Branch, MN: Specialty Press, 2005.

MacIsaac, David. *Strategic Bombing in World War Two: The Story of the United States Strategic Bombing Survey*. New York: Garland, 1976.

Marshall, Gen George C. "Responsibility of Victory." *Vital Speeches of the Day*, 15 November 1945, 77–78.

Maurer, Maurer, ed. *The U.S. Air Service in World War I*. 4 vols. Washington, DC: Office of Air Force History, 1978–79.

———. *Aviation in the U.S. Army, 1919–1939*. Washington, DC: Office of Air Force History, 1987.

McArthur, Charles W. *Operations Analysis in the US Army Eighth Air Force in World War II*. Providence, RI: American Mathematical Society, 1990.

McFarland, Keith D., and David L. Roll. *Louis Johnson and the Arming of America: The Roosevelt and Truman Years*. Bloomington: Indiana University Press, 2005.

McFarland, Stephen L. *America's Pursuit of Precision Bombing, 1910–1945*. Washington, DC: Smithsonian Institution Press, 1995.

Meilinger, Phillip S. *Hoyt S. Vandenberg: The Life of a General*. Bloomington: University of Indiana Press, 1989.

———. "Alexander P. de Seversky and American Airpower." In *The Paths of Heaven: The Evolution of Airpower Theory*, edited by Meilinger. Maxwell AFB, AL: Air University Press, 1997.

Mierzejewski, Alfred C. *The Collapse of the German War Economy, 1939–1945: Allied Air Power and the German National Railway.* Chapel Hill: University of North Carolina Press, 1988.

Miller, Roger G. *To Save a City: The Berlin Airlift, 1948–1949*. College Station: Texas A&M University Press, 2000.

Millett, Allan R, and Peter Maslowski. *For the Common Defense*. New York: Free Press, 1984.

Millis, Walter, and E. S. Duffield, eds. *The Forrestal Diaries*. New York: Viking, 1951.

Miscamble, Wilson D. "Harry S. Truman, the Berlin Blockade and the 1948 Election." *Presidential Studies Quarterly* 10 (Summer 1980): 1133–67.

Mitchell, Vance O. *Air Force Officers: Personnel Policy Development, 1944–1974*. Washington, DC: Air Force History and Museums Program, 1996.

Mitchell, Brig Gen William. "The Air Service at the Argonne-Meuse." *World's Work*, September 1919, 552–60.

———. "The Air Service at St. Mihiel." *World's Work*, August 1919, 360–705.

———. "Notes on the Multi-Motored Bombardment Group Day and Night," 1923.

———. *Our Air Force: The Keystone of National Defense*. New York: E. P. Dutton, 1921.

———. *Winged Defense*. New York: G. P. Putnam's Sons, 1925.

Mollenhoff, Clark R. *The Pentagon: Politics, Profits and Plunder*. New York: G. P. Putnam's Sons, 1967.

Moody, Walton S. *Building a Strategic Air Force*. Washington, DC: Air Force History and Museums Program, 1996.

"Mr. Secretary Johnson." *Newsweek*, 25 July 1949, 18–20.

Mueller, Karl P. "Strategic Airpower and Nuclear Strategy: New Theory for a Not-Quite-So-New Apocalypse." In *The Paths of Heaven: The Evolution of Airpower Theory*, edited by Phillip S. Meilinger. Maxwell AFB, AL: Air University Press, 1997.

"Navy Inquiry." *Aviation Week*, 19 September 1949, 16.

Neufeld, Jacob. *Ballistic Missiles in the United States Air Force, 1945–1960*. Washington, DC: Office of Air Force History, 1990.

Nichols, Maj Gen K. D. *The Road to Trinity: A Personal Account of How America's Nuclear Policies Were Made*. New York: William Morrow, 1987.

Nitze, Paul H. *From Hiroshima to Glasnost: At the Center of Decision—A Memoir*. New York: Grove Weidenfeld, 1989.

Norris, Robert S., Thomas B. Cochran, and William M. Arkin. "History of the Nuclear Stockpile." *Bulletin of the Atomic Scientists*, August 1985, 106–9.

Northedge, F. S. *The League of Nations: Its Life and Times, 1920–1940*. New York: Holmes & Meier, 1986.

Official Army Register, 1939. Washington, DC: GPO, 1939.

Olson, Mancur, Jr. "The Economics of Target Selection for the Combined Bomber Offensive." *Royal United Services Institute Journal* 107 (November 1962): 308–14.

Oppenheimer, J. Robert. "Physics in the Contemporary World." *Bulletin of the Atomic Scientists*, March 1948, 66.

Overy, Richard J. *Why the Allies Won*. London: Jonathan Cape, 1995.

Parrish, Noel F. *Behind the Sheltering Bomb: Military Indecision from Alamogordo to Korea*. New York: Arno, 1979.

Parton, James. *"Air Force Spoken Here": General Ira Eaker and the Command of the Air*. Bethesda, MD: Adler & Adler, 1986.

Patterson, Charles. *The Oxford 50th Anniversary Book of the United Nations*. New York: Oxford University Press, 1995.

Perera, Guido R. *Leaves from My Book of Life*. Vol. 2, *Washington and War Years*. Boston: [privately printed], 1975.

Perret, Geoffrey. *Winged Victory: The Army Air Forces in World War II*. New York: Random House, 1993.

Poole, Walter S. *The Joint Chiefs of Staff and National Policy*. Vol. 4, *1950–1952*. Washington, DC: Office of Joint History, 1979.

Potter, E. B. *Nimitz*. Annapolis, MD: Naval Institute Press, 1976.

Puryear, Edgar F., Jr. *Stars in Flight: A Study in Air Force Character and Leadership*. Novato, CA: Presidio, 1981.

Pyeatt, Don, and Dennis R. Jenkins. *Cold War Peacemaker: The Story of Cowtown and the Convair B-36*. North Branch, MN: Specialty Press, 2010.

Rawlings, Gen Edwin W. *Born to Fly*. Minneapolis: Great Way Publishing, 1987.

Rearden, Steven L. *History of the Office of the Secretary of Defense*. Vol. 1, *The Formative Years, 1947–1950*. Washington, DC: Office of the Secretary of Defense, 1984.

Rhodes, Richard. *Dark Sun: The Making of the Hydrogen Bomb*. New York: Simon & Schuster, 1995.

Richelson, Jeffrey T. *Spying on the Bomb: American Nuclear Intelligence from Nazi Germany to Iran and North Korea*. New York: W. W. Norton, 2006.

"Report of the Congressional Aviation Policy Board." *Air Force*, April 1948, 12–15, 38–39.

Report of the Secretary of War to the President. Washington, DC: GPO, 1923–41.

Roman, Peter J. "Curtis LeMay and the Origins of NATO Atomic Targeting." *Journal of Strategic Studies* 16 (March 1993): 46–74.

Rosen, Stephen. *Winning the Next War: Innovation and the Modern Military*. Ithaca, NY: Cornell University Press, 1991.

Rosenberg, David Alan. " 'A Smoking Radiating Ruin at the End of Two Hours': Documents on American Plans for Nuclear War with the Soviet Union, 1954–1955," *International Security* 6 (Winter 1981/82): 3–35.

———. "The Origins of Overkill: Nuclear Weapons and American Strategy, 1945–1960." *International Security* 7 (Spring 1983): 3–37.

———. "U.S. Nuclear Stockpile." *Bulletin of the Atomic Scientists*, May 1983, 25–30.

———. "U.S. Nuclear War Planning, 1945–1960." In *Strategic Nuclear Targeting*, edited by Desmond Ball and Jeffrey Richelson. Ithaca, NY: Cornell University Press, 1986.

Ross, Steven T. *American War Plans, 1919–1941*. New York: Garland, 1992.

———. *American War Plans, 1945–1950*. New York: Garland, 1988.

Ross, Steven T., and David Alan Rosenberg. *America's Plans for War against the Soviet Union, 1945–1950*. Vol. 1, *The Strategic Environment*. New York: Garland, 1989.

———. *America's Plans for War against the Soviet Union, 1945–1950*. Vol. 9, *The Atomic Bomb and War Planning: Concepts and Capabilities*. New York: Garland, 1989.

———. *America's Plans for War against the Soviet Union, 1945–1950*. Vol. 11, *The Limits of Nuclear Strategy*. New York: Garland, 1989.

———. *America's Plans for War against the Soviet Union, 1945–1950*. Vol. 13, *Evaluating the Air Offensive*. New York: Garland, 1990.

Rostow, Walt W. *Pre-Invasion Bombing Strategy*. Austin: University of Texas Press, 1981.

Sakharov, Andrei. *Memoirs*. New York: Knopf, 1990.

Sander, Alfred D. "Truman and the National Security Council: 1945–1947." *Journal of American History* 59 (September 1972): 369–88.

Schaffel, Kenneth. "Muir S. Fairchild: Philosopher of Air Power." *Aerospace Historian* 33 (September 1986): 165–71.

———. *The Emerging Shield: The Air Force and the Evolution of Continental Air Defense, 1945–1960.* Washington, DC: Air Force History Office, 1991.

Schatzberg, Eric. *Wings of Wood, Wings of Metal.* Princeton, NJ: Princeton University Press, 1999.

Schlaiffer, Robert, and S. D. Heron. *The Development of Aircraft Engines and Fuels.* Cambridge, MA: Harvard University Press, 1950.

"Science and the Citizen," *Scientific American*, November 1951, 32.

Schnabel, James F. *The Joint Chiefs of Staff and National Policy.* Vol. 1, *1945–1947.* Washington, DC: Office of Joint History, 1996.

Schnabel, James F., and Robert J. Watson. *The Joint Chiefs of Staff and National Policy.* Vol. 3, *The Korean War.* Washington, DC: Office of Joint History, 1978.

Scott, George. *The Rise and Fall of the League of Nations.* New York: Macmillan, 1973.

"Security vs. Budget." *Aviation Week*, 8 December 1947, 7, 11–13.

Setright, L. J. K. *The Power to Fly.* London: George Allen & Unwin, 1970.

Sherman, Maj William C. *Air Warfare.* New York: Ronald, 1926. (Republished by Air University Press in 2002.)

Shiner, John F. *Foulois and the U.S. Army Air Corps, 1931–1935.* Washington, DC: Office of Air Force History, 1983.

Shlaim, Avi. *The United States and the Berlin Blockade, 1948–1949.* Berkeley: University of California Press, 1983.

Slayton, Robert A. *Master of the Air: William Tunner and the Success of Military Airlift.* Tuscaloosa: University of Alabama Press, 2010.

Slessor, MRAF Sir John. *The Great Deterrent.* London: Cassell, 1957.

Smith, Jean E., ed. *The Papers of General Lucius D. Clay: Germany 1945–1949.* 2 vols. Bloomington: Indiana University Press, 1974.

Smith, Perry McCoy. *The Air Force Plans for Peace, 1943–1945.* Baltimore: Johns Hopkins University Press, 1970.

Smith, Richard K. *Seventy-Five Years of Inflight Refueling.* Washington, DC: Air Force History and Museums Program, 1998.

Spaatz, Gen Carl A. "Strategic Air Power: Fulfillment of a Concept." *Foreign Affairs*, April 1946, 385–96.

———. "The Era of Air-Power Diplomacy." *Newsweek*, 20 September 1948, 26.

Special Committee of the General Council (Drum Board). "Report on Employment of Army Air Corps under Certain Strategic Plans," September 1933, AFHRA, file 145.93-47.

Spires, David N. *Air Power for Patton's Army: The XIX Tactical Air Command in the Second World War*. Washington, DC: Air Force History and Museums Program, 2002.

"State of the Unification." *Economist*, 22 October 1949, 893–94.

Steiner, Barry H. *Bernard Brodie and the Foundations of American Nuclear Strategy*. Lawrence: University Press of Kansas, 1991.

Stoff, Joshua. *The Thunder Factory: An Illustrated History of the Republic Aviation Corporation*. Osceola, WI: Motorbooks, 1990.

Stueck, William. "The Korean War." In *The Cambridge History of the Cold War*. Vol. 1, *Origins*, edited by Melvyn P. Leffler and Odd Arne Westad. New York: Cambridge University Press, 2010.

Sturm, Thomas A. "Organizational Evolution." *Air Force Magazine*, September 1970, 58–64.

Tanner, Richard M. *History of Air-to-Air Refueling*. Barnsley, UK: Pen & Sword, 2006.

Tedder, Arthur Lord. *With Prejudice*. Boston: Houghton Mifflin, 1966.

Teller, Edward, with Judith Shoolery. *Memoirs: A Twentieth-Century Journey in Science and Politics*. Cambridge, MA: Perseus, 2001.

Thompson, Thomas W. *The Fifty-Year Role of the United States Air Force in Advancing Information Technology—A History of the Rome, New York Ground Electronics Laboratory*. Lewiston, NY: Edwin Mellen Press, 2004.

Tibbets, Brig Gen Paul W. *Return of the Enola Gay*. Columbus, OH: Mid Coast Marketing, 1998.

Tooze, Adam. *The Wages of Destruction: The Making and Breaking of the Nazi Economy*. New York: Viking, 2007.

Trest, Warren A. *Air Force Roles and Missions: A History*. Washington, DC: Air Force History and Museums Program, 1998.

Truman, Harry S. "Our Armed Forces Must Be Unified." *Colliers*, 26 August 1944, 16, 63–64.

———. *Memoirs*. 2 vols. Garden City, NY: Doubleday, 1955.

———. *Public Papers of the Presidents, 1950*. Washington, DC: GPO, 1964.

Twigge, Stephen, and Len Scott. *Planning Armageddon: Britain, the United States and the Command of Nuclear Forces, 1945–1964.* Amsterdam: Harwood, 2000.

Underwood, Jeffery S. *The Wings of Democracy: The Influence of Air Power on the Roosevelt Administration, 1933–1941.* College Station: Texas A&M University Press, 1991.

US Army Air Forces. *Mission Accomplished: Interrogations of Japanese Industrial, Military and Civil Leaders of World War II.* Washington, DC: GPO, 1946.

US Atomic Energy Commission. *In the Matter of J. Robert Oppenheimer: Transcript of Hearings before Personnel Security Board.* Cambridge, MA: MIT University Press, 1971.

US Congress, Hearings before the House Appropriations Committee. *National Military Establishment Appropriations for 1950,* 81st Cong., 1st sess. Washington, DC: GPO, 1949.

US Congress, Hearings before the Senate Appropriations Committee. *National Military Establishment Appropriations Bill for 1950,* 81st Cong., 1st sess. Washington, DC: GPO, 1949.

US Congress, Hearings before the Senate Armed Service Committee. *The National Defense Establishment (Unification of the Armed Services),* 80th Cong., 1st sess. Washington, DC: GPO, 1947.

———. *Investigation of the B-36 Bomber Program,* 81st Cong., 1st sess. Washington, DC: GPO, 1949.

———. *Investigation of the B-36 Bomber Program, H. Res. 234,* 81st Cong., 2nd sess. Washington, DC: GPO, 1950.

———. *The National Defense Program—Unification and Strategy,* 81st Cong., 1st sess. Washington, DC: GPO, 1949.

———. *Study of Airpower,* 84th Cong., 2nd sess. Washington, DC: GPO, 1956.

US Congress, Hearings before the Senate Armed Services and Foreign Relations Committees. *The Military Situation in the Far East,* 82nd Cong., 1st sess. Washington, DC: GPO, 1951.

US Congress, Hearings before the Senate Naval Affairs Committee. *On S. 2044, a Bill to Promote the Common Defense by Unifying the Departments and Agencies of the Government Relating to the Common Defense,* 79th Cong., 2nd sess. Washington, DC: GPO, 1946.

US Congress, House Select Committee on Post-War Military Policy. *Proposal to Establish a Single Department of Armed Forces,* 78th Cong., 2nd sess. Washington, DC: GPO, 1944.

US Department of Defense. *Annual Report of the Secretary of Defense.* Washington, DC: GPO, 1949–60.

US Department of State. *American Foreign Policy, 1950–1955: Basic Documents*, Vol. 2. Washington, DC: GPO, 1957.

———. *Foreign Relations of the United States (FRUS), 1932.* Vol. 1, *General.* Washington, DC: GPO, 1948.

———. *FRUS: The Conferences at Cairo and Tehran, 1943.* Washington, DC: GPO, 1961.

———. *FRUS, 1947.* Vol. 1, *General: The United Nations.* Washington, DC: GPO, 1973.

———. *FRUS, 1948.* Vol. 1, *General: The United Nations.* Washington, DC: GPO, 1976.

———. *FRUS, 1949.* Vol. 1, *National Security Affairs: Foreign Economic Policy.* Washington, DC: GPO, 1976.

———. *FRUS, 1950.* Vol. 1, *National Security Affairs; Foreign Economic Policy.* Washington, DC: GPO, 1977.

———. *FRUS, 1950.* Vol. 7, *Korea.* Washington, DC: GPO, 1976.

———. *FRUS, 1951.* Vol. 1, *National Security Affairs: Foreign Economic Policy.* Washington, DC: GPO, 1979.

———. *FRUS: 1951.* Vol. 3, *Korea.* Washington, DC: GPO, 1983.

———. *FRUS: 1952–1954.* Vol. 2, *National Security Affairs.* Washington, DC: GPO, 1984.

———. *FRUS, 1952–1954.* Vol. 15, *Korea.* Washington, DC: GPO, 1984.

———. *FRUS, 1955–1957.* Vol. 19, *National Security Policy.* Washington, DC: GPO, 1990.

Vander Meulen, Jacob A. *The Politics of Aircraft: Building an American Military Industry.* Lawrence: University Press of Kansas, 1991.

Wakelam, Randall T. *The Science of Bombing: Operational Research in RAF Bomber Command.* Toronto: University of Toronto Press, 2009.

Walker, 1LT Kenneth N. "Bombardment Aviation: Bulwark of National Defense." *U.S. Air Services*, August 1933, 15–19.

Waller, Douglas. *A Question of Loyalty: Gen. Billy Mitchell and the Court-Martial That Gripped the Nation.* New York: HarperCollins, 2004.

"War Diary." OSS London: Research and Analysis Branch [Enemy Objectives Unit or EOU], 1945. AFHRA, file 520.056-167.

Watts, Barry D. *The Foundations of US Air Doctrine: The Problem of Friction in War.* Maxwell AFB, AL: Air University Press, 1984.

Webster, Charles, and Noble Frankland. *The Strategic Air Offensive against Germany, 1939–1945.* 4 vols. London: HMSO, 1961.

Weinstein, Allen, and Alexander Vassiliev. *The Haunted Wood: Soviet Espionage in America—The Stalin Era*. New York: Random House, 1998.

Weisgall, Jonathan M. *Operation Crossroads: The Atomic Tests at Bikini Atoll*. Annapolis, MD: Naval Institute Press, 1994.

Westenhoff, Charles M. *Military Airpower: A Revised Digest of Airpower Opinions and Thoughts*. Maxwell AFB, AL: Air University Press, 2007.

Williams, Edwin L., Jr. "Legislative History of the AAF and USAF, 1941–1995." Air Force Historical Study no. 84, 1955.

Williams, George K. *Biplanes and Bombers: British Bombing in World War I*. Maxwell AFB, AL: Air University Press, 1999.

Wilson, Maj Gen Donald. "Origins of a Theory of Air Strategy." *Aerospace Historian* 18 (Spring 1971): 19–25.

Wohlstetter, Albert, Fred S. Hoffman, Robert J. Lutz, and Henry S. Rowen. *Selection and Use of Strategic Air Bases*. Santa Monica, CA: RAND, April 1954.

Wolf, Richard I. *The United States Air Force: Basic Documents on Roles and Missions*. Washington, DC: Office of Air Force History, 1987.

Wolk, Herman S. *The Struggle for Air Force Independence, 1943–1947*. Washington, DC: Air Force History and Museums Program, 1997.

Worden, R. Michael. *Rise of the Fighter Generals: The Problem of Air Force Leadership, 1945–1982*. Maxwell AFB, AL: Air University Press, 1998.

Wright, Monte Duane. *Most Probable Position: A History of Aerial Navigation to 1941*. Lawrence: University Press of Kansas, 1972.

Y'Blood, William T., ed. *The Three Wars of Lt. Gen. George E. Stratemeyer: His Korean War Diary*. Washington, DC: Air Force History and Museums Program, 1999.

Young, Ken. "No Blank Cheque: Anglo-American (Mis)understandings and the Use of the English Airbases." *Journal of Military History* 71 (October 2007): 1133–67.

Zhang, Shu Guang. *Mao's Military Romanticism: China and the Korean War, 1950–1953*. Lawrence: University Press of Kansas, 1995.

Ziegler, Charles A. "Intelligence Assessments of Soviet Atomic Capability, 1945–1949: Myths, Monopolies and *Maskirovka*." *Intelligence and National Security* 12 (October 1997): 1–24.

Zimmerman, Carroll L. *Insider at SAC: Operations Analysis under General LeMay*. Manhattan, KS: Sunflower Press, 1988.

Zuckerman, Solly. *From Apes to Warlords*. New York: Harper & Row, 1978.

United States Strategic Bombing Survey (USSBS) Reports

"Bombing Accuracy, USAAF Heavy and Medium Bombers in the ETO." Study no. 63, January 1947.

"The Campaigns of the Pacific War." Study no. 73, 1946.

"The Effects of Air Attack on the Japanese Urban Economy." Study no. 55, March 1947.

"Effects of Incendiary Bomb Attacks on Japan." Study no. 90, April 1947.

"The Effects of Strategic Bombing on German Morale." Study no. 64B, May 1947.

"The Effects of Strategic Bombing on Japanese Morale." Study no. 14, June 1947.

"The Effects of Strategic Bombing on Japan's War Economy." Study no. 53, December 1946.

"The German Anti-Friction Bearings Industry." Study no. 53, November 1945.

"German Electric Utilities Industry Report." Study no. 205, 10 August 1945.

"Oil Division Final Report." Study no. 109, August 1945.

"Over-All Report (European War)." Study no. 2, February 1947.

"Statistical Appendix to Over-all Report (European War)." February 1947.

"Strategic Bombing of the German Aircraft Industry." Study no. 4, November 1945.

"Summary Report (European War)." Study no. 1, 30 September 1945.

"Summary Report (Pacific Theater)." Study no. 1, 1 July 1946.

Microfilm Collections

All microfilm collections were published by University Publications of America.

"CIA Reports, 1946–1976," 1980.

"Official Conversations with Dean Acheson, 1949–1953," 1980.

"Public Statements by the Secretaries of Defense, Part 1: The Truman Administration, 1947–1953," 1982.

"Records of the Joint Chiefs of Staff, 1945–1953, Strategic Issues, Part 2: The United States," 1980.

"Records of the Joint Chiefs of Staff, Part 2: 1946–53: The Soviet Union," 1979.

"Records of the Joint Chiefs of Staff: The Far East," 1979.

Unpublished Works

Brown, Michael E. "Flying Blind: Decision Making in the US Strategic Bombing Program." PhD diss., Cornell University, 1983.

Dealile, Melvin G. "The SAC Mentality: The Origins of Organizational Culture in Strategic Air Command, 1946–1962." PhD diss., University of North Carolina, 2007.

Green, Murray. "Stuart Symington and the B-36." PhD diss., American University, 1969.

Kuehl, Daniel T. "The Radar Eye Blinded: The USAF and Electronic Warfare, 1945–1955." PhD diss., Duke University, 1992.

Meilinger, Phillip S. "Technology and Procurement: Factors in the Development of United States Fighter Aircraft between the World Wars." Master's thesis, University of Colorado, 1975.

Ponturo, John. "Analytical Support for the Joint Chiefs of Staff: The WSEG Experience, 1948–1976," Study S-507. Washington, DC: Institute for Defense Analyses, July 1976.

Schake, Kurt W. "Strategic Frontier: American Bomber Bases Overseas, 1950–1960." PhD diss., Norwegian University of Science and Technology, 1998.

Scrivner, John H., Jr. "Pioneer into Space: A Biography of Major General Orvil A. Anderson." PhD diss., University of Oklahoma, 1971.

Wilson, Don. "The History of President Truman's Air Policy Commission and Its Influence on Air Policy, 1947–1949." PhD diss., Denver University, 1979.

Interviews

All interviews were conducted by and are maintained by the Air Force Historical Research Agency, Maxwell AFB, Alabama. For information on access to these files, see http://www.afhra.af.mil/index.asp.

Carlton, Gen Paul K. Interview by Maj Scottie S. Thompson, 13–15 August 1979.

———. Interview by Cargill Hall, 30 September 1980.

Combs, Maj Gen Cecil E. Interview by Hugh N. Ahmann, 28–29 June 1982.

Ellis, Gen Richard H. Interview by Maurice Maryanow, 17–21 August 1987.

Finletter, Thomas K. Interview by Col Marvin Stanley, February 1967.

Gunderson, Brig Gen Brian S. Interview by Hugh N. Ahmann, 22–23 October 1987.

Harris, Lt Gen Edgar S. Interview by Lt Col David L. Young Jr., 25–26 November 1985.

Irvine, Lt Gen Clarence S. Interview by Robert M. Kipp, 17 December 1970.

Johnson, Gen Leon W. Interview by James C. Hasdorff, August 1975.

Kenney, Gen George C. Interview by James C. Hasdorff, 10–21 August 1974.

Landon, Gen Truman H. Interview by Hugh N. Ahmann, 31 May–3 June 1977.

LeMay, Gen Curtis E. Interview by Max Rosenberg, January 1965.

———. Interview by Col Bill Peck, March 1965.

———. Interview by John T. Bohn, 9 March 1971.

———. Interview by Robert M. Kipp and John T. Bohn, 16 November 1972.

———. Interview by Edgar F. Puryear Jr., 17 November 1976.

———. Interview by Charles Gross, 14 September 1978.

———. Interview by Frank Voltaggio, 4 June 1984.

Leo, Stephen. Interview by George M. Watson, 18 August 1982.

Martin, Lt Gen William K. Interview by Hugh N. Ahmann, February 1988.

Montgomery, Maj Gen John B. Interview by Capt Mark C. Cleary, 30 April–1 May 1984.

Montgomery, Lt Gen Richard M. Interview by Capt Mark C. Cleary, 28–30 June 1983.

Norstad, Gen Lauris. Interview by the author, 22 February 1984.

Quesada, Lt Gen Elwood P. Interview by Lt Cols S. W. Long and R. W. Stephenson, 12–13 May 1975.

Partridge, Gen Earle E. Interview by Lt Col Jon Reynolds, Maj Robert Bartanowicz, and Capt Phillip S. Meilinger, 16 February 1978.

Ratkovich, Maj Gen Edward. Interview by Lt Col John D. Miller, 8–9 January 1985.

Russell, Lt Gen Austin J. Interview by James C. Hasdorff, June 1988.

Sessums, Maj Gen John W. Interview by Hugh N. Ahmann, 25–28 July 1977 and 26–31 March 1978.

Smith, Lt Gen Robert N. Interview by Hugh N. Ahmann, 3–5 March 1983.

Symington, Stuart W. Interview by Hugh N. Ahmann and Herman S. Wolk, 2 May and 12 December 1978, AFHRA.

Tibbets, Brig Gen Paul W., Jr. Interview by James S. Howard, Lt Col Frederick Zoes, and Capt Barry J. Anderson, 7 February 1985.

Timberlake, Lt Gen Edward J. Interview by Burt Case, May 1965.

Wilson, Maj Gen Roscoe C. Interview by Lt Col Dennis A. Smith, 1–2 December 1983.

Index

Bomber

The Formation and Early Years of Strategic Air Command

Air University Press Team

Chief Editor
Jerry L. Gantt

Copy Editor
Sherry Terrell

Quality Review
Demorah Hayes

Cover Art
Phillip S. Meilinger Jr.

Book Design, and Illustrations
Daniel Armstrong

Composition and Prepress Production
Ann Bailey

Print Preparation and Distribution
Diane Clark